Decision Making, Learning, and Collaboration in AI-Driven Entrepreneurship

Samreen Tunio
https://orcid.org/0009-0001-1697-8519
University of Milan, Italy

Muhammad Nawaz Tunio
University of Klagenfurt, Austria

IGI Global
Scientific Publishing
Publishing Tomorrow's Research Today

Published in the United States of America by
IGI Global Scientific Publishing
701 East Chocolate Avenue
Hershey, PA, 17033, USA
Tel: 717-533-8845 | Fax: 717-533-7115
Website: https://www.igi-global.com E-mail: cust@igi-global.com

Library of Congress Cataloging-in-Publication Data

(CIP Data Pending)
ISBN13: 979-8-2600-1353-3
Isbn13Softcover: 979-8-2600-1354-0
EISBN13: 979-8-2600-1355-7
British Cataloguing in Publication Data
A Cataloguing in Publication record for this book is available from the British Library.

Table of Contents

Detailed Table of Contents

Entrepreneurial decision-making is inherently complex, shaped by uncertainty, risk perception, and cognitive biases. The integration of artificial intelligence (AI) offers novel opportunities to enhance decision quality, mitigate biases, and support adaptive risk-taking. This chapter explores how AI tools—including predictive analytics, natural language processing, and simulation models—provide insights into entrepreneurial behavior, opportunity recognition, and resource allocation. It examines theoretical foundations of risk-taking, behavioral biases, and decision-making under uncertainty, highlighting how AI augments human judgment without replacing intuition or creativity. Practical applications, case studies, and emerging trends demonstrate AI's potential to improve venture outcomes, enhance strategic flexibility, and promote inclusive entrepreneurial ecosystems. Ethical considerations, data governance, and algorithmic transparency are also discussed.

Most companies in a modern digitalized economy are resorting to artificial intelligence (AI) to assist them in making strategic and financial decisions. Yet these are choices

Entrepreneurial skill development increasingly relies on innovative educational approaches that bridge theory and practice. This chapter explores the integration of gamification and AI-driven simulations as transformative tools for cultivating entrepreneurial competencies. Gamification leverages game elements such as points, badges, and leaderboards to enhance learner engagement, motivation, and strategic thinking, while AI-driven simulations provide adaptive, immersive environments for experiential learning, decision-making, and problem-solving. The synergy between gamification and AI simulations enables personalized feedback, collaborative challenges, and realistic entrepreneurial scenarios, fostering critical skills for startup success. The chapter also addresses technological, ethical, and accessibility considerations, highlighting best practices for implementation. Emerging trends such as AR/VR integration and predictive learning analytics are discussed, emphasizing opportunities for future research and innovation in entrepreneurial education.

Artificial Intelligence (AI) is reshaping entrepreneurial education by enabling personalized learning pathways that cater to individual learner needs, preferences, and competencies. This chapter explores how AI technologies—such as adaptive learning systems, intelligent tutoring, generative AI, and learning analytics—facilitate customized instruction, real-time feedback, and experiential learning opportunities. Drawing on constructivist, experiential, and cognitive learning theories, the chapter examines the design and implementation of personalized pathways, highlighting case studies that demonstrate improved learner engagement, skill acquisition, and entrepreneurial decision-making. It also addresses key challenges, including data privacy, algorithmic bias, equity, and the balance between AI guidance and human mentorship. Finally, the chapter identifies future directions for research and practice,

Human–AI collaboration is transforming entrepreneurship by reshaping how opportunities are recognized, risks managed, and innovations developed. This chapter explores the psychological and practical dimensions of this partnership, highlighting how entrepreneurial traits such as creativity, adaptability, and emotional intelligence intersect with AI's analytical precision and predictive power. It examines the role of AI in decision-making, creativity enhancement, and stress reduction, while also addressing ethical dilemmas, cultural differences, and psychological barriers such as fear of replacement. Through case studies and conceptual frameworks, the chapter demonstrates how human–AI synergy fosters resilience and hybrid innovation models. The discussion concludes with future directions for research on entrepreneurial psychology, AI integration, and the evolution of a human–machine entrepreneurial ecosystem.

Introducing Artificial Intelligence (AI) within the entrepreneurship industry is changing the decision-making, problem-solving, and creating innovations processes. This chapter addresses the changing environment of Human-AI collaboration, and how the use of intelligent systems can contribute to cognitive resilience and allow more intelligent and data-driven decision-making among entrepreneurs. In times of challenges and growing unpredictability and complexity in the business, AI becomes a strategic ally capable of enhancing human intelligence to help entrepreneurs to process extensive information, predict the future, and minimize risks more efficiently. Nevertheless, the potentials of this collaboration do not imply the avoidance of human intuition but rather empowering it with the help of lifelong learning, flexibility, and contemplation. Cognitive, emotional, and strategic aspects of Human-AI engagement focus within this chapter allow developing a framework of developing strong entrepreneurial mindsets that would be able to use AI technologies in an ethical and effective way.

Rapidly growing beyond mere applications of artificial intelligence, it is redefining the way entrepreneurs ideate, decide and shape their businesses in turbulent and competitive markets. Besides the benefit of increased efficiency and performance, the psychological impact of human-AI collaboration is significant, especially in the development of entrepreneurial resilience, the ability to address stress, uncertainty, and numerous failures. This chapter addresses the overlap between human-AI cooperation and psychological resilience in the entrepreneurship area by discussing the way the AI systems are utilized not only as capabilities of technological technologies but also as cognitive and emotional aids in the entrepreneurship decision-making. Based on theories in the fields of entrepreneurship, human-computer interaction, and organizational psychology, the chapter examines how insights, simulations, and adaptive feedback with the help of AI can decrease cognitive overload, boost confidence, and provide reflective learning.

Artificial intelligence (AI) is quickly changing the entrepreneurial ecosystems and is providing new opportunities to become more efficient, make decisions and be competitive. To women entrepreneurs in the field, AI has a specific potential to enhance an ability to be psychologically resilient and more adaptive to the environment and find their ways through the uncertainties, extend market reach, and multi-task. The chapter review incorporates both interdisciplinary literature, reports of global entrepreneurship, and actual case studies in India and other emerging economies backe by recent developments on bridging the gender gap in the AI economy to look at the ways in which women are using AI tools in their businesses and the impact of using AI tools on business performance and personal empowerment. Results show that the adoption of AI can have a great impact in enhancing the performance of operations, confidence, and autonomy of women entrepreneurs. Nevertheless, there are still structural inequalities, such as lack of digital access, lack of AI training, financial obstacles that are gender-based, and women are still underrepresented in the development and governance of AI. These issues explain why gender-sensitive policies, inclusive digital-skilling initiatives, fair funding systems, and algorithmic bias, online security, and data privacy protection should be implemented. The chapter comes to a conclusion that the development of inclusive AI ecosystems makes AI-enabled women-based entrepreneurship one of the driving forces of the sustainable development, economic inclusion, and gender equality.

Artificial intelligence (AI) has increasingly been applied to model entrepreneurial traits, offering new insights into constructs such as creativity, resilience, and risk-taking. However, these AI systems often inherit biases from datasets, feature selection, and algorithmic processes, which can misrepresent entrepreneurial potential and perpetuate inequities across gender, socioeconomic, and cultural groups. This chapter examines the conceptual foundations of bias and fairness in AI, explores techniques for detecting and mitigating bias, and highlights ethical considerations and policy implications for equitable deployment. It emphasizes the importance of inclusive data practices, fairness-aware algorithms, explainable AI, and participatory governance to foster trust and accountability in entrepreneurial ecosystems. Future directions focus on interdisciplinary approaches, culturally sensitive Modeling, and regulatory frameworks to ensure AI supports diversity, inclusivity, and responsible innovation in entrepreneurship research and practice.

Emotional intelligence (EI) is a critical driver of entrepreneurial success, influencing opportunity recognition, leadership, team dynamics, negotiation, resilience, and well-being. Traditional methods of assessing EI, including self-report and ability-based measures, are limited by subjectivity, cultural bias, and static evaluation. Recent advances in artificial intelligence (AI) offer innovative approaches for measuring EI through natural language processing, facial expression recognition, voice analysis, and physiological sensing, providing real-time, objective, and multimodal insights.

AI-based assessments can enhance start-up team selection, investor evaluations, coaching, and stress management, while ethical considerations—such as algorithmic bias, privacy, and interpretive limitations—must be addressed. Integrating AI with EI theory enables dynamic, context-sensitive evaluation and development of emotional competencies, fostering more resilient and effective entrepreneurial ecosystems.

As AI steps in as an active partner in decision-making, leadership is shifting from cognitively exclusive authority to emotionally intelligent partnership. This chapter discusses how Emotional Intelligence (EI) enables leaders to incorporate human empathy, ethical decision-making, and psychological safety in AI-facilitated workplaces. It presents the AIRE Model (Awareness, Integration, Regulation, and Empathy)—a model blending traditional EI theory (Goleman, Mayer & Salovey) with AI-enhanced leadership practices. Practical strategies, case vignettes, and empirical findings illustrate how AI can enhance instead of displace emotional intelligence. It finally details ethical, psychological, and cultural guidelines for designing emotionally aware, sustainable leadership systems.

This chapter explores the use of Natural Language Processing (NLP) to study entrepreneurial narratives and pitches, highlighting its potential to analyze linguistic, rhetorical, and emotional dimensions of entrepreneurial communication. By applying techniques such as sentiment analysis, topic modeling, and transformer-based models, NLP enables researchers to identify persuasive elements, detect biases, and predict funding outcomes. Case studies from crowdfunding campaigns, venture capital pitches, and real-time pitch coaching illustrate practical applications for entrepreneurs, investors, and educators. While NLP offers transformative insights, challenges such as data scarcity, contextual nuances, cross-cultural biases, and ethical considerations must be addressed. The chapter concludes by outlining future opportunities, including multimodal analysis, AI-driven training, and inclusive ecosystem development,

Preface

The accelerating integration of artificial intelligence (AI) into entrepreneurial ecosystems marks a profound shift in how opportunities are identified, decisions are made, and ventures are developed. *Decision Making, Learning, and Collaboration in AI-Driven Entrepreneurship* brings together diverse scholarly perspectives to explore this transformation at the intersection of technology, human cognition, and innovation. The volume examines how AI not only enhances analytical capabilities but also reshapes behavioral, educational, and collaborative dimensions of entrepreneurship.

Entrepreneurship has always been characterized by uncertainty, intuition, and risk-taking. However, the emergence of AI introduces new mechanisms for augmenting human judgment through predictive analytics, intelligent systems, and adaptive learning environments. Rather than replacing the entrepreneur, AI increasingly functions as a strategic partner—supporting decision-making, reducing bias, and enabling more inclusive and resilient innovation ecosystems. At the same time, this transformation raises critical questions surrounding ethics, fairness, transparency, and the preservation of human creativity and emotional intelligence.

This book adopts a multidisciplinary approach, drawing on insights from behavioral finance, psychology, education, management, and data science. It explores how entrepreneurs interact with AI systems in contexts ranging from financial decision-making and talent development to leadership, communication, and resilience building. A central theme throughout the volume is the dynamic interplay between human intuition and machine intelligence, emphasizing that the future of entrepreneurship lies in their thoughtful integration.

In addition to examining practical applications, the chapters highlight emerging challenges, including algorithmic bias, data governance, digital inequality, and the psychological implications of human–AI collaboration. By addressing these issues, the book contributes to ongoing conversations about responsible AI adoption and the development of equitable entrepreneurial ecosystems worldwide.

CHAPTER OVERVIEW

Chapter 1 examines how AI-driven tools enhance entrepreneurial decision-making, risk assessment, and opportunity recognition while addressing cognitive biases and uncertainty.

Chapter 2 explores the relationship between behavioral finance theories, risk perception, and AI-supported financial decision-making in entrepreneurial contexts.

Chapter 3 investigates the use of AI in identifying and developing entrepreneurial talent through recruitment, training, and predictive assessment methods.

Chapter 4 analyzes the role of gamification and AI-driven simulations in fostering entrepreneurial skills, engagement, and experiential learning.

Chapter 5 discusses how AI enables personalized learning pathways in entrepreneurship education through adaptive systems and learning analytics.

Chapter 6 presents an integrative review of AI's impact on entrepreneurial mindset, creativity, and self-efficacy within educational frameworks.

Chapter 7 explores the evolving dynamics of human–AI collaboration and its influence on creativity, decision-making, and innovation in entrepreneurship.

Chapter 8 focuses on the development of cognitive resilience through AI-supported decision-making and human–AI interaction.

Chapter 9 examines the psychological dimensions of human–AI collaboration, particularly its role in enhancing resilience and managing entrepreneurial stress.

Chapter 10 investigates the transformative role of AI in women entrepreneurship, highlighting empowerment, challenges, and inclusive development.

Chapter 11 analyzes issues of bias and fairness in AI models of entrepreneurial traits and their implications for equitable innovation ecosystems.

Chapter 12 explores AI-based approaches to measuring emotional intelligence and their applications in entrepreneurship.

Chapter 13 discusses the integration of emotional intelligence with AI in shaping effective and empathetic entrepreneurial leadership.

Chapter 14 examines the application of natural language processing in analyzing entrepreneurial narratives, pitches, and communication strategies.

Collectively, these chapters provide a comprehensive exploration of how AI is redefining entrepreneurship—not as a purely technological shift, but as a reconfiguration of human potential, learning, and collaboration in an increasingly intelligent world.

Samreen Tunio
University of Milan, Italy

Muhammad Nawaz Tunio

University of Klagenfurt, Austria

Chapter 1
AI-Driven Insights Into Risk-Taking and Decision-Making Among Entrepreneurs

Xuan-Hoa Nghiem
http://orcid.org/0000-0003-2292-0257
International School, Vietnam National University, Hanoi, Vietnam

Mohit Yadav
http://orcid.org/0000-0002-9341-2527
O.P. Jindal Global University, India

Narayanage Jayantha Dewasiri
http://orcid.org/0000-0002-5908-8890
Faculty of Management Studies, Sabaragamuwa University of Sri Lanka, Sri Lanka & Qasim Ibrahim School of Business, Villa College, Maldives

ABSTRACT

Entrepreneurial decision-making is inherently complex, shaped by uncertainty, risk perception, and cognitive biases. The integration of artificial intelligence (AI) offers novel opportunities to enhance decision quality, mitigate biases, and support adaptive risk-taking. This chapter explores how AI tools—including predictive analytics, natural language processing, and simulation models—provide insights into entrepreneurial behavior, opportunity recognition, and resource allocation. It examines theoretical foundations of risk-taking, behavioral biases, and decision-making under uncertainty, highlighting how AI augments human judgment without replacing intuition or creativity. Practical applications, case studies, and emerging

DOI: 10.4018/979-8-2600-1353-3.ch001

trends demonstrate AI's potential to improve venture outcomes, enhance strategic flexibility, and promote inclusive entrepreneurial ecosystems. Ethical considerations, data governance, and algorithmic transparency are also discussed.

INTRODUCTION

Entrepreneurial activity has long been recognised as a process that is uncertain and ambiguous, as well as one that involves the necessary risk-taking that is calculated (McMullen and Shepherd, 2006). In dynamic and volatile settings, entrepreneurs make strategic decisions in which constrained information, and time constraints are often expected to damage rationality (Keh, Foo, and Lim, 2002). The traditional literature on entrepreneurial risk-taking and decision-making has largely been based on the psychological and behavioral theories, foregrounding heuristics, cognitive biases, and individual differences in risk perceptions (Kahneman and Tversky, 1979; Baron, 2004). Despite the substantive results of these frameworks, they are often being criticized by the complexity of the modern entrepreneurial ecosystems in which market indicators, social dynamics, and technological shocks interconnect in manners that cannot be analyzed linearly.

Artificial intelligence (AI) has emerged in recent years as a disruptive tool that can help overcome these multidimensional issues by providing new analytic methods to the perception and support of entrepreneurial decision-making (Cockburn, Henderson, and Stern, 2018). Machine learning, natural language processing and predictive analytics are AI techniques that allow identifying hidden trends in large and varied datasets that habitually escape human thinking (Jordan & Mitchell, 2015). This ability is especially relevant to entrepreneurship that is a multi-dimensional risk and is shaped by both psychological tendencies and contextual factors. Using AI, researchers and practitioners are able to dig up more information regarding the way entrepreneurs view, assess, and act upon risk under uncertain circumstances (Yadav et al., 2024).

This chapter aims at analyzing how AI-based insights may help us to better understand entrepreneurial risk-taking and decision-making. In particular, it examines the ways in which AI can supplement the existing theoretical models, reduce human biases, and provide effective instruments to entrepreneurs operating in complicated settings. Trying to fill the gap between psychological theories of business entrepreneurship and the technological progress that is already influencing the modern business practice, this chapter aims to place AI as a diagnostic and decision-support system.

Theoretical Underpinnings of Entrepreneurial Risk-Taking

Risk-taking has traditionally been perceived as one of the key features of entrepreneurship, being deeply intertwined with both old economics and modern psychology research. Early theorists like Cantillon (1755/2010) and Knight (1921) had stressed on the centrality of uncertainty in entrepreneurial behavior, distinguishing between entrepreneurs and managers on the basis of their risky behavior to take advantage of opportunity. The bifurcation of quantifiable risk and unquantifiable uncertainty proposed by Knight (1921) has continued to play a crucial role especially in explaining why the decision-making of an entrepreneur often involves taking a risk by entering a situation where the consequences are not completely foreseeable. It is on this heritage that risk-taking has been questioned by scholars as a characteristic that is a dynamic process of interaction among cognitive assessments, affective reactions, and environmental factors (Trivedi et al., 2023).

The psychological theories have been instrumental in the development of the modern perspective of entrepreneurial risk-taking. The use of prospect theory (Kahneman and Tversky, 1979) has been extensively used to identify the rationalization of the failures of entrepreneurs to assume rational economic behavior, and it has been established that people tend to overweight losses in comparison with similar gains systematically. This observation explains why entrepreneurs can be either too cautious or overcommitted depending on the way opportunities are characterized. Equally, the idea of a limited rationality (Simon, 1997) highlights the fact that entrepreneurs who are limited by information and cognitive resources utilise heuristics and simplified rules of decision making in the face of uncertainty. These heuristics often have systematic biases like overconfidence, optimistic bias or illusion of control which in turn influences the entrepreneurial risk preferences (Baron, 2004; Simon, Houghton, and Aquino, 2000; Yadav et al., 2019).

On the behavioral perspective, personality traits and motivational drives will also determine risk-taking behavior. According to the trait perspective, entrepreneurs tend to have greater tolerance to ambiguity, internal locus of control and high achievement needs compared to non-entrepreneurs (McClelland, 1961; Rauch and Frese, 2007). These psychological traits do not only predispose entrepreneurs to risk activities, but also mediate the manner in which they perceive and react to uncertain situations. Entrepreneurial risk behavior is further mediated through social and contextual factors including cultural norms, institutional settings as well as peer influence (Mitchell et al., 2002). All these theoretical strands point to the fact that entrepreneurial risk-taking is not strictly rational or strictly stochastic but the result of a complicated interplay between personal cognition, affective states, and environmental signals (Tayal et al., 2021).

Although the foundational theories are quite insightful, they also show weaknesses in their ability to capture the multidimensional and dynamic aspects of risk in the modern entrepreneurial environment. The advent of digital markets, accelerated technological change and globally integrated ecosystems has created an environment where the classical decision-making paradigms are unable to explain the speed and intricacy of risk (Grégoire, Corbett, and McMullen, 2011). This creates a strong motivation to include AI as an analytical and interpretive tool to further develop our insights on the ways in which entrepreneurs analyse and deal with risk in practice. These theoretical bases can be expanded by AI-based solutions that identify the patterns of the entrepreneurial behavior that can still be hidden in the traditional psychological or economic framework (Choudhary et al., 2024).

Decision Making in the Face of Uncertainty.

Entrepreneurial decision-making is contextually situated in uncertain situations where the results cannot only be unpredictable, but frequently unknown in advance. The business environment that entrepreneurs face is volatile, where the structure is not fully developed and customer needs change fast unlike managers who are working in relatively stable environments (McMullen and Shepherd, 2006). The fact that risk is calculable in probabilistic terms, whereas uncertainty cannot be, as pointed out by Knight in 1921, is still the backbone on explaining the entrepreneurial condition. This delineation highlights the fact that decision-making in entrepreneurial situations needs to be more than the rational optimisation; the decisions-making must have the ability to make decisions in the face of uncertainty and the lack of predictive models with certainty (Afshan et al., 2021).

A number of decision-making models have been used in explaining the ways that entrepreneurs make decisions under uncertainty. According to the rational choice model, entrepreneurs are assumed to explore options systematically, consider probabilities and maximise the utility of their expectations (March, 1994). Nevertheless, human cognition, time constraints and information overload make a strictly rational decision-making process unlikely. Simon (1997) suggests that entrepreneurs make satisfice decisions, i.e. they make a decision that is good enough and not necessarily the best. Availability, representativeness and anchoring are the heuristics commonly used by entrepreneurs when faced with high uncertainty in order to make complex judgments simple (Kahneman, 2011). Despite the fact that heuristics are quicker in making decisions, they also subject entrepreneurs to systematic biases such as overconfidence and escalation of commitment (Busenitz and Barney, 1997; Tunio et al., 2021).

The role of uncertainty in entrepreneurial decision-making is also explained by behavioral economics and psychology. Prospect theory (Kahneman and Tversky,

1979) states that entrepreneurs do not assess risky decisions based on actual results but against a reference point, and risk-seeking behaviour is common when they face possible losses and risk-aversion when they face possible gains. Such framing effect has been witnessed in investment decision making of entrepreneurs where the perception of loss or opportunity cost is a major determinant of strategic judgment (Luce and Weber, 1986). At the same time, individual differences, including ambiguity tolerance, emotional control, and previous entrepreneurial experience mediate the interpretation and action of uncertainty (Sarasvathy, 2001; Mitchell et al., 2002; Gilal et al., 2020).

The importance of effectuation in making decisions in the face of uncertainty has also been highlighted in the contemporary entrepreneurship scholarship. Sarasvathy (2001) assumed that entrepreneurs do not always have a predetermined aim; they use the available resources, experiment and co-produce opportunities with stakeholders. This is unlike causal logic which focuses on predictive planning and formal risk assessment. Effectuation is more about a less predictive, more adaptive strategy that places a premium on control over prediction in situations of high uncertainty. The result of such adaptive decision-making is the reason why entrepreneurs are usually tougher than the traditional framework implies they see uncertainty as a source of creative space and innovation, rather than a risk.

Although these theoretical developments have been made, understanding how to make decisions in the situation of uncertainty is not an easy task since traditional models are not capable of capturing the nonlinear and dynamic nature of the entrepreneurial environment. The growing sophistication of globalised markets, digital ecosystems and disruptive innovations requires new instruments to examine uncertainty more holistically. AI provides a new lens to overcome these shortcomings, providing predictive analytics, scenario modelling, and pattern recognition which can supplement human judgements in uncertain situations (Brynjolfsson and McAfee, 2017). With a combination of human flexibility with AI-contributed knowledge, entrepreneurs will be able to shift to more informed and resilient decision-making.

The AI as a Lens to understand Entrepreneurial Behavior.

Artificial intelligence (AI) has become a revolutionary tool to study the intricate behavioural patterns, providing the new insights into entrepreneurial decision-making and risk-taking. In contrast to traditional research tools that rely on surveys, self-reports, and experimental designs, AI enables the study of large-scale, unstructured, and dynamic data that reflect the reality of entrepreneurial ecosystems (Brynjolfsson and McAfee, 2017). As an example, information obtained through social media, venture-capital, online pitch, and even biometric information can be crunched through machine-learning algorithms to reveal behavioural patterns that were not previously reachable to researchers (Shrestha, Ben-Menahem, and Krogh, 2019). This ability not only makes AI a technological support but also a new perspective in light of which the cognitive, affective, and social aspects of the entrepreneurial world can be viewed in an entirely new way.

NLP and sentiment analysis are examples of AI techniques that help researchers assess the wording that entrepreneurs use in pitch decks, crowdfunding pitches, and interviews and detect implicit risk attitudes, confidence, and persuasive efforts (Huang and Pearce, 2015). Similarly, predictive analytics will be able to identify the relationship between entrepreneurial decision styles and venture performance, allowing a more subtle view of how an entrepreneur handles uncertainty. The deep-learning algorithms, which are effective in identifying non-linear and non-uniform relationships, are particularly useful in modelling the decision-making processes that the traditional linear models are barely able to represent (Jordan and Mitchell, 2015). By taking these methods, the scholars can no longer rely on the traditional models of entrepreneurial cognition but rather they are able to capture the dynamic interaction of factors that influence behaviour over time.

The ability of AI to detect and reduce cognitive biases is one of the most promising uses of AI in the study of entrepreneurship. Just like any other decision-maker, entrepreneurs are susceptible to the heuristics of overconfidence, confirmation bias, and optimism bias (Baron, 2004). AI systems that are trained on historical data will be able to indicate decisions that are significantly not in line with rational standards or areas where there are blind spots, thus providing entrepreneurs with real-time feedback that will help them understand themselves better. To illustrate, AI-based decision-support systems have the ability to simulate a variety of situations, stress-test assumptions, and counterfactuals, thus compelling entrepreneurs to rethink biased or excessively risky judgments (Dwivedi et al., 2021). This way, AI will not only become a spectator to more thoughtful and evidence-based decision-making, but also an active contributor to it.

Despite all these benefits, the use of AI as a prism through which one can view entrepreneurial behaviour is not limited to nothing. The results of algorithmic insights are extremely sensitive to the quality and representativeness of the data on which they were trained which makes one raise the issue of inherent biases within datasets (O'Neil, 2016). Additionally, AI may shed light on trends and associations, but it is often not as contextual and interpretive-rich as human cognition adds to entrepreneurial decision-making. In turn, AI is supposed to be an addition to, but not a replacement of, the human judgment and psychological theory. Combining AI with the existing behavioural models, researchers will be able to obtain a more comprehensive view of entrepreneurial behaviour that would cover not only the data-driven regularities but also the human subtleties of uncertainty-driven decision-making.

Artificial Intelligence-Based Insights on risk perception and risk assessment.

The central part of entrepreneurial decision-making is risk perception and evaluation, which determines whether an opportunity is taken or not. The self-report method and the controlled experiments have traditionally been used to study risk perception, although they have a limitation in the ability to capture the complexity and dynamism of the real entrepreneurial situation (Keh, Foo, and Lim, 2002). Artificial intelligence (AI) can be a powerful complement to these strategies because it allows recognising subtle behavioural and contextual patterns that shape the perception and assessment of risk in entrepreneurs. Using massive datasets, AI devices can discover how personal characteristics, cognitive biases, and environmental cues interact, and give finer details about risk-taking behaviour (Chaudhry et al., 2021).

Machine-learning algorithms, such as, can be used to scan historical data of venture performance to identify typical risk-evaluation strategies of successful and unsuccessful entrepreneurs (Ransbotham et al., 2021). These analyses may indicate behavioural biases, including overestimating the demand in the market or underestimating the risks of operation, which are usually obscure to human reasoning. In the same spirit, NLP has been adapted to analyze entrepreneurial communication, i.e. investor pitch, crowdfunding campaign, or interview, to identify linguistic indicators of optimism, confidence, or risk aversion (Allison, Davis, Short, and Webb, 2015). These indicators are indirect but strong indicators of the way in which entrepreneurs frame risks and opportunities and hence inform their own decision-making as well as those of stakeholders.

Predictive analytics based on AI also allow assessing risk in real time in dynamic scenarios. As an example, the simulation models can be used to create scenarios under dynamic market conditions, which in turn allows entrepreneurs to check the strength of their strategies prior to resource allocation (Brynjolfsson & McAfee, 2017). Such models provide business people with a more comprehensive picture of risk potentials by synthesising financial indicators, consumer sentiment data and competitor behaviour. Notably, these tools help not only to identify objective risk factors but also to reveal the discrepancy between actual and perceived risk, thus helping entrepreneurs to realise that their judgment is distorted by such cognitive biases like the overconfidence or optimism bias (Baron, 2004).

Furthermore, AI enables creating customised risk profiles using the information of various fields, such as psychological tests, previous entrepreneurial activity, and online footprints (Shrestha, Ben-Menahem, and Krogh, 2019). Such profiles can alert entrepreneurs to their individual risk inclinations, and offer specific advice that is a mix of intuition and evidence-based assessment. To illustrate, an entrepreneur who has a tendency to take risks should be given warnings by AI about the possibility of negative events, and a super cautious entrepreneur should be advised to explore more lucrative opportunities. This way, AI is a diagnostic and corrective system in the process of evaluating the risk of entrepreneurship (Rashid et al., 2024).

Although these are promising applications, there are challenges posed by the dependence on AI to determine risk perception and evaluation. Algorithms are limited to the quality and representativeness of training data, and there is a fear of strengthening the already existing biases or missing the contextual nuances (O'Neil, 2016). Moreover, AI models interpretability is an acute topic; machine learning can identify patterns but it does not necessarily explain the reasons why one risk is considered to be more salient than another. As a result, there is a need to combine the insights of AI with human intuition and expertise in a field. Instead of replacing human judgement, AI must be framed as a complementary resource that will improve the ability of entrepreneurs to perceive and assess risks more effectively in uncertain situations.

Practical decision-making in entrepreneurial activities with the assistance of AI.

Entrepreneurial decision-making is often limited by the scarcity of information, time, and high uncertainty. In this context, artificial intelligence (AI) systems can be a useful supplement to human thinking, offering data-driven information, simulation of situations, and real-time feedback to enhance judgment. The AI-based platforms, unlike the traditional systems of decision support, use continuous learning to adapt strategies to new conditions, as they change, and thus allow the entrepreneurs to adjust their strategies dynamically (Brynjolfsson and McAfee, 2017). This is an adaptive ability that is applicable especially in the field of entrepreneurship where the markets change very fast and opportunities have to be evaluated in a shortened time.

AI-based decision dashboards combine various types of data, including financial data and customer responses with competitor insights, into visualisations accessible to a user and help them make more informed strategic decisions (Chatterjee, Rana, Tamilmani, and Sharma, 2020). These systems allow business persons to track the key performance indicators in real-time, estimate the risk exposure, and analyze the effect of the potential decisions in various situations. Predictive analytics can also complement such dashboards with predictive trends, resource requirements, and investment results, which makes them less dependent on intuition (Jordan and Mitchell, 2015). These are not tools that can remove uncertainty but enable it to be dealt with in a more manageable way by giving probabilistic estimates of what the future might hold.

Another area where AI is greatly beneficial in entrepreneurial decision-making is simulation and scenario analysis tools. Complex market dynamics can be simulated using agent-based models and reinforcement learning algorithms and enable entrepreneurs to explore strategic alternatives in a virtual environment before implementing them (Ransbotham et al., 2021). As an example, an entrepreneur who wants to go international can use AI-driven simulations to simulate consumer reactions, regulatory shifts, and competitor reactions and get a more sophisticated view of the possible threats and benefits. Such capabilities make the process of decision-making dynamic rather than reactive so that the entrepreneurs can venture into unforeseen circumstances that would not have been considered.

Opportunity recognition, which is an essential aspect of entrepreneurship, is also a critical role of AI tools. AI systems can identify new trends and unmet demands sooner than the traditional market research approaches by analysing large volumes of unstructured information, including discussions on social media, search engine queries, or even patent applications (Nambisan, 2017). This is a competitive advantage that entrepreneur is given by this early identification and they are able to place their enterprises ahead of the others. In addition, the natural language processing (NLP) applications are able to analyse customer feedback and spot the unspoken indication of dissatisfaction or change in demand and optimise opportunity assessment.

In addition to the opportunity identification and risk assessment, AI applications can reduce the biases in decision-making. Entrepreneurs tend to be overconfident, have confirmation bias, or escalation of commitment, and it can lead to a failure in venture (Busenitz and Barney, 1997). AI based decision helps to overcome these biases by showing evidence based alternatives, pointing out anomalies, and creating counterfactuals. As an example, the recommendation systems can test the assumptions of entrepreneurs by showing how different strategies can work in different market conditions. This corrective role leads to creating a more balanced and rational decision-making process and increases the resilience of entrepreneurial activities (Dwivedi et al., 2021).

Although these advances have been made, there are no challenges in integrating AI in entrepreneurial decision-making. The use of algorithms can undermine the worth of entrepreneurial intuition and creativity, which is a critical ability to get through uncertainty (Huang and Pearce, 2015). Also, the explainability of AI models is an issue because the entrepreneurs might not be ready to make important decisions relying on obscure algorithms. Therefore, the best application of AI tools is in an integrated approach where the role of a human and machine intelligence comes into play. This model is based on AI, which offers systematic analysis and predictive ideas, and entrepreneurs, who offer contextual understanding, ethical argument, and innovative vision. This kind of synergy allows stronger, adaptive, and creative decision-making in the entrepreneurial practice.

Bias Detection and Correction through AI

As with all decision-makers, entrepreneurs are prone to cognitive and affective biases that may lead to distortion of judgement and failure of the venture. The errors of common belief, such as overconfidence, confirmation bias, optimism bias, and escalation of commitment, influence the process of risk and opportunities estimation (Busenitz and Barney, 1997; Kahneman, 2011). Such biases are especially troublesome when it comes to the world of entrepreneurship, where the decisions are usually associated with a great deal of uncertainty and lack of information. The common methods of bias mitigation like training, reflection, or group decision-making have proved to be ineffective because biases are so ingrained and are often unconscious (Baron, 2004). Artificial intelligence (AI), though, provides the potential solutions to identify, expose and address such biases through the analysis of decision patterns and offering objective counterarguments to human judgement.

The AI systems will be able to detect the biases by analyzing the differences between the decisions made by the entrepreneurs and the historical trends or rational standards. As an example, predictive analytics may identify the cases of an entrepreneur who constantly overestimates revenue forecasts in comparison with the industry averages, which is an indicator of overconfidence (Dwivedi et al., 2021). NLP can also be used to analyse the communication patterns of pitch decks, during an interview or team discussion, and identify either overuse of positive language or framing that signifies confirmation bias (Huang and Pearce, 2015). Marking these trends, AI creates a mirror that will make subconscious biases transparent in order to make the entrepreneurs see the picture more objectively.

In addition to detection, AI can play a corrective role by providing evidence-based alternatives that can address biases in decision tendencies. A counterfactual situation can be created with the help of decision-support tools such as visualizing how a venture will act in less favourable circumstances, which in turn can dispute over-optimistic assumptions (Brynjolfsson and McAfee, 2017). Similarly, the recommendation systems may open up a range of options to the entrepreneur than he or she would have independently, which reduces the narrowing effect of confirmation bias. In financial decision making, AI is able to instill discipline by suggesting diversification measure, which counters the phenomenon of escalation of commitment that usually comes out when entrepreneurs continue to invest on failing projects (Simon, Houghton, and Aquino, 2000).

One of the key aspects of AI-based bias correction is its personalisation. The algorithms of machine learning can create a personal bias profile basing on previous choices of an entrepreneur, and indicate the consistent behaviours, including a tendency to be too risk-averse or risk-seeking (Shrestha, Ben-Menahem, and Krogh, 2019). Individualised feedback would help business people to be more self-aware of their own cognitive blind spots, which would lead to a learning process that enhances the quality of decisions made in the long term. As an external cognitive assistant, AI can help entrepreneurs balance between evidence and intuition by helping them to calibrate their judgments.

Nonetheless, the use of AI as a tool to identify and rectify biases also creates serious ethical and practical issues. Algorithms are also not bias-free; when provided with biased or partial data, they can reproduce or even enhance the existing distortions (O'Neil, 2016). In addition, the overreliance of AI might decrease the independence of an entrepreneur, substituting human creativity and intuition with strict algorithmic direction. Therefore, AI is not to be seen as an alternative to human decision-making but as a complementary device. The best way to do it is to create a collaborative relationship where AI brings up possible biases but the ultimate decision is still in the hands of the entrepreneur, thus maintaining the human aspect in entrepreneurial innovation.

Difficulties and Ethical Problems.

Even though artificial intelligence (AI) has a disruptive potential to change the nature of risk-taking in entrepreneurship and decision-making, there is also a list of challenges and ethical issues that can be raised in connection with the implementation of AI. One of the main problems is the untransparency of AI algorithms, which can be referred to as the black box problem. Most machine learning models especially the deep learning systems do not give reasoned outputs and this means that entrepreneurs cannot understand or trust the recommendations at all (Burrell, 2016). This non-interpretability creates accountability concerns because entrepreneurs can be informed by insights that cannot be sufficiently disclosed to the stakeholders, investors, or regulators.

The other issue is that of data quality and bias. The AI systems depend on the data that they are trained on. In case historical data are based on systemic inequalities or partial market data, the algorithms will tend to preserve or even increase these biases (O'Neil, 2016). To illustrate, the funding recommendation systems can end up giving preferential treatment to the entrepreneurs who come out of the historically well-represented groups, which further entrenches the bias in financing a venture. Not only are such outcomes detrimental to fairness, but they also threaten to block out innovative ideas of the underrepresented groups.

Ethics are also applied to the area of privacy and data management. In order to feed AI models, entrepreneurs often use sensitive datasets, such as customer behaviour, financial records, or personal information. The absence of strict protection can lead to abuse of this information or its leakage, which is why the issue of consent, possession, and abuse is of concern (Zuboff, 2019). Abuse of consumer information in business activities may destroy trust, which is very essential to a startup that has entered a competitive market. The entrepreneurs are thus faced with the challenge of balancing the advantages of AI-based insights with responsible data management and adherence to emerging rules including the General Data Protection Regulation (GDPR).

The danger of becoming too dependent on AI tools is also a possibility, which can reduce the significance of entrepreneurial intuition and creativity. Entrepreneurship is a business that is driven by imagination, vision, and the ability to see the possibilities that the data might not show (Huang and Pearce, 2015). When decision-making is too mechanised, the ventures will lose their disruptive innovation ability and will rather tend to converge to risk-averse, data-driven homogeneity. Such a conflict highlights the importance of hybrid decision models, where AI complements and does not replace human judgment.

Lastly, when it comes to responsibility and accountability, there are still ethical debates. In case the AI-based suggestion results in poor choices, who is to be held responsible, the entrepreneur, the developer of the AI, or the data provider? (Floridi & Cowls, 2019). The spread of responsibility makes legal and ethical responsibility of practice in entrepreneurship complicated. In order to address these issues, there is a need to have transparent governance systems, ethical AI principles and training programmes to enable entrepreneurs to use AI tools in a responsible manner without losing accountability.

To conclude, although AI can enhance the accuracy of decisions and reduce the biases, its adoption in entrepreneurial practice is surrounded by a number of challenges, which go beyond technical application. Transparency, bias, privacy, over-reliance, and accountability are some of the concerns, which highlight the need to incorporate ethical considerations with technology integration. A moderate position, based on responsible innovation, will be necessary, so that AI does not undermine fairness, trust, or human creativity among the entrepreneurs.

Applications and Future Direction.

The concept of artificial intelligence (AI) being applied to entrepreneurial risk-taking and decision-making has transformed into a hypothetical idea all the way to becoming a ubiquitous phenomenon that can be observed in many industries. The scope of AI applications in the entrepreneurship domain is quite extensive, including the offer of opportunities, strategy formulation, and implementation. As an example, the growing companies more often introduce AI-based analytics systems to identify the needs of consumers by analyzing social media trends, on-line reviews, and live buying behaviors (Nambisan, 2017). These abilities enable entrepreneurs to predict market changes ahead of their rivals and they are able to produce products that meet new demands. Similarly, AI-based financial forecasting tools are useful to an entrepreneur in capital allocation and fundraising by modeling several investment options and providing evidence-based risk assessments (Jordan and Mitchell, 2015). In fields like healthcare and fintech, virtual advisors AI chatbots and decision-support systems are already used to guide entrepreneurs on how to engage with their customers and comply with regulations (Dwivedi et al., 2021).

The other application that is salient is venture capital and investment decision-making whereby entrepreneurs and investors use AI to reduce uncertainty. Machine-learning algorithms are used to study the trends in the success of startups, the experience of the founders, and the trends of the sector and predict success in a venture to guide the decision to fund a startup (Shrestha, Ben-Menahem, and Krogh, 2019). These tools can be used by the entrepreneurs to improve the pitch preparation by comparison with successful cases and outline the areas where improvement can be made. The mitigation of biases is also facilitated by AI so that the entrepreneurial projects of varied founders could be evaluated more fairly, depending on the quality and representativeness of the training data.

In the future, the future of AI in the entrepreneurial practice is in the direction of more symbiotic relations between human decision-makers and intelligent systems. The development of explainable AI (XAI) can potentially reduce the problem of transparency and allow business owners to understand why an algorithm offers specific suggestions and be able to use them in a strategy (Burrell, 2016). Similarly, real-time adaptive systems that constantly absorb the changing market conditions will provide entrepreneurs with dynamic feedback loops, which will assist in agile pivots and iterative innovation. This evolution can introduce the era of augmented entrepreneurship, when human imagination, intuition, and vision will be systematically enhanced by predictive abilities and computational skills of AI (Brynjolfsson and McAfee, 2017).

Moreover, the development of collaborative ecosystems based on AI platforms is likely to transform the entrepreneurial networks. The AI-driven markets and innovation centres can connect entrepreneurs to resources, mentors, and partners more efficiently, thus democratising knowledge and capital access (Nambisan, 2017). Also, AI can be used as a sustainable entrepreneurship tool, helping entrepreneurs to assess the environmental and social implications of their businesses and trade-off profitability and responsibility (Floridi and Cowls, 2019).

Although these trends are encouraging, to make AI potential in the entrepreneurship industry a reality, one has to address the issues of algorithmic bias, data management, and ethical responsibility. Future studies are necessary to examine how hybrid human-AI decision models can retain entrepreneurial creativity and at the same time be evidence-based. Government officials, educators, and business executives should work together to set standards that will help ethical AI use in entrepreneurial ecosystems. Finally, the future of AI in entrepreneurship is promising, which implies that, in the future, machine intelligence is not going to replace human judgment but complement it: entrepreneurs will be able to make more informed decisions, make better decisions, and build more innovative and socially responsible ventures.

CONCLUSION

The concept of artificial intelligence (AI) as part of entrepreneurial risk-taking and decision-making is a paradigm shift in how entrepreneurs approach uncertainty, opportunity, and strategy implementation. The classical theories of entrepreneurship, which are based on the psychology, economics, and decision making based on heuristics and cognitive bias, have long provided useful information about how cognitive bias, heuristics and risk perceptions influence entrepreneurial behaviour (Kahneman and Tversky, 1979; Baron, 2004; McMullen and Shepherd, 2006). The sophistication of modern entrepreneurial ecosystems, however, with the speed of technological transformation and integration of the world market requires the means that can process large, dynamic, and multi-faceted data. AI can provide this ability, improving the accuracy and timeliness of entrepreneurial decisions and at the same time offering the means of identifying and controlling cognitive biases.

AI helps entrepreneurs to understand and assess risks better, recognise emergent opportunities, and allocate resources optimally through applications like predictive analytics, natural language processing, and scenario simulation (Brynjolfsson and McAfee, 2017; Jordan and Mitchell, 2015). Moreover, analysis of the behavioural pattern with AI and formulation of evidence-based recommendations makes decision-making more thoughtful and balanced and does not replace human intuition, but complements it (Shrestha, Ben-Menahem, and Krogh, 2019). The practical implementations and empirical case studies demonstrate that AI tools may positively impact the outcomes of the ventures, increase strategic flexibility, and democratise knowledge and resource access in entrepreneurial ecosystems.

At the same time, the use of AI in entrepreneurship also introduces important ethical and operational issues, such as transparency of the algorithm, data privacy, training dataset bias, and responsibility of the decision results (O'Neil, 2016; Burrell, 2016; Floridi and Cowls, 2019). The solutions to these issues lie in a delicate balance between the technological implementation and human control over them, and in the focus on the hybrid models of decision-making that should be based on AI insights and supplemented with entrepreneurial decisions, creativity, and situational awareness. In such a way, the entrepreneurs can utilize the power of AI without losing the human characteristics of imagination, vision, and ethical responsibility needed to innovate and develop a sustainable venture.

To conclude, the future of AI and entrepreneurship suggests a future where the process of decision-making is more and more augmented, but not automated, where machine intelligence is systematically integrated with human intuition. This integration will not only lead to a smarter risk-taking and discovery of opportunities, but also a more resilient, adaptable, and inclusive entrepreneurial ecosystem. With a combination of stringent theoretical base and AI-inspired knowledge, researchers and practitioners can learn more and influence the entrepreneurial behaviour in a fast-paced digital environment. Finally, AI has the power to turn entrepreneurship into a field that is not limited by the uncertainty factor but where risk-taking is calculated and evidence-based, and spurs innovation and value generation.

REFERENCES

Afshan, G., Shahid, S., & Tunio, M. N. (2021). Learning experiences of women entrepreneurs amidst COVID-19. *International Journal of Gender and Entrepreneurship, 13*(2), 162–186. DOI: 10.1108/IJGE-09-2020-0153

Allison, T. H., Davis, B. C., Short, J. C., & Webb, J. W. (2015). Crowdfunding in a prosocial micro-lending environment: Examining the role of intrinsic versus extrinsic cues. *Entrepreneurship Theory and Practice, 39*(1), 53–73. DOI: 10.1111/etap.12108

Baron, R. A. (2004). The cognitive perspective: A valuable tool for answering entrepreneurship's basic "why" questions. *Journal of Business Venturing, 19*(2), 221–239. DOI: 10.1016/S0883-9026(03)00008-9

Brynjolfsson, E., & McAfee, A. (2017). *Machine, platform, crowd: Harnessing our digital future*. W. W. Norton & Company.

Burrell, J. (2016). How the machine 'thinks': Understanding opacity in machine learning algorithms. *Big Data & Society, 3*(1), 1–12. DOI: 10.1177/2053951715622512

Busenitz, L. W., & Barney, J. B. (1997). Differences between entrepreneurs and managers in large organizations: Biases and heuristics in strategic decision-making. *Journal of Business Venturing, 12*(1), 9–30. DOI: 10.1016/S0883-9026(96)00003-1

Cantillon, R. (2010). *Essay on the nature of trade in general* (Higgs, H., Trans.). Liberty Fund. (Original work published 1755)

Chatterjee, S., Rana, N. P., Tamilmani, K., & Sharma, A. (2020). The next generation of technology-enabled decision-making: Artificial intelligence and big data. *Journal of Business Research, 124*, 311–320. DOI: 10.1016/j.jbusres.2020.11.015

Chaudhry, I. S., Paquibut, R. Y., & Tunio, M. N. (2021). Do workforce diversity, inclusion practices, & organizational characteristics contribute to organizational innovation? Evidence from the UAE. *Cogent Business & Management, 8*(1), 1947549. DOI: 10.1080/23311975.2021.1947549

Choudhary, S., Yadav, M., & Srivastava, A. P. (2024). Cognitive biases among millennial Indian investors: Do personality and demographic factors matter? *FIIB Business Review, 13*(1), 106–117. DOI: 10.1177/23197145211057343

Cockburn, I. M., Henderson, R., & Stern, S. (2018). The impact of artificial intelligence on innovation. *The National Bureau of Economic Research Working Paper Series*, (24449), 1–37. DOI: 10.3386/w24449

Dwivedi, Y. K., Hughes, L., Baabdullah, A. M., Ribeiro-Navarrete, S., Giannakis, M., Al-Debei, M. M., Dennehy, D., Metri, B., Buhalis, D., Cheung, C. M. K., Conboy, K., Doyle, R., Dubey, R., Dutot, V., Felix, R., Goyal, D. P., Gustafsson, A., Hinsch, C., Jebabli, I., & Wamba, S. F. (2021). Metaverse beyond the hype: Multidisciplinary perspectives on emerging challenges, opportunities, and agenda for research, practice and policy. *International Journal of Information Management*, *66*, 102542. DOI: 10.1016/j.ijinfomgt.2022.102542

Floridi, L., & Cowls, J. (2019). A unified framework of five principles for AI in society. *Harvard Data Science Review*, *1*(1), 1–15. DOI: 10.1162/99608f92.8cd550d1

Gilal, F. G., Gilal, N. G., Channa, N. A., Gilal, R. G., Gilal, R. G., & Tunio, M. N. (2020). Towards an integrated model for the transference of environmental responsibility. *Business Strategy and the Environment*, *29*(6), 2614–2623. DOI: 10.1002/bse.2524

Grégoire, D. A., Corbett, A. C., & McMullen, J. S. (2011). The cognitive perspective in entrepreneurship: An agenda for future research. *Journal of Management Studies*, *48*(6), 1443–1477. DOI: 10.1111/j.1467-6486.2010.00922.x

Huang, L., & Pearce, J. L. (2015). Managing the unknowable: The effectiveness of early-stage investor gut feel in entrepreneurial investment decisions. *Administrative Science Quarterly*, *60*(4), 634–670. DOI: 10.1177/0001839215597270

Jordan, M. I., & Mitchell, T. M. (2015). Machine learning: Trends, perspectives, and prospects. *Science*, *349*(6245), 255–260. DOI: 10.1126/science.aaa8415

Kahneman, D. (2011). *Thinking, fast and slow*. Farrar, Straus and Giroux.

Kahneman, D., & Tversky, A. (1979). Prospect theory: An analysis of decision under risk. *Econometrica*, *47*(2), 263–291. DOI: 10.2307/1914185

Keh, H. T., Foo, M. D., & Lim, B. C. (2002). Opportunity evaluation under risky conditions: The cognitive processes of entrepreneurs. *Entrepreneurship Theory and Practice*, *27*(2), 125–148. DOI: 10.1111/1540-8520.00003

Knight, F. H. (1921). *Risk, uncertainty, and profit*. Houghton Mifflin.

Luce, R. D., & Weber, E. U. (1986). An axiomatic theory of conjoint, expected risk. *Journal of Mathematical Psychology*, *30*(2), 188–205. DOI: 10.1016/0022-2496(86)90013-1

March, J. G. (1994). *A primer on decision making: How decisions happen*. Free Press.

McClelland, D. C. (1961). *The achieving society*. Van Nostrand. DOI: 10.1037/14359-000

McMullen, J. S., & Shepherd, D. A. (2006). Entrepreneurial action and the role of uncertainty in the theory of the entrepreneur. *Academy of Management Review*, *31*(1), 132–152. DOI: 10.5465/amr.2006.19379628

Mitchell, R. K., Busenitz, L., Lant, T., McDougall, P. P., Morse, E. A., & Smith, J. B. (2002). Toward a theory of entrepreneurial cognition: Rethinking the people side of entrepreneurship research. *Entrepreneurship Theory and Practice*, *27*(2), 93–104. DOI: 10.1111/1540-8520.00001

Nambisan, S. (2017). Digital entrepreneurship: Toward a digital technology perspective of entrepreneurship. *Entrepreneurship Theory and Practice*, *41*(6), 1029–1055. DOI: 10.1111/etap.12254

O'Neil, C. (2016). *Weapons of math destruction: How big data increases inequality and threatens democracy*. Crown.

Ransbotham, S., Kiron, D., Gerbert, P., & Reeves, M. (2021). Artificial intelligence in business gets real. *MIT Sloan Management Review*, *63*(1), 1–14.

Rashid, A., Rasheed, R., Ngah, A. H., Pradeepa Jayaratne, M. D. R., Rahi, S., & Tunio, M. N. (2024). Role of information processing and digital supply chain in supply chain resilience through supply chain risk management. *Journal of Global Operations and Strategic Sourcing*, *17*(2), 429–447. DOI: 10.1108/JGOSS-12-2023-0106

Rauch, A., & Frese, M. (2007). Born to be an entrepreneur? Revisiting the personality approach to entrepreneurship. In Baum, J. R., Frese, M., & Baron, R. (Eds.), *The psychology of entrepreneurship* (pp. 41–65). Lawrence Erlbaum Associates.

Sarasvathy, S. D. (2001). Causation and effectuation: Toward a theoretical shift from economic inevitability to entrepreneurial contingency. *Academy of Management Review*, *26*(2), 243–263. DOI: 10.2307/259121

Shrestha, Y. R., Ben-Menahem, S. M., & Krogh, G. V. (2019). Organizational decision-making structures in the age of artificial intelligence. *California Management Review*, *61*(4), 66–83. DOI: 10.1177/0008125619862257

Simon, H. A. (1997). *Administrative behavior* (4th ed.). Free Press.

Simon, M., Houghton, S. M., & Aquino, K. (2000). Cognitive biases, risk perception, and venture formation: How individuals decide to start companies. *Journal of Business Venturing*, *15*(2), 113–134. DOI: 10.1016/S0883-9026(98)00003-2

Tayal, R., Upadhyay, R. K., Yadav, M., & Singh, R. (2021). The development and validation of the organizational effectiveness scale using confirmatory factor analysis. *Global Business Review*, *22*(3), 821–843. DOI: 10.1177/0972150918811720

Trivedi, S. K., Vishnu, S., Singh, A., & Yadav, M. (2023). Research trends in sustainable E-payment systems: A study using topic modeling approach. *IEEE Transactions on Engineering Management*, *71*, 7511–7525. DOI: 10.1109/TEM.2023.3280216

Trivedi, V., Banerji, D., & Yadav, M. (2023). Expecting the surprises: Role of hope in consumer repurchase intentions in an online shopping environment. *Journal of Strategic Marketing*, *31*(4), 794–816. DOI: 10.1080/0965254X.2021.1996449

Tunio, M. N., Chaudhry, I. S., Shaikh, S., Jariko, M. A., & Brahmi, M. (2021). Determinants of the sustainable entrepreneurial engagement of youth in developing country—An empirical evidence from Pakistan. *Sustainability (Basel)*, *13*(14), 7764. DOI: 10.3390/su13147764

Yadav, M., Rangnekar, S., & Srivastava, A. P. (2019). Demographic variables as moderators between QWL and OCB. *Industrial and Commercial Training*, *51*(7/8), 396–408. DOI: 10.1108/ICT-04-2018-0040

Yadav, R., Yadav, M., & Vihari, N. S. (2024). High-performance work system and learning orientation in offline, online, and hybrid workplaces: The mediating role of affective commitment. *The Learning Organization*, *31*(1), 122–136. DOI: 10.1108/TLO-10-2022-0118

Zuboff, S. (2019). *The age of surveillance capitalism: The fight for a human future at the new frontier of power*. PublicAffairs.

Chapter 2
Entrepreneurial Risk Perception and AI-Driven Financial Decision-Making: A Behavioral Finance Perspective

Mansi Panwar
http://orcid.org/0009-0007-0470-8216
Devi Ahilya Vishwavidyalaya University in Indore, India

Pratiksha Saxena
http://orcid.org/0009-0008-3643-1327
Amity University, Gwalior, India

Manish Dubey
Shri Vaishnav College of Arts and Commerce, Indore, India

Bhumika Ray
http://orcid.org/0009-0002-6518-7227
O.P. Jindal Global University, India

Shashi Kant
http://orcid.org/0000-0003-4722-5736
School of Management, DMI-St. Eugene University, Zambia

ABSTRACT

Most companies in a modern digitalized economy are resorting to artificial intelligence (AI) to assist them in making strategic and financial decisions. Yet these are

DOI: 10.4018/979-8-2600-1353-3.ch002

choices that are deeply rooted in behavioral and psychological factors and this is risk perception and cognitive bias. This article, entitled Entrepreneurial Risk Perception and AI-Driven Financial Decision Making: A Behavioral Finance Perspective, inculcates the theory of behavioral finance with the use of AI to interpret, base, and take action on algorithmic intelligence. This study is based on Prospect Theory, Bounded Rationality, Signaling Theory, Expectancy-Violation Theory, Emotional Contagion, and the Algorithmic Bias-Trust Framework to form an integrative model that risk perception is an intervening cognitive process between entrepreneurial biases and AI adoption. Theoretical synthesis: AI increases the accuracy of prediction and decreases information asymmetry because it combines with cognitive and emotional filters of entrepreneurs. Theoretical implications suggest that the entrepreneurs must combine human intuition and algorithmic intelligence, undergo life long behavioral-finance education, and establish the openness of explainable AI in order to influence the rational, inclusive and ethical decision-making. The paper concludes with a statement that the future of entrepreneurial finance will be defined by the co-evolution of human judgement and machine learning, in the era where technology will help but never replace human knowledge and the sense of morals.

1. INTRODUCTION

The integration of the behavioral finance knowledge and artificial intelligence (AI) applications is reorganizing the modern entrepreneurial decision-making in the financial environment and having an immense impact on how entrepreneurs grasp and manage risk (Saura and Bužinskienė, 2025; Giuggioli et al., 2024). An existing body of evidence already points to the fact that entrepreneurial psychology, and particularly, the cognitive aspects of risk perceptions, matter in their role in influencing the allocation of resources and the judgment of uncertain opportunities by founders. It has been identified that behavioral biases such as overconfidence, limited rationality, loss aversion and confirmation bias have an effect on the judgment of entrepreneurs that subsequently affect the survival of the firm and the investment outcome (Koudstaal et al., 2016; Chen et al., 2018a, b). These psychological underpinning can be more important to forecasting and improving financial decision making even at the fast, dynamic business environment.

In the meantime, AI-driven financial analytics are radically transforming the notion of uncertainty and decision-making guided by data in the mind of an entrepreneur. The developed AI techniques of machine learning, deep learning, and natural language processing go beyond the old econometric models by offering adaptive mechanisms capable of learning the complex non-linear trends evident in the performance of the market and an enterprise (Hossain, 2025). Financial analytics

Fintech such systems are used to assist businesspeople in forecasting risk in a market and to optimise portfolios and derive scenarios basing on the heterogeneous data of prices, macroeconomic data and textual releases (Jaboob et al., 2024; Foukalas, 2025). AI therefore cogitates on the decisions regarding finances to increase the level of quality and accuracy, to enhance its role in complementing the human cognition in the volatile and data-intensive decision-making situations.

In entrepreneurial finance, AI has also become a facilitator of fundraising and evaluation mechanisms. Giuggioli et al. (2024) have shown how AI can analyse entrepreneurs' verbal, emotional and behavioural cues from startup video pitches to predict fundraising success in accelerators and incubators. They find evidence of significant effects on the investors' perceptions, suggesting a connection between psychological traits and AI-supported decision outcomes. These studies show that AI not only helps investors to decide on the potential of an entrepreneur, it also allows entrepreneurs to further develop themselves and their pitch by managing perceived risk as well as increasing their chances of receiving financial support.

Yet even with increasing attention, the relationship between entrepreneurial risk perception and decision-making driven by AI continues to be somewhat underexamined. Although it is true that AI can enhance the accuracy of predictions and decrease human error, whether to trust and use digital recommendations is typically influenced by individual entrepreneurs' risk taking behavior toward uncertainty (Saura & Bužinskienė, 2025; Bonilla & Vergara 2021). Extremely risk-averse entrepreneurs may ignore the algorithmic advice even when the signals are favourable, while overconfident persons may rely too much on AI outputs, increasing their exposure to market fluctuations. The interplay of behaviour and technology highlights the requirement for a framework that takes into account psychological as well as computational aspects of entrepreneurial finance.

The interaction of behavioral finance and AI is a novel paradigm of entrepreneurial decision in the new economic background of modern society. Behavioral finance found out that financial behavior is influenced by cognitive bias and emotions; AI adds predictive power and analytical accuracy to overcome human constraints (Saura & Bužinskienė, 2025; Hossain, 2025). Together, they can transform the manner, in which business people think about danger, develop investment plans and achieve long-term economic growth. Such converging is an understanding that is important to academics and professionals seeking to design adaptive, technology-based, and psychologically informed financial ecosystems that can be used to drive innovation and resilience in uncertain markets. The objectives include:

- To investigate the connection between a perception of risk and financial actions taken by entrepreneurs in uncertain business settings.

- To explore the impact of AI-enabled tools and predictive analytics on entrepreneurs' financial decision-making and risk assessment.
- To study the interplay between AI-driven financial systems and psychological biases such as overconfidence, bounder rationality and loss aversion.
- To explore the moderating effect of AI on the relationship between entrepreneurial risk perception and investment/financing results.
- To develop a behavioral-finance-informed conceptual model incorporating entrepreneurial psychology and AI-driven financial decision making to articulate theoretically the drivers of the investor bias during an IPO.

2. LITERATURE REVIEW

Over the past years, a relatively new field is emerging where entrepreneurship studies are combined with both behavioral finance research and artificial intelligence (AI) literature in order to understand how entrepreneurs perceive and handle risk in AI-assisted decision-making situations. Entrepreneurship is characterized by uncertainty, and rational-choice models are not adequate to represent the human motivations and imperfect information underlying financial choices. New research on entrepreneurial finance, AI-mediated valuation and investor behavior have cumulatively highlighted how behavioral biases, information cues and technological interfaces structure the financial decisions in contemporary entrepreneurial ecosystems.

An increasing line of research investigates artificial intelligence in entrepreneurial finance for investment screening, startup matching, valuation approximation and success forecasting. Giuggioli et al. (2024), it is possible for AI to have a crucial role in evaluating startup pitches directly by considering entrepreneurs' verbal and non-verbal cues (e.g., confidence, emotional tone and expressiveness) from text and video data. Their findings indicate that confiders (not overconfident or emotional) founders receive more positive funding evaluation. The study recognizes that AI improves the decision-making of investors and understands the nuanced human patterns of entrepreneurs, hence making the link between psychology expression and investment performance. Cohen, Aiche and Winer (2025) in the same line created the application of artificial intelligence to enhance a matching of the angel investors and start-ups. Using AI engines such as Gemini and ChatGPT-4 based on game-theoretic approaches, they have been able to trace the most significant characteristics that influence investor behavior. Their results indicate that the addition of the not only qualitative preferences (e.g., entrepreneur preference) but also quantitative variables (e.g., venture metrics) are highly likely to enhance the accuracy of prediction in the context of investment matching, which gives a more balanced support to the process of entrepreneur financing choices.

Similarly, Zhang et al. (2023) applied the state of the art algorithms of machine learning in the process of valuing aficionado entrepreneurs. They were better than classical models in their model performances and included the number of venture capital investors and their social capital to be important to the firm valuation. It is also interesting to note that traditional indicators such as the number of patent played a relatively weaker role in predicting firm quality at early stage, implying that AI tools can explore new non-traditional indicators to explain better and predict success of entrepreneurial firms. In line with these results, Ferrati and Muffatto (2021) conducted a broad review on AI applications in entrepreneurial finance based on the Crunchbase database. Their findings suggested that machine learning through predictive models could greatly enhance venture screening, portfolio management for predicting exits and providing new theories "to make sense of the data" used by fickle decision makers in high uncertainty (Bigliardi et al. Likewise, Piskunova et al. (2021) built predictive models for startups' success with logistic regression, decision tree and random forest algorithms. Their findings from 123 Ukrainian startups found that application and adoption of machine learning to perform the classification task was a useful tool in predicting which venture would secure reinvestment, signaling AI's increasing importance as an assisting hand for decisions being made by investors and entrepreneurs.

Besides these findings, other studies have studied the effects of prompts and patterns in the process of investor communications and its influence on sick minds and funding decisions), there is more knowledge on how risk perception seems to manifest itself in how entrepreneurial finance is followed. Wang, Xu, Wu and Goh (2022) reviewed over 328 thousand crowdfunding projects placed on Kickstarter and discovered that the linguistic distortion of information - exaggeration or suppression - affected the campaign success in a net negative way. Nevertheless, they also displayed inverted U-shaped relation meaning that moderate positive framing would be beneficial to perceived quality. Interestingly, entrepreneurial biographical enhancement was positively linked to campaign success, which indicates that stories and self-presentation influence the investor trust and decision-making. This was also the case identified as worse than Raab et al. (2020), who also examined facial vigilant and neutral expressions across 18,696 crowdfunding projects in relation to the effect of these on investment. Using machine learning to determine the emotions that were expressed in the pitch pictures, the authors found that the expression of happiness and sadness was beneficial in increasing investor interest, but that taking it too far in displaying emotions undermined their intentions. The implications of these findings are the analysis of emotional and textual stimuli by AI may provide implementable advice on how entrepreneurs can strategically communicate to shift investor risk perception.

Even empirical studies in entrepreneurial finance have begun to respond to bias, discrimination and stereotype dynamics of investor investment decision-making the nature of which are increasingly becoming a problem within AI-based assessment systems. Antretter et al, (2025) examined the effect of obesity stereotype on angel investments decision making on the expectancy violation theory. The results indicated that the sociotype of obese founders is more prone to receive high ratings of warmth and low ratings of competence among the angel investors, which would lead to lower investment ratings. However, the obese initiators who indicated competence by signaling the venture through technology or express presentations effectively did not meet this expectation and were given more favorable judgments. Furthermore, the study was able to incorporate AI-generated photorealistic images as well as use physical cues, which proves that algorithmic devices are not only capable of identifying but also recreating the stereotype effects in entrepreneurial finance. This outcome also contributes to the concerns of Levy et al (2023) raised, who cautioned that AI was capable of ensuring that biases in human nature do not happen in investment contexts, though the algorithms themselves were vulnerable to systemic bias. In their proposals, they proposed that investing is an art, as well as a science where both algorithms and humans have implicit (ie, gut feeling about potential, etc) and explicit (venture capital backing) biases, and that the interaction of algorithms and human intuition and fairness, in general, in entrepreneurial finance must be better understood.

The influence of AI integration and other risk variables on financial decision-making has been explored in the context of production and enterprise, as well, which sheds light on the basis of economic implications of risk perception in the technological adoption. Mukherjee et al. (2024) examined the optimal investment problem of AI-enhanced production decisions with a mean-variance utility environment. They conclude that an increase in TFP volatility reduces investments, whereas the impact of AI use and skilled labor on productivity and capital accumulation is on production. Surprisingly, the propensity of entrepreneurial risk-taking reacted somewhat counterintuitively to the raised background risks being explained in other words, the propensity to adopt AI depends on the interaction between their perceived degree of control over uncertainty and risk attitudes. Similarly, it is argued that AI and big data is transforming the financial risk models, making them more predictive and adaptable in real-time (Hossain, 2025). His study highlighted the fact that the use of AI in financial analytics has led to the speed of action, portfolio management and scenario analysis which are crucial features that entrepreneurs need to make risk decisions in unstable markets.

In a broader sense, articles like Raza et al. (2025) and Santibanuel et al. (2024) indicate how the use of algorithmic training and big data and fintech innovations can speed the process of digitizing finance and facilitate inclusion and sustainability.

Raza et al. (2025) discovered that big data analytics combined with algorithmic systems enabled the improvement of the trading strategies and risk management, bringing us to hasten predictive results by the use of data source. Santiban, Gonza, and Galera (2024) are exploring the fintech-environmental, social, and governance (ESG) intersection in the meantime because machine learning, blockchain, and tokenisation as digital technologies are moving sustainable finance. They portray more broad-scale studies, they also locate the heart of AI disruptive power in entrepreneurial and macro-financial systems that hopes to integrate technological invention in considerate financial behaviors.

Besides venture capital and corporate finance, they have creatively proposed new decision-support techniques grounded on the AI and computation models on the literatures with the view of integrating greater accuracy and adaptability to financial decision. Ardika, Setianingrum, and Hakiem (2017) have created fuzzy Tsukamoto model to enhance the financing eligibility decision in Islamic microfinance institutions. Their model substituted the hard-coded or interpretive scoring systems with more adaptable than earlier systems which were based on the customer behaviour, business nature and personal attributes- which yielded superior decision outcomes. In the same way, Shahriar et al. (2021) have compared financial models of project evaluation of forecasting and have found hybrid AI models(Raci model, Leung model, Belton-Neesham model) in general support vector machine and other models like Monte Carlo simulation a neural network are increasingly helpful in the actual forecasting and planning. In their work, the authors underscored the importance of the reality that effective financial-related decision-making requires a capacity to minimize not only statistical error margins but also to generate reliable early warning indicators through an AI device.

The recent encounter of behavioral finance with AI has historical insight provided by past seminal works in computational economics. Giulioni et al. (2012) have structured the capital-structure decision of the firms, based on artificial agents that are replicated by human behaviour in terms of finance. They demonstrated that heuristics based on rules could replicate real characteristics of entrepreneurial financing and involved artificial agents as a viable micro basis of the stud firm behavior. Besides, they also showed that the financial behavior is not only regulated by the macroeconomic cycle but it is more and more irritated by the volatility of the demand and the accuracy of the forecast, which aligns with the recent evidence on AI-based forecasting and the judgment of entrepreneurs under uncertainty.

Combined, these empirical studies indicate that entrepreneurial finance is not only more data-driven, but it is behaviourally constrained in that perception of risk, cognitive bias and technological augmentation are interacting to produce the consequences of a decision. AI has made the predictions stronger and information asymmetry smaller, however, it also questions us morally and psychologically, as it is biased, not interpretable. The belief of entrepreneur in AI predictions, seems to depend on their individual risk-taking and on the extent of the information about the AI system that they are getting, yet at least some subgroups of investors still do not seem to be immune to nonverbal information and stereotyping even when these messages are being fed to them by an algorithm. These observations indicate the duality- of AI in entrepreneurial finance: a tool to minimize human biases, and a system that can spread it unless used with care and in a responsible manner.

In conclusion, the paper provides 4 insights of the literature review. More importantly, AI effectively increases financial predictions, valuation and business matching of an enormous amount of data. Second, human psychological roles and communication are still influential in determining investment performance even in the technology mediated environment. Third, algorithms may take on new human biases and even double them into high-stakes financial choices; hence, it is necessary to evaluate them in a moderated manner. Finally, the interaction between entrepreneurial risk perception and AI-based decision tools in terms of adoption of AI and quality of financial decisions has not yet been critically studied. This gap will require the integration of behavioral finance and computational analytics ideas -not easy! The combination of these two fields is in fact what the focus of this paper is all about.

3. THEORETICAL FRAMEWORK

In the entrepreneurship field of activities, decision making involves working with uncertainty and balancing intuition with the use of analytic thinking. Conventional financial theories often portray decision makers as the wholesomely rational full-informed act, but in the real world entrepreneurs consider the way to behave within the confines of cognitive constraints, emotions and peer pressure. Human behavior is systematically suboptimal due to being limited to boundedly rational behavior and is subject to psychological distortions the behavioral approach of behavioral finance offers a more realistic method to do so (Saura & Bužinskienė, 2025). The subjective risk estimates of the entrepreneurs are taken based on their personal experience, affective and other influences than on more objective probabilities. These perceptions have a direct impact on their investment choices, evaluation of opportunities and faith in frontier technologies such as artificial intelligence (AI).

The first theoretical foundation for this study is Prospect Theory developed by Kahneman and Tversky (1979), which explains that people make decisions on gains and losses asymmetrically through loss aversion and reference dependence. In entrepreneurial contexts, this implies that founders may either overestimate the risk for potential losses or underestimate general risks due to optimism bias. Decisions that can be made using AI Decision-making in entrepreneurship is affected by behavioral biases which, if unchecked, may distort the rational use of information (Saura and Bužinskienė, 2025),AI-based decision-making-tools may help to correct or reinforce such distortions depending on how entrepreneurs react to algorithmic outputs. The AI embedding thus dynamically interacts with the entrepreneur's biases and perceived influence in outcomes.

Related to Prospect Theory is the concept of Bounded Rationality (Simon, 1957), that decision-makers choose to satisfice rather than maximize as a result of lack of information and cognitive limitations. When making financ ial decisions, many entrepreneurs follow heuristics such as representativeness, anchoring and overconf idence. AI tools, which replicate some heuristic procedures and learning processes through learning machines, are considered as a sort of bounded rationality (Giulioni et al., 2012). Instead of removing human bias, AI only enshrines and automates decision rules, creating as a result that the quality of the decisions made through AI are reliant on the user's ability to read and understand results within his psychological frame.

Communication and perception matter, in the world of entrepreneurial finance. Signaling Theory postulates that entrepreneurs utilize information cues—product quality, financial transparency and emotional tone—to shape investors' trust (Wang et al., 2022). The linguistic framing in crowdfunding stories or pitching of startups which is full of emotion, such as tales or speech, has a great impact on the perception of risk by investors. The Expectancy-Violation Theory (Antretter et al., 2025) is another claim that states that once entrepreneurs do things that are stereotypical, i.e. prove more competent than the prejudice would suggest, they can skew the investor judgments to their advantage. All of these theories point in concert to the idea that AI-enabled analyses of communication patterns (e.g., text mining, facial recognition) emulate human processes of reading credibility and competence into behavior and that we can therefore count behavioral signals with technology.

The inclusion of AI in financial decisions has created a new cognitive intermediary: trustworthiness of algorithms. Trust in how AIs are perceived to be fair and transparent by entrepreneurs mitigates the tendency of investors to take AI advice into consideration (Levy & Liguori, 2023). The Algorithmic Bias and Trust Framework posits that human and machine biases operate together – human overconfidence or under-confidence may result in humans over-trusting or ignoring the insights of AI, while algorithms might reinforce societal / data-driven bias. Thus AI is a reparative and magnifying agent for behavioral finance. Therefore, the entrepreneur's risk perception serves as a mediator between psychological characteristics and technology adoption attitude and affects the degree of effectiveness for using AI tools in financial decisions.

Lastly, she can utilize Emotional Contagion Theory in getting an insight on the affective component of entrepreneurial decision-making. Raab et al. (2020) found that positive feelings, such as happiness or empathy when playing the pitches, can have an influential and unconscious effect on the investors. To the extent that contemporary AI systems can be programmed to process facial and linguistic emotion in serving the aim of forecasting outcomes, therefore, exnihilotechnic procedural emotional contagion occurs in algorithmic evaluation businesses - associating affect, cognition and computational processes in financial judgment.

In line with these opinions, under the influence of the above literature, we were able to propose our cognitive mediation model where the entrepreneurial risk perception serves as a cognitive mediator between psychological biases and AI-based decision support system of financial decisions. The perceptions of risk by entrepreneurs are counterintuitive influenced by counteractive biases (overconfidence, limited rationality, and loss aversion) which influence the degree of reliance on AI tools. In its turn, AI tools can provide risk-related point of view that acts as a reinforcement to the intuitions of the entrepreneurs or as the correction to the course. Framework therefore poses AI as a means of reinforcing behaviour that has otherwise talked to human cognition and not supersede it. Second, the impact of perceived risk on the decision outcome is moderated by the trust on AI, which makes technology a dual source of rational and emotional capital in entrepreneurship.

Acknowledgement This theoretical amalgamation also acknowledges that, despite the unprecedented dimensions of AI inpersistent pursuit of data-driven accuracy, human interpretation and affective stance still prevail in making entrepreneurial financial decisions. To this end, an integrative model comprising of Prospect Theory, Bounded Rationality, Signaling Theory, Expectancy-Violation Theory, Emotional Contagion and Algorithmsic Bias-Trust (ABT) are usefully applied to illuminate how entrepreneurs perceive and process AI-contingent financial advice and how they respond to the recommendation that they did.

3.1 TCCM Framework

Dimension	Description (Application in this Study)	Key References
Theory (T)	The study integrates multiple behavioral and cognitive theories including Prospect Theory, Bounded Rationality, Signaling Theory, Expectancy-Violation Theory, Emotional Contagion, and Algorithmic Bias–Trust Framework. These explain how risk perception and technology-driven insights influence financial decision outcomes.	Kahneman & Tversky (1979); Simon (1957); Saura & Bužinskienė (2025); Antretter et al. (2025); Wang et al. (2022); Raab et al. (2020); Levy & Liguori (2023)
Context (C)	The background is on the entrepreneurial finance, especially startups, and venture decisions affected by AI analytics. The framework deals with the valuation of investments, financing success and decision making on insecure, data-driven markets.	Giuggioli et al. (2024); Zhang et al. (2023); Cohen et al. (2025); Ferrati & Muffatto (2021)
Characteristics (C)	They are (1) Entrepreneurial Risk Perception, (2) Psychological Biases (Overconfidence, Bounded Rationality, Loss Aversion), (3) AI Trust and Adoption, and (4) Financial Decision Outcomes. In between these variables lie mediating and moderating relationships.	Saura & Bužinskienė (2025); Hossain (2025); Raza et al. (2025); Mukherjee et al. (2024)
Method (M)	Quantitative SEM or PLS-SEM can be used to conduct empirical testing with the help of survey data on the psychological variables and secondary measures of AI-use. Mixed-method designs (that use experimental or text-analytic data) may contribute to strength.	Zhang et al. (2023); Cohen et al. (2025); Raab et al. (2020); Ferrati & Muffatto (2021)

3.2 Representative Articles Using Theories

Theory	Representative Studies	Key Contribution / Findings
Prospect Theory	Saura & Bužinskienė (2025); Mukherjee et al. (2024)	Showed that entrepreneurs exhibit risk-seeking behavior in losses and risk aversion in gains; AI can recalibrate perceived risk-return trade-offs.
Bounded Rationality	Giulioni et al. (2012); Ferrati & Muffatto (2021)	Demonstrated that both human and artificial agents make satisficing, heuristic-based financial decisions under uncertainty.
Signaling Theory	Wang et al. (2022); Giuggioli et al. (2024)	Explained how textual and visual cues signal competence and influence investor perceptions in AI-assisted evaluations.
Expectancy-Violation Theory	Antretter et al. (2025)	Highlighted how stereotype violations (e.g., competence cues) improve angel investors' assessments of entrepreneurs.
Emotional Contagion Theory	Raab et al. (2020)	Found that positive emotional displays increase investment intentions; emotions mediate investor decision quality.
Algorithmic Bias–Trust Framework	Levy & Liguori (2023); Hossain (2025); Raza et al. (2025)	Addressed how trust and perceived fairness affect reliance on AI recommendations and decision outcomes.

4. DISCUSSION

The combination of theoretics on the perception of risk in entrepreneurship and the use of AI to coordinate financial decision-making has great implications on modern entrepreneurs, investors, as well as policy makers who operate in dynamic data oriented economies. The combination of behavioral finance and AI creates an opportunity to create psychologically inspired and technologically empowered decision environments.

Enhancing Entrepreneurial Decision Quality:

Predictive analytics, natural language processing and pattern recognition artificial intelligence systems allow predicting where entrepreneurs need to invest and raise money better. These systems are however effective as well as the cognitive orientation of risk by entrepreneurs. The training interventions that combine behavioral finance awareness (e.g., the ability to detect overconfidence or loss aversion) and AI literacy will help entrepreneurs to make balanced, evidence-informed financial decisions (Saura & Bužinskienė, 2025; Hossain, 2025).

Building Algorithmic Trust and Transparency:

Entrepreneurs distrust of algorithmic advice is one of the leading problems of the literature. Simple language predictive explanations and looking through AI interfaces can build trust in users and potentially reduce a perceived uncertainty (Levy and Liguori, 3023). Startup-built fintech dashboards with embedded explainable AI modules may assist in alleviating the problem of decision fatigue and boosting the adoption rate.

Promoting cognitive awareness and risk resilience:

IT entrepreneurship education should include behavioral finance simulations of people being made conscious of their own biases in times of uncertainty. By example, simulating the perception of risk changing in reaction to feedback and AI hints, the entrepreneurs will be able to build mental resilience and immunity to emotional over-reaction on the market volatility (Giuggioli et al., 2024; Mukherjee et al., 2024).

Foster Ethical and Fair AI Use:

The effect of algorithmic bias can reproduce the stereotypes of human investors (Antretter et al., 2025). The regulators and venture platforms should therefore implement ethical data-training requirements, fairness audit and bias-detection tools. Careful AI implementation will ensure a set of entrepreneurial profiles remain secure and democratize access to capital.

Catalysing Innovation through Data Democratisation:

Democratization of inner-circle venture intelligence to nontraditional mainstream investors can be achieved by AI-powered decision-support systems. Together with inclusive fintech, they allow small entrepreneurs with an especially strong presence in developing nations like India to make superior investment decisions and seize the growth opportunities (Raza et al., 2025; Santibañez-Gonzalez et al., 2024).

Integrating Emotional and Behavioral Intelligence:

The manner in which emotional intelligence enlightens leaders, the emotional awareness informs financial judgment. Those entrepreneurs who are aware of the essence of affect and signs of communication when engaging with investors (Raab et al., 2020; Wang et al., 2022) may be strategically inclined to frame their narrative, yet leave it sincere. The tone, sentiment and body-language analyzing AI systems must therefore not be used as a substitute but instead as a feedback mechanism of human empathy.

Continuous Learning and Human–AI Co-evolution:

Lastly, the attitude of continuous learning is needed to achieve long-term success as a digital entrepreneur. Algorithms will improve and entrepreneurs will have to change their cognitive models of decision-making. The competition between human judgment and AI analysis will further be majorly affecting the financial competitiveness. The entrepreneurs can be prepared to that hybrid decision future by conducting upskilling programs in the fields of behavioral finance, AI ethics, or data interpretation.

Ethical, Regulatory, and Practical Problems of AI-Driven Entrepreneurial Decision-Making.

Despite the fact that AI can enhance the judgment of entrepreneurs, by enhancing predictive quality and decreasing information asymmetry, its application in financial decision-making presents a set of ethical, regulatory, and practical issues that determine the perception and treatment of risk by entrepreneurs. The challenges are also interconnected with the psychological processes, which are the focus of this study, which further supports the importance of behavioral biases, trust, and cognitive frames in the adoption of AI.

Biases and Discrimination Algorithms.

Artificial intelligence models that are applied to calculate startup pitches, filter founders, or even forecast fundraising success are likely to reproduce and even compound human biases in their training data. Algorithms presented by the study by Antretter et al. (2025) can generate stereotypes concerning competence, warmth, or physical appearance, thus influencing the investment outcome. This provokes very serious moral questions: AI can seem to be objective, but it can strengthen structural inequalities unless it is strictly regulated.

Opaqueness and Unexplainability.

Another issue that arises with entrepreneurs is the black box nature of AI systems where the logic behind decisions is hard to make. The lack of explainability will decrease the level of algorithmic trust, especially with risk-averse entrepreneurs who need transparency to trust machine advice. The cognitive biases (such as loss aversion, anchoring) become more salient, contributing to the compliance or resistance to AI-generated insights when founders are unable to comprehend such an algorithm, suggesting a valuation, risk score, or an investment strategy.

Data Ethics and Privacy Threats.

Decision tools based on AI frequently are premised on copious behavioral, financial, and emotional information. This brings about the issues of consent, data security, and abuse. In the case of business leaders working within data-scarce or informal ecologies the ethical consequences of disclosing sensitive business data may considerably increase the perceived risk and deter the use of AI.

5. LIMITATIONS

Despite the fact that the consideration of the behavioral finance and artificial intelligence perspectives on entrepreneurial decision-making is important in providing conceptual insights, there are some limitations that should be identified. To start with, it can be stated that the framework suggested in the study is rather theoretical in nature hence its constraints can be associated with the inability to generalize it empirically. The correlation of the described relations among entrepreneurial risk perception and cognitive biases and the decision-making process influenced by AI might vary depending on industries, level of maturity of the technological innovation and national ecosystems. The dynamics of decision making by small businesses in the economy with a high digitalisation may be very different than that of the small business owners in resource poor areas or in traditional markets.

Second, the study being limited to a small number of psychological and technological aspects, that is, overconfidence, loss aversion, bound rationality and algorithmic trust, suggests that other aspects that affect the results have not been accounted in detail, e.g., organizational culture or intuition formation. Entrepreneurial financial behaviour is numerous-sided and the decision to concentrate on limited number of constructs might simplify the interaction of behavioural, economic and contextual concerns that are rather complex.

Third, the report on this study is speculative and interpretative because the study is not carried out using original quantitative or qualitative data. It may not be the case in real life because entrepreneurial behaviour in the context of AI-enhanced environments is subject to situational variations such as technological comfort, feelings or experience of investing. Moreover, it would be interesting to witness in future empirical studies founded on survey or experiment research or longitudinal evidence to know whether the relationships among variables are true.

The second disadvantage is that AI technologies are developing too fast. Algorithms, data structures and the regulatory environment can change rapidly therefore any specific observations can be construed as out-of-date. The level of trust in AI tools and risk perception of entrepreneurs may shift as technology keeps evolving and algorithmic transparency is different, which will require revision of the model at the interim.

As a matter of fact, SMEs could be limited by the resources and capabilities to utilize AI-based decision support fully. There may be access to data, training or cost issues in case of entrepreneurs operating in emerging markets. Thus, points of the framework parts need to be adjusted to local needs and resources so that to transcend logistical challenges and facilitate scalability or cost.

To overcome this, it is recommended that practitioners initially pilot-test AI-based financial tools on smaller projects and obtain feedback on them and then operationalize them on bigger scale. Practical and theoretical implications: We suggest that educators and policy makers should establish behavior-finance awareness programs and AI-ethics training programs to improve entrepreneurial cognitive adaptability. Such across-disciplines as behavioral economics, computer science and... are also to be incorporated by researchers.

Finally, the presented integrated framework of psychology and artificial intelligence in entrepreneurial finance is, in its turn, a theoretical innovation with the prospects to be empirically proved, but which must be approached with criticism in view of the exploratory character of the given research. The models should be updated to the latest data, adjusted to specific sectors, and stakeholders engaged in a responsible AI application to be sure that such a framework becomes relevant/ impactful.

6. IMPLICATIONS AND CONCLUSION

In conclusion, the integrated approach of entrepreneurial psychology and artificial intelligence as discussed in this paper has significant implications to the contemporary entrepreneurship and finance. The combination of behavioral-finance knowledge with AI-based analytics implies that in the field of entrepreneurship, smart survival will not be dependent on technical competence, but requires the skill of feeling the psychological changes. When entrepreneurs become aware of their own biases (e.g., overconfidence, loss aversion, and bounded rationality) and are also aware of how to interpret algorithms are such, they may have more opportunities in volatile markets and encounter data-driven but emotion-based financial decision-making (Saura and Bužinskienė, 2025; Hossain, 2025).

Implications for Practitioners

One, to consider AI as a decision-partner, but not as an intermediary, is necessary among the entrepreneurs and managers. By combining human intuition with machine accuracy, it can subjugate prejudices of the individual entrepreneur without destroying his or her creativity. Faith in technology can be built, without strangling personal judgment, by pragmatic courses on behavioral-finance awareness, digital-finance literacy, and explainable AI design. Second, the grid could be utilized by investors and venture platforms in order to enhance equity in funding: bias-detection systems and transparent algorithms to make their decision-advocated reduce stereotype-based discrimination and contribute to the inclusion of everyone in accessing capital (Antretter et al., 2025; Levy and Liguori, 2023). Third, teacher and mentors to include experiential learning, which includes AI-based market simulation with bias-reflection training to educate aspiring entrepreneurs in analytical discipline and emotion intelligence. Finally, but certainly not the least, policymakers and financial technologies innovators should make sure that the tools based on algorithms are under ethical control, auditable and in line with the human principles of financial sectors.

Implications for Theory and Research

Theoretically, the study adds to behavioural-finance studies and derives AI trust and algorithmic bias in the psychology of entrepreneurial-decision making. It reformulates risk perception as an individual cognitive distortion, but as a dynamic human-machine interaction based on the visibility of data and emotional awareness. This model can possibly be tested empirically: e.g., by structural-equation modeling, or experiments that can account levels of AI explainability, experience in entrepreneurship, and the effects of these on decision quality and investment performance.

Conclusion

In short, these findings add up to the fact that the future of entrepreneurship finance will be the future where human judgment and Artificial Intelligence develop jointly. In order to compete, you will not just be required to invest in the continuous learning but also reflectively think and responsibly use technology. The entrepreneurs with these two aspects of self-awareness, and also the AI literacy will be in a position to transform uncertainty into opportunity, where subjective risk is transformed into strategic foresight. It is the institutions and ecosystems that will support this type of hybrid intelligence, a combination of sensibilities: human and computational, that will result in innovation, equity, and sustainability of digital financial age. It is, inherently the coming together of behavioral understanding and intelligent technology that would become better than a more technical make-over: it attracts a shift to a smarter, more accommodative and healthy entrepreneurial future.

REFERENCES

Antretter, T., Lekkas, H. W., Djokovic, D., Souitaris, V., & Wincent, J. (2025). Not what you expected to see? Obesity stereotypes, expectancy violations, and angel investment decisions. *Journal of Business Venturing*, *40*(5), 106510. DOI: 10.1016/j.jbusvent.2025.106510

Ardika, B. S., Setianingrum, A. H., & Hakiem, N. (2017, November). Funding eligibility decision support system using fuzzy logic Tsukamoto:(Case: BMT XYZ). In *2017 Second International Conference on Informatics and Computing (ICIC)* (pp. 1-7). IEEE. DOI: 10.1109/IAC.2017.8280622

Bonilla, C. A., & Vergara, M. (2021). Risk aversion, downside risk aversion, and the transition to entrepreneurship. *Theory and Decision*, *91*(1), 123–133. DOI: 10.1007/s11238-020-09786-w

. Chen, J. S., Croson, D. C., Elfenbein, D. W., & Posen, H. E. (2018a). The impact of learning and overconfidence on entrepreneurial entry and exit. Organization Science, 29(6), 989–1009. https://doi.org/10.1287/orsc.2018.1225

Chen, M. H., Chang, Y. Y., & Pan, J. Y. (2018b). Typology of creative entrepreneurs and entrepreneurial success. *Journal of Enterprising Communities: People and Places in the Global Economy*, *12*(5), 632–656. DOI: 10.1108/JEC-07-2017-0041

Cohen, G., Aiche, A., & Winer, Z. (2025). Matching angels to startups using AI. *China Finance Review International*. Advance online publication. DOI: 10.1108/CFRI-04-2024-0222

. Ferrati, F., & Muffatto, M. (2021). Entrepreneurial finance: emerging approaches using machine learning and big data. *Foundations and Trends® in Entrepreneurship*, *17*(3), 232-329.

Foukalas, F. (2025). A Survey of Artificial Neural Network Computing Systems. *Cognitive Computation*, *17*(1), 4. DOI: 10.1007/s12559-024-10383-0

Giuggioli, G., Pellegrini, M. M., & Giannone, G. (2024). Artificial intelligence as an enabler for entrepreneurial finance: A practical guide to AI-driven video pitch evaluation for entrepreneurs and investors. *Management Decision*.

Giulioni, G., Bucciarelli, E., & Silvestri, M. (2012, March). Modeling firms financial behavior in an evolving economy by using artificial intelligence. In *Highlights on Practical Applications of Agents and Multi-Agent Systems: 10th International Conference on Practical Applications of Agents and Multi-Agent Systems* (pp. 333-340). Berlin, Heidelberg: Springer Berlin Heidelberg. DOI: 10.1007/978-3-642-28762-6_40

Gonzalez, E. D. S., Kandpal, V., Ozili, P. K., & Chatterjee, P. (Eds.). (2024). *Fintech for ESG and the Circular Economy*. John Wiley & Sons.

Jaboob, A., Durrah, O., & Chakir, A. (2024). Artificial intelligence: An overview. *Engineering Applications of Artificial Intelligence*, •••, 3–22.

. Kahneman, T., & Tversky, A. (1979). Prospect theory: An analysis of decisions under risk, 47(2), 263–291. DOI: 10.2307/1914185

Koudstaal, M., Sloof, R., & Van Praag, M. (2016). Risk, uncertainty, and entrepreneurship: Evidence from a lab-in-the-field experiment. *Management Science*, *62*(10), 2897–2915. DOI: 10.1287/mnsc.2015.2249

Levy, M., & Liguori, E. (2023). Algorithms and venture investment decisions: Better, fairer or biased? *Journal of Small Business and Enterprise Development*, *30*(2), 419–422. DOI: 10.1108/JSBED-09-2021-0336

Mukherjee, S., Nawazish, M., Padhi, S. S., & Jayaram, J. (2024). Optimal investment in artificial intelligence-driven production activities considering socio-economic concerns. *International Journal of Production Research*, •••, 1–25.

Raab, M., Schlauderer, S., Overhage, S., & Friedrich, T. (2020). More than a feeling: Investigating the contagious effect of facial emotional expressions on investment decisions in reward-based crowdfunding. *Decision Support Systems*, *135*, 113326. DOI: 10.1016/j.dss.2020.113326

Raza, H., Riaz, A., Riaz, N., & Ramakrishnan, S. A. L. (2025). *Algorithmic training, future markets, and big data for finance digitalization*. Elsevier., DOI: 10.4018/979-8-3693-6386-7

Saura, J. R., & Bužinskienė, R. (2025). Behavioral economics, artificial intelligence and entrepreneurship: An updated framework for management. *The International Entrepreneurship and Management Journal*, *21*(1), 1–33. DOI: 10.1007/s11365-025-01076-7

Shahriar, M. S., Hasan, K. B. M. R., Hossain, T., Beg, T. H., Islam, K. A., & Zayed, N. M. (2021). Financial decision making and forecasting techniques on project evaluation: A planning, development and entrepreneurial perspective. *Academy of Entrepreneurship Journal*, *27*(4), 1–7.

. Simon, H. A. (1957). A behavioral model of rational choice. *Models of man, social and rational: Mathematical essays on rational human behavior in a social setting*, *6*(1), 241-260.

Wang, W., Xu, Y., Wu, Y. J., & Goh, M. (2022). Linguistic information distortion on investment decision-making in the crowdfunding market. *Management Decision*, *60*(3), 648–672. DOI: 10.1108/MD-09-2020-1203

Zhang, R., Wang, J., Liu, C., Su, K., Ishibuchi, H., & Jin, Y. (2025). Synergistic integration of metaheuristics and machine learning: Latest advances and emerging trends. *Artificial Intelligence Review*, *58*(9), 268. DOI: 10.1007/s10462-025-11266-y

Chapter 3
AI-Driven Discovery and Development of Entrepreneurial Potential Innovations in Recruitment and Training

Mohan Kumar
http://orcid.org/0000-0002-5171-0892
Faculty of Commerce and Management, SGT University, India

Damith Gangodawilage
http://orcid.org/0000-0001-7968-6284
Villa College, Maldives

Jeayaram Subramanian
O.P. Jindal Global University, India

Sushma Budshra
School of Business, Galgotias University, India

ABSTRACT

Identifying and developing entrepreneurial potential is critical for fostering innovation and economic growth. Traditional methods, including psychometric tests, interviews, and experiential assessments, often face limitations in scalability, objectivity, and predictive accuracy. This chapter explores how artificial intelligence (AI) enhances recruitment and training by leveraging data-driven, adaptive, and predictive approaches. AI tools such as natural language processing, machine learn-

DOI: 10.4018/979-8-2600-1353-3.ch003

ing, gamified assessments, and adaptive learning platforms enable organizations to detect latent entrepreneurial traits, personalize skill development, and optimize talent selection. Case studies from startups, corporate innovation programs, universities, and accelerators illustrate practical applications. The chapter also addresses challenges, including algorithmic bias, fairness, transparency, data privacy, and long-term effectiveness. Finally, it highlights future research directions emphasizing multimodal data, cross-cultural validation, and ethical AI frameworks.

INTRODUCTION

With the modern economies being volatile, technologically dynamic and competitive in a global market, entrepreneurship has become a key source of innovation, job creation and economic growth (Shane, 2003; Audretsch and Thurik, 2010). The process of identifying people with high entrepreneurial abilities has thus become a critical goal in business, incubators and even policymakers. Entrepreneurial potential is a set of cognitive, behavioural, and motivational qualities, including creativity, resilience, risk-taking disposition, and opportunity recognition, that all have an impact on entrepreneurial success (Rauch and Frese, 2007; Obschonka et al., 2017). The measurement and development of these qualities have however been based on the subjective approaches of interviewing, self-report survey and experience-based assessment which tend to be biased, inconsistent and possess low predictive validity.

Artificial Intelligence (AI) is an innovative chance to improve the recruitment and training process with providing data-driven, scalable, and adaptable strategies to determine entrepreneurial potential. The tools that are AI-powered are able to process enormous amounts of behavioural, psychometric, and performance-related data to identify trends that are not immediately apparent to human evaluators (Jordan and Mitchell, 2015; Brynjolfsson and McAfee, 2017). As an example, communication styles, decision-making patterns, and problem-solving approaches can be identified as entrepreneurial attributes that can be identified by machine-learning algorithms, and adaptive AI-based training platforms can tailor the learning experience to develop entrepreneurial skills (Liu et al., 2021a)(Tayal et al., 2019; Trivedi et al., 2023a). These innovations are not only expected to make the process of bias reduction and accuracy improvement in talent identification, but they are also expected to lead to more inclusive and efficient entrepreneurial ecosystems.

This chapter explores the theoretical and practical applications and ethical concerns of using AI tools to identify and train individuals with entrepreneurial potential. It explores how AI-based recruitment systems, adaptive learning systems and predictive analytics are transforming how organisations identify and develop entrepreneurial talent. Moreover, it points out the issues and dangers of algorithmic decision-making, especially in terms of fairness, privacy, and cultural background. Through the combination of knowledge in entrepreneurship studies and the use of AI, this chapter provides a holistic view of how technology can be used to further the identification and nurturing of future entrepreneurs.

Theoretical Bases of Entrepreneurial Potential

Entrepreneurial potential is the ability of individuals to recognize, analyse and take advantage of opportunities in the face of uncertainty and mobilisation of resources (Krueger and Brazeal, 1994; Shane and Venkataraman, 2000). It does not just apply to the process of entrepreneurship but is a wider range of psychological, cognitive, and behavioural qualities that precondition entrepreneurial action. It is essential to understand these underpinnings in order to develop effective recruitment and training systems, particularly when incorporating the use of artificial intelligence in them (Trivedi et al., 2023b; Yadav et al., 2023).

Psychologically, the entrepreneurial potential is usually identified with the following personality factors: openness to experience, conscientiousness and extraversion that are positively correlated with entrepreneurial intention and success (Zhao and Seibert, 2006; Rauch and Frese, 2007). Other characteristics that have been revealed to have a big role in entrepreneurial behaviour are risk-taking propensity, locus of control, and self-efficacy (McClelland, 1961; Chen, Greene, and Crick, 1998). These characteristics are the foundations of personal differences, which determine the way that potential entrepreneurs see opportunities and react to challenges.

The cognitive theories underline the fact that entrepreneurial potential is closely connected to opportunity recognition, problem-solving abilities and creative thinking. Entrepreneurs are also likely to have distinct mental models that enable them to draw unrelated information and see new ways of doing things (Baron, 2006; Mitchell et al., 2002). The studies on entrepreneurial cognition emphasize the heuristics, biases, and intuitive decision-making as the key processes by which entrepreneurs assess uncertain conditions (Keh, Foo, and Lim, 2002). Such cognitive systems offer an excellent perspective on AI-based systems because algorithms can identify and represent trends in the decision-making process and information processing.

Motivational theories also emphasise the significance of intrinsic motivation like achievement motivation, autonomy need and persistence (Collins, Hanges, and Locke, 2004). According to the theory of achievement motivation that McClelland (1961) proposed, people who have high achievement need tend to be more involved in entrepreneurial activity, and other researchers believe that resilience and ambiguity tolerance are also important (Littunen, 2000). Such inspirational foundations give rise to the suggestion that entrepreneurial potential is not limited to quantifiable abilities but includes more profound psychological forces of action.

Altogether, entrepreneurial potential is a multidimensional construct that combines personality, cognitive skills, and motivation. The traditional models are useful in determining the entrepreneurial aptitude, yet they bring out the complexity of this construct (Tunio et al., 2021; Tunio & Tunio, 2025). The potential of AI tools is specifically due to the possibility of combining various sources of data, such as psychometric, behavioural, and performance-based, into a unified and predictive model of entrepreneurial potential.

Traditional Approaches to Identifying Entrepreneurial Talent

In the past, the process of determining the entrepreneurial talent has been based on practices that are anchored in psychology, management science, and education. Conventional methods focus on observable behaviours, self-reported traits, and structured tests with the goal of forecasting entrepreneurial success. Although these approaches have provided a rich source of information, they also have significant weaknesses in the form of subjectivity, scalability, and predictive power.

Among the most popular techniques, one can identify psychometric tests, including the Big Five Inventory (BFI) or the Myers-Briggs Type Indicator (MBTI). These measures have tried to measure stable personality scales that are associated with entrepreneurship, such as openness to experience, conscientiousness and extraversion (Zhao and Seibert, 2006)(Malhan et al., 2021; Nguyen et al., 2025). Equally, the entrepreneurial intention surveys, including the ones that were created in the context of the Theory of Planned Behaviour (Ajzen, 1991), evaluate the motivational and attitudinal elements of entrepreneurial potential. Although psychometric instruments offer standardised measurement, they have been criticised as culturally biased and have little predictive power of real-life entrepreneurial performance (Gartner, 1988) (Kumar et al., 2025a; Kumar et al., 2025c; Malhan et al., 2021; Nguyen et al., 2025).

Another of the conventional approaches is behavioural tests, which are based on the observable behaviours and previous successes as the measure of entrepreneurial skills. As an illustration, past experience in venture formation, leadership capability or innovative projects is often used as a proxy of entrepreneurial success in the future (Cooper, Woo, and Dunkelberg, 1989). Decision-making, opportunity identification, and problem solving have also been assessed using simulations, role-playing exercises and assessment centres in controlled environments (Boyatzis, 1982). Though they provide more insight into behaviour than the static tests, they are resource-intensive and cannot be easily applied to large applicant pools.

Traditional recruitment and talent identification have also been focused on interviews and expert assessment. The structured and semi-structured interviews enable the recruiters, educators, or investors to measure entrepreneurial traits like resilience, creativity, and leadership potential. Nevertheless, these ratings are very subjective and prone to bias by the interviewer, halo effects, and unequal standards (Gatewood, Shaver, and Gartner, 1995).

Lastly, academic performance, enrolment in entrepreneurship programmes, or course work that is related to innovation have been commonly used by educational and training institutions as indicators of entrepreneurial promise (Wilson, Kickul, and Marlino, 2007). Even though these measures offer some evidence of engagement, they frequently do not reflect non-linear, experiential, and risk-focused aspects of entrepreneurship.

Overall, the conventional ways of determining the talent of entrepreneurs provide valuable yet partial insights. They tend to use static, situation-specific measures that have a hard time reflecting the dynamic and complex nature of entrepreneurial potential. Such constraints open up room to artificial intelligence applications, which are able to combine various sources of data, reduce bias, and offer scalable and adaptive measures of entrepreneurial potential.

AI-Driven Tools for Recruitment

The adoption of the artificial intelligence (AI) in the recruitment process has brought a paradigm shift in the way organisations find and assess entrepreneurial potential. Contrary to the conventional approach that uses fixed metrics and subjective opinions, AI systems use massive data sets, predictive models, and adaptive algorithms to identify trends that can be used to predict entrepreneurial skills (Kumar et al., 2023, 2024). These tools improve objectivity, efficiency, and scalability of the recruitment process and are thus useful especially when organisations need individuals who have high entrepreneurial capacity.

Among the most notable uses is Natural Language Processing (NLP), which interprets communication in a resume, cover letter and during an interview. Linguistic markers and sentiment analysis can identify the signs of the entrepreneurial qualities of creativity, initiative, and leadership (van Esch, Black, and Ferolie, 2019). NLP is applied to affective computing to assess both verbal and non-verbal behavior, which can give information on confidence, adaptability, and problem-solving capacity based on automated video interview platforms, such as Winsborough, Sherman, and Hogan (2016).

Predictive analytics based on machine-learning is another effective instrument that uses historical performance data, psychometric scores, and behavioural testing to determine the likelihood of a person becoming an entrepreneur. Organisations can use training algorithms on massive datasets to discover the characteristics and skills that are always associated with venture creation, opportunity recognition, and innovation (Bogen and Rieke, 2018). Such predictive models minimize human bias and offer more stable evaluation criteria, but they should be closely monitored to avoid algorithmic discrimination.

AI-driven gamified assessment platforms are also becoming popular in the recruitment process. These are tools that simulate entrepreneurial conditions in which candidates are tested in decision making, risk taking, and strategy. Gameplay data is recorded and processed with the help of AI models that create competency profiles that are consistent with entrepreneurial potential (Langer, König, and Fitili, 2019). These platforms are more effective in engaging the applicants and generate more behavioural data than the conventional survey or interview.

Lastly, applicant tracking systems (ATS) using AI are already being widely used to process large numbers of applications and filter out applicants whose profile matches entrepreneurial positions. They apply the AI algorithms to align the skills, experiences, and behavioural indicators with the job requirements to streamline the recruitment process and focus on the entrepreneurial fit (Upadhyay & Khandelwal, 2018)(Kumar et al., 2025b; Kumar et al., 2025c).

Overall, AI-based hiring solutions go beyond the superficial assessment of the qualifications and allow the identification of the underlying entrepreneurial skills, including linguistic, behavioural, and predictive analyses. Nevertheless, as much as these technologies are expected to be more objective and efficient, they also present issues concerning transparency, ethical application, and fairness that must be well handled so that the recruitment results are not only accurate but also fair.

AI in Training and Skill Development

In addition to recruitment, artificial intelligence (AI) is also employed to develop and provide training programmes that develop entrepreneurial skills. Training with AI-enabled platforms is also personalised, adaptive, and dynamic, unlike the old-fashioned one-size-fits-all training that only considers weaknesses, strengths and developmental needs. It can be especially useful in entrepreneurship education, where such competencies as opportunity recognition, creativity, risk management, and resilience differ significantly among individuals (Neck and Corbett, 2018).

One of the most radical AI applications in the field of entrepreneurial training is adaptive learning systems. These services employ machine-learning algorithms to constantly evaluate the performance of learners to customise instructional materials according to the level of skills and learning preferences (Baker and Inventado, 2014). An example is the case of entrepreneurs who are strong in strategic planning but weak in financial forecasting, who can be offered specific modules that would help them improve in the latter. This personalised method gives full effect to the learning and makes sure that the necessary entrepreneurial skills are developed better than in an inert training setting.

Simulations based on AI and gamification are also essential in educating entrepreneurs. AI-powered business simulation games enable participants to participate in decision-making games that simulate real-world entrepreneurial problems, including market entry, resource distribution, and competitive strategy (Bellotti et al., 2013). Not only do these simulations offer a safe space to experiment with, but the data produced through behavioural simulation can be analysed by AI systems to give feedback on problem-solving, leadership, and risk-taking behaviours. The process facilitates the growth of entrepreneurial intuition and strengthens skills of analytical decision-making.

The other important use is in the field of entrepreneurship education where intelligent tutoring systems (ITS) are used. ITS platforms make use of AI to mimic the functions of human instructors, providing personalised instructions, real-time feedback, and adjustable difficulty (Nkambou, Bourdeau, and Mizoguchi, 2010). Within the entrepreneurship domain, ITS can support learners by taking them through business model creation, market research, or even the creation of innovative solutions and provide assistance that is progressively enhanced as the learner becomes more experienced.

Moreover, AI may facilitate continuous performance measurement and feedback during entrepreneurial training. Through monitoring the participation, decision-making, and performance of learners in different tasks, the AI systems can give real-time feedback and suggestions on how to enhance them (Almalki, 2020). This feedback loop makes one more self-aware and speeds up the learning process, especially when it comes to acquiring dynamic entrepreneurial skills such as resilience and adaptability.

Essentially, training solutions based on AI fill the gap between theory and practice, creating experiential and personalised learning at scale. Such technologies are useful in training future entrepreneurs to gain not only technical skills but also to gain the cognitive flexibility, creativity and persistence needed in uncertain and competitive settings. Nevertheless, their effectiveness will be determined by their wise incorporation into the entrepreneurship programmes and proper handling of the challenges related to accessibility, inclusivity, and ethical usage of data.

Case Studies and Applications

The real-life application of artificial intelligence (AI) in the hiring and education of entrepreneurial potential has shifted into a concept to a new reality in industries, higher education institutions, and entrepreneurial ecosystems. The use of AI-based systems to detect and develop entrepreneurial talent is illustrated in a number of case studies, which can provide significant value to scholars, practitioners, and policymakers.

The example of using AI-based recruitment systems in startups and companies can be considered one of them. HireVue and Pymetrics are examples of companies that use video interviews and gamified cognitive tests based on AI to assess competencies that predict entrepreneurial abilities, such as risk tolerance, adaptability, and problem-solving (Chamorro-Premuzic et al., 2016; Pymetrics, 2020). These sites scan facial expressions, linguistic patterns, and performance in a game to create predictive profiles of entrepreneurial competence. Companies that use these technologies do not only record efficiency improvements but also increased consistency in the assessment of candidates, despite the apprehensions of unfairness and bias.

Within the sphere of entrepreneurship education, the most prominent universities and incubators have incorporated the use of AI-enabled learning systems to supplement entrepreneurial education. An example of an AI-driven simulation that lets students experiment with business models in dynamic uncertain market conditions is the Sloan School of Management at MIT. The platform provides students with customized feedback and chances to optimize strategic decisions by using machine-learning algorithms to modify the situations in real time (Neck and Corbett, 2018). Similarly, data-driven personalization is used in AI-assisted adaptive platforms like Coursera and edX to provide entrepreneurship modules that are specific to the background and progression of learners.

Corporate innovation programmes have also been implemented using AI to find so-called intrapreneurs, or those employees who have an entrepreneurial potential, and can trigger internal innovation. As an example, IBM uses AI-based analytics in its talent-management systems to identify those employees who demonstrate creativity, leadership, and collaborative skills in project data and internal communications (IBM, 2019). Through early detection of such people organisations can offer them specific training and leadership opportunities in entrepreneurship and thus a culture of innovation can be created internally.

Additionally, AI tools are being used more and more by incubators and accelerators to screen startup founders and teams. FounderNest uses natural-language processing, predictive analytics, to interpret the backgrounds, networks, and communication patterns of founders, providing investors and mentors with information on entrepreneurial potential that is data-driven (FounderNest, 2021). These instruments allow making better decisions in terms of resource distribution, mentorship, and investment and increase the likelihood of venture success.

All these case studies highlight the transformative nature of AI in the recruitment and training processes. They explain that AI can offer scalable and data-driven insights into entrepreneurial potential and can offer individualised developmental opportunities. However, they also point to some fundamental issues, especially in the area of the transparency of the algorithms, data confidentiality, and the maintenance of the fairness in the diverse pools of applicants. With organisations persistently trying out these tools, careful consideration of the results and ethical protection will be necessary to make adoption responsible and fair.

Bias, Fairness, and Ethical Considerations

Although AI provides unprecedented opportunities to enhance recruitment and training to become an entrepreneur, it also raises serious ethical issues. The key concerns here include the issues of bias, fairness, transparency, and accountability. These risks left unaddressed can erode the very purpose of implementing AI to develop more precise and justifiable identification of entrepreneurial talent.

One of the most popular ethical issues is algorithmic bias. Historical data are used to train AI models, which often reflect the existing social inequalities based on gender, race, socioeconomic status, and cultural background (Barocas and Selbst, 2016). In hiring, this may lead to the biased results in which entrepreneurial potential is undervalued in under-represented groups. As an example, in case historical records are not representative of female founders or applicants to elite institutions, AI-based models could reinforce these trends unintentionally.

Another burning problem is fairness in evaluation. It is true that AI tools are capable of handling data in a consistent manner, however, fairness requires more than consistency; fairness requires contextual sensitivity. Characteristics like risk-taking or communication style can be represented differently among cultural or demographic groups, but AI systems can perceive such differences as a lack of abilities instead of the variety of manifestations of entrepreneurial skills (Mehrabi et al., 2021). Such a risk can result in the marginalization of the talented people who do not fit the dominant cultural or behavioural patterns in training data.

Explainability and transparency are also important issues. Most AIs, especially deep learning models, are black boxes, which make predictions without explaining the reasoning behind the choice (Burrell, 2016). This ambiguity is detrimental in recruiting and training entrepreneurs in that it prevents the candidates, the recruiter, or the educator to know why a system classifies someone as having high or low entrepreneurial potential. The inability to explain not just lowers the trust but also hinders the identification and rectification of bias.

Moreover, the most important is privacy and data protection. The AI-based recruitment and training tools often gather sensitive information, such as psychometric answers, behavioural trends, and biometric data during video interviews or simulations. The mishandling of such data can lead to violations of confidentiality and abuse, and it creates legal and ethical concerns (Zarsky, 2016).

In order to address these issues, researchers and professionals propose responsible AI models that focus on fairness, accountability, and transparency (FAT). The suggested solutions are the diversification of training data to provide representation, algorithmic auditing, and explainable AI methods to increase interpretability (Raghavan et al., 2020). The role of human control is also unavoidable because the application of AI-based insights to the human reason can harmonize the efficiency and ethical sensitivity.

Overall, although AI has the potential to decrease some types of subjectivity in the recruitment and training processes, it also has the potential to increase the hidden biases when not designed and implemented in a responsible manner. The need to consider ethical considerations is thus critical in order to have AI tools that will aid in the inclusion, equity, and credibility in identifying entrepreneurial potential.

Challenges in Implementing AI for Entrepreneurial Talent Development

Despite the promising opportunities of AI in improving the recruitment and training processes, its use in the process of talent development in entrepreneurship is marred by a number of challenges. These barriers are technical, organisational and socio-cultural and restrict the scalability and long-term effectiveness of AI-driven solutions and it is crucial to understand these barriers when designing more effective and sustainable systems.

In technical terms, much of the AI models are trained on large-scale datasets of high quality. However, data that are unique to entrepreneurial behaviour and performance tend to be small, scattered, or location-specific (Li et al., 2020). Entrepreneurial potential is dynamic in nature and depends on changing circumstances, networks, experience and thus making it difficult to model such constructs with fixed data inputs. Further, AI systems are often weak at transferability; models developed or trained in one cultural or organisational context may not generalise to others.

Another barrier is organisational resistance. The adoption of AI-based systems may require a change in the culture of recruitment and training that is based on human intuition and experience (Davenport and Ronanki, 2018). Managers and educators can be reluctant to embrace AI because they are afraid to lose control, they do not believe in the accuracy of the algorithms, or they are afraid that the recruitment process will be depersonalised. These cultural and psychological barriers may hinder the implementation of AI even though it has proven useful.

The cost and resource requirements also limit adoption, especially to small and medium-sized enterprises (SMEs) and start-ups. The creation or utilization of advanced AI-based recruitment and training systems is often associated with significant financial expenses on technology, infrastructure, and skills (Bughin et al., 2018).

The organisations will end up relying on the traditional, less efficient approaches to identifying entrepreneurial talent without the necessary resources.

The analysis of the long-term effectiveness is not finished yet. Although AI systems are able to forecast short-term performance or learning results, their ability to predict with accuracy the success of an entrepreneur in the long run is still unclear (Nambisan et al., 2019). The entrepreneurial careers are influenced by very unstable and situation-specific variables, like market dynamics, social networks, and institutional circumstances, which AI might be not able to fully represent. As a result, the stakeholders will be prone to over-trusting an algorithmic prediction that is not properly validated longitudinally.

Lastly, there are ethical and legal limitations that make implementation difficult. Data privacy laws like the General Data Protection Regulation (GDPR) require close attention to the data of the candidates, especially when such data includes sensitive psychometric, behavioural, or biometric data (Wachter and Mittelstadt, 2019). The organisations also need to address the issue of public trust, and the AI-based systems should be transparent, fair, and accountable.

Overall, the application of AI in talent development in the entrepreneurial domain is faced with technical constraints, organisational opposition, resource constraints, uncertainty about the long-term effectiveness, and ethical-legal issues. To eliminate these obstacles, interdisciplinary efforts, well-developed data plans, cultural sensitivity, and continuous assessment are necessary to enable AI to become an enabler as opposed to an impediment in the process of recognizing and developing entrepreneurial potential.

Future Directions and Research Opportunities

The incorporation of AI in the process of recognizing and cultivating entrepreneurial potential has not yet reached its full potential, which still offers ample opportunities to advance in the future and conduct research. With the changes in technology and the digitalisation of entrepreneurial ecosystems, new research and practice directions will appear.

One such direction is the development of multimodal data analytics. The existing AI models mostly use textual, survey-based, or performance-related information. The next generation of research may include multimodal sources of data, including voice, facial expressions, physiological signals, and digital footprint analytics, to identify more detailed and colorful signals of entrepreneurial qualities (Liu et al., 2021b). This kind of integration may enlighten such dormant potentials as resilience, flexibility and creativity, which are the core areas of entrepreneurial success.

Another frontier is personalised training through adaptive AI systems. The AI-based platforms may use the reinforcement learning and the feedback loops to adjust the training modules to the strengths and weaknesses of the future entrepreneurs (Zhou et al., 2019). Research into the benefits of personalization in learning and the speed with which it can prepare entrepreneurs compared to traditional, one-size-fits-all methods is a worthwhile research project.

Also of interest is cross-cultural validation of AI models. Cultural norms, institutional structures and social networks have a significant impact on entrepreneurial behaviour (Autio et al., 2013). The models that are created in one area might not be applicable to other areas, and this is where the global applicability is questioned. The future research would be able to experiment and refine AI recruitment and training tools in various cultural and economic settings to be inclusive and equitable.

Ethical AI models specific to entrepreneurship are yet to be developed. Bias, transparency, and accountability are well-known, but there is a lack of specific guidelines, which are specific to the entrepreneurial recruitment and training (Jobin et al., 2019). Studies may be aimed at defining standardised auditing procedures, equity measures, and human-AI interaction guidelines that will keep the utilisation of such technologies responsible.

Lastly, longitudinal impact studies cannot be ignored. The majority of contemporary AI tests focus on short-term predictive success, but the actual test is whether AI-named candidates will be successful in their entrepreneurial ventures in the long-term. Following a group of entrepreneurs who are evaluated by AI tools and comparing their performance with that of the group of entrepreneurs who are chosen through conventional means would be a way of empirically testing the value of AI in the long-term in entrepreneurial ecosystems.

Finally, the integration, personalisation, cultural sensitivity, and ethical-based AI systems should be sought in future studies. By responding to these opportunities, scholars and practitioners will be able to utilize AI not just to increase efficiency but also to substantially develop a diverse and resilient group of entrepreneurs.

CONCLUSION

The discovery and nurturing of entrepreneurial potential is an urgent task to organisations, educational institutions, and policymakers who wish to promote innovation and economic development. Conventional methods of assessment, including psychometric testing, interviews and experience-based evaluations provide useful information but often suffer as a result of subjectivity, lack of scalability and inconsistent predictive validity. The opportunity of AI is a radical solution to overcome these constraints by using data-driven, adaptive, and predictive solutions to improve the recruitment and training process.

AI-based applications, such as natural language processing, machine-learning, gamified learning, and adaptive learning platforms, can help organisations identify the latent entrepreneurial characteristics and provide personalised skill development at scale. Startups, corporate innovation programmes, universities, and accelerators are examples of case studies that demonstrate the practical applicability of these technologies in identifying and developing entrepreneurial talent. However, the implementation of AI is not without problems. The issues of bias in algorithms, fairness, transparency, data privacy, and long-term effectiveness require a special approach and ethical monitoring to implement them responsibly.

Future research opportunities focus on multimodal data integration, culturally sensitive modelling, personalised adaptive training and longitudinal validation of results. Discussing these spheres will enable AI to help in the development of a diverse, resilient, and competent entrepreneurial workforce. Overall, AI can be a strong adjunct to human judgement in the discovery and development of entrepreneurial potential as long as its application is informed by ethical considerations, stringent assessment, and a firm belief in inclusivity.

REFERENCES

Ajzen, I. (1991). The theory of planned behavior. *Organizational Behavior and Human Decision Processes*, *50*(2), 179–211. DOI: 10.1016/0749-5978(91)90020-T

Almalki, A. (2020). Intelligent learning systems: A systematic review and future directions. *Education and Information Technologies*, *25*(6), 5401–5438. DOI: 10.1007/s10639-020-10247-1

Audretsch, D. B., & Thurik, A. R. (2010). *Unraveling the shift to the entrepreneurial economy*. Springer. DOI: 10.2139/ssrn.1664466

Autio, E., Pathak, S., & Wennberg, K. (2013). Consequences of cultural practices for entrepreneurial behaviors. *Journal of International Business Studies*, *44*(4), 334–362. DOI: 10.1057/jibs.2013.15

Baker, R. S., & Inventado, P. S. (2014). Educational data mining and learning analytics. In Larusson, J. A., & White, B. (Eds.), *Learning analytics: From research to practice* (pp. 61–75). Springer. DOI: 10.1007/978-1-4614-3305-7_4

Barocas, S., & Selbst, A. D. (2016). Big data's disparate impact. *SSRN*, *104*(3), 671–732. DOI: 10.2139/ssrn.2477899

Baron, R. A. (2006). Opportunity recognition as pattern recognition: How entrepreneurs "connect the dots" to identify new business opportunities. *The Academy of Management Perspectives*, *20*(1), 104–119. DOI: 10.5465/amp.2006.19873412

Bellotti, F., Kapralos, B., Lee, K., Moreno-Ger, P., & Berta, R. (2013). Assessment in and of serious games: An overview. *Advances in Human-Computer Interaction*, *2013*, 1–11. DOI: 10.1155/2013/136864

Bogen, M., & Rieke, A. (2018). Help wanted: An examination of hiring algorithms, equity, and bias. *Technology Science*. https://techscience.org/a/2018050901/

Boyatzis, R. E. (1982). *The competent manager: A model for effective performance*. Wiley.

Brynjolfsson, E., & McAfee, A. (2017). *Machine, platform, crowd: Harnessing our digital future*. W. W. Norton & Company.

Bughin, J., Seong, J., Manyika, J., Chui, M., & Joshi, R. (2018). *Notes from the AI frontier: Modeling the impact of AI on the world economy*. McKinsey Global Institute.

Burrell, J. (2016). How the machine 'thinks': Understanding opacity in machine learning algorithms. *Big Data & Society*, *3*(1), 1–12. DOI: 10.1177/2053951715622512

Chamorro-Premuzic, T., Winsborough, D., Sherman, R. A., & Hogan, R. (2016). New talent signals: Shiny new objects or a brave new world? *Industrial and Organizational Psychology: Perspectives on Science and Practice*, *9*(3), 621–640. DOI: 10.1017/iop.2016.6

Chen, C. C., Greene, P. G., & Crick, A. (1998). Does entrepreneurial self-efficacy distinguish entrepreneurs from managers? *Journal of Business Venturing*, *13*(4), 295–316. DOI: 10.1016/S0883-9026(97)00029-3

Collins, C. J., Hanges, P. J., & Locke, E. A. (2004). The relationship of achievement motivation to entrepreneurial behavior: A meta-analysis. *Human Performance*, *17*(1), 95–117. DOI: 10.1207/S15327043HUP1701_5

Cooper, A. C., Woo, C. Y., & Dunkelberg, W. C. (1989). Entrepreneurship and the initial size of firms. *Journal of Business Venturing*, *4*(5), 317–332. DOI: 10.1016/0883-9026(89)90004-9

Davenport, T. H., & Ronanki, R. (2018). Artificial intelligence for the real world. *Harvard Business Review*, *96*(1), 108–116.

FounderNest. (2021). *FounderNest: AI-powered founder analysis*. https://www.foundernest.com/

Gartner, W. B. (1988). "Who is an entrepreneur?" is the wrong question. *American Journal of Small Business*, *12*(4), 11–32. DOI: 10.1177/104225878801200401

Gatewood, E. J., Shaver, K. G., & Gartner, W. B. (1995). A longitudinal study of cognitive factors influencing start-up behaviors and success at venture creation. *Journal of Business Venturing*, *10*(5), 371–391. DOI: 10.1016/0883-9026(95)00035-7

IBM. (2019). *AI in talent management: Identifying intrapreneurs at IBM*. IBM Research. https://www.ibm.com/research

Jobin, A., Ienca, M., & Vayena, E. (2019). The global landscape of AI ethics guidelines. *Nature Machine Intelligence*, *1*(9), 389–399. DOI: 10.1038/s42256-019-0088-2

Jordan, M. I., & Mitchell, T. M. (2015). Machine learning: Trends, perspectives, and prospects. *Science*, *349*(6245), 255–260. DOI: 10.1126/science.aaa8415

Keh, H. T., Foo, M. D., & Lim, B. C. (2002). Opportunity evaluation under risky conditions: The cognitive processes of entrepreneurs. *Entrepreneurship Theory and Practice*, *27*(2), 125–148. DOI: 10.1111/1540-8520.00003

Krueger, N. F.Jr, & Brazeal, D. V. (1994). Entrepreneurial potential and potential entrepreneurs. *Entrepreneurship Theory and Practice*, *18*(3), 91–104. DOI: 10.1177/104225879401800307

Kumar, M., Dagar, M., Yadav, M., Choudhury, T., & Luu, T. M. N. (2025a). Navigating the future: Challenges and opportunities in intelligent RPA implementation. In Intelligent Robotic Process Automation: Development, Vulnerability and Applications (pp. 393–420). IGI Global. DOI: 10.4018/979-8-3693-4365-4.ch015

Kumar, M., Jain, A., Mittal, A., Gera, R., Biswal, S. K., Yadav, M., Hung, T. H., & Priya Srivastava, A. (2024). Inclusion of Neural Networks in Higher Education: A Systematic Review and Bibliometric Analysis. 2024 4th International Conference on Innovative Practices in Technology and Management (ICIPTM), 1–6. DOI: 10.1109/ICIPTM59628.2024.10563852

Kumar, M., Nain, N., Dagar, M., Luu, T. M. N., & Kaur, K. (2025b). Redefining work and outsourcing in the AI era: Challenges and opportunities. In *Global Work Arrangements and Outsourcing in the Age of AI*. IGI Global., DOI: 10.4018/979-8-3373-1270-5.ch021

Kumar, M., Rani, P., Mangla, N., Nguyen, N. T., & Kaur, K. (2025c). Sustainable outsourcing in an AI-driven world: Ethical, economic, and environmental perspectives. In *Global Work Arrangements and Outsourcing in the Age of AI*. IGI Global., DOI: 10.4018/979-8-3373-1270-5.ch001

Kumar, M., Yadav, R., Suresh, A. S., Singh, R., Yadav, M., Balodi, A., Vihari, N. S., & Srivastava, A. P. (2023). Mapping AI-Driven Marketing: Review of Field and Directions for Future Research. 2023 2nd International Conference on Futuristic Technologies (INCOFT), 1–5. DOI: 10.1109/INCOFT60753.2023.10425169

Langer, M., König, C. J., & Fitili, A. (2019). Information as a double-edged sword: The role of computer experience and information disclosure on applicant reactions to AI-based assessments. *Computers in Human Behavior*, *97*, 123–132. DOI: 10.1016/j.chb.2019.03.029

Li, F., Duan, Y., & Fu, Z. (2020). Towards an understanding of the adoption of artificial intelligence in education: A systematic literature review. *Technological Forecasting and Social Change*, *158*, 120–178. DOI: 10.1016/j.techfore.2020.120178

Littunen, H. (2000). Entrepreneurship and the characteristics of the entrepreneurial personality. *International Journal of Entrepreneurial Behaviour & Research*, *6*(6), 295–310. DOI: 10.1108/13552550010362741

Liu, Y., Li, H., & Xu, X. (2021a). Artificial intelligence in human resource management: Applications and challenges. *Journal of Management Science and Engineering*, *6*(1), 1–12. DOI: 10.1016/j.jmse.2025.11.001

Liu, Y., Osmani, V., & Demartini, G. (2021b). Multimodal machine learning for mental health applications: Current developments and future directions. *ACM Computing Surveys*, *54*(5), 1–36. DOI: 10.1145/3214304

Malhan, D. Mohan, Preeti, Sushma, Harsh, & Nisha. (2021). Probing Anterior of Entrepreneurial Intentions of Youngsters in India, an Analytical Approach. Academy of Strategic Management Journal, Suppl. Special Issue 6, 20(October), 1–10. https://www.abacademies.org/articles/probing-anterior-of-entrepreneurial-intentions-of-youngsters-in-india-an-analytical-approach-11730.html

McClelland, D. C. (1961). *The achieving society*. Van Nostrand. DOI: 10.1037/14359-000

Mehrabi, N., Morstatter, F., Saxena, N., Lerman, K., & Galstyan, A. (2021). A survey on bias and fairness in machine learning. *ACM Computing Surveys*, *54*(6), 1–35. DOI: 10.1145/3457607

Mitchell, R. K., Smith, B., Seawright, K. W., & Morse, E. A. (2002). Cross-cultural cognitions and the venture creation decision. *Academy of Management Journal*, *43*(5), 974–993. DOI: 10.2307/1556422

Nambisan, S., Wright, M., & Feldman, M. (2019). The digital transformation of innovation and entrepreneurship: Progress, challenges and key themes. *Research Policy*, *48*(8), 103773. DOI: 10.1016/j.respol.2019.03.018

Neck, H. M., & Corbett, A. C. (2018). The scholarship of teaching and learning entrepreneurship. *Entrepreneurship Education and Pedagogy*, *1*(1), 8–41. DOI: 10.1177/2515127417737286

Nguyen, T. B., Kumar, M., Sahoo, D. K., Nain, N., Yadav, M., & Dadhich, V. (2025). Mapping the landscape of women entrepreneurs in micro and small enterprises: Trends, themes, and insights through systematic review and text mining. F1000Research, 14. DOI: 10.12688/f1000research.163030.1

Nkambou, R., Bourdeau, J., & Mizoguchi, R. (2010). *Advances in intelligent tutoring systems*. Springer. DOI: 10.1007/978-3-642-14363-2

Obschonka, M., Stuetzer, M., Gosling, S. D., Rentfrow, P. J., Lamb, M. E., & Potter, J. (2017). Entrepreneurial regions: Do macro-psychological cultural characteristics of regions help solve the "knowledge paradox" of economics? *PLoS One*, *12*(6), e0178332. DOI: 10.1371/journal.pone.0178332

Pymetrics. (2020). *How pymetrics works: AI-driven talent matching*. https://www.pymetrics.ai/

Raghavan, M., Barocas, S., Kleinberg, J., & Levy, K. (2020). Mitigating bias in algorithmic hiring: Evaluating claims and practices. *Proceedings of the 2020 Conference on Fairness, Accountability, and Transparency*, 469–481. DOI: 10.1145/3351095.3372828

Rauch, A., & Frese, M. (2007). Let's put the person back into entrepreneurship research: A meta-analysis on the relationship between business owners' personality traits, business creation, and success. *European Journal of Work and Organizational Psychology*, *16*(4), 353–385. DOI: 10.1080/13594320701595438

Shane, S. (2003). *A general theory of entrepreneurship: The individual-opportunity nexus*. Edward Elgar. DOI: 10.4337/9781781007990

Shane, S., & Venkataraman, S. (2000). The promise of entrepreneurship as a field of research. *Academy of Management Review*, *25*(1), 217–226. DOI: 10.5465/amr.2000.2791611

Tayal, R., Upadhyay, R., Yadav, M., & Singh, R. (2019). The Development and Validation of the Organizational Effectiveness Scale Using Confirmatory Factor Analysis. *Global Business Review*, *22*(3), 097215091881172. DOI: 10.1177/0972150918811720

Trivedi, S., Vishnu, S., Singh, A., & Yadav, M. (2023a). Research Trends in Sustainable E-Payment Systems: A Study Using Topic Modeling Approach. IEEE Transactions on Engineering Management, PP, 1–15. DOI: 10.1109/TEM.2023.3280216

Trivedi, V., Banerji, D., & Yadav, M. (2023b). Expecting the surprises: Role of hope in consumer repurchase intentions in an online shopping environment. In Journal of Strategic Marketing (Vol. 31, Issue 4, pp. 794–816). Taylor & Francis. DOI: 10.1080/0965254X.2021.1996449

Tunio, M. N., Jariko, M. A., Børsen, T., Shaikh, S., Mushtaque, T., & Brahmi, M. (2021). How Entrepreneurship Sustains Barriers in the Entrepreneurial Process—A Lesson from a Developing Nation. In Sustainability (Vol. 13, Issue 20). DOI: 10.3390/su132011419

Tunio, M. N., & Tunio, S. (2025). *Navigating Digital Transformation: A Systematic Review of SMEs' Transitions and Growth in the Digital Age*. Sukkur IBA Journal of Management and Business., DOI: 10.30537/sijmb.v11i2.1509

Upadhyay, A. K., & Khandelwal, K. (2018). Applying artificial intelligence: Implications for recruitment. *Strategic HR Review*, *17*(5), 255–258. DOI: 10.1108/SHR-07-2018-0051 van Esch, P., Black, J. S., & Ferolie, J. (2019). Marketing AI recruitment: The next phase in job application and selection. *Computers in Human Behavior*, *90*, 215–222. DOI: 10.1016/j.chb.2018.09.009

Wachter, S., & Mittelstadt, B. (2019). A right to reasonable inferences: Re-thinking data protection law in the age of big data and AI. *Columbia Business Law Review*, *2019*(2), 494–620.

Wilson, F., Kickul, J., & Marlino, D. (2007). Gender, entrepreneurial self-efficacy, and entrepreneurial career intentions: Implications for entrepreneurship education. *Entrepreneurship Theory and Practice*, *31*(3), 387–406. DOI: 10.1111/j.1540-6520.2007.00179.x

Yadav, R., Yadav, M., & Vihari, N. (2023). High-performance work system and learning orientation in offline, online, and hybrid workplaces: The mediating role of affective commitment. *The Learning Organization*, *31*(1), 122–136. Advance online publication. DOI: 10.1108/TLO-10-2022-0118

Zarsky, T. Z. (2016). The trouble with algorithmic decisions: An analytic road map to examine efficiency and fairness in automated and opaque decision making. *Science, Technology & Human Values*, *41*(1), 118–132. DOI: 10.1177/0162243915605575

Zhao, H., & Seibert, S. E. (2006). The Big Five personality dimensions and entrepreneurial status: A meta-analytical review. *The Journal of Applied Psychology*, *91*(2), 259–271. DOI: 10.1037/0021-9010.91.2.259

Zhou, J., Pan, Y., Wang, J., Vasilakos, A. V., & Fang, B. (2019). Artificial intelligence in personalized education. *IEEE Transactions on Systems, Man, and Cybernetics. Systems*, *49*(12), 2153–2164. DOI: 10.1109/TSMC.2019.2915125

Chapter 4
Gamification and AI-Driven Simulations in Entrepreneurial Skill Development

Priya Gaur
Centre for Online Education, GLA University, India

Gunjan Mohan Sharma
http://orcid.org/0000-0003-2272-7385
JGBS, O.P. Jindal Global University, India

Ali Najeeb
http://orcid.org/0000-0003-4663-9347
Qasim Ibrahim School of Business, Villa College, Maldives

Hung Duy Bui
Faculty of Economics, Banking Academy of Vietnam, Vietnam

ABSTRACT

Entrepreneurial skill development increasingly relies on innovative educational approaches that bridge theory and practice. This chapter explores the integration of gamification and AI-driven simulations as transformative tools for cultivating entrepreneurial competencies. Gamification leverages game elements such as points, badges, and leaderboards to enhance learner engagement, motivation, and strategic thinking, while AI-driven simulations provide adaptive, immersive environments for experiential learning, decision-making, and problem-solving. The synergy between gamification and AI simulations enables personalized feedback, collaborative chal-

DOI: 10.4018/979-8-2600-1353-3.ch004

lenges, and realistic entrepreneurial scenarios, fostering critical skills for startup success. The chapter also addresses technological, ethical, and accessibility considerations, highlighting best practices for implementation. Emerging trends such as AR/VR integration and predictive learning analytics are discussed, emphasizing opportunities for future research and innovation in entrepreneurial education.

Introduction

The development of entrepreneurial skills has become a major concern of education and career training, with entrepreneurship being generally accepted as a source of economic expansion as well as an innovation-based and self-empowering experience (Rae, 2017; Neck et al., 2018). Traditional classroom models, that are heavily based on lectures and theoretical models, often do not provide learners with the practical, adaptive, and decision-making skills to operate in dynamic entrepreneurial settings (Gartner et al., 2019). To address these shortcomings, experiential learning practices have become more popular, which focus on active learning, reflection, and practical problem-solving (Kolb, 2015). In this regard, gamification and AI-based simulations have become the revolutionary means of entrepreneurial education, where immersive, interactive, and personalized learning experiences can engage learners and support the acquisition of skills (Deterding et al., 2011; Hamari et al., 2014).

Gamification uses the game-design principles of points, badges, leaderboards, and challenges to encourage and maintain the interest of learners and promote strategic thinking, groupwork, and resilience, which are the competencies of an entrepreneur (Werbach and Hunter, 2012). In the meantime, AI-based simulations offer dynamic, scenario-based settings in which learners are able to test business decisions, strategies, and get real-time feedback, thus, acquiring problem-solving and critical-thinking skills in a risk-free environment (Luckin et al., 2016; Holmes et al., 2019). Combining gamification with AI-based simulations adds another layer of learning because it incorporates incentive and cognitive aspects with personalised and data-driven feedback to maximise performance and learning results (Johnson et al., 2020).

Nonetheless, regardless of their potential, the application of gamified AI simulation in the context of entrepreneurship education has several challenges, such as ethical considerations, the problem of accessibility, and the threat of excessive dependence on technology (Bai and Ertmer, 2021; Floridi, 2019). Moreover, the success of these strategies relies on the attentive design of instructions that would match the learning goals with the gameplay and simulation contexts. These dynamics are essential to educators, policymakers, and practitioners who want to use technology to develop entrepreneurial skills in an effective manner. The given chapter thus seeks to examine the theoretical backgrounds, practical uses, and future developments of gamification and AI-based simulations in the development of entrepreneurial skills and provide information about their possibilities, constraints, and prospects (Yadav et al., 2024).

Theoretical Foundations

The combination of gamification and AI-based simulations in entrepreneurial learning has its basis in a number of established learning theories and pedagogical models. Experience learning theory (Kolb, 2015) underlines the significance of learning based on real-life experience, reflexive observation, abstract conceptualisation and active experimentation. Within the context of entrepreneurship, learners have the advantage of simulated business environments and gamified tasks that enable them to experiment with making decisions, trying strategies, and reflecting on their results without the danger of failure in the real world (Rae, 2017). The experiences enable the acquisition of key entrepreneurial skills including opportunity identification, management, and strategic planning.

The constructivist theory of learning also justifies the application of gamified and simulation-based learning, which assumes that students can build knowledge by engaging in active learning and social interaction (Piaget, 1972; Vygotsky, 1978). Through AI-based simulations, learners are motivated to develop their knowledge of complex business processes, market forces, and managerial decision-making through iteration. The elements of gamification (collaborative challenges and peer competition) improve social learning through interaction, feedback, and shared problem-solving experiences (Deterding et al., 2011).

Self-determination theory (SDT) can also be used to shed more light on the motivational processes that lie behind gamified learning (Deci and Ryan, 2000). According to SDT, autonomy, competence, and relatedness are the main psychological needs that promote intrinsic motivation. These needs can be met through gamified learning environments, which enable learners to make purposeful decisions, give feedback on their progress, and have a collaborative or competitive interaction, and thus increase engagement, persistence, and skill acquisition (Hamari et al., 2014). In the same manner, AI-based simulations can also provide customised adaptive challenges that are within the skill level of the learner, which encourages a sense of competence and mastery (Luckin et al., 2016).

Technologically, the simulations based on AI rely on intelligent tutoring systems (ITS) and adaptive learning models, which employ machine learning algorithms and predictive analytics to track the learner behaviour, give real-time feedback and customise the instructional material (Holmes et al., 2019). Such systems are capable of replicating complicated entrepreneurial conditions, including market dynamics, financial risk and stakeholder negotiations, which allow the learners to acquire strategic thinking, problem solving and decision making confidence. The synergistic learning effect of AI adaptivity and gamification makes use of both motivational and cognitive processes to maximise the acquisition of entrepreneurial skills (Johnson et al., 2020).

Altogether, the experiential learning, constructivism, self-determination theory, and intelligent adaptive learning models support gamification and AI-based simulations in entrepreneurial education in theory. Collectively, these strategies offer a pedagogically sound, interesting, and individualized channel toward the acquisition of the competencies required to succeed as an entrepreneur in complex and dynamic settings (Trivedi et al., 2023a).

Entrepreneurial Learning through Gamification.

Gamification has become a potent pedagogical tool in entrepreneurial learning that uses game-design concepts to improve engagement, motivation, as well as skill acquisition (Werbach and Hunter, 2012). In contrast to the traditional instruction that tends to focus on passive learning, the gamified learning environment engages the learners in interactive tasks, problem-solving, and scenario-related activities. The strategy is consistent with the idea of experiential learning that allows students to learn through doing, reflecting on their actions, and testing their strategies in a secure and organized setting (Kolb, 2015; Rae, 2017).

The major components of gamification are points, badges, leaderboards, challenges, and levels, which are created to give instant feedback and support the required behaviours (Deterding et al., 2011). These factors can replicate the dynamics of the real world in a business context in the process of entrepreneurial learning, including resource management, dealings, or reaction to market dynamics. As an example, the points can be profits, badges can be mastery of certain skills, and leaderboards can encourage healthy competition between learners, which encourages persistence and strategic thinking (Hamari et al., 2014). Through these mechanisms, gamification does not only enhance the motivation of learners but also stimulates goal-setting, teamwork, and adaptable decision-making skills, which are essential entrepreneurial skills.

Gamification has been reported by empirical studies to be effective in entrepreneurship education. Competitions and simulation-based business exercises have been demonstrated to enhance engagement, creativity, and strategic thinking of learners more than traditional instructional techniques (Johnson et al., 2020; Su and Cheng, 2020). Gamified platforms enable the learner to explore the business models, make calculated risks, and get instant feedback, which promotes reflective learning and continual improvement. Moreover, gamification helps to address the self-determination theory and fulfil the intrinsic needs of autonomy, competence, and relatedness of learners, which increases intrinsic motivation and skill retention in the long run (Deci and Ryan, 2000; Hamari et al., 2014).

Although the benefits of gamification in entrepreneurial education are evident, there are challenges associated with the implementation. Badly constructed gamified experiences can result in extrinsic motivation that cannot be based on deep learning or can focus on competition instead of collaboration, which causes disengagement in some learners (Bai and Ertmer, 2021). Moreover, teachers have to make sure that the aspects of games are correlated with the learning goals and that the assessment of performance is based on the development of skills and not on the surface level success. Effective gamification must be thoroughly designed, be integrated with pedagogical objectives, and continuously measure the results of the learners (Yadav et al., 2019).

To sum up, gamification is a revolutionary business model of learning in entrepreneurship, which provides a stimulating, interactive, and motivational model of skills acquisition. Gamification can be used in conjunction with careful instructional design and combined with AI-based simulations to benefit practical skills, decision-making capabilities, and entrepreneurial preparedness of learners in the real world considerably.

Artificial Intelligence-based Simulations in Entrepreneurship.

Artificial intelligence (AI) has transformed entrepreneurial education by allowing the development of dynamic, interactive, and customised simulation settings that simulate intricate business situations (Luckin et al., 2016; Holmes et al., 2019). Simulations based on AI give learners a chance to practice entrepreneurial decision-making, resource allocation, market strategies, and risk management in a risk-free environment. These platforms enable learners to test hypotheses, observe the consequences, and optimize their strategies, which are key to successful entrepreneurship through simulating real-world dynamics and developing critical thinking, strategic planning, and problem-solving skills (Johnson et al., 2020; Floridi, 2019).

One of the main advantages of AI-based simulations is the ability to offer adaptive learning. AI systems can observe the behaviour of the learner, trace the performance and modify the complexity and content of the scenario according to the progress of a person by machine learning algorithms and predictive analytics (Holmes et al., 2019). An example of this is that a learner with a weak financial decision-making capability can be presented with simplified market situations with specific advice, whereas more advanced learners can be presented with more complicated simulations with competition, supply-chain dynamics, and changing market conditions. Such individualisation improves the level of engagement, mastery, and the ability of learners to develop competencies that match their levels of competence (Luckin et al., 2016).

Simulations of AI can also be used to facilitate the learning of metacognitive abilities through real-time feedback and reflections. Students will be able to evaluate the consequences of their actions, detect mistakes, and consider new options, which will facilitate self-regulated learning and lifelong learning (Holmes et al., 2019). In addition to this, certain platforms combine collaborative and competitive features, enabling learners to engage with others, bargain, and co-create solutions, and thus strengthen social and entrepreneurial skills in a simulated but realistic environment (Johnson et al., 2020).

In addition to cognitive and skill development, AI-based simulations provide meaningful data-driven information to educators. Learner performance, decision-making, and behavioural analytics allow instructors to detect knowledge gaps, customize interventions, and evaluate the learning outcomes with increased accuracy (Luckin et al., 2016). These insights do not only enhance the design of instruction, but they also help learners to understand their strengths, weaknesses, and growth paths, and to have a roadmap of skill improvement (Tayal et al., 2021).

However, AI-based simulations are not as easy to implement, as they are associated with ethical issues related to privacy, bias of algorithms, and accessibility (Floridi, 2019; Bai and Ertmer, 2021). It is important to ensure that the accessibility is fair, the decision-making process is transparent, and the design is inclusive to avoid possible negative outcomes of some groups of learners. Also, simulation scenarios should be thoroughly matched with learning goals to prevent superficiality or excessive focus on technical skills at the cost of the overall entrepreneurial skills.

To sum up, the AI-driven simulations are a new form of entrepreneurial education, which provides adaptive, immersive, and feedback-rich experiences that develop strategic thinking, decision-making, and problem-solving. These simulations can be used to produce interesting, customized, and efficient learning experiences when combined with gamification, which helps to close the gap between theory and practice in the field of entrepreneurship.

Combining Gamification and AI Simulations.

Gamification in combination with AI-based simulations is an effective convergence of motivational and adaptive learning approaches in entrepreneurial education. Although gamification will increase the level of engagement through its ability to use motivational drives like achievement, competition, and recognition (Werbach and Hunter, 2012; Hamari et al., 2014), AI-based simulations will be more profound as they will create dynamic and personalised learning processes that respond to the needs of specific learners (Luckin et al., 2016). Collectively, these strategies form immersive and interactive experiences that not only encourage learners to engage actively but also give them real-world experiences that allow them to apply entrepreneurial skills.

Gamification-based hybrid systems with AI simulations can be used in the context of entrepreneurial training to simulate a real startup experience, with learners moving through levels that reflect the business development stages: ideation, market validation, funding, and scaling (Su and Cheng, 2020). Extrinsic motivation is achieved through gamified features like points, badges, and leaderboards, whereas AI makes sure that the situation becomes more complex according to the performance of the learner, thus scaffolding the skills and promoting mastery (Holmes et al., 2019). This integration makes sure that the learners are not bored or pushed to death with boredom (Trivedi et al., 2023b).

One of the advantages of this integration is the possibility to create individual feedback loops. Gamified systems usually provide instant feedback on completion of a task, but when integrated with AI analytics, they are more subtle and can provide feedback on decision-making patterns, strategic advantages, and improvement opportunities (Johnson et al., 2020). As an example, students who continually make high-risk business choices can be given AI-generated hints to consider risk-management approaches and get gamified rewards on their achievements. This type of synergy between motivational reinforcement and adaptive feedback empowers engagement and skill development.

Besides, collaborative and competitive learning processes are facilitated by the combination of gamification and AI simulation. A learner can engage in team-based entrepreneurial games, where AI will dynamically simulate situations to achieve balance and fairness, and gamified leaderboards will promote healthy competition and peer learning (Deterding et al., 2011). These simulate real-life entrepreneurial ecosystems, where both collaboration and competition exist, thus equipping learners with the challenges of the real world of business (Rae, 2017).

Nonetheless, effective integration must be carefully designed. The incongruity between learning objectives and gameplay may reduce the educational utility of a game, resulting in shallow learning oriented on rewards as opposed to learning (Bai and Ertmer, 2021). Similarly, excessive use of AI adaptations with no significant gamified interactions could destroy the motivation of learners. Therefore, teachers and learning developers need to make sure that the aspects of gamification are strategically oriented to the entrepreneurial skills, and AI simulations should be transparent, ethical, and available to every learner (Choudhary et al., 2024).

Overall, a combination of gamification and AI-based simulations can be used as a synergistic method of entrepreneurial education, bringing together the motivational benefits of gamification and the adaptability and realism of AI simulations. These hybrid systems, when well-structured, have the potential to give learners interesting, customized, and realistic experiences of an entrepreneur, and fill the gap between theory and practice in creative ways.

Technological and Ethical Concerns.

The combination of gamification and AI-based simulations has both serious technological opportunities and ethical and practical concerns. Technologically, AI systems are based on sophisticated algorithms, data gathering, and predictive analytics to tailor the learning process, adjust situations, and provide feedback in real-time (Luckin et al., 2016; Holmes et al., 2019). These abilities increase the engagement of learners and their skill acquisition but require special consideration of data security, algorithm transparency, and system reliability to avoid unintended outcomes. The failure to work properly, a biased input of data, or inappropriate modeling may misguide learners or support the formation of mistaken decision-making patterns, which will negatively affect educational outcomes (Floridi, 2019).

Ethical considerations are also very important. The AI-based simulations systematically gather and process learning sensitive data, such as behavioral tendencies, performance indicators, and decision-making records (Bai and Ertmer, 2021). Schools and teachers should make sure that they are adhering to the rules of data privacy and implement open policies concerning the use of data. The issue of algorithmic bias is a major concern as the AI models, being trained on incomplete or unrepresentative data, can unintentionally discriminate against some groups of learners in favor of others (Floridi, 2019). To ensure equity and trust in AI-enhanced educational platforms, ethical design practices (including frequent audits, nonbiased datasets, and fairness monitoring) are needed.

Ethical issues also emerge with gamification, especially when it comes to motivation and engagement. Although such game mechanics as points, badges, and leaderboards can increase the motivation of learners, excessive focus on extrinsic incentives can decrease intrinsic motivation and encourage an unhealthy level of competition (Bai and Ertmer, 2021). The designers should also make sure that gamification is not merely a way of triggering a superficial engagement but in line with the learning objectives. In addition, the aspect of accessibility is also urgent: unless the principles of accommodations and inclusive design are implemented, learners with disabilities or insufficient technological access may be disadvantaged in highly gamified, AI-driven settings (Luckin et al., 2016).

The following best practices can be adopted to overcome these challenges: the adoption of transparent AI algorithms, the adoption of strong data protection protocols, the creation of friendly and accessible interfaces, and the alignment of gamification mechanics with educational objectives (Floridi, 2019; Werbach and Hunter, 2012). Fairness, accountability, and trust between the learners can be ensured with the assistance of regular feedback loops, consultations with stakeholders, and ethical oversight. When educators take the initiative to manage technological and ethical issues, they will be able to use AI and gamification in a responsible way, so that the development of entrepreneurial skills is effective and fair.

To sum up, technological changes like AI-based simulations and gamification have the potential to transform entrepreneurial education, but their application should take into account the issue of ethical, equity, and accessibility. By incorporating these factors into the instructional design, teachers can take full advantage of the pedagogical opportunities offered by AI-enhanced gamified learning without jeopardizing the rights, interest, and welfare of learners.

Future Trends and Research Directions.

Gamification and AI-based simulations in entrepreneurial education will converge and become highly innovative due to technological, data analytics, and immersive learning environments. One of the opportunities is the incorporation of augmented reality (AR) and virtual reality (VR) into gamified AI simulations to build an entirely immersive entrepreneurial ecosystem (Bacca et al., 2014; Radianti et al., 2020). These simulated experiences allow the learners to engage with the real world of business, feel the dynamics of the market, and acquire the skills of decision-making and problem-solving in a very engaging and secure environment. Teamwork, negotiation, and leadership skills required in entrepreneurship can also be developed with the help of AR and VR, as learners can collaborate in common virtual environments and develop teamwork (Radianti et al., 2020).

The other important trend is the application of predictive analytics and learning analytics to streamline individualised learning journeys. The machine can use big data to forecast performance of learners, determine possible gaps in skills, and prescribe specific interventions, which in turn will improve competency building in entrepreneurial settings (Luckin et al., 2016; Holmes et al., 2019). Further studies can examine the predictive capability of AI-based simulations to forecast the needs of learners, dynamically change the complexity of the scenario, and generate actionable information to both learners and teachers.

Another area of research is adaptive gamification. In contrast to traditional gamification, which uses the same game elements to all learners, adaptive gamification reacts to the motivations, learning styles, and progress of individual learners by varying the rewards, challenges, and feedback (Su and Cheng, 2020). The studies in this field can explore the best ratio of extrinsic and intrinsic motivation, the effect of adaptive gameplay on the retention of skills and entrepreneurial self-efficacy in the long term.

Also, ethical, equity, and accessibility aspects of AI-enhanced gamified learning are still important aspects to be explored in the future. With AI and gamification becoming more embedded in the educational platform, researchers and practitioners need to answer questions of algorithmic bias, data privacy, and inclusive design to provide a fair educational experience to diverse populations (Floridi, 2019; Bai and Ertmer, 2021).

To sum up, gamification and AI-based simulations are expected to evolve in the future to provide very immersive, adaptive, and personalised entrepreneurial learning experiences. New technologies including AR/VR, predictive analytics, and adaptive gamification provide promising opportunities to increase the level of skills, engagement of learners, and the ability to operate in the real world. These innovations should be optimised and their effects on entrepreneurial competence and outcomes researched further to improve the ethical and accessibility issues and determine their long-term effects in entrepreneurship.

Conclusion

The use of gamification and AI-based simulations has become the revolutionary way of teaching entrepreneurship, providing immersive, adaptive, and interactive ways to acquire essential entrepreneurial skills. Using the motivational principles of gamification, including points, badges, leaderboards, and challenges, teachers can increase the levels of engagement, persistence, and goal-oriented behaviour in learners (Werbach and Hunter, 2012; Hamari et al., 2014). At the same time, AI-based simulations offer data-driven, personalised learning experiences to mimic the complexity of real-world entrepreneurial situations, enabling learners to train on strategic decision-making, problem-solving, and risk management in a safe, iterative environment (Luckin et al., 2016; Holmes et al., 2019).

Gamification and AI simulations are synergistically beneficial as the motivational reinforcement of the learning process is integrated with adaptive learning pathways to maximise the acquisition of skills and competencies. Hybrid systems allow customised challenges, feedback loops, and social experiences that recreate real-world entrepreneurial systems, and promote individual development and social learning (Johnson et al., 2020; Su and Cheng, 2020). Nonetheless, these strategies should be carried out in a carefully calculated manner, taking into account the design of the instruction, its correspondence to the learning goals, as well as the preservation of ethical norms. Data privacy, algorithmic bias, accessibility, and excessive emphasis on extrinsic rewards are only some of the issues that need to be addressed to make the learning processes equitable and meaningful (Floridi, 2019; Bai and Ertmer, 2021).

In the future, the possibilities of AI-driven gamified simulations in entrepreneurship education will probably be even more expanded due to the emergence of new technologies like augmented and virtual reality, adaptive gamification, and advanced predictive analytics. These technologies give the chance to establish fully immersive, customised, and interactive learning experiences that equip learners to overcome the uncertainties and complexities of entrepreneurial projects (Bacca et al., 2014; Radianti et al., 2020). Further studies are still needed to examine the pedagogical, technological and ethical aspects of such methods and their long-term effects on entrepreneurial competence, motivation, and self-efficacy.

To conclude, gamification and AI-based simulations are the next step in the development of entrepreneurial skills that could help to fill the gap between theory and practice. These strategies can be designed and implemented in a way that ensures that the learners are able to immerse themselves in entrepreneurial issues, acquire the necessary skills, and gain the confidence required to thrive in the dynamic business environment.

References

Bacca, J., Baldiris, S., Fabregat, R., & Graf, S., & Kinshuk. (2014). Augmented reality trends in education: A systematic review of research and applications. *Journal of Educational Technology & Society, 17*(4), 133–149.

Bai, H., & Ertmer, P. A. (2021). Ethical considerations in AI-enhanced learning environments. *Educational Technology Research and Development, 69*(5), 2553–2571.

Choudhary, S., Yadav, M., & Srivastava, A. P. (2024). Cognitive biases among millennial Indian investors: Do personality and demographic factors matter? *FIIB Business Review, 13*(1), 106–117. DOI: 10.1177/23197145211057343

Deci, E. L., & Ryan, R. M. (2000). The "what" and "why" of goal pursuits: Human needs and the self-determination of behavior. *Psychological Inquiry, 11*(4), 227–268. DOI: 10.1207/S15327965PLI1104_01

Deterding, S., Dixon, D., Khaled, R., & Nacke, L. (2011). From game design elements to gamefulness: Defining "gamification." *Proceedings of the 15th International Academic MindTrek Conference*, 9–15. DOI: 10.1145/2181037.2181040

Floridi, L. (2019). *The ethics of artificial intelligence*. Oxford University Press.

Gartner, W. B., Carter, N. M., & Hills, G. E. (2019). The development of entrepreneurship: Key factors, challenges, and perspectives. *Journal of Business Venturing Insights, 11*, e00142.

Hamari, J., Koivisto, J., & Sarsa, H. (2014). Does gamification work?—A literature review of empirical studies on gamification. *Proceedings of the 47th Hawaii International Conference on System Sciences*, 3025–3034. DOI: 10.1109/HICSS.2014.377

Holmes, W., Bialik, M., & Fadel, C. (2019). *Artificial intelligence in education: Promises and implications for teaching and learning*. Center for Curriculum Redesign.

Johnson, L., Adams Becker, S., Estrada, V., & Freeman, A. (2020). *The NMC Horizon Report: 2020 Higher Education Edition*. EDUCAUSE.

Kolb, D. A. (2015). *Experiential learning: Experience as the source of learning and development* (2nd ed.). Pearson Education.

Luckin, R., Holmes, W., Griffiths, M., & Forcier, L. B. (2016). *Intelligence unleashed: An argument for AI in education*. Pearson.

Neck, H. M., Greene, P. G., & Brush, C. (2018). *Entrepreneurship education: Experiential learning approaches*. Routledge.

Piaget, J. (1972). *The psychology of the child*. Basic Books.

Radianti, J., Majchrzak, T. A., Fromm, J., & Wohlgenannt, I. (2020). A systematic review of immersive virtual reality applications for higher education: Design elements, lessons learned, and research agenda. *Computers & Education, 147*, 103778. DOI: 10.1016/j.compedu.2019.103778

Rae, D. (2017). *Entrepreneurial learning: Conceptual frameworks and applications*. Routledge.

Su, C. H., & Cheng, C. H. (2020). A mobile gamification learning system for improving the learning motivation and achievements of students. *Computers & Education*, *75*, 16–27.

Tayal, R., Upadhyay, R. K., Yadav, M., & Singh, R. (2021). The development and validation of the organizational effectiveness scale using confirmatory factor analysis. *Global Business Review*, *22*(3), 821–843. DOI: 10.1177/0972150918811720

Trivedi, S. K., Vishnu, S., Singh, A., & Yadav, M. (2023a). Research trends in sustainable E-payment systems: A study using topic modeling approach. *IEEE Transactions on Engineering Management*, *71*, 7511–7525. DOI: 10.1109/TEM.2023.3280216

Trivedi, V., Banerji, D., & Yadav, M. (2023b). Expecting the surprises: Role of hope in consumer repurchase intentions in an online shopping environment. *Journal of Strategic Marketing*, *31*(4), 794–816. DOI: 10.1080/0965254X.2021.1996449

Vygotsky, L. S. (1978). *Mind in society: The development of higher psychological processes*. Harvard University Press.

Werbach, K., & Hunter, D. (2012). *For the win: How game thinking can revolutionize your business*. Wharton Digital Press.

Yadav, M., Rangnekar, S., & Srivastava, A. P. (2019). Demographic variables as moderators between QWL and OCB. *Industrial and Commercial Training*, *51*(7/8), 396–408. DOI: 10.1108/ICT-04-2018-0040

Yadav, R., Yadav, M., & Vihari, N. S. (2024). High-performance work system and learning orientation in offline, online, and hybrid workplaces: The mediating role of affective commitment. *The Learning Organization*, *31*(1), 122–136. DOI: 10.1108/TLO-10-2022-0118

Chapter 5
AI-Enhanced Entrepreneurial Education:
Personalizing Learning Pathways

Hung Duy Bui
Faculty of Economics, Banking Academy of Vietnam, Vietnam

Gunjan Mohan Sharma
http://orcid.org/0000-0003-2272-7385
JGBS, O.P. Jindal Global University, India

Priya Gaur
Centre for Online Education, GLA University, India

Ali Najeeb
http://orcid.org/0000-0003-4663-9347
Qasim Ibrahim School of Business, Villa College, Maldives

ABSTRACT

Artificial Intelligence (AI) is reshaping entrepreneurial education by enabling personalized learning pathways that cater to individual learner needs, preferences, and competencies. This chapter explores how AI technologies—such as adaptive learning systems, intelligent tutoring, generative AI, and learning analytics—facilitate customized instruction, real-time feedback, and experiential learning opportunities. Drawing on constructivist, experiential, and cognitive learning theories, the chapter examines the design and implementation of personalized pathways, highlighting case studies that demonstrate improved learner engagement, skill acquisition, and entrepreneurial decision-making. It also addresses key challenges, including data

DOI: 10.4018/979-8-2600-1353-3.ch005

privacy, algorithmic bias, equity, and the balance between AI guidance and human mentorship. Finally, the chapter identifies future directions for research and practice, emphasizing immersive technologies, predictive analytics, and ethical frameworks to enhance the effectiveness and inclusivity of entrepreneurial education.

INTRODUCTION

Entrepreneur education has been considered as a pillar of economic growth and development, innovation, employment and advancements in the society. Traditional curricula tend to assume a uniform group of learners thus ignoring the different learning needs, paces and aspirations. With the introduction of Artificial Intelligence (AI), this paradigm has been transformed, and the individualization of the learning trajectories that are in line with the profile of a particular learner has become possible. The ability of AI to handle large volumes of data allows customizing learning experiences to help students get the most relevant content and resources in accordance with their goals and abilities (Gulla, 2025).

There are several transformative advantages to the introduction of AI in entrepreneurial education. It creates adaptive learning conditions where teaching materials and tests are adjusted dynamically based on the performance and participation of students. This active flexibility keeps the learner motivated and retains them better by introducing sufficiently challenging content (Gulla, 2025). Furthermore, AI-based applications can provide personalized feedback and guidance, creating a simulation of real-life entrepreneurial experiences and decision-making, thus filling the knowledge-practice gap (Sajja et al., 2023).

Individualized learning plans are particularly important in the context of entrepreneurship education where the diversification of ventures and the different backgrounds of students necessitate an individualized approach. Using AI, teachers can create personalized learning opportunities that address the individual interests, strengths, and weaknesses of students and thus create an inclusive and efficient learning experience (Xie, 2025). Such a shift does not only enhance the learning process but also prepares students better to cope with the complexity and challenges of the entrepreneurial environment (Choudhary et al., 2024).

This chapter discusses the application of AI in individualizing entrepreneurial education, the technology behind it, the advantages and difficulties of its application, and the effects on educators and learners. In this exploration, we will seek to give a holistic picture on how AI can be utilized to develop adaptive, engaging and effective learning pathways in the area of entrepreneurship education.

THEORETICAL PRINCIPLES OF PERSONALIZED LEARNING IN ENTREPRENEURSHIP.

Individualized learning in entrepreneurship education relies on numerous existing learning theories, each of which provides the framework of how AI can improve educational outcomes. An example of this is the constructivist theory, which assumes that, learners build knowledge by actively engaging in experiences and reflection (Piaget, 1972). This means that in the context of entrepreneurship, the learner is exposed to realistic business situations, simulation, and case studies, which helps him or her to build meaningful knowledge that can be readily applied to real-world businesses. AI complements this constructivist method by dynamically adjusting situations to the existing knowledge, interests, and advancement of the learner so as to optimize the learning process (Yadav et al., 2024).

Personalized entrepreneurial education is also based on experiential learning theory, which was popularized by Kolb (1984). The theory focuses on the cycle that includes the concrete experience, reflective observation, abstract conceptualization, and active experimentation. The use of AI technologies can support each phase with customized simulation to engage in practice, adaptive feedback to reflect, and designed advice to plan and experiment. As an illustration, AI can recreate the market environment or entrepreneurial problem, which enables learners to experiment with strategies and see the results in a risk-free setting.

The cognitive learning theories also support the application of AI in personalization by asserting the relevance of the instructional content to the cognitive ability and learning styles of learners (Sweller, 1988). AI-based adaptive learning systems are able to assess the responses and engagement patterns of learners and present information in the most effective forms to guarantee the most comprehension and retention, e.g., through visual aids, interactive tasks, or written explanations. Moreover, AI will be able to detect knowledge gaps and suggest materials or learning paths that directly address these gaps, thus making the learning process more effective and focused (Trivedi et al., 2023a).

The combination of these theoretical frameworks into the field of AI-enhanced entrepreneurship education highlights the opportunities of personalized learning to not only enhance knowledge acquisition but also critical thinking, problem-solving, and innovation. Using the constructivist, experiential, and cognitive principles, teachers can create AI-based learning experiences that are more learner-focused and results-oriented to equip students with the confidence and skills to operate in the world of entrepreneurship.

TECHNOLOGIES OF ARTIFICIAL INTELLIGENCE IN ENTREPRENEURIAL EDUCATION.

Artificial Intelligence (AI) is fundamentally changing the field of entrepreneurial education by allowing individual learning experiences that support the needs, preferences, and advancement of individual learners. At the heart of this change are a number of AI technologies that support adaptive learning, real-time feedback, and personalized content delivery.

Adaptive Learning Systems

Adaptive learning systems are AI-based systems that dynamically modify the intensity and speed of the instructional material according to the performance analysis of a learner. The systems use machine learning algorithms to identify trends in student interactions and as such, the learning experiences are tailored to individual competencies and learning pace. This flexibility will increase the interaction and knowledge retention since the learners will not feel overloaded (Kabudi, 2021).

Personalized Content Generative AI.

Generative AI and especially large language models are central to the creation of individualized learning content. These models have the capability of creating tailor made quizzes, flash cards and explanatory material that will be in accordance with what a learner already knows and what he or she wants to know. As an example, applications like Alice.Tech apply generative AI to convert generic course content into custom study resources, thus accommodating the needs of a wide range of learners and encouraging them to develop more effective study habits (Business Insider, 2025).

Intelligent Tutoring Systems.

Intelligent tutoring systems (ITS) are intelligent systems that replicate the one-on-one tutoring process by offering individualized guidance and feedback. They can examine the responses of the learners to provide focused assistance, helping students to overcome the complicated entrepreneurial ideas and situations. With the ability to adjust to the level of understanding of every learner, ITS will lead to a better understanding and critical thinking abilities, which are crucial in the success of an entrepreneur (Gulla, 2025).

Live Feedback Systems.

AI technologies allow providing instant feedback on the performance of the learners and allowing timely interventions and support. Real time feedback assists the learners to quickly know where to improve so that corrective measures can be taken to improve the learning results. This immediacy can be especially useful in entrepreneurial education, where it is essential to make decisions in time and be flexible (Tapalova, 2022).

Data-driven learning analytics.

AI systems combine and process large amounts of data about learners to provide insights on the behaviors of learning, preferences, and progress. These analytics guide the creation of individual learning journeys, so that the learning material is relevant to individual needs. With the help of data-driven insights, educators can make sound decisions to maximize the learning process and results of each student (Xie, 2025).

To sum up, AI technologies in entrepreneurial education help to develop individual learning paths that would meet the needs of every learner. Using adaptive learning systems, generative AI, intelligent tutoring, real-time feedback, and data-driven analytics, educational institutions can promote the effectiveness and engagement of their entrepreneurial programs, thus equipping students with the challenges associated with the entrepreneurial environment (Yadav et al., 2019).

Creating Individualized Learning Journeys.

The architecture of the customised learning journeys in entrepreneurial education entails the systematic mapping of the individual profiles, objectives, and capabilities of learners to AI-based learning approaches in order to maximise the learning results. The central idea of this design is that every learner has his or her unique collection of background knowledge, thinking skills, ambitions and entrepreneurial passions. With the help of AI technologies, teachers have the opportunity to trace these qualities to the personalized learning process, so that the learning process is not only relevant but also effective (Sajja et al., 2023; Xie, 2025).

Learner Profiling and Competency Mapping.

Comprehensive learner profiling is the first stage in the development of individual learning pathways. This involves gathering of information about the previous knowledge of learners, their level of skills, their preferences of learning and their entrepreneurial desires. This multidimensional data can be processed by AI algorithms to create detailed profiles of learners, which will include their strengths, weaknesses, and possible areas to improve (Kabudi, 2021). According to these profiles, teachers will be able to match competencies with learning goals, which means that every student will experience materials and tasks that will help him/her acquire the particular skills that are required to succeed in entrepreneurship (Tayal, et al., 2021).

Adaptive Learning Frameworks.

The adaptive learning models play a key role in the implementation of individualized pathways. These systems constantly provide feedback on the performance of learners in the form of quizzes, simulations, and interactions with AI-based systems. Through the analysis of engagement patterns and evaluation outcomes, AI systems are capable of dynamically changing the learning pathway - offering more challenging material to more advanced learners or introducing scaffolding to those students who need it (Gulla, 2025). This flexibility will ensure that students are able to learn at their own speed as they learn the fundamental entrepreneurial concepts and practices.

Live Feedback and Mentoring.

Good individualized learning journeys are those that involve constant feedback and mentoring. Intelligent tutoring systems and chatbots are examples of AI tools that provide real-time assistance to learners by explaining or giving hints or corrective feedback depending on their performance (Tapalova, 2022). In addition, AI can be used to support virtual mentoring by suggesting specific resources or matching learners with expert mentors according to their learning requirements. This combination of AI-based assistance and human guidance improves knowledge and makes learners more confident in their ability to make decisions in entrepreneurship.

Experiential Learning Activities Integration.

Individualized tracks also have elements of experiential learning, such as business simulations, project-based work, and entrepreneurial challenges. These activities can be designed by AI to fit the profile of the learner, simulating real-life situations that require the use of strategic thinking, problem-solving, and risk assessment (Kolb, 1984; Sajja et al., 2023). Contextualisation of learning by putting it into real entrepreneurial situations enables the learners to be in a better position to transfer theoretical knowledge into practical problems.

Constant Review and Improvement.

Lastly, the creation of individualised learning pathways must be evaluated and optimised continuously. The AI systems gather ongoing information about the learner engagement, performance and satisfaction and allow refinements to the learning path to be made iteratively (Xie, 2025). This informative methodology will make sure that the pathways are in line with the needs of learners, maximise the acquisition of skills, and eventually enable the production of competent and adaptive entrepreneurs.

Overall, the architecture of custom-designed learning journeys in entrepreneurial education is a dynamic and data-driven procedure that uses AI to match the profile of learners, adaptive models, real-time feedback, experiential learning, and ongoing assessment. Adopting this strategy, teachers will be able to design learning experiences that are personalized, interesting, and effective in equipping students with the challenges of the entrepreneurial practice (Trivedi et al., 2023b).

CASE STUDIES AND IMPLEMENTATION EXAMPLES

Entrepreneurial education that is enhanced by artificial intelligence has been implemented in various academic institutions and educational technology platforms with good success, which is a compelling indicator of its impact on individual learning and skill development. These case studies show that AI can customize learning materials, create realistic entrepreneurial experiences, and provide dynamic feedback to improve learning.

Case Study 1: Alice.Tech Individualized Learning Platform.

An example of how generative AI can be used in the development of personalized learning journeys among entrepreneurial learners is Alice.Tech, an AI-based edtech startup. The platform examines the previous knowledge, interaction history, and performance indicators of learners to create custom quizzes, learning content, and project-based activities. A case study of Alice.Tech users showed that there was a significant increase in the engagement of learners, the retention of knowledge, and the ability to solve entrepreneurial problems (Business Insider, 2025). The platform allows the dynamically adjusted content to keep the learners constantly challenged on an adequate level, thus, promoting the deeper knowledge and application.

Case Study 2: Higher Education Intelligent Tutoring Systems.

Intelligent Tutoring Systems (ITS) are AI-driven programs that have been introduced in entrepreneurship courses at universities to support and mentor students in a personalized way. As an example, the University of Toronto deployed an ITS that provides real-time feedback on business plans and simulations of students. Students said that they became more confident in their decision-making, understood more complicated entrepreneurial issues, and developed better skills in critical thinking (Sajja et al., 2023). The ITS also allows teachers to track the progress of learners and provide them with focused instruction, which means that individual support will be ongoing and data-based.

Case Study 3: Experiential Entrepreneurship Programs based on Adaptive Learning.

The experiential learning model developed by Kolb has been used in adaptive learning where AI customizes entrepreneurial simulations to the skill level and learning style of the individual learner. Students in a business school at Singapore interacted with AI-based simulations which varied market conditions, customer behaviour and competition issues according to the learner choices. The program also showed tangible gains in strategic thinking, opportunity recognition and risk-management skills, which proved the effectiveness of AI in personalizing experiential learning (Kolb, 1984; Tapalova, 2022).

LESSONS LEARNED AND BEST PRACTICES

In these implementations, there are a number of best practices that come out. To begin with, successful personalization cannot be achieved without gathering extensive data about the learner, as only in this case, AI systems will be able to adjust the content, feedback, and other types of experiences to the needs of a particular learner. Second, AI-based guidance can be used in conjunction with human mentorship to improve the learning process so that learners would be provided with both automated and professional assistance. Third, ongoing observation and repetitive optimization of learning paths should be considered essential to maintain the engagement and respond to the changing needs of learners (Gulla, 2025; Xie, 2025).

To summarize, the case studies presented above show that AI-driven customized learning paths have the potential to significantly enhance entrepreneurial education by matching the learning experience with the unique characteristics of individual learners, offering immediate feedback, and modeling real-world entrepreneurial problems. These strategies can also help educational institutions to create more exciting, dynamic, and useful programs that can better equip the students to the intricacies of the entrepreneurial environment.

CHALLENGES AND ETHICAL CONSIDERATIONS

Although AI-based entrepreneurial education has significant advantages in terms of individualization of learning trajectories, it also brings up a number of challenges and ethical issues that need to be tackled to make the application of AI-based entrepreneurial education equitable, responsible and effective. One of the most prominent challenges is the privacy and security of data. Individualized learning relies on gathering and processing enormous volumes of data on learners, such as academic achievement, behavioral tendencies, and individual tastes. It is essential to protect this sensitive data since its breach or misuse may result in privacy breaches, identity theft, or unwarranted profiling (Kabudi, 2021; Sajja et al., 2023). To ensure that learners have trust in institutions, strict data protection measures and adherence to regulations including GDPR have to be adopted by institutions.

The other issue is the bias in algorithms. Before long, AI systems have the potential to reproduce or even increase the bias found in the training data, and it results in unfair learning experiences. Students with underrepresented backgrounds can be given less favorable advice or exposed to material that does not represent their culture or socioeconomic background (Tapalova, 2022). To solve the problem of bias, AI models have to be transparent, datasets must be diverse and representative, and AI outputs must be audited on a regular basis to promote fairness and inclusiveness.

Accessibility and equity also make AI implementation more difficult. Even though AI has the potential to make learning personal, not all learners have equal access to AI-based educational technologies, especially low-resource students. Inequality in infrastructure, digital literacy, and the availability of devices may widen the educational disparities unless they are actively mitigated (Xie, 2025). It is necessary to design inclusive AI systems that can adapt to different learning settings, languages, and abilities to ensure that personalization is beneficial to every learner.

It is another challenge to balance AI-based guidance with human guidance. Although AI has the capability of delivering real-time feedback and adaptive pathways, it cannot be as supportive, motivating, and mentoring as human educators. Trusting AI too heavily can reduce the ability to learn and collaborate and mentor people, which are particularly important in entrepreneurial education (Gulla, 2025). To implement AI successfully, it is necessary to combine it with human guidance instead of replacing it.

Lastly, accountability and transparency are the most important ethical issues. The learners are supposed to know how AI systems work, how their information is utilized, and the premise of any recommendation or feedback. By providing clear accountability mechanisms, mistakes, biases, or unintended consequences can be resolved in the nearest future, which will help to maintain the integrity of the educational process (Sajja et al., 2023).

Overall, these issues and ethical implications should be discussed to enable the responsible use of AI in entrepreneurial education. Focus on data privacy, bias reduction, equity, human-AI interaction, and transparency can help educators and institutions to maximize the advantages of personalized learning and reduce possible risks.

FUTURE RESEARCH AND FUTURE DIRECTION

The future of AI-based entrepreneurial education is set to experience a transformative growth, as the machine learning, natural language processing, and immersive technologies are rapidly evolving. The incorporation of generative AI into the construction of learning experiences that are highly personalized is one of the potential opportunities. The ability to generate personalized content, simulations, and interactive case studies based on the competencies and entrepreneurial interests of learners as they evolve allows generating a certain personalization that was not possible before (Xie, 2025). The studies into the effectiveness of generative AI in the acquisition of entrepreneurial skills, creativity, and problem-solving are a promising field to be further examined.

Another technology to consider in AI-enhanced entrepreneurial education is immersive learning technologies, including virtual reality (VR) and augmented reality (AR). These technologies enable learners to explore strategies, feel the effects of decision-making, and acquire important entrepreneurial skills under risk-free environments by simulating realistic business environments and market conditions. VR/AR platforms can adapt the situation to the profiles of individual learners, combined with AI-based adaptive feedback, and, therefore, offer a highly engaging and experience-based learning pathway (Tapalova, 2022).

Research opportunities are also promising in the context of increasing sophistication of learning analytics. Longitudinal data on learners can be analyzed using AI to determine trends in the development, engagement, and performance of entrepreneurial skills, and provide forecasts about the outcomes of interventions, which can be used in personalized interventions. It is important to study how these analytics can streamline course design, mentor support, and adaptive learning pathways to enhance both educational outcomes and learner satisfaction (Sajja et al., 2023).

Ethical AI and fair access will continue to be the main themes of technology development. Studies should be done to create structures of reducing the biases of algorithms, improving transparency, and making AI-based entrepreneurial education inclusive. Researchers can look into the ways of how AI-based learning tools can be democratized in low-resource environments, which will minimize educational inequalities (Kabudi, 2021; Xie, 2025).

Lastly, interdisciplinary research, which integrates findings of AI, entrepreneurship, education, and cognitive sciences, will be necessary to get the full potential of AI-enhanced personalized learning. The longitudinal research on the effects of AI-based pathways on entrepreneurial performance, innovation ability, and professional achievement will serve as a useful resource in policy, curriculum design, and technology adoption.

Altogether, the following areas of AI-enhanced entrepreneurial education research and development in the future can be noted: generative AI, immersive technologies, predictive learning analytics, ethical frameworks, and equitable access. These channels have a potential of establishing more interactive, dynamic and efficient learning conditions that equip students to the dynamic and multifaceted entrepreneurial world.

CONCLUSION

The concept of AI-improved entrepreneurial education is a radical change in the manner in which learners gain the skills, knowledge, and mindset to succeed as entrepreneurs. Using adaptive learning systems, generative AI, intelligent tutoring, real-time feedback, and learning analytics, teachers will be able to create individualized learning journeys that match the profiles, competencies, and goals of individual learners. Such AI-based solutions not only improve engagement and knowledge retention, but also develop critical thinking, problem-solving, and innovation skills, which are crucial to coping with the dynamics of entrepreneurial projects (Gulla, 2025; Sajja et al., 2023).

There are, however, no issues with the implementation of AI in entrepreneurial education. The privacy of data, the bias of algorithms, fair access, and the equilibrium between artificial intelligence guidance and human mentorship are the issues that require a close look to guarantee ethical and inclusive learning settings (Kabudi, 2021; Tapalova, 2022). By ensuring open AI practices, a system design that is inclusive, and constant monitoring, it is possible to maximize the advantages of AI and reduce possible risks.

In the future, the combination of immersive technology, including VR/AR, a new level of generative AI, and predictive learning analytics creates promising prospects in the further personalization of the learning process and experience. The key to the full potential of AI-enhanced entrepreneurial education will be interdisciplinary research and innovative applications that will help learners to acquire the competencies and resilience needed to succeed as entrepreneurs in a rapidly changing global environment (Xie, 2025).

To sum up, AI-based personalization in entrepreneurial education has a great potential to develop customized, interactive, and efficient learning experiences. Careful incorporation of technology, pedagogy and ethics enable learning institutions to equip learners with the challenges of the modern business environment and enable the nurturing of future entrepreneurs.

REFERENCES

Business Insider. (2025, May 7). *This edtech startup bills itself as the 'Duolingo for exams.' Check out the pitch deck Alice.Tech used to raise $4.8 million.* Retrieved from https://www.businessinsider.com/pitch-deck-alice-tech-funding-ai-edtech-2025-5

Choudhary, S., Yadav, M., & Srivastava, A. P. (2024). Cognitive biases among millennial Indian investors: Do personality and demographic factors matter? *FIIB Business Review, 13*(1), 106–117. DOI: 10.1177/23197145211057343

Gulla, B. (2025). *The advantages of AI-driven personalized learning paths.* The Training Associates. Retrieved from https://thetrainingassociates.com/ai-personalized-learning-paths/

Kabudi, T. (2021). AI-enabled adaptive learning systems: A systematic review. *Journal of Educational Technology & Society, 24*(3), 1–15.

Kolb, D. A. (1984). *Experiential learning: Experience as the source of learning and development.* Prentice Hall.

Piaget, J. (1972). *The psychology of the child.* Basic Books.

Sajja, R., Sermet, Y., Cikmaz, M., Cwiertny, D., & Demir, I. (2023). Artificial Intelligence-Enabled Intelligent Assistant for Personalized and Adaptive Learning in Higher Education. *arXiv*.

Sweller, J. (1988). Cognitive load during problem solving: Effects on learning. *Cognitive Science, 12*(2), 257–285. DOI: 10.1207/s15516709cog1202_4

Tapalova, O. (2022). AIEd for personalized learning pathways. *Electronic Journal of e-Learning, 20*(5), 640–651. DOI: 10.34190/ejel.20.5.2597

Tayal, R., Upadhyay, R. K., Yadav, M., & Singh, R. (2021). The development and validation of the organizational effectiveness scale using confirmatory factor analysis. *Global Business Review, 22*(3), 821–843. DOI: 10.1177/0972150918811720

Trivedi, S. K., Vishnu, S., Singh, A., & Yadav, M. (2023a). Research trends in sustainable E-payment systems: A study using topic modeling approach. *IEEE Transactions on Engineering Management, 71*, 7511–7525. DOI: 10.1109/TEM.2023.3280216

Trivedi, V., Banerji, D., & Yadav, M. (2023b). Expecting the surprises: Role of hope in consumer repurchase intentions in an online shopping environment. *Journal of Strategic Marketing, 31*(4), 794–816. DOI: 10.1080/0965254X.2021.1996449

Xie, Y. (2025). Generative artificial intelligence in entrepreneurship education. *Scientific Reports*. Retrieved from https://www.nature.com/articles/s41598-025-09545-3

Yadav, M., Rangnekar, S., & Srivastava, A. P. (2019). Demographic variables as moderators between QWL and OCB. *Industrial and Commercial Training*, *51*(7/8), 396–408. DOI: 10.1108/ICT-04-2018-0040

Yadav, R., Yadav, M., & Vihari, N. S. (2024). High-performance work system and learning orientation in offline, online, and hybrid workplaces: The mediating role of affective commitment. *The Learning Organization*, *31*(1), 122–136. DOI: 10.1108/TLO-10-2022-0118

Chapter 6
AI-Driven Pedagogical Transformation in Entrepreneurship Education:
An Integrative Literature Review on Mindset, Creativity, and Self-Efficacy

Syed Haider Ali Shah
http://orcid.org/0000-0002-4898-3769
Department of Business Administration, Faculty of Managerial Sciences, Abdullah Gül University, Turkey

Eman Zameer Rahman
http://orcid.org/0000-0003-2420-625X
Bahria University, Islamabad, Pakistan

Fatma Selen Madenoğlu
http://orcid.org/0000-0002-5577-4471
Department of Business Administration, Faculty of Managerial Sciences, Abdullah Gül University, Turkey

Syed Bilawal Ali Shah
Department of Applied Sciences (Applied Geology), Curtin University, Malaysia

DOI: 10.4018/979-8-2600-1353-3.ch006

ABSTRACT

Artificial intelligence (AI) is rapidly transforming entrepreneurship education by reshaping how entrepreneurial competencies are cultivated. This chapter presents an integrative literature review that synthesizes empirical and conceptual research on AI-enabled pedagogy and its impact on entrepreneurial mindset, creativity, and self-efficacy. Drawing on Kolb's Experiential Learning Theory and Bandura's Social Cognitive Theory, the chapter conceptualizes AI as an amplifier of experiential and social learning rather than a substitute for human instruction. AI tools including generative models, intelligent tutoring systems, simulations, and analytics are increasingly embedded in entrepreneurship curricula to support personalized learning, real-time feedback, and immersive decision-making environments. evidence shows that such AI-supported interventions enhance opportunity recognition, innovation orientation, creative problem-solving, digital entrepreneurial skills, and entrepreneurial attitudes, while significantly increasing entrepreneurial self-efficacy and intentions when combined with robust learning designs and institutional support. Studies also highlight the role of AI literacy and AI self-efficacy as critical mediators in fostering digital entrepreneurial intention, especially in entrepreneurship contexts. However, the review also reveals concerns about over-reliance on AI, superficial learning, ethical risks, algorithmic opacity, and inequitable access. Building on the integrative review method, the chapter develops a conceptual framework that maps the pathways through which AI-enabled experiential ecosystems shape entrepreneurial mindset, creative self-efficacy, and resilience. It concludes by outlining design principles for ethically grounded, creativity-enhancing, and self-efficacy-oriented AI integration in entrepreneurship programs, and proposes a future research agenda focused on longitudinal effects, cross-cultural applications, and the measurement of psychological constructs in AI-rich learning environments.

1. BACKGROUND AND RATIONALE

Artificial intelligence has progressed from a technological specialty to a global socio-technical infrastructure that supports the various ways people work, learn, and create value. One of the areas where this transition can be seen is the higher education sector, where adaptive learning platforms, learning analytics, and more recently, generative AI systems that can interact with, create, and solve problems with students in a natural language have emerged (Park et al., 2025; Uriarte et al., 2025; Wang et al., 2022). The oldest forms of teaching entrepreneurship such as business planning, case studies, project-based learning are becoming more and more affected by these advances as teachers look to make their courses more relevant to the current data-driven, digitally-based entrepreneurial ecosystem (Rahmi et al., 2025; Ahmed et al., 2025).

Generative AI tools like ChatGPT, Claude, Gemini, and specific assistants are already employed to generate business ideas, write value propositions, conduct market analysis, and practice pitches to investors. For many students, these tools have become a cognitive partner that is present all the time, which effectively enlarges the scope of the whole semester and lets a lot more iterations of concept development and refinement than can be accomplished with human feedback alone (Ahmed et al., 2025; Xie & Wang, 2025; Motta & Galina, 2023). According to the results from experimental and quasi-experimental studies, when AI is integrated into carefully crafted learning activities, students become more innovative, acquire more advanced digital entrepreneurship skills, and develop a stronger entrepreneurial mindset than their counterparts in traditional education (Rahmi et al., 2025; Zulfiqar et al., 2025).

A broader examination of AI in educational settings indicates that the mere fact of having AI in the educational process does not ensure that students will attain a deep understanding of the subject matter. If the learners consider the outputs from AI to be infallible "answers," they may very well win the cognitive and affective battles that involve ambiguity, uncertainty, and iterative failure which are very important to attaining an authentic entrepreneurial mindset (Park et al., 2025; Zulfiqar et al., 2025; Saritepeci & Durak, 2024; Motta & Galina, 2023). In addition, there are still debates regarding the academic honesty issue, the originality of AI-assisted business plans, data protection, and the possible increase of the gap between the AI-savvy-students and the non-AI-savvy one (Park et al., 2025; Zulfiqar et al., 2025; Zhu & Luo, 2025)

The studies that delve into this intricate environment are quite a few and mostly limited to the core psychological dimensions affected by AI-driven pedagogy: the entrepreneurial mindset (whose components are opportunity recognition, resilience, and tolerance to ambiguity), creativity and creative self-efficacy, and finally entrepreneurial self-efficacy itself (Ndlovu et al., 2025; Jiatong et al., 2021; Gedeon & Huber, 2025). Various studies give evidence of major shifts in the entrepreneurial mindset and self-efficacy as well as in the experiential courses supported by AI (Ahmed et al., 2025; Uriarte et al., 2025; Wang et al., 2022), while other studies, particularly in design-based and AI-supported learning contexts, imply that AI might boost creative self-efficacy without necessarily affecting deeper mindsets in a short term (Saritepeci & Durak, 2024). Thus, the research area is both promising and split in its views.

The chapter addresses this by analyzing evidence from entrepreneurship education, AI in higher education, and entrepreneurial psychology. By adopting an integrative literature review, it becomes possible to compare conceptual models, experimental studies, survey-based structural equation models, and qualitative case studies. It also enables to derive a more holistic understanding of how AI-enabled pedagogy can be leveraged to foster future-ready entrepreneurial graduates.

2. THEORETICAL FOUNDATIONS

The theory of experiential learning regards learning as a circular process consisting of four stages: concrete experiences, reflective observation, abstract conceptualization, and active experimentation. In this context, the entrepreneurial education has been using the above mentioned methods long ago i.e. the simulations, live projects and the activities of the venture creating as a way of getting into "learning through" entrepreneurial action from (Uriarte et al., 2025; Motta & Galina, 2023) "learning about" entrepreneurship. The systematic reviews point out the role of experiential methods as a positive contributor to one's intention to become an entrepreneur and the acquisition of such skills as identifying opportunities, managing risks, and innovating (Motta & Galina, 2023; Gedeon & Huber, 2025).

AI tools can be seen as the ones increasing the duration of the cycle, so to speak, for each phase. Simulations driven by AI and virtual practice environments are opening up new avenues for concrete experiences that are richer, more complex, and closer to actual business situations, thus allowing students to try out business decisions in secure and somewhat realistic contexts (Rahmi et al., 2025; Zhang, 2025). The generative AI is acting as a reflective partner that is soon pointing out students to express their logic, discuss the opposite side, and take advantage of the feedback that is going to help them in the creation of the concept (Park et al., 2025). The use of analytics dashboards and recommender systems makes it easier for students to integrate their seemingly unrelated experiences into consistent conceptual models by uncovering the patterns in their actions and the resultant outcomes (Zhang, 2025). And finally, the tools for AI enabled prototyping, content generation, and rapid scenario testing allow much more and varied experimentation that would not be possible otherwise with the limited time of the course (Ahmed et al., 2025).

Social cognitive theory adds a complementary viewpoint by putting the focus on the main role of self-efficacy, learning through observation, and self-regulation for the purpose of changing behavior. The studies in entrepreneurship education have arrived at the same conclusion multiple times that the self-efficacy of the entrepreneur is the mediator of the relationship between education, mindset, creativity, and the intention to become an entrepreneur (Jiatong et al., 2021; Gedeon & Huber, 2025). The latest research in the fields of digital and e-entrepreneurship expands this reasoning to AI literacy and AI self-efficacy, proving that the students who are confident in identifying and assessing AI tools as well as in their ability to use them are more likely to have high digital entrepreneurial self-efficacy and strong e-entrepreneurial intentions (Duong, 2025; Duong & Vu, 2025). Entrepreneurship courses supported by Generative AI report similar results that the AI embedded instruction increases entrepreneurial self-efficacy and intention; this is especially true when there is a strong university entrepreneurial environment (Wang et al., 2022).

Theoretical perspectives of above-mentioned converge at one key notion: the integration of AI technology into teaching can significantly amplify the already known experiential and social cognitive mechanisms that lead to the development of entrepreneurial mindset, creativity, and self-efficacy. Nevertheless, this potential still depends on the careful orchestration of pedagogical practices, the setting of ethical guidelines, and, above all, the explicit commitment to keeping human agency and critical thinking alive within the AI rich learning environments.

2.1 Experiential Learning

Experiential learning theory (ELT) sees learning as a continuous cycle of four stages: concrete experience, reflective observation, abstract conceptualization, and active experimentation (Kolb). In the teaching of entrepreneurship, experiential methods like business simulations, field projects, and venture creation are firmly linked to the increase of entrepreneurial intention and the growth of entrepreneurial skills and competencies (Vankov & Wang, 2024). Reviews of literature confirm that "learning by doing" is a major factor in real opportunity recognition, risk taking, and resilience development (Motta & Galina, 2023).

AI tools can be integrated into each stage of the experiential learning cycle: for instance, games and simulations powered by AI provide learners with concrete experiences; AI generates and supports reflection (e.g., feedback via structured debriefing prompts); analytics tools bring together various factors facilitating the learning of concepts; and market testing and AI-assisted prototyping lead to quick and efficient experiments (Dunan et al., 2025; Sekli & Portuguez-Castro, 2025; Darnell & Gopalkrishnan, 2024; Ahmed et al., 2025; Sirait et al., 2025). New practices that integrate immersive fieldwork with generative AI result in a substantial increase in the entrepreneurial mindset scores, thus demonstrating that AI can enhance the effectiveness of experiential designs rather than take over (Ahmed et al., 2025).

2.2 Social Cognitive Theory and Entrepreneurial Self-Efficacy

The social cognitive theory presented by Bandura gives priority to the processes of learning through observing others, self-regulation, and self-efficacy in influencing one's behavior. In the case of entrepreneurship, self-efficacy, the conviction about one's capability to carry out entrepreneurial activities, mediates the impact of education and creativity on the formation of entrepreneurial intentions, besides its power being increased when combined with resilience (Vankov & Wang, 2024; Ginting & Azizurrohman, 2025).

Reports on studies that combine experiential entrepreneurship education with social cognitive principles show that the improvements in the multiple dimensions of entrepreneurial self-efficacy were over time and to a great extent (Vankov & Wang, 2024). It is possible that AI mediated environments would reinforce the already mentioned four classic sources of the self-efficacy: (a) mastery experiences through the means of scaffolded tasks and adaptive difficulty, (b) vicarious learning through AI generated exemplars and cases, (c) social persuasion through automated formative feedback, and (d) management of affect by reduction of anxiety through low stakes practice and simulations (Dunan et al., 2025; Sekli & Portuguez-Castro, 2025; Awad & Abdelaziz, 2025; Motta & Galina, 2023; Ahmed et al., 2025). Early research suggests that generative AI can increase students' confidence in spotting intentions and performing entrepreneurial tasks, though this may vary by tool and context (Awad & Abdelaziz, 2025; Somià & Vecchiarini, 2024; Sirait et al., 2025).

2.3 Creativity, Creative Self-Efficacy, and Entrepreneurial Intent

Creativity is one of the main reasons people will consider entrepreneurship. Creative self-efficacy, which is the belief in one's own creative capabilities, encourages one to participate in creative activities and through attitudes and creative process participation predicts the intention to become an entrepreneur (Tantawy et al., 2021). Therefore, the teaching of entrepreneurship that emphasizes creativity and engagement with creative processes can be a very efficient means to control the future of one's career in entrepreneurship.

Generative AI can be a dual effect in terms of creativity. It can increase the number of possible ideas, shape the brainstorming process, and assist the evaluation and improvement of concepts, leading to the development of creative self-efficacy and the involvement in the artistic process (Abdelmagid et al., 2025; Vecchiarini & Somià, 2023; Ahmed et al., 2025; Sirait et al., 2025).

However, if not properly scaffolding, reliance on AI outputs can lead to the displacement of original thought and can diminish the students' feeling of ownership over the ideas (Bell & Bell, 2023; Belguith, 2025). Evidence from studies is beginning to show that experiential activities with the support of ChatGPT can develop the skills of recognizing opportunities, appreciating ideas, and ethical thinking, all of which are components of creative entrepreneurship (Somià & Vecchiarini, 2024).

2.4 Entrepreneurial Mindset

The entrepreneurial mindset involves various traits such as the ability to recognize opportunities, being comfortable with uncertainty, persistence, taking initiative, and finding creative solutions. It is well established that learning in experiential and socially rich environments strengthens the entrepreneurial mindset, and a recent study has shown that non-business majors have a significantly higher entrepreneurial mindset when participating in entrepreneurship education with constructive alignment and real-world tasks (Ahmed et al., 2025). AI-assisted experiential courses have demonstrated improvements that are statistically significant (e.g., a 30% increase) in measurements of the entrepreneurial mindset, indicating that AI can promote more reflection, iteration, and feedback around the challenges of entrepreneurship (Ahmed et al., 2025). Furthermore, at the systemic level, the entrepreneurship education that targets simultaneously creativity, self-efficacy, and resilience simultaneously appears the most effective in turning the learning experiences into the sustained intentions of entrepreneurs (Vankov & Wang, 2024; Ginting & Azizurrohman, 2025).

2.5 AI in Entrepreneurship Education: Key Outcomes

After analyzing the literature of several studies, the key factors identified in AI-entrepreneurship education studies and psychological outcomes are outlined in the table.

Table 1. AI entrepreneurship education studies and psychological outcomes

Focus	Main AI role/design	Outcomes on mindset, creativity, self-self-efficacy	Citations
Digital entrepreneurship skills	Quasi-experiment using ChatGPT vs. traditional teaching	Higher innovation, creative thinking, and entrepreneurial initiative in the AI group	(Abdelmagid et al., 2025)
Entrepreneurial success tasks	Multi-case study with generative AI in business school	Perceived performance benefits via compatibility, ease of use, and info quality	(Sekli & Portuguez-Castro, 2025)
Mindset and intentions	Pre/post AI tools in entrepreneurial courses	Improved entrepreneurial attitudes and intentions	(Zulfiqar et al., 2025)
Classroom uses of ChatGPT	Student survey in entrepreneurship courses	Enhanced efficiency, process support, some creativity gains; concerns on reliability	(Vecchiarini & Somià, 2023)
Competencies (opportunities, valuing ideas, ethics)	ChatGPT to improve business model canvas	Gains in spotting opportunities, creativity, valuing ideas, and ethical thinking	(Somià & Vecchiarini, 2024)

continued on following page

Table 1. Continued

Focus	Main AI role/design	Outcomes on mindset, creativity, self-self-efficacy	Citations
Experiential + generative AI	Mixed-methods with fieldwork and AI tools	~35% increase in entrepreneurial mindset; improved opportunity recognition, problem-solving	(Ahmed et al., 2025)
AI & TikTok in student ventures	Mixed-methods SEM-PLS + interviews	AI boosts entrepreneurial knowledge and business performance directly	(Sirait et al., 2025)
Scoping review of AI in EE	Review of intelligent tech adoption in EE	Highlights potential but notes weak pedagogical designs and research gaps	(Chen et al., 2024)

3. AI-ENABLED EXPERIENTIAL ECOSYSTEMS

3.1 Personalization, Feedback, and Adaptive Learning

Different studies show that one of the major teaching benefits of AI is its ability to personalize the learning experience. Such adaptive systems depend on learner data to alter content difficulty and speed up learning; hence, they facilitate the process of acquisition of basic knowledge by students with little previous exposure to the area of entrepreneurship at their own pace (Dunan et al., 2025; Chen et al., 2024; Sirait et al., 2025). Generative AI applications such as ChatGPT grant access to explanations, offer alternative examples, and provide formative feedback on business ideas, pitches, and business models, thus making the practice and reflection more intense than the feedback from the teacher can support (Abdelmagid et al., 2025; Sekli & Portuguez-Castro, 2025; Vecchiarini & Somià, 2023; Darnell & Gopalkrishnan, 2024).

Along with AI, students can get through realistic but low-risk environments created by gamification where they can try out pricing, marketing, and strategic decisions among others and see the consequences right away, thus building up their decision-making skills and confidence (Dunan et al., 2025; Awad & Abdelaziz, 2025; Motta & Galina, 2023). While educators view these cognitive technologies as good methods to go about making learning environments experiential, collaborative, and digitally enhanced, they also mention that such a move is limited by resource constraints and data protection concerns (Belguith, 2025).

3.2 Generative AI and Creativity

Generative AI is taking over the role of the facilitator in opportunity recognition and creative problem-solving:

- Students who are exposed to ChatGPT in quasi-experimental settings have higher levels of innovation, creative thinking, and the ability to create cutting-edge digital products compared to control groups that are taught in the traditional way (Abdelmagid et al., 2025).
- Exploratory studies of students using ChatGPT to tweak their business model canvas report gains in opportunity spotting, creativity,, vision, valuing ideas, and ethical and sustainable thinking (Somià & Vecchiarini, 2024).
- Research conducted in classrooms regarding entrepreneurship and exercises has revealed that the use of AI-augmented structured prompts and templates can be extremely beneficial for students in terms of creating, and even more so, improving and criticizing their business ideas. Such processes will become very much easy for the diverse group of learners to access (Vecchiarini & Somià, 2023; Darnell & Gopalkrishnan, 2024; Ahmed et al., 2025).

These advantages are much reliant on the design of the task. Students may comply with and approve of AI outputs if there are no straight-forward prompts that urge critical examination and novel synthesis, thus bringing down the level of participation in the creative process (Bell & Bell, 2023; Vecchiarini & Somià, 2023; Belguith, 2025; Somià & Vecchiarini, 2024). Hence, the conceptual work in entrepreneurship education calls for making the generative AI a co-creator rather than a vending machine of answers, and placing the students at the hot seat of the critical editors who repeatedly confront and hone the ideas generated by the AI (Vecchiarini & Somià, 2023; Darnell & Gopalkrishnan, 2024).

4. MINDSET, SELF-EFFICACY, AND INTENTIONS

4.1 Entrepreneurial Mindset Development

The latest AI-integrated interventions have given a new ray of hope wherein AI can be the determinant of the amplification of the entrepreneurial mindset outcomes if such a case is mounted in experiential learning ecosystems that are well-designed:

- A non-business postgraduate students participated in a mixed-methods study, where the course that was based on AI--augmented, problem-based, and field trip-based learning was found to have a statistically significant effect of 35.48% increase in entrepreneurial mindset scores. It was the AI tools that assisted the students in structuring their inquiries, testing their assumptions, and making connections between their field observations and wider opportunity spaces (Ahmed et al., 2025).

- The combined applications of AI tools in the entrepreneurship curricula through longitudinal and pre/post designs have resulted in the changing of entrepreneurial attitudes and intentions for the better, which means that the learning environments with support from AI can make the students perceive the value of and the feasibility of entrepreneurial careers more (Zulfiqar et al., 2025; Sirait et al., 2025).
- Entrepreneurship education studies highlight those pedagogies that build creativity, self-efficacy, and resilience, together applying the strongest effect on entrepreneurial intentions effects which AI can potentially intensify through tailored feedback and iterative support (Vankov & Wang, 2024; Ginting & Azizurrohman, 2025).

4.2 Entrepreneurial Self-Efficacy and Competencies

There are several important empirical studies that associate the use of AI with the development of entrepreneurs' core competencies and self-efficacy:

- The experiments conducted based on ChatGPT have concluded that digital entrepreneurial skills are improved and students' assurance in their ability to organize, generate and make informed decisions in digital entrepreneurship settings is increased (Abdelmagid et al., 2025).
- The survey conducted on GenAI tools in business programs in the Middle East indicates that ChatGPT can boost start-up intentions, although the indirect effect through entrepreneurship cognition and competencies is not always significant, while AI simulations lead to better educational outcomes which in turn raise intentions (Awad & Abdelaziz, 2025).
- Undergraduate students were working on ChatGPT-enabled revision of their business model canvas in a mixed-methods explorative study and realized improvement in their competencies such as opportunity identification, value assessment, and ethical and sustainable thinking which are the main foundations of entrepreneurial self-efficacy (Somià & Vecchiarini, 2024).
- Research into entrepreneurship education on a larger scale invariably shows that it is mainly through self-efficacy that the impact of education and creativity on the intention to become an entrepreneur is realized, with the mediation being the strongest among those students who are very resilient. This

indicates that AI-enabled experiences should not only be about teaching but also include the essential traits of perseverance and the ability to cope with difficult situations as well (Vankov & Wang, 2024; Ginting & Azizurrohman, 2025).

4.3 Creativity, Creative Self-Efficacy, and Intent

5. ETHICAL, COGNITIVE, AND PEDAGOGICAL IMPACTS

5.1 Risks of Over-reliance and Superficial Learning

A number of researches caution that the ease with which AI can be used may lead to the learning of the surface type and the critical thinking may also be diminished if proper guidelines are not given. Students may place too much trust in the outputs of AI, do less practicing of the analytical skills and also avoid the discomfort that usually comes with deep entrepreneurial learning and is the driving force behind it (Chen et al., 2024; Somià & Vecchiarini, 2024). Other worries are possible decline in academic integrity, less paper originality, and a gap among students having various levels of AI literacy.

5.2 Data Privacy, Transparency, and Power Asymmetries

The engagement of digital data generated by learners in AI systems brings up concerns regarding privacy, consent, and non-transparency of algorithms. In Europe and other areas with rigid regulatory structures, educators highlight the importance of not only transparent data practices but also informed consent in the use of AI-powered analytics (Belguith, 2025). The over centralization of decision making in such non-transparent systems may pose a conflict with the objectives of entrepreneurship education which are autonomy and empowerment.

5.3 Equity and Access

It is possible that AI will eliminate the existing barriers to access and make it available to everyone, no matter their location, high-quality mentoring and feedback which is typical for the AI-assisted resource-poor environments (Dunan et al., 2025). However, the differing access to devices, connectivity, and paid AI features could very well lead to a situation where the already existing educational inequalities are causing even more serious problems, thus risking their being amplified. The research on the adoption of AI in emerging economies spotlights infrastructure, digital literacy, and cost as the main barriers to inclusive AI-driven entrepreneurship education (Sirait et al., 2025).

5.4 Educator Roles and Professional Development

The shift of the educator's role towards that of a curator, coach, and ethical guide is brought about by the assumption of routine instructional tasks by AI. Qualitative study with university lecturers indicates the ambivalence of this situation as the educators admit to being excited about AI's potential but at the same time uncertain about its influence over assessment, classroom dynamics, and their own workload (Chen et al., 2024). Ongoing professional development and institutional support are crucial for helping educators in shaping AI-aligned experiential activities, overcoming challenges, and keeping the human factor strong in teaching.

6. CONCEPTUAL FRAMEWORK: AI-ENABLED PEDAGOGY AND ENTREPRENEURIAL PSYCHOLOGY

The synthesis of the literature that has been reviewed allows us to conceptualize AI-enabled entrepreneurship education as an experiential, socially embedded eco-system where AI not only plays a role of amplifying but also the roles of Kolbian learning cycles and social cognitive mechanisms.

6.1 Key Pathways

The main pathways include AI augmented experiences, AI-supported reflection and conceptualization, Creative co-production with AI, and social learning with and around AI (Tantawy et al., 2021; Vecchiarini & Somià, 2023; Darnell & Gopalkrishnan, 2024; Abdelmagid et al., 2025; Belguith, 2025; Sekli & Portuguez-Castro, 2025; Vankov & Wang, 2024; Ginting & Azizurrohman, 2025).

- **AI augmented experiences** - The applications of AI in the classroom not only help the students learn better but also make teaching activities more creative and fun.
- **AI supported reflection and conceptualization** - The use of technology in the classroom not just through the teacher but also the students is going to make the former more reflective and creative by the use of different means.
- **Creative co-production with AI** - Brainstorming, and testing ideas not only diplomats the problem but also boosts the skill of the students in the area of

the teacher's choice and the creative engagement process in the classroom as long as they are given the power to influence the deciding process as active critics.

- **Social learning with and around AI** - The learning by doing and peer support that AI help to create and the shared feedback of output generated by AI would not only facilitate learning indirectly, socially motivate the learners, and thus lead to the development of an entrepreneurial mindset and resilience in the students.

6.2 Moderators

Effects are moderated by student characteristics (Somià & Vecchiarini, 2024; Vankov & Wang, 2024; Ginting & Azizurrohman, 2025), pedagogical design quality (Darnell & Gopalkrishnan, 2024; Motta & Galina, 2023; Ahmed et al., 2025; Chen et al., 2024), and institutional context (Dunan et al., 2025; Belguith, 2025; Chen et al., 2024; Sirait et al., 2025).

- Student characteristics, such as initial self-confidence, ability to bounce back from difficulties, and tech-savvy.
- Pedagogical design quality, such as alignment of teaching and assessment, clear creativity goals, and critical AI literacy.
- The institutional setting, which includes among other things resources, data policies, and support for innovation.

6.3 Implications for Curriculum Design and Practice

Literature review has revealed (Sekli & Portuguez-Castro, 2025; Darnell & Gopalkrishnan, 2024; Motta & Galina, 2023; Ahmed et al., 2025; Sirait et al., 2025; Abdelmagid et al., 2025; Vecchiarini & Somià, 2023; Somià & Vecchiarini, 2024; Tantawy et al., 2021; Ahmed et al., 2025; Vankov & Wang, 2024; Ginting & Azizurrohman, 2025; (Bell & Bell, 2023; Belguith, 2025; Chen et al., 2024; Dunan et al., 2025), the following design principles emerges:

1. Experiential, real-world tasks should incorporate AI rather than isolating it as a separate subject; this will make sure that every AI-enabled activity corresponds to a specific entrepreneurial problem
2. Creative process engagement should be the goal of the design, and students should be required to keep records of idea generation, evaluation, and selection processes, clearly indicating their own contributions and the AI suggestions

3. Self-efficacy and resilience should be scaffolded through progressively challenging AI-supported projects, regular feedback, and reflection on failures, which aligns with social cognitive theory
4. AI literacy and critical use should be included in teaching, such as the limitations, bias, hallucinations, and ethical use, so that students learn to critique rather than copy AI outputs
5. Human-centered assessment should be kept, with a focus on oral defenses, reflective journals, and peer reviews that highlight over-reliance on AI and reward original synthesis and judgment
6. Equity and access issues should be addressed by providing institutional licenses, baseline training, and alternative low-tech pathways where required.

7. RESEARCH GAPS AND FUTURE DIRECTIONS

Alongside the mentioned projects, the area still lacks substantial longitudinal research that would depict how the changes in the educational setting brought about by AI could positively affect the learners' mindset, creativity, self-confidence, and even their behavior to become entrepreneurs during a period of years (Zulfiqar et al., 2025; Awad & Abdelaziz, 2025; Ahmed et al., 2025; Vankov & Wang, 2024; Ginting & Azizurrohman, 2025). Also rare were the cases when researchers directly assessed students' creative self-efficacy and resilience in an AI-rich learning environment (Somià & Vecchiarini, 2024; Tantawy et al., 2021; Ginting & Azizurrohman, 2025). The development of AI tools has not yet been fully explored in terms of teaching and learning purposes. For instance, the development of domain-specific tools as well as agent-based simulations are quite advanced but their pedagogical affordances have not been widely studied (Dunan et al., 2025; Awad & Abdelaziz, 2025; Chen et al., 2024; Sirait et al., 2025).

The authors mention that the lack of cultural and institutional context comparative studies is one of the major issues the academic community is facing. This is especially true in the case of the Global South region despite the fact that some researchers already focused on Indonesia, the Middle East, and China (Dunan et al., 2025; Awad & Abdelaziz, 2025; Sirait et al., 2025; Vankov & Wang, 2024; Ginting & Azizurrohman, 2025). There is a need for more sophisticated pedagogical designs that integrate AI for diagnosis, prediction, intervention, and recommendation within explicit entrepreneurial learning trajectories (Motta & Galina, 2023; Chen et al., 2024).

8. CONCLUSION

The literature that has been reviewed has brought to light that AI, particularly generative AI, has the potential to greatly improve the entrepreneurs' mindset, the digital entrepreneurship skills, and the key competencies of opportunity recognition, creativity, and ethical thinking provided that they are all incorporated into well-designed experiential and social learning environments. At the same time, reliance on AI, ethical issues, and unequal access will continue to be the main challenges that the educational institutions will have to face and consequently will need the right curriculum design, strong institutional policies and educator's empowerment to come up with solutions.

An integrative framework that combines experiential learning and social cognitive theory with AI enabled pedagogy shows the way how AI can be a powerful reflector, experimenter, and self-regulated learner amplifier instead of being a human judge substitute. The main challenge for the upcoming generation of entrepreneurship education is not just to “add AI” to the courses already in place, but also to transform the learning ecosystems in such a way that the very use of AI becomes the ground for nurturing creativity, self efficacy, resilience, and ethical entrepreneurial mindsets.

REFERENCES

Abdelmagid, A., Jabli, N., Ibrahim, A., & Teleb, A. (2025). *Generative artificial intelligence (ChatGPT) technology and its impact on the development of digital entrepreneurship skills among university students*. International Journal of Innovative Research and Scientific Studies., DOI: 10.53894/ijirss.v8i2.5885

Ahmed, F., Lo, Y., & Chen, S. (2025). Developing Entrepreneurial Mindset Among Non-Business Majors Through Experiential Learning and AI Tools. *European Conference on Knowledge Management*. DOI: 10.34190/eckm.26.1.3762

Awad, A., & Abdelaziz, E. (2025). ENTREPRENEURSHIP EDUCATION: A STUDY OF HIGHER EDUCATION INSTITUTIONS IN THE MIDDLE EAST. *Journal of Southwest Jiaotong University*, (2). Advance online publication. DOI: 10.35741/issn.0258-2724.60.2.3

Belguith, M. (2025). *Adoption of AI in entrepreneurship education: University teachers' perceptions*. International Journal of Advances in Educational Research., DOI: 10.62941/ijaer.v2i1.151

Bell, R., & Bell, H. (2023). Entrepreneurship education in the era of generative artificial intelligence. *Entrepreneurship Education*, *6*(3), 229–244. DOI: 10.1007/s41959-023-00099-x

Chen, L., Ifenthaler, D., Yau, J., & Sun, W. (2024). Artificial Intelligence in Entrepreneurship Education: A Scoping Review. *Education + Training*, *2023*(6), 589–608. Advance online publication. DOI: 10.1108/ET-05-2023-0169

Darnell, J., & Gopalkrishnan, S. (2024). Entrepreneurship teaching exercises: Integrating generative AI. *Discover Education*, *3*(1), 172. Advance online publication. DOI: 10.1007/s44217-024-00261-0

Dunan, A., Mudjiyanto, B., Setiawan, A., Syarifuddin, S., Pala, R., Rustam, M., Dirgahayu, D., Buyamin, B., Nuryana, M., & Hartiningsih, H. (2025). Artificial Intelligence in E-Entrepreneurship Training. *International Journal of E-Entrepreneurship and Innovation*, *15*(1), 1–22. Advance online publication. DOI: 10.4018/IJEEI.386065

Duong, C. (2025). AI literacy and higher education students' digital entrepreneurial intention: A moderated mediation model of AI self-efficacy and digital entrepreneurial self-efficacy. *Industry and Higher Education*. Advance online publication. DOI: 10.1177/09504222251370089

Duong, C., & Vu, T. (2025). *Entrepreneurial education and higher education students' e-entrepreneurial intention: a moderated mediation model of generative AI incorporation and e-entrepreneurial self-efficacy*. Higher Education, Skills and Work-Based Learning., DOI: 10.1108/HESWBL-12-2024-0390

Gedeon, S., & Huber, F. (2025). *Using AI-Enabled Images and Comic Narrative to Enhance Entrepreneurship Education*. Entrepreneurship Education and Pedagogy., DOI: 10.1177/25151274251358708

Ginting, Y., & Azizurrohman, M. (2025). *Linking Entrepreneurship Education to Entrepreneurial Intentions: A Social Cognitive and Resource-Based Perspective. The Asian Journal of Technology Management*. AJTM., DOI: 10.12695/ajtm.2025.18.1.4

Jiatong, W., Murad, M., Bajun, F., Tufail, M., Mirza, F., & Rafiq, M. (2021). Impact of Entrepreneurial Education, Mindset, and Creativity on Entrepreneurial Intention: Mediating Role of Entrepreneurial Self-Efficacy. *Frontiers in Psychology*, *12*, 724440. Advance online publication. DOI: 10.3389/fpsyg.2021.724440 PMID: 34497568

Motta, V., & Galina, S. (2023). Experiential learning in entrepreneurship education: A systematic literature review. *Teaching and Teacher Education*, *121*, 103919. Advance online publication. DOI: 10.1016/j.tate.2022.103919

Ndlovu, E., Ebewo, P., Mlotshwa, S., & Shumba, K. (2025). Entrepreneurial Coaching and Self-Efficacy: A Systematic Review of Its Pedagogical Integration into Entrepreneurship Education. *Education Sciences*, *15*(2), 237. Advance online publication. DOI: 10.3390/educsci15020237

Park, J., Kim, S., & Lee, S. (2025). AI and Creativity in Entrepreneurship Education: A Systematic Review of LLM Applications. *AI*, *6*(5), 100. Advance online publication. DOI: 10.3390/ai6050100

Rahmi, E., Darmansyah, D., Yulastri, A., & Handrianto, C. (2025). *Bridging Entrepreneurship Education and Digital Transformation: A Novel Experiential Learning Model for Entrepreneurial Mindset Development*. International Journal of Learning, Teaching and Educational Research., DOI: 10.26803/ijlter.24.4.29

Saritepeci, M., & Durak, H. (2024). Effectiveness of artificial intelligence integration in design-based learning on design thinking mindset, creative and reflective thinking skills: An experimental study. *Education and Information Technologies*, *29*(18), 25175–25209. DOI: 10.1007/s10639-024-12829-2

Sekli, M., & Portuguez-Castro, M. (2025). Fostering entrepreneurial success from the classroom: Unleashing the potential of generative AI through technology-to-performance chain. A multi-case study approach. *Education and Information Technologies, 30*(10), 13075–13103. DOI: 10.1007/s10639-025-13316-y

Sirait, H., Basuki, R., Djubair, R., Hardipura, G., & Endri, E. (2025). Exploring the Diffusion of Digital Technologies in Higher Education Entrepreneurship: The Impact of the Utilization of AI and TikTok on Student Entrepreneurial Knowledge, Experience, and Business Performance. *Administrative Sciences, 15*(7), 285. Advance online publication. DOI: 10.3390/admsci15070285

Somià, T., & Vecchiarini, M. (2024). Navigating the new frontier: The impact of artificial intelligence on students' entrepreneurial competencies. *International Journal of Entrepreneurial Behaviour & Research, 30*(11), 236–260. Advance online publication. DOI: 10.1108/IJEBR-08-2023-0788

Tantawy, M., Herbert, K., McNally, J., Mengel, T., Piperopoulos, P., & Foord, D. (2021). Bringing creativity back to entrepreneurship education: Creative self-efficacy, creative process engagement, and entrepreneurial intentions. *Journal of Business Venturing Insights, 15*, e00239. Advance online publication. DOI: 10.1016/j.jbvi.2021.e00239

Uriarte, S., Baier-Fuentes, H., Espinoza-Benavides, J., & Inzunza-Mendoza, W. (2025). Artificial intelligence technologies and entrepreneurship: A hybrid literature review. *Review of Managerial Science*. Advance online publication. DOI: 10.1007/s11846-025-00839-4

Vankov, D., & Wang, L. (2024). *Education program and experiential learning in Chinese entrepreneurship education: A year-long social cognitive theory intervention's impact on self-efficacy and intention's impact on self-efficacy and intention.* International Journal of Innovation Studies., DOI: 10.1016/j.ijis.2024.07.002

Vecchiarini, M., & Somià, T. (2023). Redefining entrepreneurship education in the age of artificial intelligence: An explorative analysis. *International Journal of Management Education, 21*(3), 100879. Advance online publication. DOI: 10.1016/j.ijme.2023.100879

Wang, S., Sun, Z., & Chen, Y. (2022). Effects of higher education institutes' artificial intelligence capability on students' self-efficacy, creativity and learning performance. *Education and Information Technologies, 28*(5), 4919–4939. DOI: 10.1007/s10639-022-11338-4

Xie, Y., & Wang, S. (2025). Generative artificial intelligence in entrepreneurship education enhances entrepreneurial intention through self-efficacy and university support. *Scientific Reports*, *15*(1), 24079. Advance online publication. DOI: 10.1038/s41598-025-09545-3 PMID: 40618006

Zhang, H. (2025). AI-driven innovation and entrepreneurship education: A K-means clustering approach for Chinese university students. *Discover Artificial Intelligence*, *5*(1), 127. Advance online publication. DOI: 10.1007/s44163-025-00341-6

Zhu, J., & Luo, L. (2025). Designing the Future of Entrepreneurship Education: Exploring an AI-Empowered Scaffold System for Business Plan Development. 2025 5th International Conference on Artificial Intelligence and Education (ICAIE), 184-193. DOI: 10.1109/ICAIE64856.2025.11158485

Zulfiqar, S., Sarwar, B., Huo, C., Zhao, X., & Mahasbi, H. (2025). AI-powered education: Driving entrepreneurial spirit among university students. *International Journal of Management Education*, *23*(2), 101106. Advance online publication. DOI: 10.1016/j.ijme.2024.101106

Chapter 7
Human–AI Collaboration in Entrepreneurship

Satya Subrahmanyam
http://orcid.org/0000-0003-0441-2742
Holy Spirit University of Kaslik, Lebanon

Fleur C. Khalil
http://orcid.org/0000-0001-8306-3370
Holy Spirit University of Kaslik, Lebanon

ABSTRACT

Human–AI collaboration is transforming entrepreneurship by reshaping how opportunities are recognized, risks managed, and innovations developed. This chapter explores the psychological and practical dimensions of this partnership, highlighting how entrepreneurial traits such as creativity, adaptability, and emotional intelligence intersect with AI's analytical precision and predictive power. It examines the role of AI in decision-making, creativity enhancement, and stress reduction, while also addressing ethical dilemmas, cultural differences, and psychological barriers such as fear of replacement. Through case studies and conceptual frameworks, the chapter demonstrates how human–AI synergy fosters resilience and hybrid innovation models. The discussion concludes with future directions for research on entrepreneurial psychology, AI integration, and the evolution of a human–machine entrepreneurial ecosystem.

DOI: 10.4018/979-8-2600-1353-3.ch007

1. INTRODUCTION

1.1 Contextualizing the Rise of AI in Entrepreneurial Ecosystems

Artificial intelligence (AI) as a rapidly growing field has become one of the most disruptive factors in the contemporary business ecosystem, altering the principles of entrepreneurship. Conventionally, human creativity, intuition, and decision-making under uncertainty were the key tools to entrepreneurial activity. The past ten years have also been marked by a rapid increase in the number of AI applications helping business owners to utilize the power of data-driven insights, predictive analytics, and intelligent automation to generate and capture value (Dwivedi et al., 2021). NLP, machine learning, and computer vision are becoming more and more integrated into the processes of entrepreneurship, whether in the process of recognizing opportunities and conducting market research, or in interacting with customers and streamlining operations (Cockburn et al., 2018).

In entrepreneurial ecosystems, AI functions not merely as a tool but as a catalyst that fosters innovation and lowers barriers to entry. Digital platforms and cloud-based AI solutions provide startups with access to sophisticated analytical capabilities previously reserved for large corporations. This democratization of technology has contributed to the rise of "AI-first" startups, where algorithmic intelligence is central to business models (Rai et al., 2019). Entrepreneurs today operate within ecosystems where the interplay between human ingenuity and AI capabilities is becoming essential for survival and competitiveness.

1.2 Human–AI Collaboration as a Paradigm Shift in Entrepreneurship

While the early discourse on AI focused heavily on automation and the replacement of human labor, recent perspectives emphasize collaboration between humans and AI as a paradigm shift in entrepreneurship. Human–AI collaboration refers to the integration of AI systems with human judgment, creativity, and social intelligence to achieve outcomes that neither could accomplish alone (Subrahmanyam, 2025b). Unlike earlier technological disruptions, AI does not merely augment productivity - it fundamentally reconfigures the entrepreneurial process by enabling entrepreneurs to think, act, and scale differently.

Entrepreneurs can use AI-driven tools to identify emerging market trends, optimize product design, and personalize customer experiences on a scale, while retaining human-centered capabilities such as empathy, negotiation, and ethical reasoning (Daugherty & Wilson, 2022). This synergy highlights a shift from an efficiency-driven perspective of technology adoption toward a co-creative model, where entrepreneurs collaborate with AI as a cognitive partner. The entrepreneurial ecosystem thus evolves into a hybrid environment, where strategic decision-making blends machine intelligence with human vision.

This paradigm shifts challenges traditional notions of entrepreneurial agency. In AI-enabled ecosystems, entrepreneurs are no longer the sole drivers of innovation; instead, they operate in symbiosis with intelligent systems that actively shape ideation, experimentation, and execution (Shrestha et al., 2019). Such reconfiguration necessitates rethinking skill sets, leadership models, and ethical considerations to ensure that the human–AI relationship remains complementary and sustainable.

1.3 Objectives and Scope of the Chapter

This chapter aims to explore the evolving role of human–AI collaboration within entrepreneurial ecosystems, with a particular emphasis on its implications for innovation, competitiveness, and organizational transformation. By contextualizing AI not as a disruptive threat but as a collaborative partner, the chapter seeks to reframe entrepreneurship in the digital era. The objectives are threefold. First, to analyze how AI is integrated into entrepreneurial practices, highlighting opportunities and challenges across different stages of the entrepreneurial lifecycle. Second, to examine the nature of human–AI collaboration, focusing on the complementarities between human creativity, intuition, and ethics, and AI's analytical, predictive, and automation capacities. Third, to evaluate the implications of this collaboration for entrepreneurial ecosystems, including shifts in organizational culture, business models, and the broader socio-economic landscape.

The scope of this chapter extends beyond a purely technological discussion to consider the human, social, and cultural dimensions of AI adoption in entrepreneurship. It emphasizes that while AI provides unprecedented opportunities for scaling and efficiency, the success of entrepreneurial ventures ultimately depends on the quality of human–AI interaction. As such, this chapter contributes to a growing body of literature that underscores the importance of developing strategies, mindsets, and policies that foster collaborative intelligence rather than competition between humans and machines.

In doing so, the chapter situates human–AI collaboration as a critical frontier in entrepreneurship research and practice. It not only sheds light on the ongoing transformation of entrepreneurial ecosystems but also provides insights for policymakers, educators, and practitioners seeking to prepare future entrepreneurs for a hybrid, AI-augmented business environment.

2. THE PSYCHOLOGICAL FOUNDATIONS OF HUMAN–AI COLLABORATION

The psychological foundations of human–AI collaboration provide insight into how entrepreneurs adapt and thrive in an evolving digital landscape. By blending entrepreneurial traits such as creativity, adaptability, and risk-taking with AI's cognitive augmentation, entrepreneurs can enhance decision-making and innovation. At the same time, trust, control, and perceptions of fairness shape the willingness to rely on AI systems. Understanding these psychological drivers reveals how human intuition and emotional intelligence complement AI's analytical power in entrepreneurial ecosystems.

2.1 Entrepreneurial Mindset: Creativity, Risk-Taking, and Adaptability

At the heart of entrepreneurship lies a distinct mindset characterized by creativity, risk-taking, and adaptability. Entrepreneurs often thrive on uncertainty, viewing challenges as opportunities for innovation and growth. Creativity allows them to generate novel ideas and solutions, risk-taking drives them to pursue ventures with uncertain outcomes, and adaptability enables them to pivot strategies in response to shifting market conditions (Obschonka & Audretsch, 2020). These qualities are foundational for navigating highly dynamic and competitive ecosystems.

The introduction of AI into entrepreneurial processes reshapes how these psychological traits are expressed and operationalized. For instance, AI-powered tools can amplify creativity by providing entrepreneurs with data-driven inspiration, uncovering hidden market trends, and even co-creating new product designs. Likewise, risk-taking behaviors can be informed by predictive analytics and scenario simulations, reducing uncertainty without eliminating entrepreneurial daring. Adaptability, meanwhile, is supported by AI's real-time feedback loops, allowing entrepreneurs to adjust strategies swiftly. While AI provides analytical depth and operational agility, the entrepreneurial mindset remains distinctly human - anchored in vision, ambition, and resilience that machines cannot replicate (Amankwah-Amoah et al., 2021).

2.2 Cognitive Augmentation: How AI Extends Human Decision-Making Capacity

Human cognition is bound by limitations in memory, attention, and processing speed. Entrepreneurs often face complex decisions under pressure, where incomplete information and cognitive biases can distort judgment. AI addresses these limitations by augmenting human decision-making capacity. Machine learning algorithms, for example, can process vast datasets to reveal patterns and correlations that would otherwise escape human detection (Subrahmanyam, 2024a).

This cognitive augmentation does not imply the replacement of human decision-makers but rather their empowerment. Entrepreneurs can delegate routine analysis, forecasting, and optimization tasks to AI systems, freeing cognitive resources for strategic thinking and creative problem-solving (Jarrahi, 2018). AI-enabled financial models help entrepreneurs evaluate investment opportunities with greater accuracy, while natural language processing tools allow them to monitor customer sentiment in real time.

The interaction between human intuition and AI's computational capacity results in a form of "hybrid intelligence" that is more powerful than either entity alone. Nonetheless, reliance on AI requires entrepreneurs to remain vigilant about algorithmic biases, transparency, and the interpretability of machine-generated recommendations (Dwivedi et al., 2021). The success of cognitive augmentation ultimately depends on entrepreneurs' ability to critically assess AI outputs and integrate them into their broader strategic vision.

2.3 Trust, Control, and the Psychology of Relying on AI in Business

Trust is a central psychological factor in the adoption and effective use of AI within entrepreneurship. Entrepreneurs must not only understand AI capabilities but also feel confident in relying on them. Research shows that the degree of trust in AI systems is influenced by their perceived accuracy, transparency, and alignment with human values (Longoni et al., 2019). Excessive trust may lead to over-reliance, where entrepreneurs unquestioningly accept algorithmic outputs, while insufficient trust may result in under-utilization, negating potential benefits.

Control is closely tied to trust. Entrepreneurs prefer to retain decision authority, even when AI provides superior analytical insights. A lack of perceived control may create psychological resistance and fear of being sidelined by machines (Shrestha et al., 2019). Building "calibrated trust" therefore becomes essential - where entrepreneurs learn to rely on AI in areas where it excels, while retaining human oversight in domains that require ethical judgment, empathy, or contextual reasoning (Daugherty & Wilson, 2022).

The psychology of relying on AI in business thus requires balance: entrepreneurs must manage the tension between confidence in human intuition and deference to algorithmic intelligence. Designing explainable AI (XAI) systems, fostering digital literacy, and promoting transparency are crucial strategies to strengthen trust and ensure sustainable collaboration.

2.4 Emotional Intelligence and Human Intuition as Complements to AI

Despite its computational power, AI lacks emotional intelligence and an intuitive understanding of human relationships. Entrepreneurship, however, is not purely analytical - it is relational, requiring empathy, persuasion, negotiation, and leadership. Emotional intelligence (EI) enables entrepreneurs to navigate interpersonal dynamics, build trust with stakeholders, and foster strong team cultures (Côté, 2014).

AI complements but cannot replace these abilities. Customer service chatbots can automate responses, but only human entrepreneurs can interpret subtle emotional cues or resolve conflicts with empathy. While AI can predict consumer preferences, it cannot replicate the relational bonds entrepreneurs build with investors, employees, and communities. Intuition, shaped by experience and tacit knowledge, often guides entrepreneurs in ambiguous situations where data is scarce or incomplete (Azoury et al., 2024).

Figure 1. Psychological Foundations

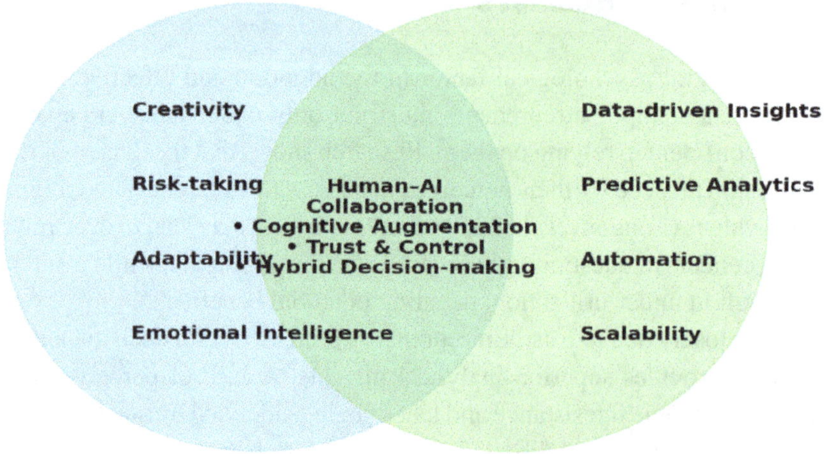

Source: Author (2025)

Thus, emotional intelligence and intuition remain indispensable human advantages in AI-augmented entrepreneurship. They ensure that technology remains aligned with human values and that business decisions are not solely data-driven but also ethically grounded and socially responsible. The interplay of human EI and AI analytics strengthens resilience, adaptability, and long-term sustainability in entrepreneurial ventures.

3. AI AS A PARTNER IN ENTREPRENEURIAL DECISION-MAKING

Artificial intelligence (AI) has transformed the face of entrepreneurial decision-making. Historically, entrepreneurs used to base their opportunities, risk evaluation, and strategic decisions on personal experience, intuition, and scanty information. AI is used today as a cognitive partner, which allows providing data-driven insights, predictions, and decision support to become more adaptable and competitive regarding entrepreneurship. This relationship is not the venture of replacing the entrepreneur, but rather, it is forming a human-AI alliance that will utilize the advantages of each entity.

3.1 AI-Driven Opportunity Recognition

The key to entrepreneurship is opportunity recognition. Businesspeople are always investigating the environment about gaps, unmet needs and emerging trends. The process is greatly improved based on the advanced analysis and trend forecasting of the market with the help of AI. Machine learning algorithms have the potential to analyze large amounts of structured and unstructured data and discover weak signals of change of which human entrepreneurs are not always aware (Subrahmanyam, 2024b). Social media discussion, consumer reviews and news articles can be analyzed with natural language processing tools to point out emerging consumer needs or discontent with available products.

AI supports ideation by generating novel product or service concepts. Generative AI, in particular, is increasingly used to create prototypes, simulate product-market fits, and inspire entrepreneurs with design alternatives (Dwivedi et al., 2021). This expands the entrepreneur's creative horizon, allowing them to test and refine ideas faster and more cost-effectively. Table 1 summarizes how AI contributes to opportunity recognition across entrepreneurial activities.

Table 1. AI Contributions to Entrepreneurial Opportunity Recognition

Entrepreneurial Activity	AI Application	Impact on Decision-Making
Market Analysis	Big data analytics, NLP	Identifies hidden patterns and emerging markets
Trend Forecasting	Machine learning, predictive modeling	Anticipates industry shifts and consumer behavior
Ideation Support	Generative AI, design simulations	Enhances creativity and rapid prototyping
Customer Insight	Sentiment analysis, recommender systems	Identifies unmet needs and customer preferences

3.2 Risk Assessment and Mitigation Through Predictive Analytics

Entrepreneurship is inherently risky, involving uncertainty about resources, markets, and competitors. While risk cannot be eliminated, AI enhances risk management by providing predictive insights. Through scenario modeling and probability forecasting, AI systems can estimate the likelihood of various outcomes, enabling entrepreneurs to prepare for contingencies (Rai et al., 2019).

Startups can use AI-powered financial tools to predict cash flow fluctuations, assess investment risks, or anticipate supply chain disruptions. AI-driven simulations allow entrepreneurs to evaluate different strategies under varying conditions, reducing the potential for costly misjudgments. Importantly, these tools allow entrepreneurs to approach risk not as a deterrent but as a manageable variable, increasing their confidence in pursuing bold initiatives (Amankwah-Amoah et al., 2021).

3.3 Cognitive Load Reduction: Freeing Entrepreneurs for Strategic Thinking

Entrepreneurs often face cognitive overload due to the breadth of decisions they must make daily - ranging from operational details to strategic planning. AI alleviates this burden by automating routine tasks, filtering relevant information, and offering decision recommendations. AI-enabled dashboards consolidate key performance indicators, providing real-time insights without requiring entrepreneurs to process raw data manually.

By reducing cognitive load, AI allows entrepreneurs to allocate more mental resources to strategic and creative activities (Jarrahi, 2018). Instead of being consumed by operational firefighting, entrepreneurs can focus on long-term visioning, partnerships, and market positioning. This shift enhances both the efficiency and quality of entrepreneurial decision-making. Table 2 illustrates the contrast between decision-making before and after AI integration.

Table 2. Cognitive Load Reduction Through AI Integration

Decision-Making Area	Traditional Approach	AI-Augmented Approach	Benefit
Market Monitoring	Manual data collection, fragmented sources	Automated dashboards, real-time analytics	Faster and more accurate insights
Financial Planning	Historical data, static projections	Predictive modeling, dynamic scenario testing	Improved forecasting and adaptability
Customer Engagement	Direct feedback, surveys	Sentiment analysis, behavioral prediction	More precise and personalized strategies
Operations Management	Reactive problem-solving	Proactive issue detection through AI monitoring	Reduced errors and proactive risk mitigation

3.4 The Role of AI in Reducing Biases Versus Introducing New Algorithmic Biases

Bias is a persistent challenge in entrepreneurial decision-making. Entrepreneurs' judgments are often influenced by cognitive biases such as overconfidence, confirmation bias, and anchoring (Tversky & Kahneman, revisited in contemporary AI contexts). AI promises to reduce these biases by introducing objectivity, consistency, and data-driven reasoning. AI-based hiring platforms can be designed to minimize human prejudices in recruitment by focusing on performance indicators rather than subjective impressions (Subrahmanyam, 2024a).

AI itself is not immune to bias. Algorithmic systems inherit biases from the data they are trained on and the assumptions embedded in their design (Mehrabi et al., 2021). For entrepreneurs, this introduces a paradox: while AI can help correct human biases, it may simultaneously embed new algorithmic biases that are less transparent. Biased AI-driven predictions in areas such as credit scoring, investment evaluation, or customer profiling can lead to unfair outcomes and ethical dilemmas.

To navigate this tension, entrepreneurs must cultivate digital literacy, ensuring they understand the limitations of AI models and implement safeguards such as explainable AI (XAI) and diverse training datasets. The ultimate responsibility for ethical decision-making rests with the entrepreneur, who must integrate AI insights with human judgment to strike a balance between efficiency and fairness.

AI is no longer a passive tool but an active partner in entrepreneurial decision-making. It enhances opportunity recognition through market analysis and ideation, mitigates risks with predictive analytics, and reduces cognitive load by automating routine tasks. At the same time, it challenges entrepreneurs to confront the complexities of algorithmic bias and ensure ethical responsibility in AI adoption. The psychological and managerial implications of this partnership underscore a fundamental transformation in entrepreneurship: decisions are no longer made by humans alone but emerge from a hybrid collaboration that blends human creativity and judgment with AI's analytical precision.

4. ENHANCING CREATIVITY AND INNOVATION THROUGH HUMAN–AI SYNERGY

Entrepreneurship is all about creativity and innovation, which allows individuals and organizations to create unique value propositions, disrupt the market, and sustain the competitive edge. In the past, creativity has been regarded as a human characteristic, which is exclusive to humans and is based on imagination, intuition, and cultural context. The advent of artificial intelligence (AI) has presented possibilities of greater innovation improvement and scaling. Human-AI synergy, in which entrepreneurs are partners with AI systems, as opposed to tools, represents a paradigm shift in the way ideas are generated, developed, and commercialized.

4.1 AI as a Co-Creator: From Product Design to Marketing Strategies

AI's role in creativity has expanded beyond process automation to becoming a genuine co-creator. Entrepreneurs are increasingly using AI systems in domains such as product design, branding, and marketing strategy. Generative AI tools can propose design alternatives, produce visual or textual content, and simulate consumer responses to new products. AI-assisted design platforms allow startups to experiment with prototypes rapidly, reducing the cost and time of traditional research and development (Subrahmanyam & El Samra 2025).

In marketing, AI serves as a creative partner by generating campaign content, tailoring messaging to consumer segments, and predicting which strategies are likely to resonate. Natural language processing tools can generate slogans or ad copy, while image recognition systems support visual branding. This co-creation not only boosts efficiency but also fosters greater personalization in innovation, as AI tailors solutions to specific market niches (Rai et al., 2019).

4.2 Human Creativity Plus Machine Precision: Hybrid Innovation Models

Human creativity and AI precision form complementary forces in innovation. While humans excel at divergent thinking, empathy, and conceptual abstraction, AI specializes in convergent thinking, pattern recognition, and optimization. Hybrid innovation models that combine these strengths offer a powerful framework for entrepreneurship (Jarrahi, 2018).

Entrepreneurs may use AI to analyze massive datasets for consumer preferences, identify design constraints, or simulate product performance under various conditions. Based on these insights, human innovators provide the imaginative leap - envisioning how the product fits into broader social, cultural, or ethical contexts. The result is an iterative loop where human creativity generates ideas, AI refines them through data-driven analysis, and humans reinterpret outputs for novel applications.

This process reduces uncertainty in innovation while preserving the imaginative essence that distinguishes groundbreaking ventures. In practice, hybrid innovation models are increasingly applied in industries ranging from fashion and media to healthcare and financial technology, where precision and creativity must coexist.

4.3 Case Studies of Startups Leveraging AI for Idea Generation and Prototyping

Several startups illustrate the transformative potential of AI in creative entrepreneurship. **Runway**, a generative AI platform for video editing and content creation, empowers entrepreneurs and small businesses to produce professional-quality media without extensive technical expertise. This democratizes access to high-end creative tools and accelerates product development cycles (Amankwah-Amoah et al., 2021).

Another case is **Spacemaker AI**, a Norwegian startup acquired by Autodesk, which uses AI to generate architectural designs optimized for light, energy, and space efficiency. By providing multiple design alternatives in real time, the platform enables architects and real estate entrepreneurs to focus on vision and aesthetics while AI handles complex calculations (Dwivedi et al., 2021).

In fashion, startups such as **Stitch Fix** use AI to personalize clothing recommendations, blending stylist creativity with predictive analytics. Here, innovation emerges not just from AI's recommendations but from the synergy of human stylists interpreting data to enhance customer experience.

These examples demonstrate that AI is not replacing creativity but expanding the innovation frontier by making ideation and prototyping faster, more precise, and more market-driven.

4.4 The Psychological Drivers of Innovation When Working Alongside AI

The integration of AI into creative processes introduces important psychological dynamics that influence innovation. Entrepreneurs often experience enhanced self-efficacy when AI augments their abilities, giving them confidence to tackle complex challenges (Shrestha et al., 2019). The perception of AI as a collaborator rather than a competitor fosters a mindset of exploration and experimentation, critical drivers of entrepreneurial innovation.

At the same time, the use of AI requires psychological adaptation. Entrepreneurs must develop trust in AI systems without becoming overly reliant on them, balancing human intuition with algorithmic recommendations. This involves recalibrating their role—from being sole creators to orchestrators of a human–machine creative ecosystem (Daugherty & Wilson, 2022).

Working with AI can reduce the fear of failure. Since AI enables rapid prototyping and iteration, entrepreneurs may be more willing to experiment with bold ideas, knowing that feedback loops are faster and less costly. This iterative cycle strengthens resilience and fosters a culture of innovation. On the other hand, psychological risks such as creative complacency or overconfidence in AI outputs must also be managed, underscoring the importance of critical thinking and ethical responsibility (Obschonka & Audretsch, 2020).

Human–AI cooperation is changing entrepreneurship's creativity and innovation. AI collaborates in product design and marketing, whereas hybrid innovation models combine human creativity with machine accuracy. Startups like Runway, Spacemaker AI, and Stitch Fix demonstrate how AI-enhanced creativity can speed up and improve ideation and prototyping. How entrepreneurs use AI depends on the psychological drivers of innovation - confidence, trust, resilience, and experimentation. The future of innovation depends on combining human ingenuity with AI intelligence to push entrepreneurship's limits.

5. EMOTIONAL AND SOCIAL DIMENSIONS OF HUMAN–AI ENTREPRENEURSHIP

The emotional and social dimensions of human–AI entrepreneurship highlight the complex interplay between trust, fairness, and collaboration in digital business environments. Entrepreneurs must navigate the psychological impact of relying on AI, from managing stress and cognitive overload to balancing autonomy with algorithmic support. Equally important are perceptions of fairness, accountability, and empathy in AI-driven decisions. Exploring these dimensions underscores how human emotional intelligence and social awareness complement AI's objectivity, shaping effective and ethical entrepreneurial practices.

5.1 Building Trust between Entrepreneurs, Teams, and AI Systems

Trust is fundamental in shaping the adoption and effective use of artificial intelligence (AI) in entrepreneurial contexts. Entrepreneurs must not only trust AI systems themselves but also foster confidence among their teams and stakeholders. Trust in AI is influenced by transparency, explainability, and perceived reliability of algorithms (Dwivedi et al., 2021). When entrepreneurs understand how AI models function and can validate their recommendations, they are more likely to integrate these systems into decision-making. Employees within entrepreneurial ventures are more willing to adopt AI tools when leaders demonstrate confidence in them and highlight their benefits. Building this trust also requires addressing concerns of job displacement, ethical use of AI, and maintaining human oversight to ensure that technology is viewed as an enabler rather than a threat (Mariani et al., 2021).

5.2 AI in Managing Entrepreneurial Stress and Cognitive Overload

Entrepreneurship is associated with high levels of stress due to uncertainty, resource constraints, and constant decision-making. AI can play a supportive role by reducing cognitive overload and managing entrepreneurial stress. Cognitive overload often emerges when entrepreneurs are overwhelmed by vast amounts of data, which hinders their ability to make effective decisions (Al-Mamary, 2025). AI tools streamline this process by filtering information, identifying patterns, and presenting actionable insights. Predictive analytics can reduce uncertainty in market forecasting, thereby alleviating stress associated with ambiguous conditions. AI-driven platforms that automate repetitive administrative tasks provide entrepreneurs with more cognitive bandwidth to focus on strategic and creative work (Subrahmanyam, 2025a). This delegation of routine workload to AI allows entrepreneurs to maintain psychological resilience, improving both productivity and wellbeing.

5.3 Perceptions of Fairness, Autonomy, and Accountability in AI-Supported Decisions

A critical dimension of integrating AI into entrepreneurship relates to perceptions of fairness, autonomy, and accountability. Entrepreneurs and stakeholders are sensitive to whether AI-driven decisions are perceived as equitable and unbiased. While AI can help eliminate certain human biases, it also introduces risks of algorithmic bias due to skewed training data or flawed design (Mehrabi et al., 2021).

This duality means entrepreneurs must balance reliance on AI with mechanisms for human oversight to ensure fairness.

Autonomy is another key psychological factor, as entrepreneurs may feel constrained if AI systems dominate decision-making. Maintaining a sense of control is crucial for sustaining entrepreneurial motivation and innovation (Obschonka & Audretsch, 2020). Clear governance structures that delineate accountability between human leaders and AI systems further reinforce ethical use and trust. When entrepreneurs emphasize responsible AI practices, they not only safeguard organizational reputation but also strengthen long-term relationships with customers and stakeholders.

5.4 Human Empathy versus AI Objectivity in Leadership and Stakeholder Relations

Leadership in entrepreneurial ecosystems requires balancing human empathy with AI's objectivity. AI systems excel in rational decision-making, data-driven insights, and consistency, but they lack emotional intelligence and cultural sensitivity. Entrepreneurs, in contrast, bring empathy, compassion, and contextual understanding, which are critical in managing teams and nurturing stakeholder relationships (Huang & Rust, 2018). While AI can predict consumer behavior, only human entrepreneurs can interpret how social dynamics, emotional cues, and ethical considerations should shape customer engagement.

The tension between empathy and objectivity creates opportunities for hybrid leadership models, where entrepreneurs leverage AI's analytical rigor while maintaining the human touch in communication and relationship management. This synthesis ensures that decisions are not only efficient but also socially responsible and emotionally resonant. Such balance enhances organizational culture, fosters inclusivity, and positions the entrepreneur as a credible leader in an AI-augmented environment (Brynjolfsson & McAfee, 2017).

Figure 2. Emotional and Social Dimensions

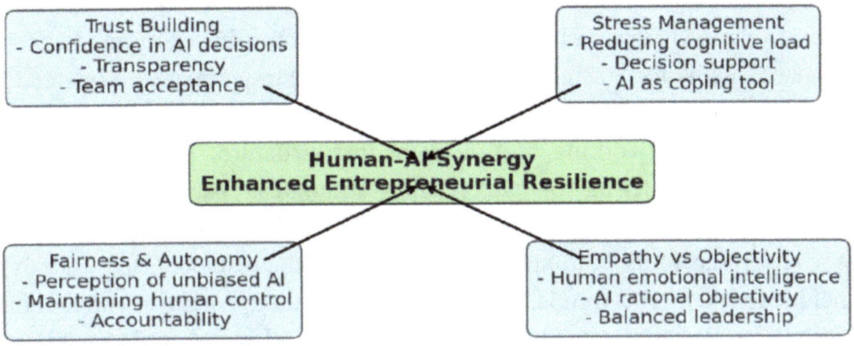

Source: Author (2025)

The emotional and social dimensions of human–AI entrepreneurship highlight the necessity of integrating psychological and relational factors into technological adoption. Building trust, reducing stress, ensuring fairness, and balancing empathy with objectivity are essential in maximizing the potential of AI while preserving the human essence of entrepreneurship. Successful entrepreneurs will be those who can navigate these complexities, positioning AI not as a replacement but as a collaborative partner in entrepreneurial endeavors. The result is a more resilient, innovative, and socially responsible entrepreneurial ecosystem.

6. CASE STUDIES OF HUMAN–AI COLLABORATION IN STARTUPS

Case studies of human–AI collaboration in startups illustrate the real-world dynamics of integrating advanced technologies into entrepreneurial ventures. They highlight how AI-powered accelerators and incubators are supporting entrepreneurs in scaling, innovation, and market expansion. At the same time, these cases reveal challenges such as over-reliance on AI or insufficient human oversight. By examining both successes and failures across diverse cultural contexts, these studies provide valuable lessons on psychological adaptation and effective human–AI synergy in entrepreneurship.

6.1 AI-Powered Accelerators and Incubators Supporting Entrepreneurs

In recent years, AI-powered accelerators and incubators have emerged as critical support mechanisms for startups, offering entrepreneurs access to advanced data analytics, mentorship, and market intelligence. Unlike traditional incubators, which focus primarily on networking and physical infrastructure, AI-driven platforms provide predictive modeling for market entry strategies, customer segmentation, and funding opportunities (Subrahmanyam, 2025c). Platforms such as Y Combinator's AI-driven tools help startups evaluate product-market fit by analyzing customer feedback, market trends, and competitive landscapes. European incubators like Station F in Paris are increasingly incorporating AI-based tools to streamline investor matching and optimize resource allocation (Nambisan et al., 2019). These accelerators act as both advisors and technological partners, reducing uncertainty in early decision-making and empowering entrepreneurs to experiment with innovative business models.

6.2 Success Stories: Entrepreneurs Using AI for Scaling and Market Expansion

Several startups have successfully leveraged AI as a collaborative partner for scaling operations and entering new markets. A notable example is **Zebra Medical Vision**, an Israeli health-tech startup that uses AI algorithms to analyze medical imaging data. By integrating AI into diagnostic processes, Zebra Medical Vision not only reduced healthcare costs but also scaled globally by partnering with hospitals in the United States and Europe (Topol, 2019). Their success demonstrates how AI can enhance both efficiency and credibility, enabling startups to attract strategic partnerships and investments.

Another case is **Stitch Fix**, a U.S.-based fashion startup that utilizes AI to provide personalized clothing recommendations. The platform combines machine learning with human stylists, creating a hybrid model where AI suggests products while human experts ensure that cultural, emotional, and aesthetic factors are considered (Huang & Rust, 2018). This synergy allowed Stitch Fix to rapidly expand its customer base and establish itself as a leader in personalized retail, highlighting how AI-human collaboration can balance precision and creativity in scaling businesses.

In the fintech sector, **Klarna**, a Swedish startup offering "buy now, pay later" services, employed AI to predict consumer creditworthiness with high accuracy. By combining AI-driven credit scoring with human oversight, Klarna minimized default risks and expanded into multiple countries (Obschonka & Audretsch, 2020).

These examples show that AI not only reduces operational risks but also facilitates global expansion by tailoring strategies to diverse consumer markets.

6.3 Insights from Failures: Over-Reliance on AI or Lack of Human Oversight

Despite notable successes, several startups have failed due to over-reliance on AI or insufficient human oversight. One such case is **X.ai**, a scheduling assistant startup that aimed to fully automate meeting coordination through natural language processing. While technology was innovative, the company struggled with contextual misunderstandings and cultural nuances in communication. Its inability to balance AI with human intervention ultimately limited customer adoption and led to its acquisition in 2021 (Dwivedi et al., 2021).

Another example comes from predictive hiring startups that relied excessively on AI algorithms for recruitment decisions. Startups such as **HireVue** faced backlash due to algorithmic bias, particularly in facial recognition and natural language processing, which disproportionately disadvantaged candidates from minority backgrounds (Mehrabi et al., 2021). The public criticism highlighted the dangers of neglecting fairness and accountability in AI applications.

These failures underscore the need for human oversight in AI-driven entrepreneurship. Entrepreneurs must not only evaluate the technical accuracy of AI tools but also consider ethical, cultural, and psychological dimensions of decision-making. Over-reliance on AI without adequate safeguards can damage brand reputation, erode trust, and hinder long-term sustainability.

6.4 Cross-Cultural Insights: Different Psychological Acceptance of AI Collaboration

The success and acceptance of AI-human collaboration in entrepreneurship also depend on cultural factors. Cross-cultural studies reveal that psychological trust in AI varies significantly across regions. In East Asia, where technological adoption is generally high, entrepreneurs and consumers often display greater openness to AI collaboration, influenced by collective cultural values and trust in institutional frameworks (Fossen et al., 2024). Chinese startups in e-commerce and health-tech are increasingly leveraging AI for personalized customer experiences, with strong consumer adoption.

In contrast, Western contexts often emphasize individual autonomy and skepticism toward algorithmic control. European entrepreneurs, for instance, face stricter regulatory environments under the General Data Protection Regulation (GDPR), which fosters caution in AI adoption and requires more transparent systems (Floridi & Cowls, 2019). In the United States, while startups rapidly integrate AI for competitive advantage, consumer concerns about privacy and algorithmic bias shape the pace of adoption.

Cultural attitudes also influence employee acceptance of AI collaboration within startups. Research shows that in collectivist cultures, teams are more likely to perceive AI as a supportive partner, while in individualistic cultures, AI may be viewed as a threat to personal autonomy (Cummings-Koether et al., 2025). These insights highlight the importance of context-sensitive strategies for integrating AI into entrepreneurial ecosystems.

Case studies of human–AI collaboration in startups illustrate both the transformative potential and inherent challenges of this partnership. Success stories demonstrate that AI can drive scalability, innovation, and market expansion when combined with human creativity and oversight. Conversely, failures highlight the risks of excessive reliance on algorithms without ethical and cultural considerations. Finally, cross-cultural insights reveal that psychological acceptance of AI varies across regions, suggesting that entrepreneurs must adopt context-specific approaches when deploying AI solutions. Together, these lessons emphasize that the future of entrepreneurship lies in hybrid models where human ingenuity and AI intelligence work in synergy, guided by trust, fairness, and cultural sensitivity.

7. CHALLENGES AND ETHICAL DILEMMAS

The integration of AI into entrepreneurship introduces complex challenges and ethical dilemmas that extend beyond technological capabilities. Entrepreneurs must address psychological barriers such as fear of replacement, loss of autonomy, and over-dependence on intelligent systems. Ethical issues, including algorithmic bias, transparency, and responsibility, further complicate adoption. Concerns over data privacy and intellectual property emerge in AI-supported ventures. Exploring these challenges highlights the need to balance human intuition with algorithmic logic while ensuring responsible and ethical innovation.

7.1 Psychological Barriers: Fear of Replacement, Loss of Autonomy, Over-Dependence

The integration of artificial intelligence (AI) in entrepreneurship brings significant psychological challenges for founders, employees, and stakeholders. A common concern is the fear of replacement, where entrepreneurs and workers worry that automation may reduce their relevance in decision-making and value creation

(Mariani et al., 2021). While AI enhances efficiency, over-reliance may undermine human confidence and perceived worth within entrepreneurial ventures.

Another psychological barrier is the loss of autonomy, as entrepreneurs often pride themselves on independent thinking and risk-taking. If algorithms dictate strategic choices, entrepreneurs may feel constrained, reducing their motivation and sense of agency (Dwivedi et al., 2021). There is the risk of over-dependence on AI, where entrepreneurs defer too much to machine recommendations without applying critical judgment. Such dependency can reduce adaptability, especially in uncertain environments where intuition and creativity are vital (Brynjolfsson & McAfee, 2017).

Table 3. Psychological Barriers in Human–AI Entrepreneurial Collaboration

Barrier	Description	Implications for Startups
Fear of Replacement	Anxiety that AI may reduce the entrepreneur's or employee's role.	Lower morale, resistance to AI adoption, potential skill neglect.
Loss of Autonomy	Concern that entrepreneurs may lose decision-making control to algorithms.	Reduced motivation, weakened entrepreneurial spirit.
Over-Dependence on AI	Excessive reliance on machine recommendations without critical thinking.	Poor adaptability, vulnerability to AI errors or bias.

7.2 Ethical Challenges in Entrepreneurial AI Use

The ethical dilemmas surrounding entrepreneurial AI adoption include algorithmic bias, lack of transparency, and blurred responsibility. AI systems learn from historical datasets, which may embed existing societal biases. Startups that rely heavily on such systems risk perpetuating discrimination, especially in hiring, lending, or consumer profiling (Mehrabi et al., 2021). Transparency is another critical issue - entrepreneurs must explain AI's decision-making logic to stakeholders, but "black box" algorithms often obscure interpretability.

Responsibility also poses a challenge: when an AI system makes a flawed decision, accountability becomes ambiguous. Should entrepreneurs, developers, or AI vendors bear responsibility? This uncertainty raises ethical and legal dilemmas, especially in regulated sectors such as finance and healthcare (Floridi & Cowls, 2019).

Table 4. Ethical and Legal Challenges of AI in Entrepreneurship

Challenge	Key Issues	Entrepreneurial Implications
Algorithmic Bias	AI reproduces or amplifies social and cultural biases in datasets.	Risk of discrimination lawsuits, reputational harm.
Transparency	Black box models limit explainability of AI-driven decisions.	Reduced trust among stakeholders and customers.
Responsibility	Ambiguity over who is accountable for AI-driven outcomes.	Legal liability concerns, difficulty in assigning blame.
Data Privacy	Use of personal data may conflict with GDPR, CCPA, or other laws.	Regulatory penalties, customer distrust.
Intellectual Property (IP)	Ambiguity in ownership of AI-generated innovations and content.	Legal disputes, lack of clarity in co-created ventures.

7.3 Data Privacy and Intellectual Property Concerns in Co-Created Ventures

The main issues related to AI-enabled entrepreneurship are data privacy and intellectual property (IP). Entrepreneurs are relying on customer data to develop their products, make them personalized and gain insights into the market. Inappropriate use or misappropriation of personal information can be in conflict with such laws as General Data Protection Regulation (GDPR) in Europe or California Consumer Privacy Act (CCPA) in the United States (Obschonka & Audretsch, 2020). Strong data governance practices are essential to the entrepreneur adopting a balance between innovation and compliance.

In addition, co-created ventures involving human–AI collaboration raise intellectual property dilemmas. If AI contributes to ideation, design, or content generation, questions arise about ownership: should IP belong to the entrepreneur, the AI developer, or jointly to both? Current legal frameworks often lag behind such technological realities, creating uncertainty for startups in creative industries (Calo, 2017).

7.4 Navigating the Balance between Human Intuition and Algorithmic Logic

One of the most profound dilemmas in entrepreneurial AI adoption is balancing human intuition with algorithmic logic. Entrepreneurs are valued for their gut feelings, creativity, and adaptability - qualities that often lead to breakthrough innovations. AI excels in processing vast datasets, identifying trends, and making evidence-based predictions (Huang & Rust, 2018). The challenge is integrating these two modes of decision-making without one overshadowing the other.

Over-emphasizing AI risks stifling creativity, while ignoring AI insights reduces competitiveness in data-driven markets. Hybrid decision-making models - where entrepreneurs use AI for cognitive augmentation while retaining final control - offer a promising pathway (Al-Mamary, 2025). These models enable startups to harness machine precision while preserving human agency, accountability, and innovation.

Human–AI collaboration in entrepreneurship holds enormous potential, but it also raises complex psychological, ethical, and legal dilemmas. Entrepreneurs face internal barriers, such as fear of replacement and loss of autonomy, alongside external pressures relating to bias, transparency, responsibility, and data governance. Intellectual property concerns further complicate AI-enabled innovation, especially in creative and knowledge-intensive industries. The key to navigating these challenges lies in developing hybrid approaches that balance algorithmic precision with human intuition, supported by strong ethical frameworks and transparent governance. Startups that proactively address these dilemmas are more likely to sustain competitive advantage while preserving trust and responsibility in the age of AI.

8. THE FUTURE OF HUMAN–AI COLLABORATION IN ENTREPRENEURSHIP

The future of human–AI collaboration in entrepreneurship promises a shift toward deeper integration, where machines act as cognitive companions and strategic co-creators. Emerging technologies such as generative AI and intelligent assistants are set to transform idea incubation, strategy development, and decision-making. At the same time, entrepreneurs must adapt psychologically to working alongside AI as co-entrepreneurs. Reimagining entrepreneurship as a human–machine ecosystem highlights opportunities for innovation, resilience, and ethically balanced business practices in a rapidly evolving landscape.

8.1 Emerging Trends in Cognitive AI Companions and Entrepreneurial Assistants

The future of entrepreneurship will be increasingly shaped by cognitive AI companions, functioning not just as tools but as intelligent partners. Unlike traditional automation, cognitive AI systems can process contextual data, adapt to dynamic environments, and deliver personalized insights. These entrepreneurial assistants are designed to augment human cognition by providing real-time recommendations, identifying market gaps, and simulating scenarios that support agile decision-making

(Subrahmanyam, 2025b). For entrepreneurs, cognitive AI companions represent a shift from static business analytics toward dynamic collaboration, where the machine learns from the entrepreneur's behavior and adapts accordingly. This trend aligns with the increasing demand for speed, accuracy, and foresight in entrepreneurial ecosystems characterized by uncertainty.

8.2 Potential of Generative AI in Idea Incubation and Personalized Strategy

Generative AI has emerged as a transformative tool for entrepreneurs, enabling the incubation of new ideas and the design of innovative business strategies. By generating prototypes, marketing copy, design suggestions, or even customer personas, generative AI reduces barriers to creativity while ensuring efficiency (Dwivedi et al., 2022). Startups are already leveraging large language models and generative design tools to brainstorm solutions, test market hypotheses, and personalize customer experiences. In entrepreneurship, this allows for rapid iteration cycles where ideas are evaluated and refined in days rather than months. Generative AI provides tailored strategies by integrating diverse datasets, offering entrepreneurs a nuanced understanding of consumer behavior and emerging trends.

8.3 Human Psychological Adaptation to AI as Co-Entrepreneurs

The integration of AI into entrepreneurship raises not only technological but also psychological challenges. Entrepreneurs must adapt to viewing AI as a co-entrepreneur rather than merely an instrument. This requires cultivating trust, balancing reliance on AI with human intuition, and developing new skills to complement AI's strengths (Longoni et al., 2019). While AI excels in rational decision-making, humans bring creativity, empathy, and moral reasoning that remain essential to entrepreneurship. As AI becomes embedded in business practices, entrepreneurs must overcome fears of replacement and instead embrace AI as a collaborative force that enhances resilience and innovation. Psychological readiness, including openness to change and digital literacy, will determine how effectively entrepreneurs harness AI as a partner.

8.4 Reimagining Entrepreneurship as a Human–Machine Ecosystem

Looking ahead, entrepreneurship will evolve into a human–machine ecosystem, characterized by symbiotic decision-making and hybrid leadership models. Rather than framing the relationship as human versus machine, the future lies in synergistic collaboration where humans set visions, values, and ethical boundaries while AI executes analysis and optimizations at scale (Shrestha et al., 2019). This ecosystemic view reframes entrepreneurship as a distributed intelligence system that integrates emotional intelligence with algorithmic logic. AI could guide entrepreneurs toward equitable hiring or sustainable supply chain practices, while humans provide the contextual awareness necessary to align business decisions with societal goals. Eventually, this reimagining has the potential to make entrepreneurship not only more innovative but also more inclusive and ethically grounded.

Figure 3. The Future of AI-Human Collaboration

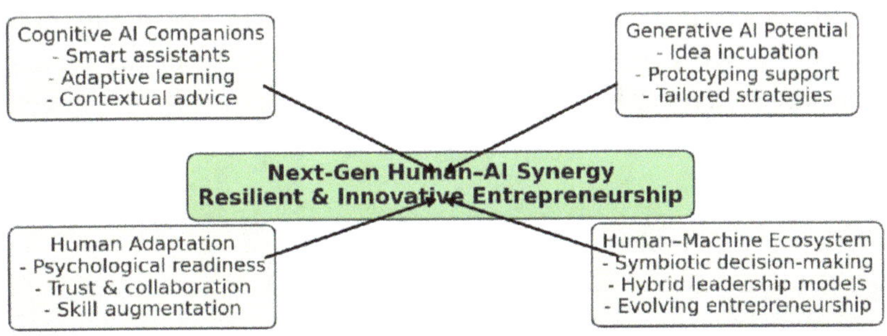

Source: Author (2025)

The future of human–AI collaboration in entrepreneurship points to deeper integration where AI functions as a cognitive partner, generative innovator, and strategic co-pilot. Entrepreneurs who adapt psychologically and strategically to this shift will benefit from enhanced creativity, agility, and resilience. The transition toward a human–machine ecosystem challenges conventional ideas of entrepreneurship, but it also opens new pathways for innovation and sustainable growth. The synergy between human ingenuity and AI precision is poised to redefine the entrepreneurial journey, making it more adaptive to the complexities of an uncertain global economy.

9. CONCLUSION

The integration of human and artificial intelligence in entrepreneurship represents a profound shift in how businesses are imagined, created, and scaled. On the psychological level, collaboration with AI challenges entrepreneurs to navigate issues of trust, autonomy, and identity while leveraging emotional intelligence and intuition to complement machine objectivity. On the practical level, AI enhances opportunity recognition, risk assessment, and innovation by reducing cognitive load and offering data-driven insights that extend human decision-making capacity. The essence of effective collaboration lies in achieving balance - where human creativity, empathy, and vision guide the entrepreneurial journey, while AI contributes precision, scalability, and predictive analytics. This synergy creates hybrid innovation models that are not only efficient but also adaptable to complex and uncertain environments.

Looking forward, the implications for entrepreneurial psychology and AI integration are significant. Research must explore how entrepreneurs psychologically adapt to AI partners, how biases - both human and algorithmic - are managed, and how cultural contexts shape acceptance of AI collaboration. By reframing entrepreneurship as a human–machine ecosystem, future scholarship can deepen understanding of resilience, creativity, and ethics in this new paradigm. Eventually, human–AI collaboration signals not the replacement of human ingenuity but its augmentation, paving the way for a more innovative and inclusive entrepreneurial future.

REFERENCES

Al-Mamary, Y. H. (2025). The transformative power of artificial intelligence in entrepreneurship: Exploring AI's capabilities for the success of entrepreneurial ventures. *Future Business Journal, 11*(1), 104. Advance online publication. DOI: 10.1186/s43093-025-00533-7

Amankwah-Amoah, J., Khan, Z., Wood, G., & Knight, G. (2021). COVID-19 and digitalization: The great acceleration. *Journal of Business Research, 136*, 602–611. DOI: 10.1016/j.jbusres.2021.08.011 PMID: 34538980

Azoury, N., Subrahmanyam, S., & Sarkis, N. (2024). The influence of a data-driven culture on product development and organizational success through the use of business analytics. [JoWUA]. *Journal of Wireless Mobile Networks, Ubiquitous Computing and Dependable Applications, 15*(2), 123–134. DOI: 10.58346/JOWUA.2024.I2.009

Brynjolfsson, E., & McAfee, A. (2017). The business of artificial intelligence: What it can — and cannot — do for your organization. *Harvard Business Review.* https://hbr.org/2017/07/the-business-of-artificial-intelligence

Calo, R. (2017). Artificial intelligence policy: A primer and roadmap. *U.C. Davis Law Review, 51*(2), 399–435. https://lawreview.law.ucdavis.edu/archives/51/2/artificial-intelligence-policy-primer-and-roadmap

Cockburn, I. M., Henderson, R., & Stern, S. (2018). The impact of artificial intelligence on innovation: An exploratory analysis. In Agrawal, A., Gans, J., & Goldfarb, A. (Eds.), *The economics of artificial intelligence: An agenda* (pp. 115–146). University of Chicago Press., DOI: 10.7208/chicago/9780226613475.003.0004

Côté, S. (2014). Emotional intelligence in organizations. *Annual Review of Organizational Psychology and Organizational Behavior, 1*(1), 459–488. DOI: 10.1146/annurev-orgpsych-031413-091233

Cummings-Koether, M. J., Durner, F., Shyiramunda, T., & Huemmer, M. (2025). Cultural dimensions of artificial intelligence adoption: Empirical insights for Wave 1 from a multinational longitudinal pilot study. *arXiv*. https://arxiv.org/abs/2510.19743

Daugherty, P. R., & Wilson, H. J. (2022). *Radically human: How new technology is transforming business and shaping our future.* Harvard Business Review Press.

Dwivedi, Y. K., Hughes, L., Baabdullah, A. M., Ribeiro-Navarrete, S., Giannakis, M., Al-Debei, M. M., Dennehy, D., Metri, B., Buhalis, D., Cheung, C. M. K., Conboy, K., Doyle, R., Dubey, R., Dutot, V., Felix, R., Goyal, D. P., Gustafsson, A., Hinsch, C., Jebabli, I., & Wamba, S. F. (2022). Metaverse beyond the hype: Multidisciplinary perspectives on emerging challenges, opportunities, and agenda for research, practice, and policy. *International Journal of Information Management*, *66*, 102542. Advance online publication. DOI: 10.1016/j.ijinfomgt.2022.102542

Dwivedi, Y. K., Hughes, L., Ismagilova, E., Aarts, G., Coombs, C., Crick, T., Duan, Y., Dwivedi, R., Edwards, J., Eirug, A., Galanos, V., Ilavarasan, P. V., Janssen, M., Jones, P., Kar, A. K., Kizgin, H., Kronemann, B., Lal, B., Lucini, B., & Williams, M. D. (2021). Artificial intelligence (AI): Multidisciplinary perspectives on emerging challenges, opportunities, and agenda for research, practice, and policy. *International Journal of Information Management*, *57*, 101994. Advance online publication. DOI: 10.1016/j.ijinfomgt.2019.08.002

Floridi, L., & Cowls, J. (2019). A unified framework of five principles for AI in society. *Harvard Data Science Review*, *1*(1). Advance online publication. DOI: 10.1162/99608f92.8cd550d1

Fossen, F. M., McLemore, T., & Sorgner, A. (2024). Artificial intelligence and entrepreneurship. *Foundations and Trends® in Entrepreneurship, 20*(8), 781–904. https://doi.org/DOI: 10.1561/0300000130

Huang, M. H., & Rust, R. T. (2018). Artificial intelligence in service. *Journal of Service Research, 21*(2), 155–172. DOI: 10.1177/1094670517752459

Jarrahi, M. H. (2018). Artificial intelligence and the future of work: Human–AI symbiosis in organizational decision making. *Business Horizons*, *61*(4), 577–586. DOI: 10.1016/j.bushor.2018.03.007

Longoni, C., Bonezzi, A., & Morewedge, C. K. (2019). Resistance to medical artificial intelligence. *The Journal of Consumer Research*, *46*(4), 629–650. DOI: 10.1093/jcr/ucz013

Mariani, M. M., Pérez-Vega, R., & Wirtz, J. (2021). AI in marketing, consumer research and psychology: A systematic literature review and research agenda. *Psychology and Marketing*, *39*(4), 755–776. DOI: 10.1002/mar.21619

Mehrabi, N., Morstatter, F., Saxena, N., Lerman, K., & Galstyan, A. (2021). A survey on bias and fairness in machine learning. *ACM Computing Surveys*, *54*(6), 1–35. DOI: 10.1145/3457607

Nambisan, S., Wright, M., & Feldman, M. (2019). The digital transformation of innovation and entrepreneurship: Progress, challenges and key themes. *Research Policy*, *48*(8), 103773. DOI: 10.1016/j.respol.2019.03.018

Obschonka, M., & Audretsch, D. B. (2020). Artificial intelligence and big data in entrepreneurship: A new era has begun. *Small Business Economics*, *55*(3), 529–539. DOI: 10.1007/s11187-019-00202-4

Rai, A., Constantinides, P., & Sarker, S. (2019). Next-generation digital platforms: Toward human–AI hybrids. *Management Information Systems Quarterly*, *43*(1), iii–ix. https://wrap.warwick.ac.uk/id/eprint/113653/. DOI: 10.25300/MISQ/2019/431E0

Shrestha, Y. R., Ben-Menahem, S. M., & Von Krogh, G. (2019). Organizational decision-making structures in the age of artificial intelligence. *California Management Review*, *61*(4), 5–18. DOI: 10.1177/0008125619862257

Subrahmanyam, S. (2024a). AI integration in HR processes. In Kaur, J. (Ed.), *Embracing transhumanism and genomics in human resources management* (pp. 69–100). IGI Global Scientific Publishing., DOI: 10.4018/979-8-3693-7668-3.ch004

Subrahmanyam, S. (2024b). Role of data analytics and big data in operational decision-making and performance improvement. In Martínez-Falcó, J., Sánchez-García, E., Marco-Lajara, B., & Visser, G. (Eds.), *Convergence of technology and operations management in modern businesses* (pp. 105–140). IGI Global Scientific Publishing., DOI: 10.4018/979-8-3693-6200-6.ch003

Subrahmanyam, S. (2025a). Business, Digital Transformation, and Entrepreneurship. In Ordóñez de Pablos, P. (Ed.), *Shaping Green and Inclusive Economies Through Innovative Entrepreneurship* (pp. 1–34). IGI Global Scientific Publishing., DOI: 10.4018/979-8-3373-1097-8.ch001

Subrahmanyam, S. (2025b). Human Factors and Workforce Adaptation in Digital Transition. In Martínez-Falcó, J., Sánchez-García, E., & Marco-Lajara, B. (Eds.), *Navigating Digital Transformation Through Business Process Management* (pp. 95–126). IGI Global Scientific Publishing., DOI: 10.4018/979-8-3373-3336-6.ch005

Subrahmanyam, S. (2025c). Shaping Tomorrow's Talent Strategies with Predictive Workforce Intelligence. In Badouch, M., & Boutaounte, M. (Eds.), *Emerging Technologies for Recruitment Strategy and Practice* (pp. 211–236). IGI Global Scientific Publishing., DOI: 10.4018/979-8-3373-6516-9.ch008

Subrahmanyam, S., & El Samra, H. (2025). Startups and AI: Fostering Entrepreneurship in the MENA Region. In Azoury, N., & Yahchouchi, G. (Eds.), *AI in the Middle East for Growth and Business* (pp. 77–92). Palgrave Macmillan., DOI: 10.1007/978-3-031-75589-7_6

Topol, E. J. (2019). High-performance medicine: The convergence of human and artificial intelligence. *Nature Medicine*, *25*(1), 44–56. DOI: 10.1038/s41591-018-0300-7 PMID: 30617339

KEY TERMS AND DEFINITIONS

Algorithmic Bias: The unintended and systematic errors in AI outputs caused by biased training data or flawed algorithms, which can shape entrepreneurial decisions and outcomes if not properly managed.

Cognitive Augmentation: The process by which AI enhances human mental capacities, such as processing large datasets, identifying hidden patterns, or generating insights, thereby freeing entrepreneurs for higher-level strategic thinking.

Entrepreneurial Mindset: A set of cognitive and psychological traits—such as creativity, adaptability, resilience, and risk-taking—that enable entrepreneurs to identify opportunities and drive ventures forward, now augmented through AI tools.

Entrepreneurial Stress: The psychological strain experienced by entrepreneurs due to high uncertainty, workload, and decision-making pressure, which AI can help alleviate through automation, forecasting, and supportive analytics.

Ethical AI in Entrepreneurship: The responsible use of AI in entrepreneurial ventures, addressing fairness, transparency, accountability, and data privacy to ensure sustainable and trustworthy business practices.

Generative AI: A form of artificial intelligence capable of producing new content, ideas, designs, or strategies, offering entrepreneurs novel ways to incubate ventures, prototype products, and personalize customer engagement.

Human–AI Collaboration: The interactive partnership where entrepreneurs and AI systems work together to enhance decision-making, creativity, and business innovation, combining human intuition with machine intelligence.

Human–Machine Ecosystem: A reimagined entrepreneurial environment where humans and AI function as co-entrepreneurs, each contributing unique strengths to drive innovation, adaptability, and value creation in business ecosystems.

Hybrid Innovation: A collaborative model of creativity where human imagination and emotional intelligence merge with AI's analytical precision and computational capabilities to generate novel business solutions.

Trust in AI: The psychological state where entrepreneurs are willing to rely on AI systems for support in decision-making, balancing confidence in technology with awareness of its limitations and biases.

Chapter 8
Human-AI Collaboration in Entrepreneurship:
Building Cognitive Resilience for Smarter Decision Making

Kamini Pareek
http://orcid.org/0009-0003-3994-7285
Poornima University, Jaipur, India

Ayesha Farooqi
http://orcid.org/0009-0000-4556-4211
Poornima University, Jaipur, India

Nikhil Kumar Goyal
http://orcid.org/0009-0007-4532-8033
Poornima University, Jaipur, India

ABSTRACT

Introducing Artificial Intelligence (AI) within the entrepreneurship industry is changing the decision-making, problem-solving, and creating innovations processes. This chapter addresses the changing environment of Human-AI collaboration, and how the use of intelligent systems can contribute to cognitive resilience and allow more intelligent and data-driven decision-making among entrepreneurs. In times of challenges and growing unpredictability and complexity in the business, AI becomes a strategic ally capable of enhancing human intelligence to help entrepreneurs to process extensive information, predict the future, and minimize risks more efficiently. Nevertheless, the potentials of this collaboration do not imply the avoidance of human intuition but rather empowering it with the help of lifelong learning, flexibility, and contemplation. Cognitive, emotional, and strategic aspects of Human-AI

DOI: 10.4018/979-8-2600-1353-3.ch008

engagement focus within this chapter allow developing a framework of developing strong entrepreneurial mindsets that would be able to use AI technologies in an ethical and effective way.

1: INTRODUCTION

1.1 Changing Landscape of Entrepreneurship in the AI Era

The current business environment has gone through a radical change because of the advent of artificial intelligence (AI) and its associated technologies. In contrast to the business world that did not rely mainly on human intuitions and experience in the past when making decisions, the current entrepreneurs are in a world that is well surrounded with data and algorithms. With AI technologies, predictive analytics to natural language processing, it is possible to analyze the markets, predict trends and opportunities with precision never seen before. This move has resulted in a new definition of entrepreneurial intelligence an intelligence balance between human creativity and empathy with computational power and efficiency of computers (Vecchiarini & Somià, 2023).

AI-based tools are becoming the tools of entrepreneurs to perform the tasks such as developing a product, making financial forecasts, and engaging a consumer. This rising reliance on AI does not lessen the strength of human capabilities, on the contrary, it supplements them and relocates thinking effort with routine mental tasks, permitting the entrepreneur to concentrate on creativity, emotional intelligence, and bubbles. This is why the fusion of human ingenuity and machine intelligence is not merely one of the technological innovation levels - it is the very beginning of a new level of thinking collaboration which is already in progress of being put into place to alter the very common sense of entrepreneurship (Primario et al., 2024).

1.2 Learning the Concept of Cognitive Resilience

Cognitive resilience is characterized as the ability of the individuals to be in a position to adjust, recuperate and make sound decisions under the uncertainty or stress. It is a key aspect in the world of entrepreneurship as the business environment is a volatile one and a person has to be capable of learning and evolving. In case it is coupled with AI, cognitive resilience will gain a new dimension. The patterns of stress can be detected, and the behavioral information can present AI systems with the opportunities to make specific suggestions, which will enable an entrepreneur to be focused and not stressed in making the much-needed decisions.

Figure 1. Representation of cognitive resilience mechanisms in the aging brain

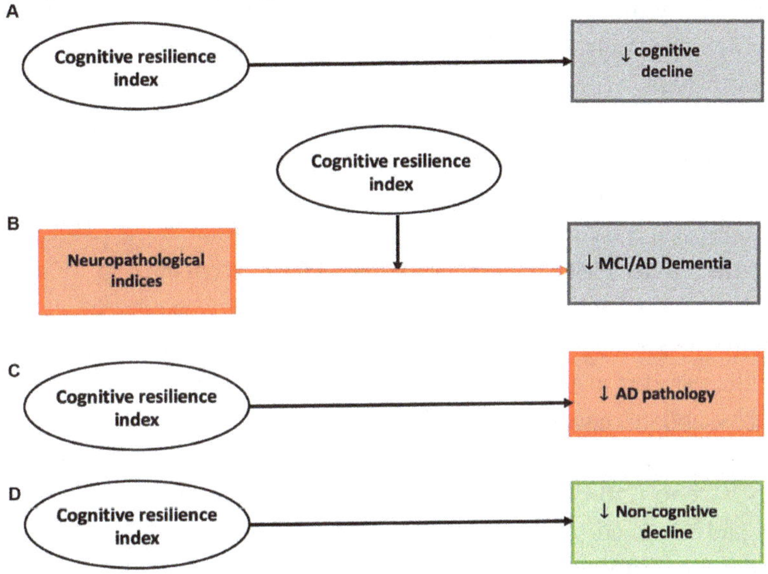

The combination of the human mind and AI intelligence creates a hybrid resilience, where people introduce their instincts of creativity, empathetic, and moral rationale, and AI introduce their instinct of speed, accuracy, and depth. Such co-operation promotes the flexibility of the mental aspect of an entrepreneur, which can react more adequately to any form of interference in the market or other tools such as supply chain, or technology failure. Therefore, cognitive resilience in an AI future is not primarily a matter of emotional stability but adaptability on a strategic level that is upheld through intelligent systems (Su & Liu, 2023).

1.3 Automation to Collaboration AI Role Evolution

When AI first entered the world in entrepreneurship, it was mainly understood as the means of automation - doing things much cheaper and easier than a human being. Despite this, the role of AI technologies began to increase as they moved beyond automation to strategic partnership. Business owners are now seeking AI systems as collaborators in the generation of their ideas, the management of innovations, and even to strategize. One can simulate the market responses, the attitude of customers and propose alternations to the design using the machine learning algorithms, and analyze these conditions with the use of creativity and intuition by entrepreneurs.

Such a working relationship implies the paradigm shift toward thinking of human-versus-machine to human-with-machine. Instead of treating AI as the reason to stop being an autonomous entrepreneur, now it is perceived as a co-creator, the intelligent ally that could provide human judgment with an objective analysis of information. The entrepreneurs of the new generation should then be trained to live and work with AI, acquire both digital literacy and ethical consciousness in addition to business culture. It is not aimed at removing human decision-making but improving it, in cases of a symbiotic relationship, it will be a blend of the finest of both mental worlds (Weng et al., 2022).

1.4 Promise and Paradox of Human–AI Partnership

Although the Human -AI collaboration can be described as a great innovation potential, the paradox also exists. AI, on the one hand, makes work more efficient, reduces risks, and increases the potential of the human factor; on the other, it is connected with difficulties in such areas as dependency, trust, ethical decision-making. Strategists have to find the balance between the delegation of decision-making to machines and the need to keep accountable when the generation of outcomes is influenced by algorithms.

Figure 2. Benefits of collaboration between human and AI

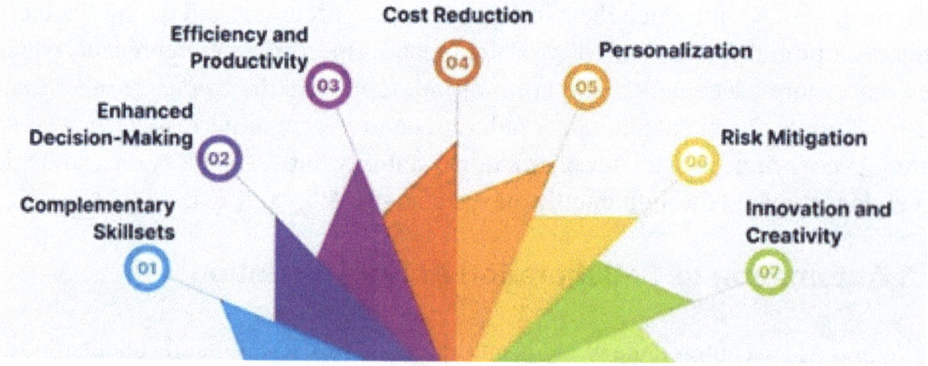

What can be used to resolve such predicaments is development of what researchers refer to as cognitive complementarity a balanced cognitive division of labor between human beings and AI systems. Human beings are supposed to think critically, learn morally and creatively but systems of AI cannot do anything but process data and identify patterns. They are able to pool together to form a cognitively strong system that is capable of fostering smarter and more ethical entrepreneurship. As this aspect dictates, the use of AI in business is not just a technological fad; but there is a cognitive revolution, that is, one that is redefining the manner in which an idea is being formulated and decisions are being made and businesses sustain existence in the digital age (Eltanahy et al., 2020).

2: COGNITIVE FOUNDATIONS OF HUMAN–AI INTERACTION IN ENTREPRENEURSHIP

2.1 Nature of Human Cognition in Entrepreneurial Decision-Making

The decision-making process of an entrepreneur is always complicated because it is intuitively, experience-based, and creative. Human cognition enables business people to make meaning to uncertain information, clearer opportunities, and imagine creativity in situations where there is ambiguity. Humans have emotional intelligence and contextual awareness, unlike machines, and that is what allows them to judge adaptively even without all the information. Cognitive flexibility also allows the entrepreneurs to alternative between divergent and convergent thinking processes, which encourage the exploration of new ideas and implementation of available strategies (Colombo & Piva, 2020).

Nonetheless, such a human mental faculty is limited in part by such shortcomings as the flaws of thinking and emotions as well as information saturation. When under pressure, entrepreneurs tend to make overconfidence errors, anchoring bias, confirmation bias, and so forth. Such psychological biases may cause a change in judgment and a lack of strategic clarity. AI systems - when carefully designed - might compensate for such cognitive weaknesses by providing objective analysis of data as well as a system for probabilistic analysis. Human intuition and machine accuracy combined in this way, therefore, preconditions one of the new cognitive paradigms in entrepreneurship the paradigm that raises the accuracy of decisions but does not suppress creativity.

2.2 Machine Cognition and Artificial Intelligence: A Supplement of Human Thinking

Artificial intelligence is developed based on the concept of machine intelligence, i.e. the computational capacities to perceive, learn, reason and make predictions based on a large amount of data. Machine cognition in entrepreneurship is a complement to the human thinking by demonstrating the hidden patterns and relations that can not be seen using human means. AI-based systems have the ability to work with huge amounts of data concerning consumer behaviors, market trends, monetary indicators and as such, hopefully give entrepreneurs the real-time data to act strategically (Mico & Cungu, 2023).

Machines do not experience fatigue, emotional diversion or subjective interpretation as do human beings. They are the best cognitive partners to use in an environment of data-intensive decisions since they are always consistent and can be scaled. Yet, machine cognition lacks empathy, lack of moral understanding, it cannot have that glimmer that it's the human source of innovation. Thus, the best way is cognitive synergy, that is, the interpretative intensity of the human mind and the computer-driven computational intensity. When entrepreneurs learn to combine these complementary intelligences, it can be possible to develop a robust decision framework, which happens to be analytical, adaptive and visionary at the same time (Roumelliotis & Tselikas, 2023).

2.3 Cognitive Synergy: A combination of Human Intuition and AI Rationality

The smooth process of uniting human thinking and AI-based reasoning is known as cognitive synergy and improves the quality of the decision made. This synergy produces a creative feedback in the entrepreneurial framework as humans offer contextual data and creative assumptions, and AI systems either confirm this data, improve it, or disapprove it through empirical data. This kind of dynamic interaction helps business people in the field of creating opportunity and threats in a more efficient manner in a manner that encourages resilience in the unpredictable business circumstances (Cribben & Zeinali, 2023).

Specifically, AI can recreate market forces, foresee what can rock the market, and the businessperson collects it to make flexible business strategies that are informed by intuitive and long-term sight. There is also cognitive synergy in the reflection of decision-making whereby the AI suggestions will be reviewed critically by the human beings before being implemented. It is not about giving over to machines and instead about leverage AI as a cognitive reflection and thus helps to identify blind spots and create a more aware mind. It is a symbiotic relationship that breeds a smarter decision-making ecosystem one in which human and machine intelligence mutually depends on each other to learn.

2.4 Cognitive Overload and AI Implication in the Bookshelf of Mental Strain

Cognitive overload on the modern entrepreneur is an increased amount of information, skillet and the unnecessary flow of new developments in the market and decision-making. Combining or handling various activities like financing, operations, innovation and marketing at the same time usually results in psychological exhaustion, lack of creativity and making optimal decisions. Intelligent recommendation systems can help to reduce this load by means of automating data analysis, prioritizing information, and offering a decision support with the use of artificial intelligence technologies (BaiDoo-Anu & Anash, 2023).

Indicatively, market reports can be summarized using natural language processing tools, and business performance summarized using AI-based dashboards in formats easy to understand. This mental offloading will enable the entrepreneurs to spend mental resources on strategic thinking and innovation as opposed to daily analysis. Moreover, AI can also serve as a reflection partner, which will in addition to decreasing cognitive load will also make the mind mindful by providing feedback on the decision habits and the tendency of behaviour. Entrepreneurs can maintain cognitive equilibrium with the aid of such help and be in a stronger position to address complex entrepreneurial issues that contain strength and clarity (Brailas, 2024).

3: BUILDING COGNITIVE RESILIENCE THROUGH HUMAN–AI COLLABORATION

3.1 The Concept of Cognitive Resilience in Entrepreneurship

Cognitive resilience can be interpreted as the ability of the mind to overcome adversities, adapt to ambiguity, and go on continuing to perform well under pressureful situations. This resilience is not an option to an entrepreneur but is a necessity. Any entrepreneurial road is characterized by uncertainty be it the volatility of the market, risk of financial institution, or the failure of innovation. Differentiation between successful and unsuccessful entrepreneurs lies in the capacity to stand calmly regardless of the situation, to make rational analysis, and quality decisions during adversity.

AI has become an important partner in the development of this type of resilience. AI systems can also help entrepreneurs deal with stress, uncertainty, and risk better by offering predictive knowledge, emotional support by conversational agents, and real-time risk analysis. To take an example, predictive models could explain that the supply chain will be disrupted or the customer would have churned, and the entrepreneur would prepare a response to it. Stress is not killed by AI but rather it alters the way it is processed by entrepreneurs, through the ability to turn uncertainty and confusion into clarity with the help of the data-driven insights provided. It is a supportive role that can assist business people in retaining mental energy, improvement of focus and rapid recovery following business failures (McCaffrey & Spector, 2018).

3.2 Continuous Cognitive Reinforcement and Adaptive Learning

A cognitive resilience is mainly nurtured in a culture where learning and adaptation are the continuous processes. In processing this flexibility, AI systems enhance it by acting as smart learning counterparts. AI provides business leaders with data insights, predictive models, and feedback mechanisms that empower them to define the outcomes of their decisions and the actions they are required to take to improve on the same. Considering the case in point, it is important to note that machine learning algorithms can study historical business behavior, map efforts of success and failure, and provide business solutions on upcoming projects (Lake et al., 2017).

It is with this continually changing interaction that what we can perhaps refer to as adaptive cognition- an activity through which business persons are developing their judgment capacities at the moment- occurs. The fallacy feedback between human experience and the AI analysis process fosters resilience via changing every failure into a learning experience. In addition, AI can be used to individualize learning, considering whatever an entrepreneur thinks and how much he/she takes risks and how he/she reacts to his/her situation. This personalization guarantees that an entrepreneur does not get sand-blasted with information on the internet but gets informed with a curated context-relevant information that increases levels of learning as well as confidence. With time, this adaptive reinforcement fosters the development of the growth mentality - the building block of cognitive resistance in the practice of entrepreneurship (Hollan et al., 2000).

3.3 Stress Work and Stress Management with the help of AI

Emotional regulation is of great significance in mental fortitude. Market reaction, funding issues, or competition can cause emotional turbulence among entrepreneurs since they are never sure of how they will react. Stress may lower the level of creativity and be clouded by stress making people burnt out when left unmanaged. In this case, AI technologies will help with the solutions that are used to track emotional health and support in real-time. The case of AI-driven mental health apps explains that voice tones, or facial expressions, or typing behaviors can be analysed to find out the expression of any symptoms of stress or exhaustion. These systems in turn propose mindfulness meditation, rest or adaptive processes which improve focus and mental stability.

Also, AI-based chatbots and digital coaches can be used to offer cognitive behavioral therapies to help entrepreneurs respond constructively to their negative feelings. They provide a most non judgmental escape and a safe launching point to self scrutiny and emotional release, an option that most businessmen lack in an employment scenario where stress is the order of the day. AI enhances resilience indirectly with the help of emotional balance, which allows the entrepreneur to be long-term motivated and creative. This is not only resulting in making better stress management but also better cognitive flexibility which is a key factor in making rational and innovative decisions despite the stressing circumstances (Graesser et al., 2018).

3.4 Risk and Artificial Intelligence Conscientiousness to Decision Making: AI-Augmented Environments

The selfcience to make a decision amidst the unpredictable is also an issue that is addressed by cognitive resilience. AI maximizes this belief by providing business owners with evidence-based information that makes intuition qualified and reliability of uncertainty low. AI-based simulations and simulations with predictive analytics can assist an entrepreneur in determining the potential outcomes of the situation and making crucial decisions. This critical vision makes them risk taking so that they can proceed with new ventures that they would have considered too risky (Deng & Yu., 2023).

As an example, AI can process financial information, customer needs, and competitive plans to determine the potential success of a new product release. Enlightened with such information, entrepreneurs are able to make calculated risks with more confidence. Notably, the human factor is always in focus, AI should serve as an informational, but not deciding power. Entrepreneurs are able to develop a positive and strong mindset by balancing confidence that has been established by data with human intuition thus being able to endure both good and bad events in a cool manner. The entrepreneur is no longer afraid of uncertainty; he or she embraces it as an incentive to explore and be creative with the assistance of the cognitive safety net of AI (Xia et al., 2022).

4: HUMAN–AI CO-CREATION AND INNOVATIVE THINKING IN ENTREPRENEURIAL CONTEXTS

4.1 The Emergence of Co-Creation in the Digital Entrepreneurial Era

The combination of human creativity and artificial intelligence has given birth to the emergence of co-creation, a process of human and machine brainstorming to create ideas, solutions, and innovations. Previously, entrepreneurial creativity was understood as a purely human activity, which is motivated by imagination, intuition, and emotional intelligence. Nonetheless, development of AI tools generative design, natural language processors, predictive modeling, etc have transformed the way innovation occurs. Entrepreneurs no longer view AI as a tool of analysis, but rather as a creative collaborative resource in brainstorming, ideation, and experimentation.

This paradigm shift creates the possibility of democratizing innovation and entrepreneurs with different levels of expertise can get access to advanced tools of designing, simulation, and prototyping. As an example, AI-powered systems can immediately create images of product ideas, refine products according to customer feedback and find solutions to these products, basing them on real-time data. These co-creation relationships give rise to a perpetual cycle of innovation - AI optimizes what the entrepreneur envisions, and the entrepreneur restyles what AI creates. Creativity is accelerated through the synergy which enables startups to transition between ideation and implementation within an amazing speed and accuracy (Li et al., 2024).

In addition, this team work diminishes stagnation of creativity. Cognitive blockers are fixation or tunnel vision; this has a tendency to enable the entrepreneur to think in a single direction, and this means that they become restricted to thinking in a single direction. AI interferes with the placement of new patterns, unusual links or unusual combinations of designs that awaken the imagination of humans. Therefore, the concept of co-creation turns not only into an efficiency process but also cognitive growth, as it challenges the boundaries of thinking that the entrepreneurs had before.

4.2 Innovation Processes of Human Intuition and Machine Intelligence

Intuition/Intelligence Sensitiveness/Delicateness central entrepreneurial innovation is at the center of innovation. Human intuition develops emotional depth, empathy and situational consciousness where artificial intelligence gives information founded on facts and precision of calculations. Their synergistic combination is able to create collaborative intelligence that is able to transform entrepreneurial innovation. As an illustration, during the engagement of new product or service designing, AI can analyze millions of reviews left by the customers, determine new demands, and propose a design change that will give an even greater satisfaction to the customers. On her part, the entrepreneur derives such enlightenment in empathy as innovation to be consistent with human value and beauty.

Figure 3. Illustration of innovation processes bridging human intuition and machine intelligence

This collision is rather evident in the following fields as fashion tech, healthcare start up or the digital creation of content through which both analytical anomie and emotional appeal matter. The collaboration of humans and AI helps businesspersons to make assumptions quicker, operate a simulation, and manipulate innovative approaches. It transforms intuition into intelligent making decisions instead of guessing. The creative compass is the human mind, which is controlled by experience and imagination, and AI is the engine that will analyze and substantiate that creativity (Luan et al., 2024).

In addition, this collaboration can be used to cope with cognitive exhaustion that may be caused by innovation overload. In case AI works on complicated computations and data synthesis, entrepreneurs have an opportunity to utilize their brain power to the conceptualization and foresight. This separation of cognition in labor improves the overall creativity productivity and at the same time innovates have been human-centered, moral and socially relevant (Guo & Wang, 2024).

4.3 AI as an impetus behind Design Thinking and Prototyping

The phenomenon of design thinking, which also involves empathy, ideation, prototyping, or testing, has always been a vital part of entrepreneurship. This approach has been given a new dimension with the introduction of AI. AI is able to create prototypes quickly, simulate user interaction, as well as forecast user response using behavioral data. Entrepreneurship is able to visualize ideas prior to investing a lot of resources, and this means that there is less design risk and a faster turnaround to market.

As an example, artificial intelligence such as a generative design application or a creativity platform based on natural languages can explore thousands of design options in just a few minutes. These systems propose the best solutions which will satisfy the user expectations as well as environmental and economic limitations. Consequently, entrepreneurs are in a position to make sustainable, efficient and user friendly design decisions (Epstein et al., 2023).

Moreover, AI improves the empathic aspect of the design thinking. When sentiment analysis is used to evaluate user emotions, AI systems can give information on how consumers can think of a product or service. The entrepreneurs can incorporate them as part of the design process and can produce something that appeals to both the functional and emotional levels. As such AI is not only a technological device, but it is also an empathetic companion, a less robotic innovation, the kind that can transform the inherent creativity that human beings hold into a feasible, marketable product.

4.4 Dynamics of Human -AI Creativity: Problems and Opportunities

On the one hand, the unity of creativity of people and machine has enormous potential that may be used, however, it is associated with new issues. One of their major problems is the over-reliance on the algorithmic suggestions, unintentionally, and perniciously, the insistence of which weakens creativity. Entrepreneurs might be inclined to be biased in their attempts to use AI outputs that might be based on primarily the patterns of data available, rather than the actual innovations. This makes creative independence significant in ensuring that AI becomes a companion, as opposed to a dictator in the innovation process.

Moreover, there is the issue of intellectual property and authorship issues in the work of co-creations. In a product design or song where an AI system has been integrated or in a marketing concept, ownership and originality have become an issue. It is in such moral aspects that a sound regulatory framework is required that will dictate the creative contribution process by humans and machines (Radford et al., 2018).

The opportunities are transformative inasmuch as they exist. When leveraged to its advantage, the Human-AI co-creation may enable entrepreneurs to achieve the level of creativity, velocity and personalization never witnessed previously. Through the aid of AI, they can test on the concepts they could not previously conceive due to the capacity of resources or thoughts. Human intuition and AI analytical skills can assist an entrepreneur in not only coming up with technologically better solutions, but creating emotionally resonant and socially feasible solutions. The prospect position of entrepreneurship, in consequence, is the possibility of the ones to acquire this interactivity, to make AI more of a helper in the creation process and less of an automation machine.

5: DECISION INTELLIGENCE AND STRATEGIC FORESIGHT OF HUMAN AI ENTREPRENEURIAL SYSTEMS

5.1 Interpreting Decision Intelligence in the Entrepreneurship Environment

A blend of data science, behavioral psychology, and artificial intelligence to make smarter and livelier decisions is decision intelligence. Not only does decision intelligence provide to the entrepreneurs with automation of choices, but the quality of choices made, and situational awareness of every choice made. The traditional decision-making models will no longer be effective in unpredictable and information-saturated environment that is characteristic of a rapidly changing business environment. Entrepreneurs require the systems that could exploit the fine details in the realities and carve opportunities and replicate the future - things that AI-enhanced decision making systems could do with more recent capabilities and aspirations to achieve.

AI-driven decision intelligence systems are used to combine information in real-time, predictive analytics, and human intelligence to create the entire picture of the business problems. As an example, when an entrepreneur prefers to enter a new market, AI can potentially gather sentiments of customers, competitor strategies and macroeconomic forces and offer evidence-based recommendations. In his or her turn, the human entrepreneur puts the contextual knowledge into the game, considering the cultural peculiarities, ethical considerations, and emotional appeal. This integration ensures that decision making process can be expedien and more deliberated and less susceptible to contingencies (Kelly et al., 2023).

The real strength in decision intelligence is that it can change reactive entrepreneurs into active strategists. Rather than reacting to market shifts once they take place, the entrepreneurs are able to foresee the disruptions and adjust their business models to them. This is why decision intelligence is viewed as a compass by which the strategic actions and operational actions are guided, and AI and human foresight are intertwined with each other.

5.2 The Predictive and Prescriptive Analytics and their use in Strategic Foresight

Two of the fundamental pillars of AI based strategic foresight are predictive and prescriptive analytics. Predictive analytics can assist entrepreneurs in knowing what is expected to occur based on analyzing past data and determining a trend or an anomaly. Prescriptive analytics takes it one step further- it advises on certain measures to take towards attaining desired results. The combination of these analytical methods into a single potent decision-support ecosystem generates a transformation of uncertainty to an intelligent chance (Alpaydin, 2021).

To give an example, an AI-based forecasting tool will forecast consumer demand fluctuations or changes in raw material prices, and, as a result, the entrepreneurs will be able to modify the production schedule and prices based on the forecasts they will make.

Nonetheless, the various advantages of predictive and prescriptive analytics are not only in the correctness of data but the transparency of their meaning as well. An entrepreneur should know the rationale behind a model suggesting a specific decision. Therefore, the principles of explainable AI (XAI) are necessary to ensure facts and confidence. When the entrepreneurs understand the reasoning behind the predictions of AI, they would be able to incorporate human intuition more efficiently, which would result in the creation of a synergistic decision-making process based on logic and intuition. Entrepreneurs can also make calculated risks as the interpretability provides them with a confident ability to convert foresight into a strategic advantage (Kelleher, 2019).

5.3 The Misfit between Human Judgment and AI-Based Decision Systems

Even though AI has the ability to process data at a way no human would be able to, humans will always be valuable in making decisions related to the business. The intelligence of AI does not possess the ethics, compassion, and situational awareness that constitute the core of human thinking. Thus, a hybrid intelligence framework that can be developed by combining human judgments with AI-enabled decision systems can be formed in which machines handle the quantitative aspects of a problem, and humans address its qualitative aspects.

The real world interpretation of this is that an entrepreneur should not leave the decision-making authority to machines but can treat AI as an ally in thinking and confirmation. Indicatively, AI can propose that a line of one product be scrapped because of low profitability. However, the entrepreneur may also see merits of having it in the short run, in terms of brand recognition, or stock alliances. This kind of human intervention avoids algorithmic rigidity, and ensures that decisions are made according to long term vision and not short term measures (Zou et al., 2009).

Furthermore, the human control contributes to the protection of the algorithmic bias and ethical blinds. Through bias or biased input, artificial intelligence, in fact, can enhance disparities or generate biased advice. Such a synthesized combination of human and artificial cognition is what decision intelligence is all about, an ecosystem with data, ethics and intuition coming together in an effort to influence innovation.

5.4 Future-Oriented Thinking and the future of AI in Scenario Planning

Entrepreneurship is driven by the power of anticipation which involves strategic planning of and foresight of several potential scenarios. The use of AI has reshaped scenario planning which was a manual and imaginative task. AI systems (with advanced simulations and probabilistic modeling) are able to generate thousands of possible futures as variables in the previous variables may change (e.g. market trends, geopolitical shifts, or technological disruptions). This is where entrepreneurs can assess in which scenarios their business models would work best (under different hypothetical conditions).

Such progressive mentality allows an entrepreneur to create dynamic plans that they will not collapse due to unforeseen alterations in the external circumstances. As an example, AI will be able to model the potential effect of climate policies on global logistics, enabling a startup to prepare more environmentally friendly supply chain designs. Likewise, AI will be able to forecast the trend of consumer behavior in the coming decade, enabling businesspeople to synchronize their innovation pipelines and emerging preferences (Li, 2017).

In addition to analytics, AI can help people be more creative in their scenario planning because it can present options that are counterintuitive, i.e., options that the human can conceal under human cognitive biases or limited imagination. Such AI generated surprises can promote the entrepreneur to widen the mindset and develop strategic agility. This interaction between the human imagination and the AI simulation is what then advances to dynamic foresight by the entrepreneurs continuously learning, adapting and evolving on the basis of predictive understanding.

Essentially, AI has turned foresight into an interactive process, which is not a static prediction activity. Entrepreneurs can no longer conceive the future as a thing to be foreseeable but as a thing to be co-created - through dialogic (iterative) interaction between human vision and machine computation. It is the beginning of a new step in the history of decision intelligence: a human-informed, algorithm-supported collaboration founded on the need to develop resilient future-oriented businesses.

6: CULTIVATING THE ENTREPRENEURIAL MINDSET FOR HUMAN–AI SYNERGY

6.1 The Evolution of the Entrepreneurial Mindset in the Age of AI

The entrepreneurial attitude has always been linked to creativity, flexibility, and taking risks. Nevertheless, as AI is introduced to the fields of entrepreneurship, there is a need to redefine what such an attitude will imply. The creativity of a entrepreneur and strategic foresight are no longer a key to success in the digital age but it is as well how the entrepreneur can operate with smart systems. The new entrepreneur should learn technological empathy, the ability to value, read, and cooperate with AI tools and not to lose human intuition and moral judgment.

This new way of thinking has been described as open to experimenting and valuing data-driven thinking. Entrepreneurs have to know how to be precise in their analytical and imaginative in their exploration. Such collaboration forms a two-way way of thinking-human sensitivity and machine rationality which improves the decisions and innovations at the same time (Susi & Ziemke, 2001).

In addition, continuous learning is another entrepreneurial characteristic of the AI era. The technology changes fast, and the entrepreneurs who are able to apply the concept of lifelong learning can be more prepared to incorporate AI innovations in their business. Therefore, entrepreneurial thinking in the modern context requires developing a combination of cognitive acuity, affective intelligence, and technological literacy the hybrid skill, which enables people to succeed in a complex AI-enhanced world.

6.2 Emotional Intelligence and Moral Sensibility of Human-AI Collaboration

Although AI adds the element of analysis, emotional intelligence (EI) is the core of successful leadership and entrepreneurship. EI is the ability to be empathetic, self-aware, and interpersonally sensitive, and AI, in spite of all its sophistication, cannot mimic it. High emotional intelligent entrepreneurs are able to operate their team, have better relations with their clients and make more human orientated decisions despite the recommendations provided by AI.

With adaptive intelligence, emotional intelligence will facilitate making sure that human values are central in a collaborative ecosystem where AI has to engage in data-driven tasks. The entrepreneurs have to understand AI insights in terms of ethical and emotional prism (how judgments influence people, communities, and stakeholders). As an example, an artificial intelligence-based job search application can suggest people according to productivity indicators, whereas an emotionally intelligent entrepreneur will apply diversity, inclusiveness and team bond. This moral decency does not allow technology to eclipse the human essence of being an entrepreneur. Entrepreneurs establish organizational cultures to appreciate both human beings and technological development when both emotional and ethical factors are combined with technical expertise. This ensures that such cultures build resilience, creativity, and moralism in the AI-driven business world.

6.3 The Growth Mindset: Change in AI-Driven Change

Our world is subject to a change in technology rapidly, and the growth mindset, the idea that any ability can be built through working on it, through learning and resilience, is important. The field of AI technologies constantly develops, and those entrepreneurs who are not ready to accept change run a risk of being obsolete. It is the development of a growth mentality that enables entrepreneurs to view AI as not a threat, but as a cognitive and professional development opportunity.

Growth entrepreneurs perceive AI failures or errors as learning experiences, and not as discouraging events. As an illustration, when an AI system makes incorrect forecasts, a resilient entrepreneur looks into the root cause known as a problem of data or models rather than discarding the technology completely. Such adaptive approach promotes the iterative enhancement, the smarter AI incorporation, and the enhancement of the output of the decision.

More so, an attitude of growth stimulates interdisciplinary learning. The entrepreneurs who have reached the highest level of success in the AI era will be those who work across fields: getting a combination of technical knowledge with a business strategy, psychology, and design thinking. They are continuously researching on ways that AI can be employed to address emerging issues or improve customer experience. This form of attitude is a source of innovation, and long term sustainability in the sense that it brings the flexibility in the very fabric of entrepreneurship.

6.4 Development of Learning and Collaborative Organisations

Entrepreneurship spirit is not an individualistic process but must be incorporated into the culture of the organization. During the period of artificial intelligence (AI) era, the companies must forego the hierarchical hierarchy of command and adopt a participatory learning strategy where both human and AIs jointly develop an innovation. It involves the idea of constructing the notion of transparency, endorsing experimentation, and granting employees an imaginative mindset not to fear AI-based tools (Sharkey, 2016).

In this change leaders should play-important role. They are supposed to turn into the facilitators of collaboration between a man and smart systems ensuring that technology implementation does not harm the team interactions but enhances them. Provision of regular training, promotion of digital literacy, as well as stimulation of curiosity are among the mechanisms that would ensure such environment where AI becomes the extension of human capability.

Also, the institutions, which focus on the group learning, are more flexible. The less information is shared throughout the departments due to the wisdom generated by AI engines, the more discerning and holistic decision making can be made. The organization is an organism learning process, and possesses the ability of sensitizing changes in the environment, and adjusting its strategies quickly. This wisdom of the crowd is the force driving resilient and futuristic businesses to trust human genius and analytical power of the artificial intelligence.

In conclusion, the enterprise attitude of the human-AI synergy is not only the that technology experience which should be refined, but the development of a new attitude to take learning, empathy, flexibility and cooperation. Such an attitude that will be internalized by entrepreneurs will not only render them successful in the age of AI but will be at the vanguard of creating a just and intelligent future of the entrepreneurship world.

7: FUTURE DIRECTIONS AND EMERGING PARADIGMS IN HUMAN–AI ENTREPRENEURSHIP

7.1 The Future Landscape of Human–AI Synergy in Entrepreneurship

The future of entrepreneurship will be significantly influenced by the fact that the human ingenuity and artificial intelligence are getting more and more converged. With AI systems turning beyond their current state of assistants to potentially strategic partnerships, the idea generating processes of the entrepreneurship, its market research, risk-taking process, and innovations will also change. Near-future entrepreneurs will not merely utilise AI; they will co-create with AI and there will be a constant feedback between human intuition and machine intelligence.

This change will change to what can be called Cognitive Symbiotic Entrepreneurship - the paradigm when AI serves as an extension, not as a substitute, of human cognition. Entrepreneurs use AI in this model to make predictions about consumer behavior and calculate simulations of market conditions, use of the enormous amounts of data available to them, therefore attractive their assumptions are based on emotional intelligence, moral thought and creative guidance, which are formed by human knowledge and experience. The result is joint-intelligence system, which integrates the finest in both worlds of speed and sensitivity, precision and purpose.

Furthermore, AI technologies will be democratized, which will allow even minor businessmen and startup to use sophisticated analytics and automation. With increased availability of AI tools at lower prices, the innovation barriers will reduce tremendously. The trend will strengthen inclusivity of the entrepreneur people of all backgrounds and places leading to global inclusivity and also resulting into socio-economic balance due to involvement in technology. Simply put, there will not be a competition between humans and AI in the future because entrepreneurship will be based on cooperation that can utilize the complementary advantages available to both sides.

7.2 Business Innovations that Transform the Decision-Making of an entrepreneur

In addition to conventional AI systems, it is also worth remembering that a surge of emerging technologies, including quantum computing, blockchain, and extended reality (XR), will transform the entrepreneurial activity. Through quantum computing, there will be the ability to run complex financial models, risk models, supply chain optimization on the super-fast speeds, which are currently consuming resources and time so much. The business people who own quantum-enhanced artificial intelligence systems will be able to play around with business situations of all kinds simultaneously which will allow them to make decisions far quicker, and make them in an informed manner.

The sphere of blockchain technology will continue to revolutionize the concept of trust in the ecosystem of the business and transparency. Combining blockchain and AI together, entrepreneurs will be able to develop autonomous systems of trust, or networks in which they are able to have contracts, payments, and data validation being used in an automatic manner. This synergy does not only guarantee efficiency in operations but also ethical accountability since all transactions are stored in a secure and audit-able manner.

In the meantime, customer interaction, promotion and create products will be transformed by extended reality (AR/VR/MR). Business people will also engage in collaborations with AI-driven virtual environments to see the business idea, model user experiences, and test innovations immersively. A combination of these technologies will result in what is being referred to by some researchers as the Entrepreneurial Metaverse; A digital ecosystem where creativity, Data and collaboration come together in real time. A combination of these innovations points to the changing of the future entrepreneurial environment towards the more immersive, decentralized, and intelligent direction.

7.3 The Rise of Cognitive Digital Twins in Entrepreneurship

The creation of cognitive digital twins, virtual representations of entrepreneurs or businesses that constantly learn and develop based on real-world information, is one of the most interesting directions of AI-driven entrepreneurship. These online sources have the ability to model the outcomes of the decisions, predict the possible risks and trial the strategies before being introduced into the actual market. To entrepreneurs, the cognitive twins make recommendations, or advice, based on their behavior, and then offer personal advice, based on their objectives and interests.

As an example, a startup founder could ask his or her digital twin about the viability of launching a new product, and be presented with data-driven information that relies on the trends of the consumer population, resource distribution, and past success trends. According to the theory, more over time, the more the digital twin learns, big data, and generalizes based on small data, the closer it resembles the way the entrepreneur thinks, although with the power of computational intelligence that is represented by AI.

At the organizational level, its cognitive twins of companies can study operations, customer responses, and variations in the market in real-time and make predictive choices. This type of technology can lower the degree of uncertainty and improve the strategic agility of the business enabling it to quickly shift its focus towards volatile markets. Finally, cognitive digital twins are a new paradigm of proactive entrepreneurship, i.e. taking action based on foresight instead of reaction.

7.4 International and Social Implications of the Human-AI Entrepreneurship

The impact of AI-based entrepreneurship on the global and societal scale already will increase as the latter grows in scale. On the one hand, AI is a democratized chance because it gives individuals access to the might of decision-making tools, but on the other hand, AI raises the issues relating to inequality, bias, and ethical leadership. The business persons of future will not just be called upon to transform into good innovators but also responsible ones.

The further role of AI in the world of entrepreneurship presupposes the high level of attention to diversity and humanistic principles. Emerging economies and, in particular, can leverage the potential of AI to build digital transformation and scalable business models. This will also mean the equal access to technology, education and digital infrastructure. To establish a healthier ecosystem where AI entrepreneurship is ethical, governments and institutions should work together and develop an environment in which innovation supports sustainability and social development.

Additionally, there will be a change in the social attitude to entrepreneurship. As the process of human-AI cooperation becomes more advanced, entrepreneurs will be perceived as intelligence ecosystem curators more often, as the professionals who coordinate information, algorithms, and human creativity to deliver meaningful results. Their task will be more than money-making as it will help define the interaction of technology and humankind. In this way, the future entrepreneur should find the right balance between the technological skills and moral leadership so that AI-based enterprises are a benefit that change communities and the world.

7.5 The Way Forward: to Conscious and Strengthened AI-facilitated Entrepreneurship

Conscious entrepreneurship, or a system where innovation, ethics, and human well-being exist as a whole, is the final path that human-AI cooperation in the field of entrepreneurship is heading to. Under this model, entrepreneurs would apply AI to work on improvements in efficiency, but also empathy, inclusivity and environmental awareness. The aim is to develop businesses that think, feel and develop in a responsible manner.

The skill that characterises this age will be cognitive resilience. Algorithms bias, regulation of AI, and digital fatigue will be some of the challenges entrepreneurs will have to fight, which will require the capacity to be mentally adaptable and ethically rooted. Individuals who develop resilience will be in positions to move through uncertainty confidently, by always matching technological power to human use Kaya-Capocci, 2023.

The last one is that the future of entrepreneurship is not eradication of the human population and implementation of machines but also re-invention of intelligence itself. Entrepreneurs are able to make the world an era of collaborative intelligence, where innovation should reward wisdom and human gains no longer should humanity be anesthetised by profits but rather benefit our society in a positive way.

CONCLUSION

Human cooperation and AI represents a breakthrough trend in the sphere of entrepreneurship which alters the current pattern of innovation, strategy and decision-making in the contemporary business world. The article has followed the connection between human cognition and artificial intelligence as the aspect that makes a person able to survive the uncertainty where cognitive resilience is the most important factor to survive the era of high-speed and change of technology. The entrepreneurs, who manage to use AI successfully, not only enjoy the fruits of the computational efficiency, but it also has an adaptive companion that can extend intuition, make future more adaptable, and facilitate strategic decisions. The combined systemic knowledge and creative skills of data and human exceptionalism result in the creation of a vibrant, strong, and progressive mind of the present-day entrepreneur.

Human-AI synergy has not merely the limitations to an individual cognition but to organizational and social as well. Co-creation, scenario planning, and predictive analytics are simple to back with the use of algorithms enabling businesspeople to make smarter choices, and innovative ecosystems. In the meantime, there is still an ethical and emotional aspect of the entrepreneurship in the limelight and the technology must be applied and maintained without compromising on the human values. One of the ways that the intelligent system can be utilized by the future generation of entrepreneurs to enhance their capacity to work more effectively and explore more innovative opportunities is the concept of cognitive digital twins, decision intelligence structures, and AI-enhanced design thinking.

In conclusion, the next phase of entrepreneurship is the integration of conscious, strong and multi-dimensional thinkers who can at least cross the AI-improved weather. The clues to success will be the ability to develop an appropriate balance between the technological proficiency with the technology, human judgment and perpetual learning. It is not only by adopting such paradigm of collaborative intelligence that entrepreneurs can drive sustainable business development onward, but also contribute to the poster image of a society in which innovation, empathy and strategic foresight are kept in a state of perfect harmony. The era of Human-AI entrepreneurship is bound to strengthen the future thus, providing a fresh look at the latter: smartness will require co-branding, choices will be wiser and strong will become one of the attributes of entrepreneurial genius.

REFERENCES

Alpaydin, E. (2021). *Machine learning*. MIT Press. DOI: 10.7551/mitpress/13811.001.0001

BaiDoo-Anu, D., & Ansah, L. O. (2023). Education in the era of generative artificial intelligence (AI): Understanding the potential benefits of ChatGPT in promoting teaching and learning. *Journal of AI, 7*(1), 52–62. https://doi.org/DOI: 10.61969/jai.1337500

Brailas, A. (2024). Postdigital duoethnography: An inquiry into human–artificial intelligence synergies. *Postdigital Science and Education, 6*(2), 486–515. DOI: 10.1007/s42438-024-00455-7

Colombo, M. G., & Piva, E. (2020). Start-ups launched by recent STEM university graduates: The impact of university education on entrepreneurial entry. *Research Policy, 49*(6), 103993. Advance online publication. DOI: 10.1016/j.respol.2020.103993

Cribben, I., & Zeinali, Y. (2023). The benefits and limitations of ChatGPT in business education and research: A focus on management science, operations management and data analytics. SSRN *Electronic Journal*. DOI: 10.2139/ssrn.4404276

Deng, X., & Yu, Z. (2023). A meta-analysis and systematic review of the effect of chatbot technology use in sustainable education. *Sustainability (Basel), 15*(4), 2940. Advance online publication. DOI: 10.3390/su15042940

Eltanahy, M., Forawi, S., & Mansour, N. (2020). Incorporating entrepreneurial practices into STEM education: Development of interdisciplinary E-STEM model in high school in the United Arab Emirates. *Thinking Skills and Creativity, 37*, 100697. Advance online publication. DOI: 10.1016/j.tsc.2020.100697

Epstein, Z., Hertzmann, A., Akten, M., Farid, H., Fjeld, J., Frank, M. R., Groh, M., Herman, L., Leach, N., Mahari, R., Pentland, A. S., Russakovsky, O., Schroeder, H., & Smith, A. (2023). Art and the science of generative AI. *Science, 380*(6650), 1110–1111. DOI: 10.1126/science.adh4451 PMID: 37319193

Graesser, A. C., Fiore, S. M., Greiff, S., Andrews-Todd, J., Foltz, P. W., & Hesse, F. W. (2018). Advancing the science of collaborative problem solving. *Psychological Science in the Public Interest, 19*(2), 59–92. DOI: 10.1177/1529100618808244 PMID: 30497346

Guo, K., & Wang, D. (2024). To resist it or to embrace it? Examining ChatGPT's potential to support teacher feedback in EFL writing. *Education and Information Technologies, 29*(7), 8435–8463. DOI: 10.1007/s10639-023-12146-0

Hollan, J., Hutchins, E., & Kirsh, D. (2000). Distributed cognition: Toward a new foundation for human–computer interaction research. *ACM Transactions on Computer-Human Interaction*, *7*(2), 174–196. DOI: 10.1145/353485.353487

Kaya-Capocci, S. (2023). The trends in entrepreneurship and STEM education studies: A bibliometric study. *İnönü Üniversitesi Eğitim Fakültesi Dergisi, 24*(2), 869–892. DOI: 10.17679/inuefd.1320031

Kelleher, J. D. (2019). *Deep learning.* MIT Press. DOI: 10.7551/mitpress/11171.001.0001

Kelly, A., Sullivan, M., & Strampel, K. (2023). Generative artificial intelligence: University student awareness, experience, and confidence in use across disciplines. *Journal of University Teaching & Learning Practice*, *20*(6). Advance online publication. DOI: 10.53761/1.20.6.12

Lake, B. M., Ullman, T. D., Tenenbaum, J. B., & Gershman, S. J. (2017). Building machines that learn and think like people. *Behavioral and Brain Sciences*, *40*, e253. DOI: 10.1017/S0140525X16001837 PMID: 27881212

Li, T., Ji, Y., & Zhan, Z. (2024). Expert or machine? Comparing the effect of pairing student teacher with in-service teacher and ChatGPT on their critical thinking, learning performance, and cognitive load in an integrated-STEM course. *Asia Pacific Journal of Education*, *44*(1), 45–60. DOI: 10.1080/02188791.2024.2305163

Li, Y. (2017). Deep reinforcement learning: An overview. *arXiv*. https://arxiv.org/abs/1701.07274

Luan, L., Lin, X., Dai, Y., Hu, S., & Sun, Q. (2024). Exploring the cognitive dynamics of artificial intelligence in the post-COVID-19 and Learning 3.0 era: A case study of ChatGPT. *Asian Journal of Distance Education*, *19*(2), 1–10. DOI: 10.5281/zenodo.10990472

McCaffrey, T., & Spector, L. (2018). An approach to human–machine collaboration in innovation. *Artificial Intelligence for Engineering Design, Analysis and Manufacturing*, *32*(1), 1–15. DOI: 10.1017/S0890060416000524

Miço, H., & Cungu, J. (2023). Entrepreneurship education, a challenging learning process towards entrepreneurial competence in education. *Administrative Sciences*, *13*(1), 22. Advance online publication. DOI: 10.3390/admsci13010022

Primario, S., Rippa, P., & Secundo, G. (2024). Rethinking entrepreneurial education: The role of digital technologies to assess entrepreneurial self-efficacy and intention of STEM students. *IEEE Transactions on Engineering Management*, *71*, 2829–2842. DOI: 10.1109/TEM.2022.3199709

Radford, A., Narasimhan, K., Salimans, T., & Sutskever, I. (2018). *Improving language understanding by generative pre-training* (Technical report). OpenAI.

Sharkey, A. J. C. (2016). Should we welcome robot teachers? *Ethics and Information Technology, 18*(4), 283–297. DOI: 10.1007/s10676-016-9387-z

Su, Y., & Liu, Z. (2023). A study of ChatGPT empowering college students' innovation and entrepreneurship education in the context of China. *International Journal of New Developments in Education, 5*(13), 1–7. DOI: 10.25236/IJNDE.2023.051301

Susi, T., & Ziemke, T. (2001). Social cognition, artefacts, and stigmergy: A comparative analysis of theoretical frameworks for artefact-mediated collaborative activity. *Cognitive Systems Research, 2*(4), 273–290. DOI: 10.1016/S1389-0417(01)00053-5

Vecchiarini, M., & Somià, T. (2023). Redefining entrepreneurship education in the age of artificial intelligence: An explorative analysis. *International Journal of Management Education, 21*(3), 100879. Advance online publication. DOI: 10.1016/j.ijme.2023.100879

Weng, X., Chiu, T. K. F., & Tsang, C. C. (2022). Promoting student creativity and entrepreneurship through real-world problem-based maker education. *Thinking Skills and Creativity, 45*, 101046. Advance online publication. DOI: 10.1016/j.tsc.2022.101046

Xia, Q., Chiu, T. K. F., Lee, M., Sanusi, I. T., Dai, Y., & Chai, C. S. (2022). A self-determination theory (SDT) design approach for inclusive and diverse artificial intelligence (AI) education. *Computers & Education, 189*, 104582. Advance online publication. DOI: 10.1016/j.compedu.2022.104582

Zou, J., Han, Y., & So, S.-S. (2009). Overview of artificial neural networks. In *Artificial neural networks: Methods and applications* (pp. 14–22). Springer.

Chapter 9
Human-AI Collaboration and Psychological Resilience in Entrepreneurship

Dharmendra Kumar Gupta
http://orcid.org/0009-0003-9219-9757
Poornima University, Jaipur, India

ABSTRACT

Rapidly growing beyond mere applications of artificial intelligence, it is redefining the way entrepreneurs ideate, decide and shape their businesses in turbulent and competitive markets. Besides the benefit of increased efficiency and performance, the psychological impact of human-AI collaboration is significant, especially in the development of entrepreneurial resilience, the ability to address stress, uncertainty, and numerous failures. This chapter addresses the overlap between human-AI cooperation and psychological resilience in the entrepreneurship area by discussing the way the AI systems are utilized not only as capabilities of technological technologies but also as cognitive and emotional aids in the entrepreneurship decision-making. Based on theories in the fields of entrepreneurship, human-computer interaction, and organizational psychology, the chapter examines how insights, simulations, and adaptive feedback with the help of AI can decrease cognitive overload, boost confidence, and provide reflective learning.

DOI: 10.4018/979-8-2600-1353-3.ch009

1. INTRODUCTION

1.1 The Changing Nature of Entrepreneurial Work in the AI Era

Entrepreneurship as a concept has always been one that is characterized by a lack of certainty and risk-taking as well as a constant necessity to make decisions based on imperfect information. Conventionally, successful entrepreneurs depended mostly on intuition, personal experience and social networks besides the few analytical tools to cope with unstable markets. Nevertheless, the fast-growing development of artificial intelligence has started to break the nature of the entrepreneurial environment completely. The ideation, market analysis, financial forecasting, customer engagement, and operational optimization systems are now all events where AI is integrated to transform the way entrepreneurs operate, therefore changing not only what they do, but also their way of thinking, making decisions, and changing (OECD, 2017).

This change opens an opportunity of transition between the human-focused and cognitive process of entrepreneurship and a model of human-AI interaction. Within the new paradigm, AI systems can help businessmen by working with gigabytes of data, finding hidden connections, and providing predictive information on demand. Consequently, the interpretation of AI outputs, questioning algorithmic suggestions, and including machine intelligence and human decision-making have become more and more relevant to the work of entrepreneurs. This partnership brings forth new openings in strategic flair and new psychological needs (of trust, comptence, and control).

Notably, uncertainty is not removed with the introduction of AI, but it is reconfigured. Inasmuch as AI can minimize the informational uncertainty, now entrepreneurs have to deal with the epistemic uncertainty regarding algorithmic opacities, data bias, and system trust. Therefore, human-AI partnership cannot be seen simply in terms of technology and technological capabilities, but it also involves cognitive and emotional experiences of the entrepreneurs who will work with intelligent systems (Carayannis & Grigoroudis, 2023).

1.2 Defining Human–AI Collaboration in Entrepreneurial Contexts

Human-AI collaboration can be defined as a symbiotic partnership with humans and artificial intelligence systems contributing to the creation of value and the solution to the problem and decision-making. This is not limited to automation but also to augmentation in any area of human endeavor because in the field of entrepreneurship AI is not designed to displace or substitute human actions but can assist them. Entrepreneurs will stay in the center, vision, ethical decision-making and understanding of the situation, and AI serves as an analysis companion, facilitating exploration and analysis (Kumari et al., 2026).

This interaction dynamic is basically interactive. Entrepreneurs engage in active control of AI results by generating data selection, parameter tuning, and interpretive framing whereas AI devices reflect on entrepreneurial cognition by emphasizing risks, opportunities, and other possible solutions. This two-way communications make collaboration distinguishable against the use of tools and place AI as an extension of cognition in the business process. This is why the role of the entrepreneur becomes one of organizing and coordinating the human and machine intelligence, rather than being a single decision maker.

The level of collaboration, however, differs greatly based on the design of the system and the competence of users. The artificial intelligence interfaces that are not well constructed, or recommendation systems that are opaque, are capable of mitigating trust and inducing cognitive load, whereas explainable and transparent systems have potential to promote confidence and learning. Human-AI teamwork in entrepreneurship, therefore, should be perceived as a socio-technical relationship that is determined by design decision-making, organizational culture, and personal psychological characteristics (Kallmuener, 2024).

1.3 Entrepreneurship, Uncertainty and Psychological Strength

Entrepreneurship is a psychologically challenging activity that is characterized by persistent uncertainty, financial strain, social responsibility, and failure. Essential entrepreneurial resources are therefore psychological resilience or the capacity to withstand stress, be able to recover after failures, and be able to continue functioning adaptively. Resilience helps an entrepreneur to endure in times of trouble, perceive failure as a learning experience and be motivated in times of prolonged uncertainty.

The response of AI to the world of entrepreneurship has complicated ramifications towards resiliency. On the one hand, AI can decrease mental load, complicated analyses, and provide simulating scenarios, as well as evidence-based choices. These capabilities will have the capacity to buffer stress and also improve the sense of control and competence among entrepreneurs. Conversely, reliance on the results of the algorithm may result in the emergence of other vulnerabilities, such as the development of the decision paralysis, the lack of self-efficacy, and anxiety in situations where AI suggestions do not correlate with the intuition made by the individual (Conz & Magnani, 2020).

The concept of resilience when it comes to human and AI collaboration therefore involves the necessity of shifting away an individual-focus to a relation-focused understanding. The quality of interaction between entrepreneurs and intelligent systems besides personal coping strategies is the source of psychological resilience.

Adaptive capacity can be empowered, instead of being disempowered, by AI being designed and applied as an assistance, and not as an authoritative decision-maker (Bilgram & Laarmann, 2023).

1.4 Rationale and Scope of the Chapter

Although the topic of AI-driven entrepreneurship is gaining traction today, literature on the subject is mostly centered on the outcome performance in terms of efficiency, scalability, and innovation. Less focus has been placed on the psychological aspects of the collaboration of human and AI especially that of resilience. This is a big gap since the success of an entrepreneur in business is reliant not only on his or her strategic choices but also on the ability of an entrepreneur to require time to endure emotional stress and uncertainty.

This is where this chapter comes in by placing psychological resilience as the main prism through which to study human-AI collaboration in entrepreneurship. It investigates the ways AI systems affect entrepreneurial thought and affect emotion control and confidence, and investigates possible threats associated with over-reliance, agency loss, and ethical dilemma. Combining the findings of entrepreneurship studies, psychology, and human-focused AI, the chapter provides a comprehensive understanding of collaboration as a technological and psychological event.

After all, this discourse preconditions the further parts of the paper, which will explore the idea of AI as a cognitive partner, the effect of AI on decision-making in the circumstances of uncertainty, and the principles of governance that must be in place to make sure that the collaboration between human and AI will boost, instead of undermine, entrepreneurial resilience.

Figure 1. Human–AI Collaboration Framework for Building Psychological Resilience in Entrepreneurship

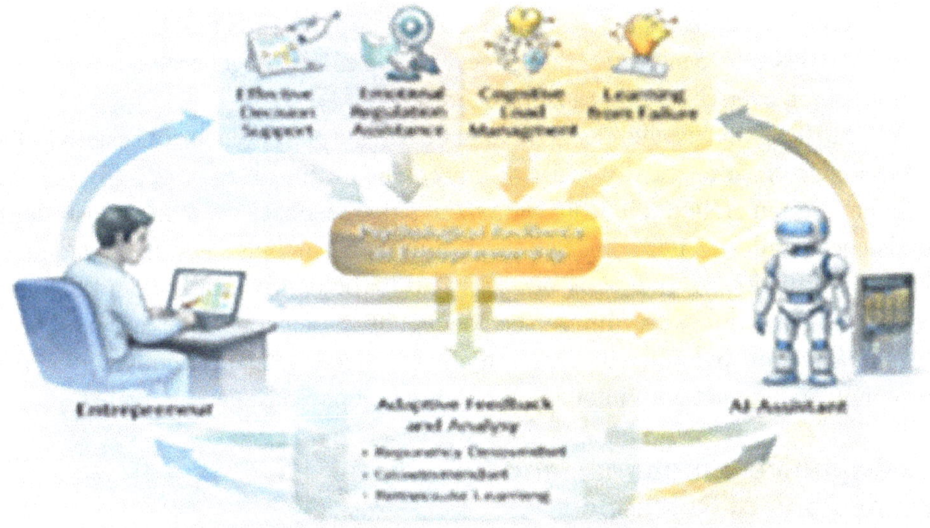

2. CONCEPTUAL FOUNDATIONS OF PSYCHOLOGICAL RESILIENCE IN ENTREPRENEURIAL HUMAN–AI COLLABORATION

2.1 Psychological Resilience as a Core Entrepreneurial Capability

Psychological resilience is often considered a basic entrepreneurial strength, since the entrepreneur is regularly confronted with an uncertain, ambiguous, and high-stakes decision making, which characterizes enterprise. The term resilience is considered to be a dynamic and context-sensitive capacity instead of being a static personality trait that allows the people to respond to stressful situations, downturns, and sudden change in a constructive manner. Resilience in entrepreneurship is demonstrated by the maintenance of motivation, emotional management, cognitive flexibility and failing to achieve an outcome through rejection as a learning process instead of viewing it as a personal failure (Kumari & Goyal, 2026).

In AI-based entrepreneurial systems, the concept of resilience gains some more complication. The entrepreneurs are now also responding to algorithmic feedback, predictive suggestions as well as automated reviews rather than market volatility and resource limitations alone. These aspects determine risk perception by entrepreneurs in terms of risk control, hence emotional reaction to success and failure. The idea of resilience here is based not solely on internal coping skills but also on how the entrepreneur is able to interpret, challenge, and assimilate AI-generated information without being overwhelmed or losing interest.

More to the point, psychological resilience will aid entrepreneurial sustainability in the long run. Strategically resilient entrepreneurs find it easier to tolerate experimentation in an iterative way, receive negative feedback, and sustain strategic persistence. With AI improving the speed of decision-making, as well as the intensity of information, resilience is necessary so that cognitive fatigue and emotion burnout do not occur. Accordingly, the concept of resilience is necessary and not a peripheral feature, but rather a core ability that moderates the efficiency with which entrepreneurs interact with intelligent systems (Shepherd & Patzelt, 2011).

2.2 Cognitive, Emotional, and Behavioral Dimensions of Resilience

The psychological resilience in entrepreneurship can be viewed in cognitive, emotional, and behavioral aspects that are interrelated and each of which is impacted by the human-AI cooperation. Sense-making, reframing problems, and adaptive learning are the mental processes that comprise the cognitive dimension. It is possible that AI systems can serve cognitive resilience through structured analyses, scenario modeling and pattern recognition to assist business owners to make sense of the complex environments. Nevertheless, a high level of algorithmic reasoning can undermine independent decision-making when entrepreneurs refer too much to the results produced by machines.

The emotional aspect of resilience relates to the management of stress, anxiety, and self-sloshing, which exist in the entrepreneurial paths. Emotional volatility can be minimized by AI-based tools that can give predictive information or early warnings to make one feel prepared. Simultaneously, the contradictory advice or unjustified conclusion of the AI systems may result in frustration and emotional tension, especially when entrepreneurs take the decisions they do not clearly comprehend. The resilience to emotions is thus based on transparency, readability, and belief in AI systems (Korzynski, 2023).

Behavioral resilience in terms of capability to operate fruitfully in cases of pressure, be able to persist in adverse circumstances, and respond strategies to feedback. Simulations and other virtual experiments can make AI-powered decision support foster experimentation and the process of learning over time by reducing the perceived cost of failure. Such tools support adaptive behaviors when put into proper use. On the other hand, strict algorithmic prescriptions can inhibit entrepreneurial agency, decrease the exploratory action and diminish resilience in the long run. Human agency and AI guidance interaction is the key to behavioral resilience (Bowman, 2023).

2.3 Theoretical Perspectives Theoretical Relations between Resilience and Human-AI Interaction

A number of theoretical approaches can be used to describe the interaction between psychological resilience and human-AI partnership in the context of entrepreneurship. Socio-cognitively, AI can be regarded as an artificial intelligence which more effectively extends the informational processing ability of the human mind. This extension can contribute to resilience, as it will decrease the cognitive load and enable entrepreneurs to perform on a higher-order strategy. The socio-cognitive theory, however, also cautions against excessive reliance on external help because it can result in the internal ability to cope and find solutions to problems.

Regarding stress and coping theory, AI systems affect the primary appraisal (how entrepreneurs assess the stressors) and the secondary appraisal (how able they are to cope with them). Timely and correct AI feedback can change anyone who feels uncertain about a risk that can be addressed as a manageable risk and help develop better coping strength. Definitely, however, the behavior of opaque AI or inconsistent AI can increase stress by adding elements over which people have no control in the decision-making process. In this regard, resilience is determined by the way AI changes the way the entrepreneur rates control and predictability (Dell'Acqua et al., 2023).

The theories of human centred AI and human computer interaction add to the need to align the system-design and the human psychological needs. The more autonomous, competent, and related AI systems, the more resilience is likely to be enhanced. In a world where the entrepreneurs are no longer stified by AI, and are instead given their power within their hands, collaboration becomes psychologically enabling, and not-inclusive. These views emphasize the fact that resilience is built up in the relations, not inherent to one (Sharma et al., 2026).

2.4 Collaborative Intelligence as the Source of Resilience

Resilience as applied to entrepreneurship should not be considered as a condition of successful collaboration between human beings and artificial intelligence but rather as an emerging consequence of collaborative intelligence. When entrepreneurs are involved in reflexive and iterative forms of interaction with AI systems, they become more tolerant to uncertainty, perceive better in learning, and they are better able to control their emotions. With time, such an interaction will potentially develop a type of distributed resilience in which adaptive capacity will be shared between human and technological elements.

This distributed resilience is based on the calibration of each other. Entrepreneurs understand how to follow the recommendations of AI and how to follow intuition or background knowledge, and AI systems, through feedback, respond to user preferences and decision-making styles. This adaptation to each other contributes to prolonged interaction and lessens psychological loading. Resilience therefore comes as a result of harmonious cooperation and not preeminence by either human or machine intelligence (Drydakis, 2022).

This section throws into focus the necessity of purposeful design and utilization of AI in entrepreneurship by constructing the conception of resilience as a relational, dynamic one. Technology does not necessarily offer psychological resilience, and thus, it should be supported in an active way with transparent systems, reflection, and the process of learning. This theoretical background preconditions the discussion of particular processes according to which AI can impact the entrepreneurship decision-making and capability in the further sections.

3. AI AS A COGNITIVE AND STRATEGIC PARTNER IN ENTREPRENEURIAL DECISION-MAKING

3.1 From Automation Tools to Cognitive Partners

The domain of artificial intelligence has increasingly become more than an automation device used at the back-end to increasingly become a proactive cognitive and strategic companion in entrepreneurial decision-making. The initial uses of AI in the field of entrepreneurship placed great emphasis on operational effectiveness, including the automated accounting system, inventory management system, or customer segmentation. These applications minimally influenced strategic thinking, although they accepted the workload that is done manually. The modern AI systems are, nevertheless, becoming more integrated in high-level entrepreneurial activities, such as opportunity, market forecasting, product and strategic planning.

This shift is a paradigm shift in the cognitive environment of entrepreneurship. The AI systems can now help the entrepreneurs process large and unstructured data, detect patterns in them, and give them alternative possibilities to explore, which would be mentally strenuous to individuals working alone. In this way, AI supplements human decision-making instead of substituting it, allowing entrepreneurs to look into a broader decision space. Strategic power of AI benefits in that it is capable of assisting sense-making in the case of uncertainty, which is a trait of most entrepreneurial environments. The collaboration is intellectually empowering when entrepreneurs view AI as a kind of partner, as opposed to a commanding power (Shahadat et al., 2020).

Nonetheless, making AI a cognitive partner also creates issues in the aspect of interpretation and judgment. Outputs of AI are usually probabilistic and situation-specific and need a human inference to convert outputs into concrete strategic decisions. It is thus necessary that entrepreneurs acquire meta-cognitive skills to criticize AI recommendations. This reciprocal engagement enhances ability to strategize but leaves the hu-man- ag-ency intact i.e. without which decision-making in entrepreneurial and entrepreneurial direction is not possible.

3.2 Improving the Recovery of Opportunities and Strategic Foresight

Among the greatest contributions made by AI to the field of entrepreneurship is the improvement of the opportunity recognition and strategic foresight. Traditionally, entrepreneurs use intuition, experience, and a few market signals to discover the opportunity in the market. AI systems increase this ability by considering a variety of sources of information including consumer behavior, social media trends, supply chain dynamics, and macroeconomic indicators. This broad analysis helps the businesspersons to identify the emergent tendencies and unmet demands in advance than they otherwise could have (Tolner et al., 2021).

AIs enabled foresight tools enable entrepreneurs to test various serve as a simulator to simulate future conditions, examine risks and weigh strategic options, then deploy resources. These features minimize the amount of uncertainty and facilitate better decision-making. Psychologically, this foreseeable clarity leads to the elimination of anxiety and self-confidence, which prove the resilience of the entrepreneurs. When evidence-based decisions are supported with evidence, entrepreneurs feel better placed to deal with volatility as opposed to relying on guesses.

Simultaneously, the idea of strategic vision that is backed by AI does not exclude uncertainty but transfigures it. The entrepreneurs are taught to perceive uncertainty as a solvable factor as opposed to a huge threat. It is this reframing that makes proactive experimentation, as well as the adaptation planning, possible. Applied in the reflective mode, AI-based foresight enhances the capacity to act strategically and psychologically prepared, helping entrepreneurs to overcome complications and turbulence in the exact markets (Shore et al., 2024).

3.3 Underpinning Cognitive Load Management and Reflective Thinking

The decision-making of entrepreneurs is associated with high cognitive load, which arises because of time pressure, information overload, competing priorities. To support the system to handle this cognitive load, AI systems are important in sorting out information, prioritizing data, and offering recommendations in a structured format. AI enables an entrepreneur to use mental resources more effectively by filtering noises and prioritizing the important signals.

Such cognitive unloading leaves room of deliberative thought, which is one of the elements that constitute strategic resilience critically. Reflection helps entrepreneurs to learn through what has been done, re-evaluate assumptions, and improve mental models. This aspect of the reflective process is assisted by AI tools that give feedback, performance dashboards and post-decision analytics that help reveal the specifics of the outcome and relate it to the previous ones. With this kind of feedback loops, there is always learning and modifying behavior (Farooqi et al., 2026).

However, AI systems can be well managed under cognitive loads to ensure their usefulness. Badly constructed interfaces or too many notifications can be a source of mental stress instead of it being reduced. Entrepreneurs will thus need to practice selective attention to the AI tools and then use the tools as part of decision-making processes in a manner that will enhance clarity and not distraction. Coordinated with the human cognitive cycles, AI is a stabilizing system increasing concentration, decision-making, and long-term stability (Sauser, 2018).

3.4 Strategy Independence and the danger of Algorithms Dependence

Even though the use of AI is associated with substantial cognitive and strategic benefits, its increasing power provokes doubts regarding strategic independence and reliance on algorithms. The entrepreneurs can tend to postpone serious decisions to the AI systems over time, especially when the system proves to be accurate or efficient. In the long run, this respect might undermine independent decision-making, decrease the risky innovations of creativity, and compromise the experiential learning, as discussed in the book that lies at the core of entrepreneur effective development.

The entrepreneurial identity and toughness are based on strategic autonomy. The key difference between entrepreneurship and routine management is the capability to make non-standard decisions, offering no guarantee, and the readiness to act upon them even with no certainty whatsoever. When AI systems rule strategic decisions, then entrepreneurs would be more of a worker instead of an innovator. This transition has an eroding effect on the psychological tenacity, a lack of the feeling of possession and thriftiness that drives endurance (Bachtiar, 2023).

To reduce this risk, AI will have to be situated as an advisory tool and not prescriptive. Business people must aggressively doubt AI results, apply contextual understanding and reserve the ultimate decision-making authority. This strategy maintains strategic independence yet it has the advantage of computational intelligence. Finally, high and tough human-AI interaction should rest heavily on the active process of balancing technology and human cognition, which should ensure that AI enhances and not limits the entrepreneurial strength (Lestari et al., 2024).

4. PSYCHOLOGICAL RESILIENCE IN HUMAN–AI COLLABORATIVE ENTREPRENEURSHIP

4.1 Understanding Psychological Resilience in Entrepreneurial Contexts

Psychological resilience in entrepreneurship can be described as the ability of entrepreneurs to positively adjust to adversity, future uncertainty and prolonged pressure so as to proceed with the creation of opportunities. Entrepreneurial environments are volatile by nature which are marked with financial risks, market ambiguity, resource limitations and failure. As this occurs, resilience is not simply a personal trait but a dynamic action that is informed by cognitive, emotional and social aspects. It helps businesspeople to overcome losses, not to lose motivation and re-evaluate strategies without becoming crippled by stress or burnout (Ajzen., 1991).

In the context of human and AI collaborative entrepreneurship, the concept of resilience gets more dimensions. In addition to being subjected to the forces of the external market, entrepreneurs have to learn to live with the constant communication with intelligent systems that dictate the level of performance, decision-making and the strategy of the company. This ableism and coping necessitate emotional disciplinary response, trust on judgment and capacity to integrate machine-generated information without a sense of being undermined. Human intuition and algorithmic intelligence can therefore be effectively collaborating and maintained by psychological steadiness.

Notably, resilience ought to be viewed as something that can be learned and culturally specific as opposed to being natural. Resilience can be enhanced by being exposed to supportive mechanisms, reflective processes, and feedback. When properly designed and implemented ethically, AI can be a source of resilience and a resource provoking neither cognitive nor emotional discomfort.

4.2 AI as a Stress Mitigation and Emotional Support

AI gradually start to act as the support system of entrepreneurs in terms of emotions and psychological support. Uncertainty is minimized by decision-support systems, smart dashboard, and predictive analytics systems that bring clarity and structure that can relieve the anxiety around high stakes decision making. Emotional stability and confidence can be achieved when the entrepreneur feels that they have the information and are ready to take action since they are more likely to feel in control.

Adaptive interfaces, conversational agents and coaching capabilities are also some of the features of Dynamic interfaces in certain AI tools, which provide guidance, reminders, and reflexive prompts. In particular, although these systems do not substitute human relationships, they offer the non-judgmental feedback that is consistent and, therefore, particularly useful at the time of isolation or when the pressure is high. In entrepreneurs with limited access to mental support, networks, or mentors (especially in the early stages), this type of support based on AI can add value to the resilience associated with emotions (Bandura, 1986).

The beneficial effects that AI meditated support has on the psyche, however, hinge on trust and transparency. To educate entrepreneurs and prevent false assurance or overconfidence, entrepreneurs need to be aware of the extent and the limitations of AI recommendations. Uncertainty passed on by AI systems in easy languages and allowing humans to reflect on such information will foster healthier coping behaviors and enhance a resilient state of mind instead of being dependent (Ayala & Manzano, 2014).

Figure 2. AI-Supported Decision-Making and Stress Mitigation Cycle in Entrepreneurship

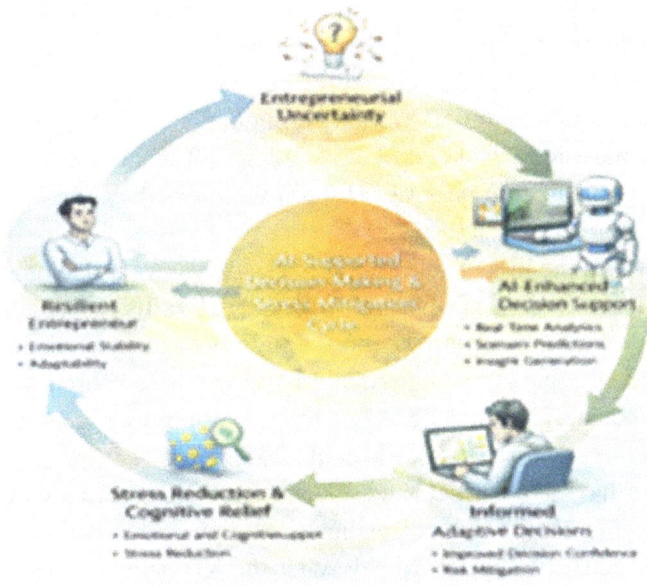

4.3 Learning by Doing Wrong with AI-Augmented Reflection

Failure is an unavoidable aspect of the entrepreneurial process, but it can be an emotional cost, which should include doubt in oneself, tense emotional reactions, and fear of decision-making in the future. The psychological resilience defines how a failure will be a learning experience or a reason to check out. The AI systems can positively contribute to the reframing failure by helping build a more structured and data-driven reflection instead of a self-judging emotional approach.

AI can allow business people to separate the personal and the business because it operates through post-action analytics, performance diagnostics, and scenario analysis. Identifying the external variables, market forces, and strategic trade-offs, AI assists the entrepreneurs to view failure as a multifactorial interaction, but not a personal weakness. This cognitive re-framing is essential in recovery of emotions and long-term entrepreneurial involvement (Goyal et al., 2026).

Additionally, the reflection based on AI would favor experimentation by reducing the perceived cost of failure. Entrepreneurs become more ready to make calculated risks when they could simulate other strategies and become able to learn out of the past data. Such a learning strategy leads to adaptive resilience, which allows entrepreneurs to persevere, be creative, and change through recurrent challenges.

4.4 Threats to Human-AI Collaboration from a Psychological Resilience

Overcoming the possible positive aspects, human-AI collaboration also gives rise to psychological risks which, when not addressed, can destroy resilience. Among the risks, one can single out cognitive overload brought about by the massive amounts of information, messages, or contradictory advice. The more entrepreneurs are bombarded with information generated by AI, the more they can be fatigued and stressed by these rather than less.

The other issue is the loss of self-efficacy. The excessive usage of AI may make entrepreneurs doubt their intuition and professional skills, especially when the decisions provided by AI are opposite to the judgment of man. This stress might cause low confidence and anxiety, particularly where there is high pressure. Also, obscure or inadequately articulated AI systems may produce a feeling of loss of control, frustration, and distrust (Baron et al., 2016).

Entrepreneurs have to be critical and selective when interacting with AI systems in order to protect their psychological resilience. Design concepts such as readability, end user control and flexibility are crucial. When the AI systems do not interfere with human entrepreneurial autonomy, but assist in making decisions, then it is beneficial to the entrepreneurial resilience. In conclusion, the future of human-AI cooperation is rooted in establishing a balanced relationship between the technological capacity and the psychological requirements of human beings in a manner that ensures that innovation promotes well-being and performance (Branicki et al., 2018).

5. STRATEGIES FOR STRENGTHENING RESILIENT HUMAN–AI ENTREPRENEURIAL ECOSYSTEMS

5.1 Designing Human-Centered AI for Entrepreneurial Well-Being

Designing artificial intelligence systems that are designed with the purpose of aiding human requirements is the initial step to reinforcing psychological resilience in human-AI entrepreneurial ecosystems. These systems lay emphasis on usability, transparency, and emotional sustainability and optimization of performance. In the case of entrepreneurs, AI tools must be collaborative tools and not dictators. Interfaces explaining recommendations clearly, visualizing uncertainty and providing users with the ability to question assumptions can help entrepreneurs to have a sense of agency and control that are central to getting through pressure.

Emotional conditions of entrepreneurs are also taken into consideration in human-centered AI. Cognitive overload can be avoided by use of adaptive systems that moderate information flow in relation to user context (stress, workload or urgency of a decision). Responding to the rhythms of the human body through designing technology, the AI systems will decrease anxiety and increase concentration. Such correspondence strengthens the ordeal of resilience because using AI as an additional skill-enhancing tool instead of depending on it to build stress or dependence will not lead to dependence (Bollough & Renko, 2013).

5.2 Mastering the Art of Entrepreneurship to work with AIs efficiently

Achieving psychological strength in AI-enhanced entrepreneurship is not an isolated act of technology but it is a process that involves facilitation of harmonious human capacities. To be productive regarding AI systems, entrepreneurs need to develop digital literacy, critical thinking and emotional intelligence. The knowledge of AI model generation can help businesspersons make insights interpretations that do not confuse them into blind trust. The competence creates confidence and minimizes uncertainty-related stress (Duchek, 2018).

Equally are reflexive and self-regulation skills. Entrepreneurs with the ability to watch their emotional reactions on AI-driven feedback, including performance reviews or risk warnings, are in a better position to positively utilize this information. Incubator programs and training must hence be combined with AI fluency with techniques of resilience, such as mindfulness, adaptive goal-setting and reflective learning. All these competencies contribute to an ability of the entrepreneurs to stay flexible and psychologically strong in the process of making complicated decisions (Duckworth et al., 2007).

5.3 Mechanisms of Institutional and Organizational support

In addition to personal abilities, strong human-AI entrepreneurial systems require institutions that are supportive. Improportionality: Accelerators, innovation centers, and venture networks have a critical role in development of norms of responsible use of AI applications and psychological health. Institutions can decrease the isolation through encouraging collective learning, peer support, and collective experimentation with AI tools and normalize obstacles to AI-integrated entrepreneurship.

The ethical implementation of AI, privacy of data, and accountability also add to the resilience since it creates a sense of trust in policies and organizational guidelines. When the entrepreneur is assured that they are in a secure environment by the transparent governance systems, cognitive and emotional resources of the entrepreneur are liberated towards innovations as opposed to defensive coping. Institutional support is therefore more of a stabilising force, that strengthens both personal resilience as well as collective adaptability of the entrepreneurial ecosystem (Kumari et al., 2026).

5.4 Toward Sustainable and Resilient Human–AI Futures

The future sustainability of human-AI entrepreneurship will require the process of reconciliation and compatibility of technological progress and human psychology needs. The resilient ecosystems are instances that progress over time and learn through failures, adjust their governance structures and perfect AI design habits. Business people should be prompted to see AI as a growing companion that would develop in tandem with their own learning and emotional development (Fredrickson, 2001).

Human and AI collaboration can be transformed to bring about a more resilient than vulnerable relationship by incorporating these three aspects of human-centered design, skill building, and institutional backing. Such ecosystems are not only beneficial to the performance of entrepreneurship but also physical safety, creativity, and prolonged involvement. By doing so, resilience will be a collaborative obligation that is spread among individuals, technologies, and institutions and create a more human and sustainable future of AI-enabled entrepreneurship (Connor & Davidson, 2003).

6. FUTURE PROSPECTUS AND RESEARCH FOCUS OF HUMAN-AI COOPERATION AND ENTREPRENEURIAL RESILIENCE

6.1 Extending the Cognitive and Emotional Capabilities of AI in Entrepreneurship

The future directions of human-AI collaboration in the realm of entrepreneurship presuppose a change in the approach to the task-based assistance and the move towards the systems that actively maintain the process of cognitive reflection and emotional control. With more complexity in the process of making decisions in the entrepreneurial sphere, AI tools are projected to help with data-based analysis, as well as, frame problems, work with uncertainty, and facilitate sense-making. Such developments can help business people to find their way in ambiguities more easily by providing alternative ways of thinking which helps to reveal some of the hidden assumptions, facilitating thoughtful thinking when they are stressed.

The emotional aspect of the entrepreneurship also plays an important role, especially when it comes to the situations, where there is unrelenting uncertainty, financial risk and social responsibility. Subsequent AI systems can also be developed to pick up on such emotional trends as burnout, decision fatigue, or too much risk aversion, through monitoring data on behavior and interaction. Such systems when made in an ethical manner would make entrepreneurs wait, reconsider priorities or seek human assistance which would make them psychologically stronger. Nevertheless, the psychological consequences of emotional AI of AI are insufficiently studied in the long term and should be outlined in a systematic way (Chadwick & Raver, 2020).

The personalization of AI support is one more direction of importance. There is a vast variation in the cognitive style, emotional levels, and the ability to endure the entrepreneur. Future AIs can modify the strategy of their interaction according to the features of each certain profile, providing their decision support and feedback. Although personalization can improve resilience, it also creates some issues with the autonomy and dependency. Studies are thus needed to establish how individualized AI can be empowering and not restrictive to the entrepreneurial agency psychologically.

6.2 Mental Hazards of Deep AI Integration

The closer the AI systems are to the operations of an entrepreneur, the greater the chances of ethical and psychological risks. Among the issues that are problematic is the gradual decay of the self-efficacy as the entrepreneurs over-relied on AI-generated suggestions. The excessive use of algorithmic advice can undermine the belief in personal judgement especially in the time of failure or doubt which are the natural characteristics of the entrepreneurial activity. This phenomenon indicates the necessity of the AI systems that supplement the reflective autonomy instead of the human decision-making.

Another emerging threat is psychological accessFirst is dependency on AI psychologically. Perpetual engagement with intelligent systems that provide validation, reassurance or a strategic direction could end up replacing the human coping behavior and social support systems unwittingly. This dependency may impair the resilience of an entrepreneur in the long term, as it may affect the ability to cope with stress without the help of external support. The future studies are advised to investigate the ways in which the limits between positive AI support and the unhealthy dependency can be determined and adhered to (Corner et al., 2017).

Corruption issues of transparency, accountability, and emotional manipulation are also ethical problems. Considering that AI can create subliminal influences on choices or influence the answers to options through framing choices or expressions, they may influence emotion without formal consciousness. This is quagmire of consent and mind-controlling regarding a high-stakes entrepreneurship. To ensure mental health and innovation remain intact, it will be necessary to build ethical guidelines on how to create AI systems that have emotional consciousness (Dandotiva et al., 2026).

6.3 Advancing Research Methodologies for Studying AI-Enabled Resilience

The methodological tools needed to gain a clear insight into the psychological resilience in human-AI entrepreneurial ecosystems must capture a dynamic interaction and subjective experience. The conventional performance-based measurements are inadequate when it comes to emotional adaptation, coping mechanisms and long-term mental consequences. The interdisciplinary approach involving psychological, human-computer interaction, entrepreneurship research, and data science knowledge should be used in the future.

Longitudinal research designs are one that are specifically relevant in measuring the impact of repeated AI interaction on bending over time. Monitoring the activities of entrepreneurs at various phases of venture development, researchers would be able to define the need to strengthen adaptive abilities or establish cognitive dependence. This type of research can also inform on the dynamics of resilience that change with the presence of success, failure, and environmental shock under AI-supported environments (Chen & Zhang, 2021).

Secondly, simulation and experimental approaches provide potential opportunities of isolating causes and effects. Simulated entrepreneurial decision-making conditions with the support of AI can be used to find out which aspects of the system support confidence, learning, and emotional stability. Qualitative approaches, reflective diaries, and in-depth interviews can also be used to understand the interpretations and emotional experiences of AI collaboration by the entrepreneurs to complement quantitative data.

6.4 Policy, Education and Entrepreneurial Practice Implications

Human–AI collaboration frameworks of the future should be able to bring the research results into clear policy, education, and entrepreneurship ecosystem strategies. The policymakers should be instrumental in setting up the rules that will facilitate the use of AI in a psychologically sustainable manner, with a significant focus on transparency, explainability, and human control. Policies that recognize mental well-being as an acceptable aspect of responsible AI embrace will be very important in determining tough entrepreneurial landscapes.

There should be the integration of AI literacy with resilience-focused training in learning institutions and incubation programs. Instead of concentrating only on the technical capabilities, the process of training entrepreneurship needs to deal with emotional intelligence, moral reasoning, and the contemplative use of AI tools. Training entrepreneurs to be able to critically assess AI outputs and contain their emotional reaction will improve the ability to innovate and the ability to endure psychologically (Bakker et al., 2014).

On the ecological level, it is essential to promote robust human-artificial intelligence entrepreneurship through the collective responsibility. Investors, accelerators, and technology providers have to cooperate to facilitate AI systems that encourage long-term health, but not short-term performance increases. By incorporating resilience as a design and assessment attribute, future entrepreneurial systems can be in a position to guarantee that AI-based innovation supports human prosperity in addition to economical achievement (Goyal et al., 2026).

CONCLUSION

The human-AI partnership is quickly transforming the entrepreneurial environment, bringing in new types of mental aid, strategic vision, and planning abilities. The importance of AI in the field of entrepreneurship, as has been argued in this chapter, cannot be measured using the criteria of efficiency or performance outcome but rather through psychological implications toward the entrepreneurs. Psychological resiliency is another critical process that results in the rise of innovativeness with the introduction of AI-based entrepreneurship or even vulnerability, dependency, and emotional load. Considering AI systems configured as, and worked as co-workers, as opposed to dictatorial replacements, it is possible to build confidence, learning, and adaptative decision-making in uncertain conditions.

Simultaneously, the implementation of AI in the entrepreneurial process also brings in complicated psychological and ethical, as well as social issues. The over-dependence on algorithmic suggestions, weakening self-efficacy, and the subtly emotional power of intelligent systems are a threat to the resilience in the long-term. These difficulties indicate the need to uphold human control, introspection, and emotional independence concerning AI-based entrepreneurship. The concept of resilience, here, is more directly not an individual, but a dynamic phenomenon that is created through the technology design, the institutions norms and the socio-cultural expectations of the entrepreneurial process and innovation.

The second point highlighted in the chapter is the fact that the human-AI entrepreneurship based on resilience needs coordinated activities on several levels. Entrepreneurs need skills in critical AI literacy and emotional self-control, institutions need to create ecosystems that are supportive and based on ethics, policymakers need to acknowledge the aspect of psychological well-being as the whole of responsible AI governance approach. Studies and practice should allow them to go beyond the range of narrow productivity indicators to emotional sustainability, learning ability and long-term adaptability as primary measures of success.

Finally, human-AI collaboration has transformative potential in the field of entrepreneurship, yet its potential can be fulfilled only once the human psychological resilience becomes the subject of designing, governing, and practicing. Trends In this direction, AI can not only enhance the economic development of industries but also ensure well-being and lasting well-being and flourishing of human populations in the entrepreneurial landscape, since it can become appealing to not only human values but also emotional needs.

REFERENCES

Ajzen, I. (1991). The theory of planned behavior. *Organizational Behavior and Human Decision Processes, 50*(2), 179–211. DOI: 10.1016/0749-5978(91)90020-T

Ayala, J.-C., & Manzano, G. (2014). The resilience of the entrepreneur. *Journal of Economic Psychology, 42*, 126–135. DOI: 10.1016/j.joep.2014.02.004

Bachtiar, N. K., Setiawan, A., Prastyan, G. A., & Kijkasiwat, P. (2023). Business resilience and growth strategy transformation. *Journal of Innovation and Entrepreneurship, 12*(1), 77. DOI: 10.1186/s13731-023-00345-5

Bakker, A. B., Demerouti, E., & Sanz-Vergel, A. I. (2014). Burnout and work engagement. *Annual Review of Organizational Psychology and Organizational Behavior, 1*(1), 389–411. DOI: 10.1146/annurev-orgpsych-031413-091235

Bandura, A. (1986). *Social foundations of thought and action*. Prentice Hall.

Baron, R. A., Franklin, R. J., & Hmieleski, K. M. (2016). Entrepreneurial stress and well-being. *Journal of Management, 42*(3), 742–768. DOI: 10.1177/0149206313495411

Bilgram, V., & Laarmann, F. (2023). Accelerating innovation with generative AI. *IEEE Engineering Management Review, 51*(2), 18–25. DOI: 10.1109/EMR.2023.3272799

Bowman, S. R. (2023). Eight things to know about large language models. *arXiv:2304.00612*.

Branicki, L. J., Sullivan-Taylor, B., & Livschitz, S. R. (2018). Entrepreneurial resilience and SMEs. *International Journal of Entrepreneurial Behaviour & Research, 24*(7), 1244–1263. DOI: 10.1108/IJEBR-11-2016-0396

Carayannis, E. G., & Grigoroudis, E. (2023). *Handbook of research on artificial intelligence, innovation and entrepreneurship*. Edward Elgar. DOI: 10.4337/9781839106750

Chadwick, I. C., & Raver, J. L. (2020). Psychological resilience and venture survival. *Entrepreneurship Theory and Practice, 44*(2), 233–255. DOI: 10.1177/1042258718801597

Chen, Y., & Zhang, Y. (2021). Fostering resilience in new venture teams. *Group & Organization Management, 46*(4), 773–816. DOI: 10.1177/10596011211033164

Connor, K. M., & Davidson, J. R. T. (2003). Development of the CD-RISC. *Depression and Anxiety, 18*(2), 76–82. DOI: 10.1002/da.10113 PMID: 12964174

Conz, E., & Magnani, G. (2020). A dynamic perspective on the resilience of firms. *European Management Journal, 38*(3), 400–412. DOI: 10.1016/j.emj.2019.12.004

Corner, P. D., Singh, S., & Pavlovich, K. (2017). Entrepreneurial resilience and venture failure. *International Small Business Journal, 35*(6), 687–708. DOI: 10.1177/0266242616685604

Dell'Acqua, F., ... (2023). Navigating the jagged technological frontier. *Harvard Business School Working Paper*. https://doi.org/DOI: 10.2139/ssrn.4573321

Drydakis, N. (2022). Artificial intelligence and reduced SMEs' business risks. *Information Systems Frontiers, 24*(4), 1223–1247. DOI: 10.1007/s10796-022-10249-6 PMID: 35261558

Duchek, S. (2018). Entrepreneurial resilience. *The International Entrepreneurship and Management Journal, 14*(2), 429–455. DOI: 10.1007/s11365-017-0467-2

Duckworth, A. L., Peterson, C., Matthews, M. D., & Kelly, D. R. (2007). Grit and perseverance. *Journal of Personality and Social Psychology, 92*(6), 1087–1101. DOI: 10.1037/0022-3514.92.6.1087 PMID: 17547490

Farooqi, A., Das, D., Tripathi, M., Dutta, R., Goyal, N. K., & Sheikh, M. F. (2026). Navigating ethical frontiers in AI-driven geriatric care. In *AI for geriatric care in an aging society* (pp. 243–266). IGI Global., DOI: 10.4018/979-8-3373-5462-0.ch009

Fredrickson, B. L. (2001). The broaden-and-build theory. *The American Psychologist, 56*(3), 218–226. DOI: 10.1037/0003-066X.56.3.218 PMID: 11315248

Goyal, N. K., Gulati, K., Avasthi, A., Kapoor, S. K., Keswani, B., & Gupta, S. (2026). Securing the imagination: Security and privacy challenges in generative AI systems. In *Generative AI-powered data architectures* (pp. 239–266). IGI Global., DOI: 10.4018/979-8-3373-5616-7.ch010

Goyal, N. K., Kumar, S., Dutta, R., Kothari, V., & Sinha, S. K. (2026). Empowering elderly care through artificial intelligence. In *AI for geriatric care in an aging society* (pp. 1–28). IGI Global., DOI: 10.4018/979-8-3373-5462-0.ch001

Korzynski, P., Mazurek, G., Altmann, A., Ejdys, J., Kazlauskaite, R., Paliszkiewicz, J., Wach, K., & Ziemba, E. (2023). Generative artificial intelligence as a new context for management theories. *Central European Management Journal, 31*(1), 3–13. DOI: 10.1108/CEMJ-02-2023-0091

Kumari, M., & Goyal, N. K. (2026). Artificial intelligence in the cryptocurrency ecosystem. In *Innovations in cryptocrime and financial fraud* (pp. 245–282). IGI Global., DOI: 10.4018/979-8-3373-0675-9.ch007

Kumari, M., Kumawat, R., Dutta, R., Khan, S. T., Goyal, N. K., & Sheikh, M. F. (2026). Wireless Communication and IoT Integration in Smart Clothing. In Saxena, P., Singh, M., Singh, S., & Rashid, M. (Eds.), *Next-Generation Electronic Textiles and Conductive Materials for Smart Wearables* (pp. 195–232). IGI Global Scientific Publishing., DOI: 10.4018/979-8-3373-4287-0.ch008

Kumari, M., Kumawat, R., Tripathi, M., Suganthi, K., Goyal, N. K., & Sheikh, M. F. (2026). Blockchain for transparency and traceability in supply chains. In *Maximizing operational efficiency at the intersection of supply chain management and marketing* (pp. 35–64). IGI Global., DOI: 10.4018/979-8-3373-3109-6.ch002

Lestari, E. D.. (2024). SMEs' business resilience post-COVID-19. *Cogent Business & Management*, *11*(1), 2301135. DOI: 10.1080/23311975.2023.2301135

OECD. (2017). *Enhancing the contributions of SMEs in a global and digitalized economy*. OECD Publishing.

Sauser, B. (2018). Resilience of SMEs and community impact. *Natural Hazards*, *90*, 79–99. DOI: 10.1007/s11069-017-3034-9

Shahadat, M. M. H.. (2020). Digital technology adoption in SMEs. *Global Business Review*.

Sharma, P., Kumawat, R., Jain, G., Keswani, G., Goyal, N. K., & Sheikh, M. F. (2026). Machine learning-based intrusion detection systems for HIoT. In *Resilient healthcare IoT systems* (pp. 185–214). IGI Global., DOI: 10.4018/979-8-3373-7610-3.ch007

Shepherd, D. A., & Patzelt, H. (2011). Sustainable entrepreneurship. *Entrepreneurship Theory and Practice*, *35*(1), 137–163. DOI: 10.1111/j.1540-6520.2010.00426.x

Shore, A., Tiwari, M., Tandon, P., & Foropon, C. (2024). Building entrepreneurial resilience using generative AI. *Technovation*. Advance online publication. DOI: 10.1016/j.technovation.2024.103063

Tolner, F., Eigner, G., & Barta, B. (2021). Resilience interpretations of SMEs. *IEEE SAMI Proceedings*, 495–500.

Chapter 10
From Innovation to Resilience:
AI-Driven Transformation in Women Entrepreneurship

Gurpreet pal Kaur
http://orcid.org/0000-0001-7475-3548
Lovely Professional University, India

Mushtaq Ahmed Shah
http://orcid.org/0000-0002-3177-9622
Lovely Professional University, India

ABSTRACT

Artificial intelligence (AI) is quickly changing the entrepreneurial ecosystems and is providing new opportunities to become more efficient, make decisions and be competitive. To women entrepreneurs in the field, AI has a specific potential to enhance an ability to be psychologically resilient and more adaptive to the environment and find their ways through the uncertainties, extend market reach, and multi-task. The chapter review incorporates both interdisciplinary literature, reports of global entrepreneurship, and actual case studies in India and other emerging economies backe by recent developments on bridging the gender gap in the AI economy to look at the ways in which women are using AI tools in their businesses and the impact of using AI tools on business performance and personal empowerment. Results show that the adoption of AI can have a great impact in enhancing the performance of operations, confidence, and autonomy of women entrepreneurs. Nevertheless, there are still structural inequalities, such as lack of digital access, lack of AI training, financial obstacles that are gender-based, and women are still underrepresented in the development and governance of AI. These issues explain why gender-sensitive

DOI: 10.4018/979-8-2600-1353-3.ch010

policies, inclusive digital-skilling initiatives, fair funding systems, and algorithmic bias, online security, and data privacy protection should be implemented. The chapter comes to a conclusion that the development of inclusive AI ecosystems makes AI-enabled women-based entrepreneurship one of the driving forces of the sustainable development, economic inclusion, and gender equality.

1. INTRODUCTION

Women entrepreneurs have been remarkable in the past years to convert their challenges into growth opportunities. Research points out that female-owned businesses are strategic in their use of digital technologies, community-based business models, alternative financing models, to address structural limitations and emerge successful though facing systemic obstacles (Tripathi &Trivedi, 2025). In the eyes of most women, entrepreneurship is not only a way of doing business, but also a way of economic empowerment and sustainable development even in rural locations (Azad & Marinova, 2025). Nevertheless, gender issues such as availability of finance, care giving duties and lack of industry contacts still act as barriers to their development. In this environment, psychological stability and adaptive leadership can prove to be key characteristics in uncertainty navigation (Yadav et al., 2024). At the same time, the emergence of AI and digital technologies opens new opportunities to increase efficiency, innovativeness, and sustainability, and the digital transformation has become one of the key enablers of inclusive entrepreneurship (Xanthopoulou & Sahinidis, 2025). Combined, the two trends suggest a closer look at how AI can help women to reclaim the principles of entrepreneurship in an ever-changing digital economy.

This question is even more pressing in the world that undergoes a high rate of digital change. In the developing economies, the continued growth of digital infrastructure, abundance of smartphones, and emergence of online marketplaces are transforming how business is conducted (Mulenga, 2025). According to the recent literature, there is a significant number of women entrepreneurs who implement AI-based solutions (i.e., AI-enhanced accounting and digital management) to improve the quality of financial reporting and decrease the operational load (Yadav et al., 2024). Several researchers suggests that AI technologies empower female founders, as well, to reinforce the personal branding and positioning on the market in culturally specific environments (Putri & Sonni, 2025). In addition, the increasing technology preparedness and acceptance of AI among young entrepreneurs in the emerging markets imply that the tools are moving beyond specialized usage to general business tools (Games et al., 2025). However, to female entrepreneurs who combine business and social duties, the implementation of AI can only be fully achieved with digital infrastructure availability, mentoring, and ecosystem (Tripathi & Trivedi, 2025).

The current chapter investigates into the intersection of gender, entrepreneurship, psychology and technology in the quest to comprehend how women use AI to create resilience and agency in dynamic worlds. Recent reports show that female entrepreneurs more frequently adopt online resources and new business approaches to break the system limits and guarantee their long-term expansion (Tripathi & Trivedi, 2025). Innovation and education have become the most important facilitators of psychological resilience and adaptive capacity enabling women to overcome financial, cultural, and policy-related obstacles (Sunny & Singh, 2025). Meanwhile, the opportunities of sustainable and empowered women-led enterprises are redefining the possibilities of digital ecosystems and AI-powered entrepreneurship models such as mentorship, platform access, and inclusive finance (Camps et al., 2026). These changing ecosystems underscore the role of adopting AI in re-inventing entrepreneurship itself - as a way of becoming resilient, autonomous, and having a long-term social impact (Raman et al., 2025).

In order to be clear with the analysis, some key terms must be stated. Psychological resilience is the ability of a person to withstand the challenges and remain driven by stress, i.e., a skill tied to entrepreneurial achievements and flexibility in unstable digital-tech conditions (Ahmad et al., 2025). Resilience in entrepreneurship does not just exist as a personality factor but evolves as a result of learning, the psychological capital, and supportive ecosystems (Zhang & Li, 2022). Adaptive capacity means being able to predict change and modify strategies in business based on uncertainty and technological changes. The flexibility of AI-powered tools helps to be able to make data-driven choices and implement change (Kariv et al., 2025). AI-enabled entrepreneurship refers to the type of business that incorporates smart technology, such as predictive analytics, automation, and other smart systems that enhance the performance of businesses in terms of response to market demands and efficiency (Kusetogullari et al., 2025). Lastly, gendered issues are those structural and social obstacles that limit women entrepreneurs such as network access, mentorship, and work-life balance issues that are highly important to well-being in new start-ups (Ammirato et al., 2024).

This chapter does not present AI in a universal manner as the solution but rather as a context-specific enabler that responds to the local ecosystem and gendered limitations in the developing and emerging economies (Kusetogullari et al., 2025). The transformational potential of AI is that it will increase the resilience and agency of women in entrepreneurship and develop adaptive capacities to uncertain settings (Kariv et al., 2025). Nevertheless, such advantages are conditional on the availability of enabling infrastructure, inclusive design, mentoring, and systemic support, which determine the ability to change the established business practices and leadership standards during the digital age (Ahmad et al., 2025).

2. CONCEPTUAL BACKGROUND

To come up with insights on how women entrepreneurs can create resilient futures using AI, it is necessary to base the discussion on the theoretical approaches of entrepreneurial psychology, gender studies, and technology-enabled entrepreneurship. In the context of entrepreneurial psychology, psychological resilience is considered as the capability to stay motivated, emotionally stable, and able to solve a problem despite the uncertainty (Ahmad et al., 2025). Entrepreneurs tend to repeatedly work in circumstances with incomplete information, unstable markets, and continuous pressure to make decisions where resilience is not only a coping mechanism but a strategic resource to keep the commitment and recognize opportunities when faced with stress (Zhang & Li, 2022). Studies highlight that resilience is dynamic as opposed to being static, and it is influenced by cognitive flexibility, self-efficacy, and availability of social and professional networks (Q. Zhu & Zhang, 2022). In the case of women entrepreneurs especially those operating in resource limited or socially constraining conditions, resilience is a decisive factor of entrepreneurial survival and growth and mediates the influence of structural inequities on entrepreneurship and adaptable responses to uncertainty (Ammirato et al., 2024).

The second conceptual strand is gendered entrepreneurship, and the study through which the social standards, institutional frameworks, and cultural demands specifically influence the experience of women in entrepreneurship. In contrast to the gender-neutral framework, studies in the area prove that women face compounded obstacles, such as limited access to capital, the lack of inclusion in power circles, and biases in the entrepreneurial ecosystems (Ammirato et al., 2024). The unequal distribution of caregiving obligations and restricting women to mobility and involvement in business ventures by the society compound these difficulties (Ayoko et al., 2021). Moreover, gender ideals have a long-term impact on how women are perceived as risk-takers and effective leaders, which has reflected in their confidence, access to mentorship, and business development opportunities (Ahmad et al., 2025). Such a dual tasking, that is, the need to reconcile the domestic expectations and the business demands is a determinant of material and psychological conditions of entrepreneurship and resilience is only helpful but critical to maintaining the continuity of entrepreneurship in gendered spaces (Zhang & Li, 2022).

The third theoretical pillar of the chapter focuses on the development of the digital technology and artificial intelligence (AI) in entrepreneurship. The digital transformation is transforming the way entrepreneurs acquire information, engage with markets and scale business ventures (Zhang & Li, 2022). Specifically, AI transforms the conventional processes of entrepreneurship and introduces automation, analytics, and decision support based on algorithms into the day-to-day tasks (Kusetogullari et al., 2025). The use of automation technologies minimizes the administrative load, and entrepreneurs can focus on strategic decision-making, and AI-based analytics can increase the level of insight into how customers act, what trends in the market, and how they perform (Ahmad et al., 2025). Machine learning and predictive modelling enable entrepreneurs to forecast changes in the market, allocate resources in the most efficient way, and individualize interactions, enhancing responsiveness in the face of uncertainty (Kariv et al., 2025). Finally, AI has opportunity recognition capabilities because it can uncover latent patterns and allow altering fundamental entrepreneurial functions, which are planning and execution, as well as scaling and innovation (Ammirato et al., 2024).

By uniting these threads, the conceptual background implies that the crossroad of psychological strength, gendered entrepreneurship, and AI-facilitated business practices builds a unique model through which the future of women in the context of entrepreneurship can be perceived. Psychological resilience offers the inner strength to handle uncertainty and survive in a state of adversity (Ahmad et al., 2025), whereas gendered entrepreneurship highlights the structural and sociocultural obstacles external to women, which define their entrepreneurship experience (Ammirato et al., 2024). In the meantime, the technology provided by AI-enabled entrepreneurship implies the introduction of technological mechanisms that will be able to increase adaptability, decision-making, and opportunities recognition in dynamic markets (Kusetogullari et al., 2025). Taken together, these areas demonstrate that women entrepreneurs can use AI not only to break through but to transform structured inequalities and create more empowered and stronger entrepreneurial possibilities (Kariv et al., 2025).

3. AI OPPORTUNITY TO WOMEN ENTREPRENEURS

The increased and continuous adoption of artificial intelligence (AI) and digital technologies in the entrepreneurial ecosystems represents a disruptive opportunity to women entrepreneurs, particularly in the context in which women previously had very limited access due to structural, financial, and mobility limitations. Recent research shows that AI-enabled applications and digital platforms could lead to better decision-making, increased operational scope, and the flexibility needed to allow women to adhere to many social and professional roles (Kusetogullari et al.,

2025). All these developments make AI an inclusion, empowerment, and resiliency catalyst in women-run businesses (Ahmad et al., 2025).

One of the most important benefits of AI is the fact that it could even the playing field in the world of the entrepreneurship. Studies have shown that AI-enhanced digital ecosystems reduce geographic, infrastructural, and entry barriers to markets, which means that women can be involved in them even in case of mobility or cultural limitations (Ammirato et al., 2024). Online shops, supply chain, and no-contact sales are made possible by digital platforms and automation and open up opportunities to participate to more people in previously male-dominated or bigger-enterprise-only business (Zhang & Li, 2022). Moreover, algorithmic credit evaluation and digital lending, which are AI-based financial inclusion technologies, have the potential to minimize gender disparities in financing because they rely on business information instead of individual characteristics (Kariv et al., 2025).

The second opportunity is presented by the ability of AI to promote efficiency and decision-making based on the data. Women entrepreneurs are being evidenced to be implementing AI analytics, customer segmentation, and inventory management to enhance performance and simplify work (Ahmad et al., 2025). The market of predictive analytics and AI-powered financial management solutions can decrease the cognitive burden of companies by automating their accounting, prediction, and resource management, allowing entrepreneurs to allocate resources to strategic growth and innovation instead (Q. Zhu & Zhang, 2022). Through the combination of these technologies, women entrepreneurs will be able to intensify strategic agility, gain better knowledge of customers, and increase their market presence to a new level, i.e., reshaping how they work, but how they lead the digital economy (Kusetogullari et al., 2025).

There is also the element of increased flexibility and better work-life balance, which is a key issue of concern by women entrepreneurs who are at the same time running businesses and are raising families. The research indicates that women become more inclined to using AI-based digital platforms to balance time limitations, retain control over the working process, and remain productive (Ammirato et al., 2024). The automation of repetitive administrative tasks, enabled by AI, such as chatbots, scheduling, and automated billing and content-generation tools, reduces the number of repetitive administrative duties and allows women to use their time more productively as an entrepreneur and a homeowner (Ahmad et al., 2025. This allowed to create more efficient time management and reduce stress levels by providing entrepreneurs with more autonomy in its working processes. Besides, women who have not had the necessary technical education can create marketing content, analyse the data and handle the communication effectively using generative AI tools (Kusetogullari et al., 2025). In a rural or resource-restricted context of women, additional participation and experimentation in entrepreneurship are further extended by AI-powered mobile apps that provide voice assistance, templates, and contextualized advice (Zhang and Li, 2022).

Besides this, AI enhances the adaptive capacity which is a crucial aspect of entrepreneurial resilience. AI allows women entrepreneurs to identify the emerging risks and dynamically change the strategies with the help of real-time analytics, feedback dashboards, and automated alerts (Kariv et al., 2025). These systems improve confidence, agility, and decision-making initiatives in fast-changing markets when combined with online learning and capacity-building systems (Zhu and Zhang, 2022). Overall, the growing amount of empirical and theoretical data confirms the view that AI presents women in the business with a complex combination of opportunities, consisting of minimizing structural and temporal barriers coupled with the empowerment of strategic choices and the increase of work-life integration (Ammirato et al., 2024). Assist women to surpass issues of scale, mobility and time, AI is a key facilitator of empowerment and mental health, not only a technological breakthrough but also a socio-economic revolution in the digital business arena (Kusetogullari et al., 2025).

4. GENDERED CHALLENGES, RISKS & BARRIERS IN AI ADOPTION

Although AI has great potential in the business of women entrepreneurs, it is not necessarily empowering. The structural, sociocultural, and psychological barriers mediate its possible advantages and determine the capacity of women to accept, believe, and make good use of AI devices (Ammirato et al., 2024). These gendered limitations as displayed in Figure 1 need to be made clear in order to make sure that technological innovation does not reinforce the existing inequalities.

Another significant issue is the digital gender inequality that is especially severe in the developing and emerging economies. Studies have indicated that women are still disadvantaged in the access to digital devices, connections, and digital literacy, which restrict their potential to engage with AI (Zhang & Li, 2022). These gaps are influenced by the socio-economic differences and cultural values that put the power of technology use and the ability to allocate household resources in the hands of men (Ahmad et al., 2025). Besides, the digital divide goes beyond access to encompass confidence, training, and exposure to technology-intensive settings especially in the rural areas (Kariv et al., 2025). This results in women not having access to, and the capability to, exploit AI platforms when they exist, and there remains a cycle where the neediest people in technology empowerment are not yet beneficiaries of digital transformation (Kusetogullari et al., 2025).

Figure 1. Barriers in AI Adoption

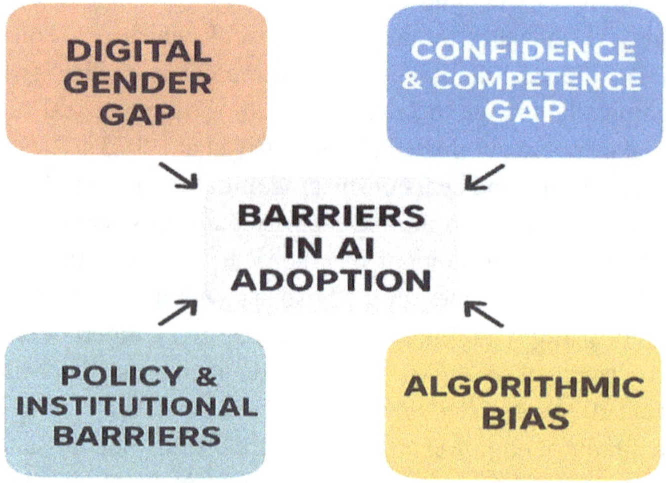

The second obstacle is associated with the confidence gap and perceived competence penalty that women face when adopting AI. Research has shown that women are less likely to use generative AI compared to men regardless of their awareness of the tool and its advantages mainly because of psychological and social negative influences, including the fear of making a mistake in the public, moral concerns, and the fear of judgment (Q. Zhu & Zhang, 2022). In the workplace, gendered expectations tend to increase the focus on technical performance of women, which causes a competence penalty, which deters experimentation (Ammirato et al., 2024). Moreover, the issue of data privacy, harassment on the Internet, and online safety also contribute to the fact that women do not trust AI systems (Ayoko et al., 2021). Collectively, these structural and psychological obstacles limit the confidence of women, their innovativeness and their ability to use AI equally, i.e. the need to design inclusively, to offer necessary ethical safeguards, and to provide specific digital upskilling to help bridge the empowerment divide.

The third group of obstacles occurs because of policy, infrastructure, and institutional barriers that restrict the female participation in AI and digital entrepreneurship. Studies indicate that most innovation ecosystems continue to be gender-blind in terms of policy and funding provisions to enable women to adopt the digital world, causing chronic disparities in access to capital and investment preparedness of AI-based tools (Ammirato et al., 2024). Poor digital infrastructure, such as inaccessible connectivity and the lack of artificial intelligence not only locally but also globally, contributes to the impossibility of equitable participation, especially in the developing economy (Zhang & Li, 2022). Research highlights the need to have inclusive training courses and culturally-related frameworks to develop the digital capabilities of women, without which women will continue to be the peripheral group in technology-driven economies (Ahmad et al., 2025). The institutional biases of the entrepreneurial support systems and financing options are likely to favour male-dominated industries, limiting the scalability of the women-led digital start-ups (Kariv et al., 2025).

Another difficulty is an algorithmic bias and other design practices that do not consider the social and cultural background of women. Training AI systems on non-representative data poses a threat of increasing gender inequalities in credit scoring, recruitment, and provision of digital services (Kusetogullari et al., 2025). Those biases are indicated to be present in less accurate systems to female users, such as the voice recognition or automated models of financial assessment, which could accidentally work against women in business (Ayoko et al., 2021). These types of algorithmic inequalities undermine trust in AI and do not allow women to use it as a strategic enabler (Q. Zhu & Zhang, 2022).

Altogether, AI has the power of transformation, but women are still limited by intersecting gendered obstacles to adoption, including access, confidence, institutional structure, and algorithmic representation. These challenges require not just technological creativity but also non-discriminatory policy frameworks, equal or fair funding frameworks, and a gendered digital capacity building approach to make AI not a form of empowerment, but of exclusion (Ammirato et al., 2024).

5. HOW AI CAN DEVELOP PSYCHOLOGICAL RESILIENCE AND ADAPTIVE CAPACITY

AI can be not only useful to improve the performance of businesses but also help women entrepreneurs increase their ability to adapt and their psychological strength. The resilience of the entrepreneurship is due to cognitive, emotional, and behavioural processes that result in successful reactions to uncertainty (Ahmad et al., 2025). AI assists with these processes by making decisions better, saving time, building new networks and learning continuously and autonomously, enabling women to get a better understanding of the fluctuating markets and social limits as illustrated in Figure 2 (Zhang & Li, 2022). One key way in which AI can build resilience is resilience to uncertainty in the decision-making process. Women entrepreneurs are prone to making decisions in the face of uncertainty in the setting where market information is not easily available. This uncertainty is prevented or diminished through the use of AI analytics and forecasting tools which produce real-time data on consumer behaviour, market trends, and operational performance (Kariv et al., 2025). This set of tools will minimize cognitive load, decrease stress levels and allow more confident and evidence-based decisions, which will lead to a sense of control and agency, a psychological basis of resilience (Ammirato et al., 2024)

Adaptive capacity is also enhanced through AI in terms of better management of time and resources. It happens to use cognitive resources that could be utilized in innovation and strategic development in routine administrative work, e.g., scheduling, invoicing, or content creation. Automation systems powered by AI can simplify such operations and decrease the occurrence of burnout and make entrepreneurship more sustainable (Zhu et al., 2025). To women who juggle between their family and career, automation would enhance efficiency, as well as aid work-life balance and psychological health (Kusetogullari et al., 2025). As a technological and emotional asset, AI will not only boost resilience and flexibility in female-run businesses by creating time to reflect and learn, but also by encouraging emotional resiliency and adaptability (Ahmad et al., 2025).

Figure 2. AI Builds Resilience and Adaptability

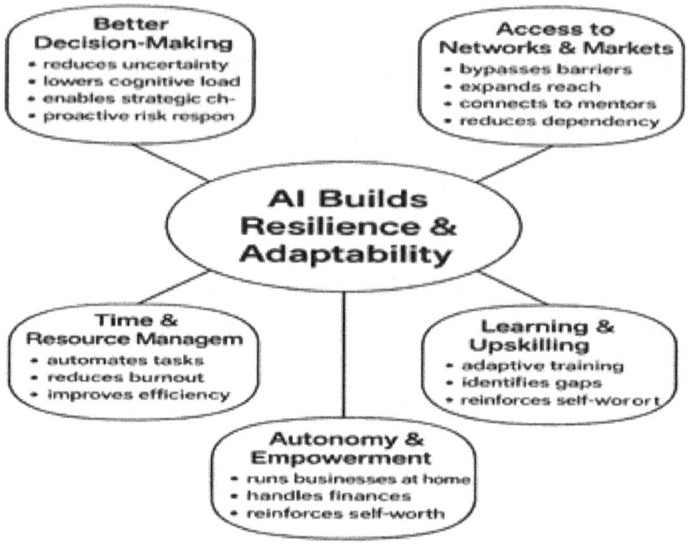

The other important system by which AI can contribute to resilience is the increased access to networks, markets, and resources that are made available through AI-driven digital platforms. The practice of traditional social norms and mobility, and poor infrastructure tend to limit the interaction of women with customers, suppliers and colleagues. The e-commerce and fintech systems powered by AI assist women to overcome these obstacles and increase their activity beyond local geographies and create social capital within the digital ecosystems (Ammirato et al., 2024). Entrepreneurial platforms that are driven by algorithms also links women to mentors, investors and training, enhances confidence, adaptability, and resilience (Ahmad et al., 2025). The use of AI-enhanced digital platforms will help women entrepreneurs become part of global value chains, which strengthens the strength of women-led business ventures by reducing reliance on local networks, which can be bias toward gender (Zhang & Li, 2022).

The role of AI in learning and upskilling is also essential in the formation of psychological resilience. Learning platforms and personalised mentorship systems that use AI offer a type of self-paced learning and identify areas in which the knowledge is weak and help the person to develop competence on a continual basis (Zhu et al., 2025). Getting access to such digital training enhances self-efficacy which is a fundamental pillar of resilience since women can learn to master new technologies and business processes (Kariv et al., 2025). Digital upskilling projects like in India demonstrate that AI-based learning increases the rate at which women engage in e-commerce, financial management, and marketing, as opposed to relying on the normal training system that is male dominated (Kusetogullari et al., 2025).

Another route is that of autonomy and empowerment which are part of the psychological resilience. To most women, being an entrepreneur is an exercise of freedom over the confining social conventions. This autonomy is enhanced by AI by allowing women to operate digital businesses remotely, on their own, and using AI-based fintech solutions that help them control and make their finances transparent (Ammirato et al., 2024). This autonomy fosters the sense of confidence, lessens the reliance on informal male networks and enforces a feeling of agency and competence, which consequently boosts resilience and persistence in the face of setbacks (Ahmad et al., 2025).

Together, these processes data-based decision-making, time-saving, extended digital networks, lifelong learning, and enhanced autonomy will form an enabling ecosystem of the psychological resilience and adaptive ability of women entrepreneurs. AI therefore not only becomes a tool, but a transformative facilitator, remaking the experience of women entrepreneurs and enabling them to survive in complicated, unpredictable conditions (Kusetogullari et al., 2025).

6. CASE STUDIES, EVIDENCE AND EMPIRICAL INSIGHTS

Real-life evidence shows that women entrepreneurs are actively using AI to build psychological resilience, adaptive capacity, and sustainable businesses despite persistent gendered constraints (Table 1). In India, Hindustan Unilever's Project Shakti has enabled rural women micro-entrepreneurs to use AI-supported digital ordering and demand forecasting tools, reducing decision fatigue, improving confidence, and leading to reported income increases of 30–40 percent within a year. Similarly, women sellers on Meesho's social commerce platform leverage AI-driven product recommendations, pricing intelligence, and customer analytics to make informed decisions, experiment with markets, and balance entrepreneurial activity with household responsibilities, thereby strengthening self-efficacy and adaptability. SEWA's digital and fintech initiatives further demonstrate how AI-based credit scoring, mobile payments, and digital bookkeeping tools enhance financial decision-making and emotional security among informal women entrepreneurs by reducing dependence on moneylenders and improving long-term planning. At the ecosystem level, global accelerators such as She Loves Tech provide AI mentoring, funding, and peer networks that help women founders overcome gender bias in venture capital access while reinforcing entrepreneurial identity and resilience. Together, these cases illustrate how AI-enabled tools and platforms, when embedded in supportive ecosystems, can mitigate sociocultural barriers, empower women psychologically and economically, and foster inclusive and sustainable entrepreneurial pathways in the digital era.

Table 1. Women entrepreneurs AI Empirical Insights

Case / Initiative	Context	AI Tools / Interventions	Key Psychological & Business Outcomes
Project Shakti (HUL, India)	Rural women micro-entrepreneurs distributing FMCG products	AI-supported digital ordering, demand forecasting, inventory recommendations	Reduced decision fatigue; increased confidence and autonomy; income growth of 30–40%; improved adaptability to disruptions
Meesho Women Sellers (India)	Home-based women entrepreneurs in Tier-II/III cities	AI-driven product recommendations, pricing intelligence, customer analytics	Enhanced self-efficacy; faster learning and experimentation; improved work–life balance; scalable digital entrepreneurship
SEWA Digital & FinTech Initiatives (India)	Informal women entrepreneurs in handicrafts, agriculture, services	AI-based credit scoring, digital payments, bookkeeping tools	Improved financial decision-making; reduced reliance on moneylenders; increased psychological security and planning ability
She Loves Tech Accelerator (Global)	Women-led AI and tech startups	AI mentoring, prototyping support, grants, investor matching	Stronger entrepreneurial identity; resilience to rejection; improved access to capital and networks
Etsy Women Sellers (Global)	Women artisans and creatives balancing care and business	AI recommendation algorithms, sales forecasting, marketing analytics	Reduced uncertainty and stress; income stability; sustainable business scaling without physical expansion

7. POLICIES, ECOSYSTEM & INSTITUTIONAL SUPPORT FOR INCLUSIVE AI-ENABLED WOMEN ENTREPRENEURSHIP

According to recent studies, an inclusive and resilient AI-enabled entrepreneurial environment that will empower women will require more than an uptake of technology, it will require a systemic ecosystem-wide approach. Research highlights that policy frameworks, education, and access to innovation should converge to eliminate financial, cultural, and digital barriers to the potential of women to be entrepreneurs (Sunny & Singh, 2025). In addition to this, another study finds that sustainable empowerment is constrained by incorporating digital interventions, skill building, and micro-enterprise development into inclusive institutional regimes (Alamuri et al., 2025). Collectively, these works portend that the potential of AI to transform women entrepreneurs can be fulfilled, but only when all of the mentioned factors work synergistically: skilling, access to funds, women-friendly design, mentorship, and social reform as shown in Figure 3.

Among the most essential facilitators of the inclusive AI-based entrepreneurship, skilling and training programs that entail digital literacy, AI tools and data-driven decision-making can be distinguished. Although there is a high interest rate among many women in the world of AI, the available literature illustrates that knowledge gaps in technical expertise and confidence remain a barrier to the adoption. Research indicates that to increase women economic independence and their involvement, particularly in rural regions, specific digital skills and vocation programs are important (Alamuri et al., 2025). The Sakti Café model of public- private-collaboration illustrates how empowering women financially and operationally could be achieved through training in the basics of AI, e-commerce, and digital marketing (Dash, 2025). Equally, when technology education is combined with financial literacy, women entrepreneurs will have the capacity to successfully incorporate AI solutions in their businesses.

To be the most effective, these programs should be multilingual, affordable, flexible, and aware of time constraints of women, especially those who combine their entrepreneurial direction with the need to take care of children. Skilling programs, designed inclusively can lead to increased digital confidence and reduce barriers to adoption and enable women to make meaningful use of AI to build on their business resiliency and competitiveness.

The second important pillar in an inclusive AI ecosystem is the financial inclusion and fair access to capital. Research indicates that adoption of AI is usually accompanied by expenses on infrastructure, software, and also skills training; expenses that are unaffordable to a good number of women because of structural financial marginalization. The discriminatory lending, insufficient collateral, and a poor financial literacy status still limit women entrepreneurial development as the level of innovation potential increases (Sunny and Singh, 2025). Likewise, combining financial literacy and access to technology is critical in inclusion of women entrepreneurs in AI-based small businesses in a sustainable way (Akponeware et al., 2022). Good digital infrastructure is also a requirement. The women-led micro-enterprises, especially in rural India, require access to cheap internet, gadgets, and safe payment systems in order to be empowered. Enhanced privacy of data, cybersecurity and regulatory protections are also of paramount importance, since safety issues are disproportionately impacting women in their online activities. Collectively, these results support the idea that inclusive AI entrepreneurship should be supported by a strong digital infrastructure and financial access which would help provide equity in the engagement and stability.

Figure 3. Policy Framework for Inclusive AI-Enabled Women's Entrepreneurship

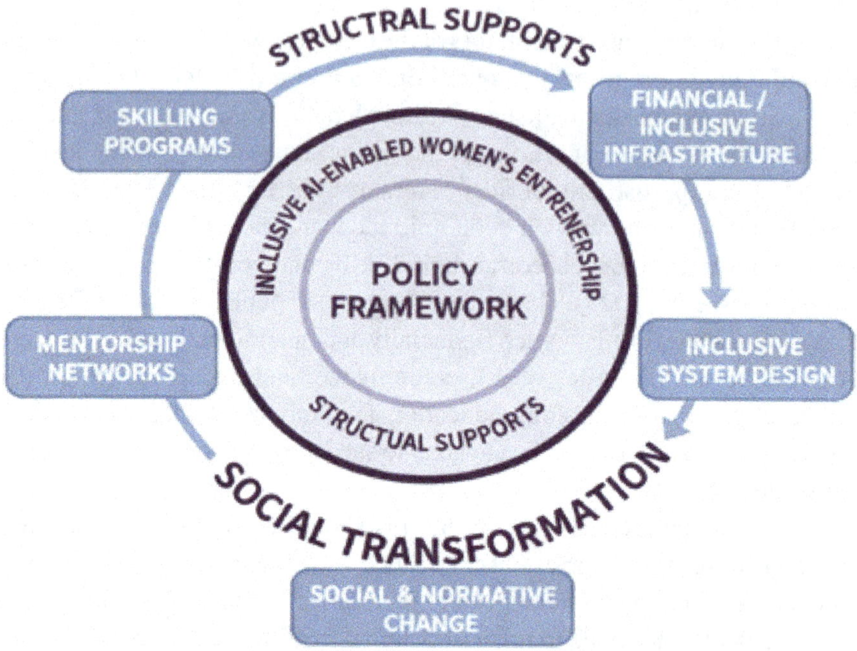

Mentorship, peer networks and gender sensitive design is a third critical element of an inclusive AI ecosystem in developing AI products. The developed mentorship programs and peer support help women in business to overcome the barriers of technological embracement, gain confidence, and become effective users of digital technology in their business (Tripathi and Trivedi, 2025). Likewise, social and economic resilience in women entrepreneurs is established through community-based mentorship programs that provide opportunities to learn and solve problems together (Dash, 2025). Meanwhile, not much of the literature cautions that a gender-blind AI design can be subject to reproducing bias, excluding women users, and strengthening the status quo, unless the processes of development proactively incorporate the experiences and cultural contexts of women (Alameeri et al., 2025). The inclusion of women in the AI co-design processes and at the same time the maintenance of linguistic and cultural inclusivity, data privacy and safety can make digital tools truly empowering tools of various entrepreneurial communities.

Lastly, social and normative change ought to be advocated to see to it that women enjoy some equal benefits of AI-driven entrepreneurship. The gender norms and institutional obstacles remain barriers to the women entrepreneurial independence, and the culturally responsive policies and the social campaigns are necessary to change the attitude of the community (Alameeri et al., 2025). Similarly, it is crucial that women address socio-cultural and regulatory limits to be able to make maximum use of innovation and technology in their business (Sunny & Singh, 2025). The presented community-driven programs show that grassroots efforts, mentorship, and awareness efforts can be used to normalize the use of technology among women, gain visibility, and become more empowered in making decisions. With the changing of social norms being the combined operation of governments, NGOs, and educational institutions, women are becoming more confident and freer to be creative, trial, and error and run AI-enhanced enterprises successfully.

To conclude, women should have an inclusive AI-enabled entrepreneurship based on the multi-layered ecosystem: the availability and relevance of training; equal financial and digital resources; facilitated mentoring and gender-sensitive technological design; and advocacy of sociocultural change. However, it is only when these factors are combined that AI can become a real empowerment tool in the form of reinforcing the psychological strength of women, enhancing opportunity, and empowering women to establish sustainable, adaptable, and future-proof enterprises.

8. IMPLICATIONS AND FUTURE RESEARCH

The introduction of AI into women entrepreneurship is a historic event both in terms of achieving gender-inclusive economic engagement and a difficult area of research, policy, and ethical issues. The innovative force that can change the lives of women entrepreneurs will rely on the ability to tackle structural disparities using evidence-based policy and gender-sensitive structures (Sunny & Singh, 2025).

Similarly, other ethical and cultural aspects, including the bias of AI systems and institutional inequity, should be prioritized in research and policy-making in the future.

One of the implications in future studies is the need to resolve the long-standing issue of a lack of gendered data and in-depth analytical frameworks of AI adoption. Although innovation and technology are advantageous to women entrepreneurs, current analyses do not take into account gendered disparities in access and performance, which constrains the effectiveness of policies (Sunny and Singh, 2025). On the same note, there is a tendency towards short-term studies on women entrepreneurship that do not keep abreast of changing psychological and social aspects of life like resilience, confidence, and a sense of perceived autonomy. In order to develop the discipline, longitudinal and multidimensional studies should be conducted to follow the impact of AI integration on the good performance of women in business, their emotional state, and flexibility in the long run. The inclusion of the psychological constructs e.g. self-efficacy, entrepreneurial stress and empowerment will be a supplement to the existing models and will create more comprehensive theories of technology-enabled and gender-inclusive entrepreneurship.

To inform policy and practice, it is indicated that the inclusionary AI policies are urgently required with a direct focus on the gendered barriers to adoption. The digital interventions, skills training, and micro-enterprise assistance should be referenced in national schemes to spur fair contribution among the women entrepreneurs (Alamuri et al., 2025). Similarly, the reforms in the policy should be access-based, mentorship, and innovation hubs to eliminate systemic barriers and enable women to have a meaningful access to AI technologies. Infrastructure (digital) must be empowered with low-cost internet, safe payment systems, and increased financial inclusion, as well. Educating women on the use of technology and providing women with access to financial literacy and gender-sensitive lending systems can help women transition to long-term AI adoption. These policies that encourage mentorship networks, incubators, and hubs designed to support women, therefore, create an ecosystem that is holistic and creates confidence and a bridge between digital opportunity and legal long-term entrepreneur empowerment.

Figure 4. AI & Women Entrepreneurship Future Direction

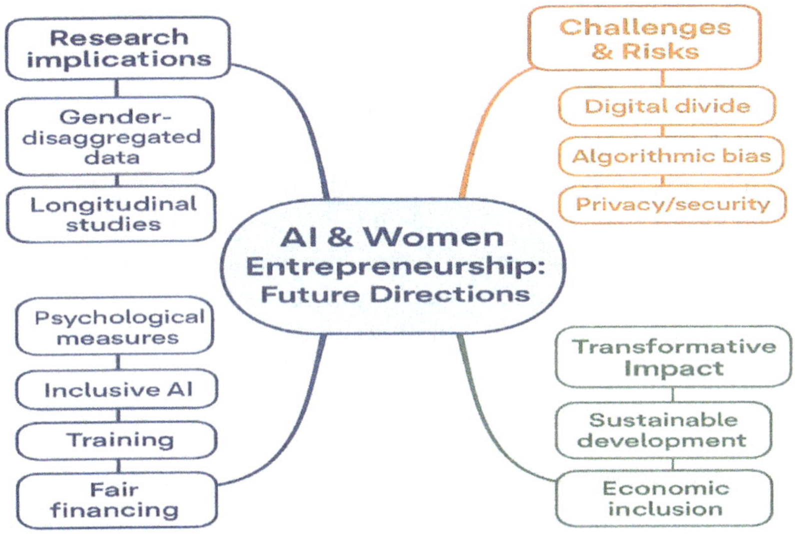

Nevertheless, there are a number of ongoing challenges and risks that are to be followed. The digital gender divide is among the most urgent challenges- without the equal access to the devices, connectivity, and abilities, AI implementation can be used to reinforce the socio-economic disparities. Women cannot be empowered through innovation only unless the financial, cultural and structural inequities are set aside. The other possible threat is AI bias, which has been demonstrated to recreate discriminatory judgments by learning on biased information and thereby heightening marginalization in the financial sector and publicity to female-owned business ventures.

The issue of privacy, cybersecurity, online safety are also relevant. Together with responsible governance systems, safe digital spaces are needed to allow women to become confident AI-powered ecosystem participants. In the future, comprehensive AI implementation can have revolutionary social payoffs wherein women dominated digital businesses improve social welfare, community stability, and economic diversity in a region. In conclusion, to achieve the potential of AI in women entrepreneurship we need to act both in research, policy and practice. As illustrated in Figure 4, by dismantling systemic barriers, ensuring algorithmic fairness, strengthening digital and financial ecosystems, and promoting gender-equitable design, stakeholders can transform AI into a catalyst for sustainable empowerment and inclusive economic growth.

9. CONCLUSION

This chapter has shown that artificial intelligence has the power to transform women's entrepreneurship by strengthening psychological resilience, adaptive capacity, and access to economic opportunity. Empirical studies demonstrate that AI tools enable women to manage uncertainty, improve decision-making, enhance efficiency, and expand their market. These technologies offer cognitive and operational support that reduces stress and builds confidence, helping women pursue entrepreneurial ventures with greater autonomy and strategic clarity. However, these benefits depend on complementary systems—robust digital infrastructure, equitable financial access, inclusive skilling, and supportive policies—to prevent AI from deepening gender inequalities (Sunny & Singh, 2025). The persistent digital divide, algorithmic bias, and socio-cultural barriers underscore the urgency of gender-sensitive AI design that reflects women lived realities.

Future research should integrate economic, social, and psychological dimensions—tracking long-term outcomes such as well-being, autonomy, and resilience through gender-disaggregated and longitudinal studies. Simultaneously, policy action must promote equitable AI access, inclusive digital ecosystems, and cultural change that expands women's mobility and confidence. Ultimately, the integration of AI into women's entrepreneurship offers a path toward a more inclusive and resilient economic future—one in which women are not only beneficiaries of technology but active innovators shaping the evolution of entrepreneurial ecosystems.

REFERENCES

Ahmad, S., Zhang, Q., Hussain, M. A., & Mahmood, S. (2025). Entrepreneurial success through learning, capital, and work engagement: Market and service orientation perspective. *Acta Psychologica*, *258*, 105188. DOI: 10.1016/j.actpsy.2025.105188 PMID: 40609188

Akponeware, A., Dawood, N., Rodriguez-Trejo, S., & Dawood, H. (2022). An integrated empirical analysis of UK rail industry's carbon assessment: An industry perspective. *Case Studies on Transport Policy*, *10*(1), 315–330. DOI: 10.1016/j.cstp.2021.12.012

Alameeri, K., Zakaria, N., & Rahman, S. A. (2025). Women's Entrepreneurship in the UAE: Exploring Cultural, Societal, and Structural Challenges through a Conceptual Lens. *International Review of Management and Marketing*, *15*(5), 414–421. DOI: 10.32479/irmm.19844

Alamuri, S., Aluvala, R., & Chittipaka, V. (2025). Innovative Pathways for Empowerment of Rural Women through Sustainable and Diversified Livelihoods. In R. Nagariya, P. Dhaundiyal, K. Mathiyazhagan, & V. Mishra (Eds.), *Proceedings of the International Conference on Sustainable Business Practices and Innovative Models (ICSBPIM-2025)* (Vol. 349, pp. 381–393). Atlantis Press International BV. DOI: 10.2991/978-94-6463-872-1_25

Ammirato, S., Felicetti, A. M., Troise, C., Santoro, G., & Rozsa, Z. (2024). Human resources well-being in innovative start-ups: Insights from a systematic review of the literature. *Journal of Innovation & Knowledge*, *9*(4), 100580. DOI: 10.1016/j.jik.2024.100580

Ayoko, O. B., Caputo, A., & Mendy, J. (2021). Management research contributions to the COVID-19: A bibliometric literature review and analysis of the contributions from the *Journal of Management & Organization*. *Journal of Management & Organization*, *27*(6), 1183–1209. DOI: 10.1017/jmo.2021.70

Azad, M., & Marinova, D. (2025). Small Business Entrepreneurship Among Rural Women: A Strategy for Sustainable Development – A Case Study of Mazu Village. *Humanities and Social Sciences*, *13*(5), 486–497. DOI: 10.11648/j.hss.20251305.19

Camps, C., Kraus, S., Thomas, A., Tiberius, V., & Jones, P. (2026). Digital Entrepreneurship: A review, research synthesis, and development of a framework. *Technology in Society*, *84*, 103124. DOI: 10.1016/j.techsoc.2025.103124

Dash, S. (2025). Sakti Cafe: Empowering Women's Financial Independence and Livelihood Advancement in Odisha, India. *Asian Journal of Education and Social Studies, 51*(4), 200–210. DOI: 10.9734/ajess/2025/v51i41861

Games, D., Masli, E., Sari, D., Triani, L., & Komalasari, S. (2025). Generational cohort and technology readiness and acceptance of artificial intelligence among young high-growth entrepreneurs. *Digital Transformation and Society*, 1–21. DOI: 10.1108/DTS-02-2025-0040

Kariv, D., Attar, I., Haber, Y., & Elyoseph, Z. (2025). AI-simulated entrepreneurship under uncertainty: Forecasting university-driven capability evolution. *The Journal of Technology Transfer*. Advance online publication. DOI: 10.1007/s10961-025-10306-7

Kusetogullari, A., Kusetogullari, H., Andersson, M., & Gorschek, T. (2025). *GenAI in Entrepreneurship: A systematic review of generative artificial intelligence in entrepreneurship research: current issues and future directions* (Version 1). arXiv. DOI: 10.48550/ARXIV.2505.05523

Mulenga, R. (2025). THE DIGITAL EVOLUTION OF BUSINESS, EDUCATION, AND GOVERNANCE IN EMERGING ECONOMIES. *International Journal of Innovative Technologies in Economy, 3*(51). Advance online publication. DOI: 10.31435/ijite.3(51).2025.3429

Putri, V. C. C., & Sonni, A. F. (2025). AI-Driven Personal Branding for Female Entrepreneurs: The Indonesian Hijabi Startup Ecosystem. *Journalism and Media, 6*(3), 131. DOI: 10.3390/journalmedia6030131

Raman, R., Alka, T. A., Suresh, M., & Nedungadi, P. (2025). Social entrepreneurship and sustainable technologies: Impact on communities, social innovation, and inclusive development. *Sustainable Technology and Entrepreneurship, 4*(3), 100110. DOI: 10.1016/j.stae.2025.100110

Sunny, B., & Singh, A. (2025). Analysing the Role of Innovation in Enhancing Women-Led Entrepreneurial Ventures. In R. Nagariya, P. Dhaundiyal, K. Mathiyazhagan, & V. Mishra (Eds.), *Proceedings of the International Conference on Sustainable Business Practices and Innovative Models (ICSBPIM-2025)* (Vol. 349, pp. 1073–1089). Atlantis Press International BV. DOI: 10.2991/978-94-6463-872-1_66

Tripathi, P., & Trivedi, A. (2025). *Breaking Barriers Through Innovation: The Rise of Women Entrepreneurs*. Cureus Journal of Business and Economics., DOI: 10.7759/s44404-025-05917-0

Xanthopoulou, P., & Sahinidis, A. (2025). Mapping the Intersection of Entrepreneurship, Digitalization, and the SDGs: A Scopus-Based Literature Review. *Sustainability (Basel)*, *17*(18), 8420. DOI: 10.3390/su17188420

Yadav, U. S., Vyas, S., Kanchan, , Ghosal, I., & yadav, A. K. (2024). Impact of entrepreneurial leadership, Social media, digital technology, Entrepreneurial orientation and innovation on business performance in the handicraft sector: Talent management as mediating construct. *Journal of Innovation and Entrepreneurship*, *13*(1), 72. DOI: 10.1186/s13731-024-00434-z

Zhang, L., & Li, J. (2022). Analysis of the influence of entrepreneurial psychology on the index system of digital development of the equipment manufacturing industry. *Frontiers in Psychology*, *13*, 1026603. DOI: 10.3389/fpsyg.2022.1026603 PMID: 36425832

Zhu, H., Zeng, W., & Chen, L. (2025). Transforming molecular diagnostics learning: The power of gamification in higher medical education. *Frontiers in Education*, *10*, 1502203. DOI: 10.3389/feduc.2025.1502203

Zhu, Q., & Zhang, H. (2022). Teaching Strategies and Psychological Effects of Entrepreneurship Education for College Students Majoring in Social Security Law Based on Deep Learning and Artificial Intelligence. *Frontiers in Psychology*, *13*, 779669. DOI: 10.3389/fpsyg.2022.779669 PMID: 35369210

Chapter 11
Bias and Fairness in AI-Driven Models of Entrepreneurial Traits Toward Equitable Innovation Ecosystems

Mohan Kumar
http://orcid.org/0000-0002-5171-0892
SGT University, India

Jeayaram Subramanian
O.P. Jindal Global University, India

Damith Gangodawilage
http://orcid.org/0000-0001-7968-6284
Qasim Ibrahim School of Business, Villa College, Maldives

A. S. Suresh
DBS Global University, Dehradun, India

ABSTRACT

Artificial intelligence (AI) has increasingly been applied to model entrepreneurial traits, offering new insights into constructs such as creativity, resilience, and risk-taking. However, these AI systems often inherit biases from datasets, feature selection, and algorithmic processes, which can misrepresent entrepreneurial potential and perpetuate inequities across gender, socioeconomic, and cultural groups. This chapter examines the conceptual foundations of bias and fairness in AI, explores

DOI: 10.4018/979-8-2600-1353-3.ch011

techniques for detecting and mitigating bias, and highlights ethical considerations and policy implications for equitable deployment. It emphasizes the importance of inclusive data practices, fairness-aware algorithms, explainable AI, and participatory governance to foster trust and accountability in entrepreneurial ecosystems. Future directions focus on interdisciplinary approaches, culturally sensitive Modeling, and regulatory frameworks to ensure AI supports diversity, inclusivity, and responsible innovation in entrepreneurship research and practice.

INTRODUCTION

The introduction of artificial intelligence (AI) into the study of entrepreneurship has opened up new possibilities in the explanation of the psychological dispositions that guide entrepreneurial behaviour. Other constructs that were historically examined with the help of psychometric tests and self-reports include risk-taking, creativity, resilience, and motivation (Rauch and Frese, 2007; Zhao and Seibert, 2006). The current AI-driven models, in their turn, allow analysing massive behavioural, cognitive and social data to predict and assess entrepreneurial potential with accuracy like never before (Nambisan, 2017)(Choudhary et al., 2021). Although such models are efficient and scalable, they also present some serious concerns about prejudice and equality. AI bias may be caused by various factors, such as training data that is not representative, imperfect annotation, and societal stereotypes, which eventually results in misguided results in trait modelling (Mehrabi et al., 2021). The issues of such distortions are particularly troublesome in the field of entrepreneurship, where biased algorithms can help to support the existing disparities between the genders, cultures, or socioeconomic groups (Fossen and Sorgner, 2021).

Fairness, in this case, can be seen both in terms of the fair treatment of people regardless of their demographic status and the fact that AI models are supposed to be based on a fair and non-discriminatory perception of entrepreneurial potential. Since entrepreneurship is being seen as a source of economic growth and innovation, especially in the context of heterogeneous world markets (Shane and Venkataraman, 2000), fairness in AI-based evaluations is a moral and a practical necessity. Lack of bias will lead to the continuation of structural disadvantage, which limits opportunities of underrepresented entrepreneurs and the diversity of entrepreneurial ecosystems (Caliskan et al., 2017)(Trivedi et al., 2023a). In this chapter, the author investigates the complexity of bias and fairness in AI models of entrepreneurial characteristics, their theoretical background, practical consequences, and how to create more equitable systems. Centralising the bias and fairness in the AI-based entrepreneurship research, this discussion will help to promote responsible innovation that considers the importance of technology development and ethical responsibility.

Learning the Characteristics of an Entrepreneur

Entrepreneurial qualities have been a point of focus in entrepreneurship literature wherein scholars have attempted to determine the individual qualities that make the entrepreneur stand out as a non-enterprise. Entrepreneurial intentions and behaviour are always associated with such traits as risk-taking, achievement need, innovativeness, self-efficacy, and resilience (Rauch and Frese, 2007; Zhao and Seibert, 2006). The risk-taking, especially, is generally considered to be one of the key characteristics, which can help the entrepreneur to make a decision when uncertain and be ready to take a chance that other people might not take (Stewart and Roth, 2001). Correspondingly, resilience and persistence are essential to be able to survive the downs and changes in the dynamic entrepreneurial landscape, and creativity and innovativeness are essential in generating new business ideas and competitive advantage (Hmieleski and Baron, 2009)(Tayal et al., 2019). These characteristics combined determine how people find opportunities, marshal resources and long-term survival of ventures.

Conventional methods in the study of entrepreneurial characteristics have immensely depended on psychometric tests, personality tests and questionnaires. An example of this is the Big Five personality model, which has been extensively used to investigate relationships between the general personality dimensions (e.g. openness to experience and conscientiousness) and entrepreneurial performance (Zhao et al., 2010). Despite the insights that such approaches have provided, they are inadequate in the context of the dynamic and context-dependent nature of entrepreneurial behaviour. The characteristics can vary between cultures, industries, or venture development phases, which makes one doubt the existence of universal trait models (Schlaegel and Koenig, 2014). Additionally, self-reported scales are susceptible to social desirability bias, response style, and recall bias, which can bias the results and limit the predictive validity of trait measures (Podsakoff et al., 2003).

With the emergence of AI-based approaches, there is a new possibility to investigate the characteristics of entrepreneurs on a large scale and more objectively. Digital footprints (activity on social media, online interactions, business correspondence, etc.) can be analysed using machine learning and natural language processing to deduce psychological characteristics (Kosinski et al., 2016). This data-driven solution will be able to record behavioural trends in real-time to provide a more sophisticated and context-sensitive perception of entrepreneurial tendencies. Furthermore, AI models have the ability to combine multimodal data, such as linguistic indicators to biometric ones, to identify hidden characteristics that can be difficult to detect in other forms (Hofmans et al., 2020)(Tunio & Tunio, 2025). These developments do not only contribute to the predictive capacity of entrepreneurial trait studies, but also allow the determination of new, emergent traits that apply to digital and globalised entrepreneurial ecosystems.

However, validity, interpretation, and fairness issues are also present in the transition to AI-based trait modelling. In contrast to conventional psychometric tests, AI-based models are frequently based on black box algorithms, which make it hard to determine whether the identified traits are a true psychological construct or a result of biased data (Floridi and Cowls, 2019). Moreover, entrepreneurial characteristics are not fixed but change as a result of experience, learning and contextual pressures (Baum and Locke, 2004)(Yadav et al., 2019). This dynamic nature can only be captured using the models that are sensitive to temporal and situational variations as opposed to the models that view traits as stable indicators. Therefore, even though AI has an enormous potential in terms of developing the research on entrepreneurial characteristics, it should be utilized with the consideration of the methodological rigor and ethical consequences.

AI Model Prejudice: Theoretical Underpinnings

Prejudice within AI models is a multidimensional phenomenon that presents a direct threat to the credibility and impartiality of results in modelling of entrepreneurial traits. Fundamentally, the concept of bias refers to systematic errors in collecting, training, or predicting data that result in unfair or inaccurate outcomes (Mehrabi et al., 2021). Even though simplification and error are part of all models, bias becomes an issue when it harms a group or group of people at a rate that is disproportionate to others and only contributes to the inequalities that already exist. As an example, an AI model, which has been trained on previous data regarding successful entrepreneurs, can be biased in three ways: it can overvalue attributes characteristic of dominant groups, including male, Western, or affluent entrepreneurs, and undervalue equally applicable attributes present in women or entrepreneurs in emerging economies (Fossen and Sorgner, 2021)(Tunio et al., 2021). These imbalances are dangerous because they can bias forecasts of entrepreneurial potential and reduce inclusiveness of entrepreneurial ecosystems (Trivedi et al., 2023b; Yadav et al., 2023).

Researchers usually divide bias in AI models into a number of different types. Biases in data Unrepresentative or incomplete training data can cause data bias, such as when digital traces of entrepreneurial activity are mostly captured in technologically advanced areas, entrepreneurs in resource-constrained environments have been underrepresented (Suresh and Guttag, 2021). The source of algorithmic bias is when the model itself enhances the difference in favour of optimisation processes, e.g. when the model favours accuracy by compromising equity between demographic groups (Friedman & Nissenbaum, 1996). Human bias is a phenomenon that shows the impact of researchers, practitioners, or annotators who introduce their assumptions and stereotypes at labeling practices or feature selection (Barocas and Selbst, 2016). These categories frequently have interaction in the subtle forms, and bias detection and correction is an extremely complicated task.

One of the most important differences in this conversation is one related to bias and error. Whereas error is defined as random deviation that influences the quality of prediction, bias is directional and systematic and tends to cause consistent disadvantages to particular groups (Hardt et al., 2016). As an illustration, when an AI model predicts lower creativity of female entrepreneurs with repeated accuracy because of biased training data, it is bias and not error. This difference is important since mistakes can be reduced by promoting model modifications but biases tend to need proactive correction measures to deal with their causes (Kumar et al., 2025; Mohan Kumar, Yadav & Sahoo, 2025). Additionally, biases have social implications, unlike random errors, which can be used to construct the understanding of who is perceived as a typical or a high-potential entrepreneur.

Bias has also got a cultural aspect especially where entrepreneurial characteristics are concerned. Different cultures perceive the conceptualisation of characteristics like risk-taking, resilience, or innovativeness differently (Hofstede, 2001). Examples of risk-taking include the Western entrepreneurial system that may see risk-taking as a sign of bravery, but collectivist cultures may consider this differently and assess risk based on a sense of community. In case AI models are based on Western-centric data only, they will be prone to generating culturally biased portrayals of entrepreneurial competence. Therefore, bias in trait modelling is not only technologically flawed but also epistemologically based on the universality of the entrepreneurial construct (Floridi and Cowls, 2019).

The fact that AI models continue to be biased highlights the importance of critically reviewing the values and design decisions that are entrenched in computational systems. AI models are not neutral; they mirror human preferences regarding what data to be included, what features to be prioritised and what results to be optimised (Crawford, 2021)(Yadav et al., 2025). The acknowledgement of such options as value-based in nature redefines bias as a technical problem but a highly social and moral one. In the field of entrepreneurship this awareness involves the understanding of how biased models can unintentionally favor some archetypes at the expense of others, thus affecting access to funding, training or policy support.

By decanaling the conceptual base of prejudice, researchers and practitioners will be able to proceed to creation of fairness-conscious AI systems that trade off predictive accuracy with ethical responsibility. The concept of bias as a natural danger in AI-based trait modelling is key to making sure that technological innovation will bring more inclusive and fair entrepreneurial environments into play.

Equity in AI: Theoretical Viewpoints

Equity in AI has become one of the most urgent issues of designing and implementing predictive models, especially when they are in the area of human potential and opportunity. Fairness in the context of entrepreneurial trait modelling is not limited to technical accuracy, but also to equity, justice, and inclusivity. Fairness involves the fact that AI systems do not have a systematic disadvantage against people without considering gender, ethnicity, socioeconomic status, or culture (Barocas et al., 2019). Due to the fact that entrepreneurial ecosystems are dependent on diversity of thought, background and approach, equity in AI-based evaluation is not only an ethical concern but also a practical means of maintaining innovation (Kumar et al., 2023; Nguyen et al., 2025). Devoid of equity, AI systems threaten to reduce the very concept of entrepreneur potential, support inequalities in society, and negate the validity of entrepreneurship studies and practice.

Social and political philosophy, especially traditions of distributive justice and equality, is also frequently used as a theoretical basis of fairness in AI. Demographic parity, in turn, presupposes that the results of AI systems should not depend on such attributes as gender or ethnicity that are under protection (Dwork et al., 2012). An AI model of entrepreneurial success should thus not intentionally give larger scores to male entrepreneurs than female entrepreneurs when other relevant factors are held constant. Equal opportunity focuses on the fact that people of equal ability or qualification must be given equal chances of positive results (Hardt et al., 2016). In entrepreneurial trait modelling, this would imply that two persons who have the same resilience or creativity would get the same prediction irrespective of their demographic background. Individual fairness is based on the notion that similar people should receive similar treatment (Dwork et al., 2012), which is specifically applicable in the business world, where subtle personal traits and situational aspects determine performance.

In addition to computational definitions, fairness has a contextual and cultural aspect as well. What can be fair in one entrepreneurial ecosystem, may not be in another, based on the local norms, values and institutional arrangements (Hofstede, 2001)(Kumar et al., 2025). As an example, fairness in a society that is highly collectivist can be achieved by rewarding joint leadership and community strength as some of the entrepreneurial capabilities, instead of focusing on such more individualistic characteristics as aggressive risk-taking. This highlights the idea that fairness is not a one-dimensional value but it needs to be receptive to the socio-cultural context within which AI models are utilized (Binns, 2018). As a result, AI-based entrepreneurship research is not only a technical construct but also a normative construct that is formed based on cultural anticipations, societal values, and moral standards.

The other important dimension is that of fairness versus accuracy. In most situations, pasting fairness restrictions may decrease predictive accuracy, creating conflicts between technical model optimisation and fairness (Chouldechova and Roth, 2020). As an example, an AI model that is trained to optimise predictive accuracy can recreate past inequalities inadvertently, but a model that is conscious of fairness may compromise predictive accuracy to achieve fairer results. Such a trade-off begs ethical questions: which models should be of most interest to entrepreneurship researchers and policymakers: those that are most accurate or those that are most fair? The solution is not merely technical but also can be based on larger social goals, including inclusive entrepreneurial ecosystem building.

The lack of transparency and accountability are the preconditions to the attainment of fairness in artificial intelligence. Without clear and explainable rationale of predictive decisions, stakeholders cannot determine whether models behave fairly or are systematically biased. Explainable AI (XAI) is suggested as the way of improving interpretability, which will allow researchers, entrepreneurs, and policymakers to examine model behaviour and results (Doshi-Velez and Kim, 2017). Transparent systems not only create a sense of trust, but also enable the stake holders to challenge unjust results and therefore create a feedback loop that gradually enhances fairness. Such transparency may be useful in the context of entrepreneurial trait modelling as it may help the more accurate and clear expression of the operationalisation of constructs like creativity or resilience thus alleviating the threat of covert bias.

In general, fairness in artificial intelligence is a multidimensional construct that requires balancing of the technical, ethical, and cultural factors. The conceptual frameworks, such as demographic parity, equal opportunity, and individual fairness, provide good points of departure in operationalising fairness in the context of entrepreneurial trait modelling. However, the concept of fairness should be placed within more extensive social values and business standards to prevent the simple imitation of the prevailing views. To fulfill this, it is necessary that methodological rigor is combined with a long-term commitment to ethical contemplation and participatory design, which would make AI applications in the field of entrepreneurship research serve different populations in an equitable and conscientious manner.

In their application in the context of entrepreneurial characteristics, AI models reproduce and increase many types of bias that exist both in the data and in algorithms. Since such constructs as risk-taking, resilience, and creativity are abstract in nature, their operationalisation depends on the proxy indicators, which are survey responses, linguistic or behavioural indicators. This reliance establishes many chances of bias, especially in situations where the proxies are unable to reflect the depth or cultural diversity of entrepreneurial behaviour (Pankaj et al., 2023) (Floridi and Cowls, 2019). As an illustration, risk-taking can be deduced on the basis of financial investment behavior, but these measures may not capture those entrepreneurs in resource-constrained environments who undertake non-financial risks, including reputational or social risks. The AI models can therefore produce systematically biased images of entrepreneurial potential, benefiting some groups and disadvantaging others.

Data collection and representation bias is one of the most common causes of distortion in AI-based trait modelling. Training datasets are often assembled in large amounts using digital traces, such as LinkedIn profiles, startup registries, and crowdfunding platforms, which are mostly biased towards capturing entrepreneurs who have access to digital infrastructure (Nambisan, 2017). Such selective inclusion unwillingly leaves actors in informal economies, rural areas, or developing regions out, creating a digital divide in the form of biased predictors of traits. Historical data also hew to the overrepresentation of male, Western, and well-capitalised businesspersons, thus inculcating the structural inequalities to survive into AI models (Fossen and Sorgner, 2021). Consequently, the models can stereotype these dominating groups as the norm with which all other entrepreneurs can be compared, and these stereotypes can strengthen the stereotyping of successful entrepreneurship.

The problem of bias in the selection of features and labels to characteristics presents more issues. The AI models are based on annotated training data to learn the relationship between attributes and definite entrepreneurial qualities. Nevertheless, the labelling process can be quite subjective, as it depends on the assumptions of researchers or annotators (Barocas and Selbst, 2016). As an example, linguistic signs of creativity could be found on the basis of Western idioms or phrases, thus, overlooking culturally specific types of innovative communication. Equally, the operationalisation of entrepreneurial resilience can be achieved by the post-failure financial recovery, ignoring the psychologically or socially oriented resilience which is also relevant in various cultures. These labelling processes reduce the conceptual breadth of the entrepreneurial characteristics to give biased models that cannot describe its diversity.

There is also prejudice in the model training and evaluation. The accuracy of the predictions made by machine-learning algorithms is maximized, which often leads to unfairness (Chouldechova and Roth, 2020). As an example, an algorithm can always forecast greater entrepreneurial potential in the case of people in urban centres since training data is biased to more successful ventures in those areas. Without the fairness restrictions, the model can consider urban background as an indicator of entrepreneurial capability, and rural entrepreneurs will be disadvantaged regardless of their genuine qualities. Moreover, measures of evaluation like overall accuracy or F-1 score do not tend to capture differences between subgroups, allowing biased models to be considered successful at the cost of misclassifying underrepresented groups of people (Mehrabi et al., 2021).

An example of the consequences of these prejudices can be captured in real-life situations. Recruitment technology that learns to find the entrepreneurial talent the accelerator or venture-capital portfolio wants, such as the assertiveness of communication style men tend to have more often than women, can overvalue those traits and undervalue collaborative or empathetic leadership styles that women tend to have more frequently (Feldman, 2021). Cross-cultural differences may also be neglected; AI systems that are created in the United States might lack the ability to forecast entrepreneurial potential in collectivist cultures where entrepreneurship is integrated into families or communities (Hofstede, 2001). In these instances, prejudice does not simply influence the abstract research outcomes, but it generates concrete implications of access, opportunity, and recognition of resources.

With entrepreneurial trait modelling the cumulative nature of bias makes it extremely difficult to counteract. The lack of data, feature selection, and algorithmic optimisation are synergistic with each other, thereby increasing disparities. This may result in biased labelling of risk-taking, which, in turn, may be used to socialize women entrepreneurs, creating positive feedback loops of exclusion (Suresh and Guttag, 2021). This compounding consequence proves that bias in AI is not a singular flaw but a system-wide issue that requires intentional actions at various levels, such as data gathering to algorithm design to policy management.

Altogether, the biases of AI models of entrepreneurial characteristics are the result of interactions between the constraints of data, the subjective labelling policies, and the algorithm optimisation procedures. Unchecked, these biases run the risk of becoming structural inequalities, and thus, become the way perceptions of who is considered to be an entrepreneurial and who is not are formed. Identifying and separating these sources of bias is a very important initial move in creating fair and inclusive AI systems that can better represent the actual diversity of entrepreneurial potential.

The existence of biased AI models in the analysis of entrepreneurial traits creates serious implications on the lives of individuals, organisations, and societies. In the nearest, these models risk to categorize entrepreneurial potential in a wrong way, resulting in the underestimation or disregard of people with real potentials because of false forecasts. As an example, the underestimation of women as risk-takers, as a consequence of underrepresentation in training data, can lead to them being locked out of incubators, funding, or mentorship programmes (Feldman, 2021). On the other hand, when the traits of overrepresented groups are overestimated, the limited resources may be wasted on biased archetypal entrepreneurs and thus the main purpose of trait modelling, which is to find and develop viable entrepreneurs can be compromised.

Another important negative impact involves the continued existence of inequalities within demographic and cultural lines. Entrepreneurship has always been touted as a form of economic mobility especially among the marginalised groups (Shane, 2009). Prejudiced AI systems, in their turn, can recreate structural inequalities by coding existing inequalities into algorithmic forecasts. Entrepreneurship Models that have been mostly trained on Western data might not identify culturally encoded manifestations of entrepreneurial resilience in collectivist cultures (Hofstede, 2001), and socioeconomic biases can punish the low-income entrepreneurs whose online patterns have no indicators to represent, such as elite education or venture-capital networks, understood as predictors of entrepreneurial success (Fossen and Sorgner, 2021). Such dynamics pose a threat of reducing the entrepreneurial pipeline to a homogeneous group and thus suppressing diversity and innovation.

Individual misclassifications are not the only ethical and societal implications. To create innovation and social development, entrepreneurial ecosystems require fairness and inclusivity. When AI systems are made controllers of possibilities, whether by recruiting or funding tools, programme applications, or even hiring algorithms, discriminatory formulas can become institutionalized in the name of impartiality (Crawford, 2021). This does not only damage those who are being excluded but it also destroys institutional credibility and trust of the people. Unfair results of AI-driven tools can make stakeholders give up on the use of potentially valuable innovations, and strengthen the stereotypes about the archetypal entrepreneur, as well as marginalising the under-represented groups (Caliskan et al., 2017).

Economically, biased trait modelling may lead to the resources in the entrepreneurial ecosystem being allocated inefficiently. Data-driven tools have attracted more and more venture-capital funds, accelerators, and policy actors that seek to determine which entrepreneurs and ventures are promising (Nambisan, 2017). The institutional preference of specific groups of people in society is discriminatory in the manner that the resource distribution is based on a few groups, which diminishes the variety of innovations that are released in the market. This kind of concentration reduces the resilience and flexibility of the whole entrepreneurial ecosystem, which is heterogeneous (Aldrich and Fiol, 1994). Therefore, bias will reduce equity and efficiency at the same time and provide a long-term cost on the economic development and innovation.

Lastly, biased trait modelling has ramifications to research and theory construction in entrepreneurial psychology. Researchers are more likely to use AI-based approaches to confirm or disprove hypothetical concepts of entrepreneurial characteristics (Obschonka and Stuetzer, 2017). In case of biased underlying models, results can be artefacts of data as opposed to real psychological phenomenon, thus misleading academic knowledge of entrepreneurship. This danger becomes a cycle of Western-centric or male-centric notions of what creativity is, or what resilience is, which, when applied to education, training or policy, may promote a limited understanding of entrepreneurial behaviour and stifle inclusiveness in global frameworks.

To sum up, the consequences of biased trait modelling are characterized by the misclassification of individuals, the overall inequity in the entrepreneurial ecosystem, the misappropriation of resources, and the theory. These results highlight the importance of urgently developing fairness-conscious AI solutions that can optimise predictive accuracy and ensure inclusivity, diversity, and ethical integrity. The task of responding to such consequences is not a technical task at all; it is a social necessity considering the contribution of entrepreneurship to the generation of innovation, jobs, and social mobility.

Methods of Bias Detection

The identification of bias in artificial intelligence systems that forecast characteristics of an entrepreneur is a critical point in guaranteeing that predictive systems are both veritable and equitable. Since entrepreneurial psychology works with complex constructs (e.g., the creativity, resilience, and risk-taking) the data or algorithm biases can easily skew assessments to an unchecked extent. These bias detection methods can be generalized into data-level methods, algorithmic-level audits, and outcome-level methods, where each of these approaches targets different points in the modeling pipeline.

On the data level, bias detection entails the examination of representativeness and balance of training data. Inequity in sample structure—such as an overrepresentation of male entrepreneurs or some people in a wealthy economy, etc.– can produce biased baselines that influence the model forecasts (Mehrabi et al., 2021). Data-distribution analysis and statistical parity checks are commonly used methods used to assess the presence of sufficient representation of salient demographic groups. The computation of group-wise proportions of such attributes as gender, socioeconomic status, or geographic origin can reveal their imbalances, which later turn into biased predictions (Barocas et al., 2019). Trait-related features Visual analytics such as t-sne plotting or clustering maps may be used to further indicate patterns of underrepresentation or clustering bias.

In the algorithmic level, bias detection is based on identifying the way models interpret and give importance to the input features. One method that has been commonly used is feature-importance analysis, which investigates whether the sensitive variables (e.g., gender, ethnicity) or their proxies dominate the predictions of entrepreneurial characteristics. Counterfactual fairness testing is a test that determines whether the manipulation of sensitive attributes, keeping all things unchanged, changes the model outputs (Kusner et al., 2017). In case, an AI system, when switching a gender of an applicant which is a man to a woman, the risk tolerance score reduced, the model can be declared as biased. Other ones, including individual-fairness audits and causal-inference models, aim to decouple the occurrence of relationships between demographic factors and trait results as indicative of true relationships or simply the result of biased correlations (Kilbertus et al., 2017).

At the outcome level, the measures of fairness are used to evaluate the equity of model predictions among groups. The commonly used metrics include statistical parity, which measures the difference in outcome rates between disparate groups; equal opportunity, which measures the equality of true-positive rates across demographics; and predictive parity, which measures whether positive predictions are equally accurate across groups (Hardt et al., 2016). Within the framework of entrepreneurial trait modelling, these measures may question whether women and men who are rated as highly creative actually perform equally, or whether socioeconomic groups that are branded as resilient show equal success rates as an entrepreneur. The simultaneous application of a set of fairness measures can help a researcher to indicate several dimensions of bias that a single measure might miss.

Biases have also been enhanced by emergent methods in explainable AI (XAI). The SHAP (SHapley Additive Explanations) and LIME (Local Interpretable Model-agnostic Explanations) tools enable the researcher to understand whether the predictions concerning the traits depend on sensitive or unimportant characteristics (Ribeiro et al., 2016; Lundberg and Lee, 2017). As an illustration, SHAP analysis, which shows an exaggerated effect of university attended on entrepreneurial motivation predictions, can have a latent socioeconomic bias. Systematic disadvantages involving demographic groups can be revealed through parallel audit studies that simulate different entrepreneur profiles and monitor predictive variations.

Practically, a powerful bias detection approach requires a multi-method approach. There is no particular method that can fully describe the delicate forms of bias in trait modeling. Through a combination of dataset audits, algorithm fairness testing, and outcome-level assessment, researchers have a comprehensive view of future disparities. Importantly, bias identification needs to become more of a cyclic process rather than a single event that is embedded into the process of AI development (Raji and Buolamwini, 2019). Constant monitoring will ensure that when models are re-trained using new data, fairness considerations will be part of their implementation in entrepreneurial settings.

Mitigation Strategies of a Bias-Free Environment: How to be Fair

To deal with bias and promote fairness in AI models of entrepreneurial characteristics, a multifaceted collection of strategies at the data, algorithmic, and governance levels is needed. Since bias may be introduced at several points, such as data collection and feature engineering, as well as, model deployment, successful mitigation needs proactive, iterative, and context-based interventions. Fairness in the entrepreneurial sphere where AI-assisted evaluation might affect funding, mentorship, and resource distribution ceases to be an issue of technical interest and turns into an ethical and socioeconomic necessity.

On the data level, an effective approach will be to improve the representativeness and inclusiveness of training datasets. Demographic disparities can be overcome by data augmentation methods like oversampling of underrepresented groups or artificial data creation (Chawla et al., 2002). In addition, bias-conscious sampling approaches that guarantee equal representation of gender, ethnicity and socioeconomic status are becoming a norm. This would require the inclusion of heterogeneous datasets in the entrepreneurial context that represent a sample of entrepreneurs living in different geographic areas, industries, and cultures, as opposed to dominant western, male-dominated samples (Obschonka & Stuetzer, 2017). Open data practices such as datasheets on datasets (Gebru et al., 2018) also enhance accountability by clearly defining data sources, data collection procedures, and possible biases.

Fairness can be promoted at the algorithmic level with the help of pre-processing, in-processing, and post-processing interventions (Mehrabi et al., 2021). Pre-processing techniques manipulate data before training; examples include reweighting examples, removing sensitive features and the attributes that are sensitive, and their proxies. In-processing methods alter the learning algorithm itself so as to penalize discriminatory results. Fairness-conscious optimisation incorporates rules to create equal opportunity in groups, thus eliminating unfair disadvantages to underrepresented entrepreneurs (Zafar et al., 2017). Post-processing techniques modify the outputs post-training, including tuning decision thresholds independently to different population groups to balance false-positive and false-negative errors (Hardt et al., 2016). Predicting objectivity of forecasts on the aspect of resilience or risk tolerance can be aided by such interventions in the context of entrepreneurial trait modelling.

Explainable AI (XAI) methods are also significant to mitigate bias. Making models more transparent, such tools as SHAP or LIME allow the stakeholders to understand what characteristics make predictions over traits and what may potentially be sources of unfairness (Ribeiro et al., 2016; Lundberg and Lee, 2017). As an illustration, when the variable of university ranking turns out to be a salient predictor of entrepreneurial potential, organisations can wonder whether the variable is just a socioeconomic proxy. This way, explainability does not only make it easy to detect bias, but also enables corrective action to be taken based on ethical and domain-specific priorities.

In addition to technical solutions, the system of governance and accountability is essential to instill fairness in AI systems deployed in the entrepreneurial ecosystem. One of them involves the creation of ethics rules and fairness audits that would ensure that AI models are properly evaluated by an independent body prior to their implementation (Raji and Buolamwini, 2019). Monitoring systems enable the models to be fair since they are constantly updated with new information or implemented in different settings. Among the most crucial ones is the multistakeholder involvement, including entrepreneurs, investors, policymakers, and ethicists, and contributing to fairness definitions with an array of different views on what equitable outcomes would be provided. These forms of participation ensure that fairness is not reduced to the role of mere technical specialists only and that AI practice is consistent with the rest of the social values (Crawford, 2021).

Moreover, entrepreneurial AI systems can be made fair through policy intervention and legal provisions. The rules like the AI Act of the European Union focus on transparency, accountability, and safeguarding against algorithmic discrimination (European Commission, 2021). The compliance with these rules will make sure that AI-based funding choices, recruitment, or training programme selection will not reinforce existing inequities. A more holistic approach to ethical deployment is achieved by combining policy frameworks and organisational best practices, including principles of fairness-by-design.

Lastly, awareness and education development of practitioners is a long-term approach. Training that involves both technical and ethical aspects of AI fairness is needed by data scientists, entrepreneurship educators, and policymakers. Such programs as fairness toolkits, capacity-building workshops can help practitioners learn the dangers of bias and apply appropriate mitigation strategies in practice (Mitchell et al., 2019). Such education is necessary in entrepreneurial ecosystems to make sure that the decision-makers can be prepared to approach AI recommendations critically instead of thinking that they are some unquestionable commands.

To conclude, decreasing bias and promoting fairness require measures at various levels, including inclusive data practices and fairness-conscious algorithms; transparent and explainable systems; governance and accountability systems; and supportive legal frameworks and stakeholder education. As far as the entrepreneurial traits modelling is concerned, these strategies protect the diversity and inclusivity that are a must in innovation and sustainable economic development. Fairness in AI goes beyond correcting technical mistakes, and it entails the creation of mechanisms that are representative and advocative of larger responsibilities to equity in entrepreneurship.

Ethical Implications and Policy Implications

The use of AI in simulating entrepreneurial qualities raises some disturbing moral questions that transcend the technical domain. In its essence, entrepreneurship is not an economic activity but a social and cultural process that is influenced by personal identities, opportunities and limitations. The implementation of AI in this sphere requires careful consideration of autonomy, equity, accountability, and transparency since the results of such systems can have a direct impact on the availability of resources, opportunities, and recognition. Failure to adhere to ethical protection would unintentionally strengthen structural inequalities, reinforce stereotypes, or damage trust in entrepreneurial ecosystems.

One of the major ethical issues is the issue of autonomy and informed consent. AI-based evaluations are often based on large volumes of data collected through social media, online platforms or biometric data, and in many cases without the knowledge or permission of the entrepreneurs (Crawford, 2021). This situation brings up critical concerns of privacy of data, its ownership and the right of individuals to manage the use of their information. In the case of entrepreneurs who work in uncertainty and risk, opaque data utilization may enhance vulnerability. The ethical practice requires clear reporting of data collection procedures, consent procedures, and the planned uses of AI-generated trait assessments.

Another area of concern is equity and justice. As described above, biased AI models may distort entrepreneurial potential both in terms of gender, socioeconomic, and cultural backgrounds, which limits opportunities of marginalized groups (Caliskan et al., 2017). Ethically, these differences are not acceptable since they go against the principles of fairness and inclusivity that should guide innovation ecosystems. The implementation of equity requires both technical bias-reduction approaches and the desire to incorporate a wide range of views into the process of designing and assessing AI systems. The models used in ethical entrepreneurship research must consider global diversity without using Western and male-based datasets (Obschonka and Stuetzer, 2017).

Responsibility and accountability are two issues that are very close. The question as to who is responsible when AI models deliver biased or harmful results is still a burning issue. Such misclassification can deny entrepreneurs financing or lock them out, but the responsibility can be distributed between the data scientists, the providers of the platform, or the decision-makers in the institution (Jobin et al., 2019). Ethical systems must have well-defined accountability systems, such as appeal and redress mechanisms. Entrepreneurs need to be able to challenge algorithm decisions and receive substantial explanations of trait classifications.

One of the ethical principles is transparency. The AI systems often act as black boxes, making it difficult to trace the process of converting the particular inputs to the outputs (Burrell, 2016). Opaque models can create distrust and opposition especially where they seem to favour certain groups. Increasing transparency would go beyond using XAI techniques but also a wider understanding of algorithmic literacy, so that users, such as entrepreneurs, investors, and policymakers, can understand the advantages and shortcomings of such tools. Even technically correct models can still lack in ethics without transparency.

Such ethical issues lead to important policy implications. The policymakers are also significant in setting standards and rules that are conducive to both innovation and protection against harm. An example of this is the proposed AI Act by the European Union, which outlines risk-based systems to regulate AI, which require increased transparency, accountability, and regulation of systems that are categorized as high risk (European Commission, 2021). Given the likely impact of entrepreneurial trait modelling on career paths and resource acquisition, it arguably belongs to this high-risk category. Similar policies in other countries might necessitate fairness audits, bias reporting, and independent certification before the implementation of AI tools in the context of entrepreneurial ecosystems.

The global aspect of fairness should be met through policies at a time. Entrepreneurial ecosystems cut across developed economies and developing areas. Policymaking systems should therefore prevent the application of western-based models of entrepreneurship that overlook cultural norms and practices (Hofstede, 2001). International cooperation and regulations that are culturally sensitive and encourage inclusiveness, instead of standardization, are necessary.

Lastly, there should be policies that promote capacity building and moral innovation. To encourage the creation of fairness-conscious artificial intelligence, governments and institutions can fund the research on bias-reduction methods, provide interdisciplinary partnerships between computer scientists and entrepreneurship researchers, and fund the creation of open-access datasets, which are diverse and representative. When policy is aligned with ethical principles, the stakeholders can make sure that AI models of entrepreneurial traits are not only the most efficient at predictive performance, but also able to enhance equity, innovation, and trust in the entrepreneurial ecosystems.

Overall, ethical issues associated with AI in entrepreneurial trait modeling have to do with autonomy, equity, accountability, and transparency, whereas the policy implications consist of regulation, global inclusivity, and capacity building. All these factors support the need to include ethical consideration in the development and implementation of AI systems. Ethics should be considered as a core rather than a peripheral issue when it comes to responsible use of AI in the entrepreneurship.

Future Directions

With AI gradually becoming a focus of entrepreneurial research and practice, the analysis of bias and equitability in modeling entrepreneurial characteristics is on the verge of drastic change. The next steps in this area are methodological innovations, interdisciplinary integration, cultural sensitivity, policy formulation, and ethical stewardship, which should help develop AI systems that are predictive and equitable.

One of the largest research possibilities in the future is the creation of more sophisticated bias mitigation methods that are specifically adapted to the entrepreneurial trait modeling. In some cases, general-purpose fairness interventions, including reweighting datasets or putting fairness constraints on model outputs, have been demonstrated to be effective (Zafar et al., 2017; Mehrabi et al., 2021), but in many cases, entrepreneurial qualities are multidimensional, context-specific, and culturally sensitive. It is recommended that future efforts should be directed at the development of algorithms that are capable of capturing this complexity without being unfair to demographic groups. Indicatively, causal inference methods with fairness restrictions might be more effective at separating actual differences in traits and biased data artifacts (Kilbertus et al., 2017).

Another important direction is the interdisciplinary approach. By combining Computer science, psychology, sociology, and entrepreneurship research expertise, scholars can enhance conceptualization of trait and operationalization of fairness. The use of behavioral, cognitive, and social data in AI models will probably make them stronger and more representative, which will cut the chances of bias due to limited proxies (Obschonka and Stuetzer, 2017). In addition, interdisciplinary cooperation may inform ethical and cultural choices, where AI systems are not only representative of a variety of entrepreneurial behaviors but also not favor a set of norms.

A research problem is also the cultural and contextual sensitivity of AI models. The majority of existing AI applications are being trained on data representative of Western, urban and male-dominated entrepreneurial systems, which restricts their generalizability to other countries (Hofstede, 2001). The next generation of research must focus on the development of culturally heterogeneous datasets and context-specific modelling approaches that will allow AI to identify other types of entrepreneurial resilience, creativity, and innovation. The cross-cultural validation studies will be required in order to make sure that AI systems will not unintentionally promote a single standard of entrepreneurship across all scenarios.

Policy wise, it is becoming urgent to have regulatory and governance systems that are developed in line with the technological abilities. Although efforts like the European Union AI Act are a starting point (European Commission, 2021), additional specifications of how fairness is determined in predictive models of human qualities, accountability and redress mechanisms, and coordination across national borders should be considered in the future so that ethical race-to-the-bottom situations can be avoided. Also, the policies should promote transparency, bias metrics reporting, and lifecycle monitoring of AI systems.

The next generation of entrepreneurial AI systems is likely to be explainable AI (XAI) and human-centred design. The interpretability-enhancing techniques not only enable the researchers and practitioners to identify bias but also increase the levels of trust and uptake by the entrepreneur and investors (Ribeiro et al., 2016; Lundberg and Lee, 2017). Further studies might concentrate on creating domain-specific interpretability instruments that explain the methods of assessing complex characteristics like risk-seeking or opportunity recognition so that stakeholders may have a more significant comprehension, challenge, and enhance model results.

Lastly, participatory design and ethical stewardship ought to be the key factors in developing this field. The design, evaluation, and implementation of AI systems can be designed to promote fairness, inclusivity and social legitimacy by involving different stakeholders, including entrepreneurs in under-represented groups, investors, policymakers and ethicists. The participatory systems will be necessary to make sure that AI does not just robotsify the existing biases but also creates fair entrepreneurial environments (Crawford, 2021).

Overall, the future of AI in entrepreneurial trait modelling lies on the cross-road of technical innovation, interdisciplinary research, cultural sensitivity, policy formulation, and ethical involvement. Following these guidelines, researchers and practitioners will be able to create AI models that can predict entrepreneurial potential precisely, as well as maintain fairness, inclusiveness, and trust, promoting the science and practice of entrepreneurship.

CONCLUSION

The artificial intelligence use in research and evaluation of entrepreneurial characteristics provides the revolution of research, application, and policy. AI can offer more information about complex constructs of psychology, including creativity, resilience, risk-taking, and opportunity recognition, thereby allowing a more specific prediction, customized training, and support of entrepreneurs. Nevertheless, all these opportunities, as this chapter has revealed, come with serious risks of prejudice and considerations of fairness inherent in datasets, algorithmic procedures, and predictive results.

Biases in AI models of entrepreneurial characteristics can manifest themselves at various levels - data collection and feature selection, model training and deployment; they can be disproportionately harmful to under-represented populations, such as women, ethnic minorities, and entrepreneurs who are low-resource or non-Western (Feldman, 2021; Hofstede, 2001). When unchecked, the biases can mis-categorize the potential of entrepreneurship, strengthen social disparities, and undermine confidence in AI-based systems. In addition to the effects at the individual level, biased AI systems may pervert entrepreneurial ecosystems, allocate resources unevenly, and influence the theoretical insights in a manner that benefits the dominant cultural and demographic groups.

The promotion of fairness in AI is a complex matter. Methods of bias detection, such as data audits, algorithmic fairness testing, outcome-level evaluations, and explainable AI, allow researchers and practitioners to detect and counter bias. Others that can be used to complement bias mitigation include inclusive data collection, fairness-conscious algorithms, transparency and interpretability, participatory design, ethical governance, and alignment with regulatory frameworks such as the European Union AI Act (European Commission, 2021; Crawford, 2021). It is important to incorporate these strategies in the lifecycle of AI to ensure that the predictive accuracy and ethicality are preserved.

The responsible use of AI in entrepreneurship revolves around ethical considerations. Autonomy, equity, accountability, and transparency are not the optional but the fundamental principles that inform the design, evaluation, and implementation of AI systems. There is a need to have policies and governance structures, as well as stakeholder education and capacity building, to make sure that AI can facilitate and not limit the equitable entrepreneurial opportunity (Jobin et al., 2019). Such combination of ethics and policy is especially significant in the international contexts, where culturally particular expressions of entrepreneurial characteristics can vary as compared to those that are defined in standard datasets.

In the future, the discipline would have innovations on bias mitigation, interdisciplinary research, culturally sensitive modelling, and participatory governance. The next generation of AI systems should not just be an upgrade to the current decision making systems and processes, but should actively encourage fairness, inclusiveness and social trust. With a focus on technical rigor coupled with ethical thinking and alignment of policies, AI can be transformed into a resource that facilitates the improvement of the entrepreneurial ecosystem, diverse talent, and equitable innovation and economic growth.

To sum up, despite the potential of AI to develop the field of entrepreneurial psychology, its usage should be accompanied by the alertness of the bias issue, the adherence to the principle of justice, and the strong ethical and regulatory system. It is only through the combination of these principles that AI can become the potential tool of understanding and cultivating entrepreneurial talent and foster inclusiveness, diversity, and justice in the larger entrepreneurial environment. The future of AI in entrepreneurship therefore lies not only on the level of predictive sophistication but also on the ability of AI to be used as a fair, transparent and socially responsible tool in human development.

REFERENCES

Aldrich, H. E., & Fiol, C. M. (1994). Fools rush in? The institutional context of industry creation. *Academy of Management Review*, *19*(4), 645–670. DOI: 10.2307/258740

Barocas, S., Hardt, M., & Narayanan, A. (2019). *Fairness and machine learning: Limitations and opportunities*. MIT Press.

Barocas, S., & Selbst, A. D. (2016). Big data's disparate impact. *SSRN*, *104*(3), 671–732. DOI: 10.2139/ssrn.2477899

Baum, J. R., & Locke, E. A. (2004). The relationship of entrepreneurial traits, skill, and motivation to subsequent venture growth. *The Journal of Applied Psychology*, *89*(4), 587–598. DOI: 10.1037/0021-9010.89.4.587 PMID: 15327346

Binns, R. (2018). Fairness in machine learning: Lessons from political philosophy. *Proceedings of the 2018 Conference on Fairness, Accountability, and Transparency*, 149–159. DOI: 10.1145/3287560.3287572

Burrell, J. (2016). How the machine 'thinks': Understanding opacity in machine learning algorithms. *Big Data & Society*, *3*(1), 1–12. DOI: 10.1177/2053951715622512

Caliskan, A., Bryson, J. J., & Narayanan, A. (2017). Semantics derived automatically from language corpora contain human-like biases. *Science*, *356*(6334), 183–186. DOI: 10.1126/science.aal4230 PMID: 28408601

Chawla, N. V., Bowyer, K. W., Hall, L. O., & Kegelmeyer, W. P. (2002). SMOTE: Synthetic minority over-sampling technique. *Journal of Artificial Intelligence Research*, *16*, 321–357. DOI: 10.1613/jair.953

Choudhary, S., Yadav, M., & Srivastava, A. P. (2021). Cognitive Biases Among Millennial Indian Investors: Do Personality and Demographic Factors Matter? *FIIB Business Review*, *13*(1), 106–117. DOI: 10.1177/23197145211057343

Chouldechova, A., & Roth, A. (2020). A snapshot of the frontiers of fairness in machine learning. *Communications of the ACM*, *63*(5), 82–89. DOI: 10.1145/3376898

Crawford, K. (2021). *Atlas of AI: Power, politics, and the planetary costs of artificial intelligence*. Yale University Press.

Doshi-Velez, F., & Kim, B. (2017). Towards a rigorous science of interpretable machine learning. *arXiv preprint* arXiv:1702.08608.

Dwork, C., Hardt, M., Pitassi, T., Reingold, O., & Zemel, R. (2012). Fairness through awareness. *Proceedings of the 3rd Innovations in Theoretical Computer Science Conference*, 214–226. DOI: 10.1145/2090236.2090255

European Commission. (2021). *Proposal for a regulation laying down harmonised rules on artificial intelligence (Artificial Intelligence Act).* COM(2021) 206 final.

Feldman, M. (2021). Gender, leadership, and entrepreneurial ecosystems. *Small Business Economics*, *56*(2), 529–541. DOI: 10.1007/s11187-019-00276-5

Floridi, L., & Cowls, J. (2019). A unified framework of five principles for AI in society. *Harvard Data Science Review*, *1*(1). Advance online publication. DOI: 10.1162/99608f92.8cd550d1

Fossen, F. M., & Sorgner, A. (2021). Digitalization of work and entry into entrepreneurship. *Journal of Business Research*, *125*, 548–563. DOI: 10.1016/j.jbusres.2019.09.019

Friedman, B., & Nissenbaum, H. (1996). Bias in computer systems. *ACM Transactions on Information Systems*, *14*(3), 330–347. DOI: 10.1145/230538.230561

Gebru, T., Morgenstern, J., Vecchione, B., Vaughan, J. W., Wallach, H., Daumé, H.III, & Crawford, K. (2018). Datasheets for datasets. *Communications of the ACM*, *64*(12), 86–92. DOI: 10.1145/3458723

Hardt, M., Price, E., & Srebro, N. (2016). Equality of opportunity in supervised learning. *Advances in Neural Information Processing Systems*, *29*, 3315–3323.

Hmieleski, K. M., & Baron, R. A. (2009). Entrepreneurs' optimism and new venture performance: A social cognitive perspective. *Academy of Management Journal*, *52*(3), 473–488. DOI: 10.5465/amj.2009.41330755

Hofmans, J., Wille, B., & Schreurs, B. (2020). Person-centered methods in vocational research. *Journal of Vocational Behavior*, *118*, 103398. DOI: 10.1016/j.jvb.2020.103398

Hofstede, G. (2001). *Culture's consequences: Comparing values, behaviors, institutions and organizations across nations* (2nd ed.). SAGE Publications.

Jobin, A., Ienca, M., & Vayena, E. (2019). The global landscape of AI ethics guidelines. *Nature Machine Intelligence*, *1*(9), 389–399. DOI: 10.1038/s42256-019-0088-2

Kilbertus, N., Rojas-Carulla, M., Parascandolo, G., Hardt, M., Janzing, D., & Schölkopf, B. (2017). Avoiding discrimination through causal reasoning. *Advances in Neural Information Processing Systems*, *30*, 656–666.

Kosinski, M., Stillwell, D., & Graepel, T. (2016). Mining big data to extract patterns and predict real-life outcomes. *Psychological Methods, 21*(4), 493–506. DOI: 10.1037/met0000105 PMID: 27918179

Kumar, M. Yadav, M., & Sahoo, A. (2025). The Importance of Collaboration Skills in Workforce Preparation From Textbooks to Teamwork. In Revitalizing Student Skills for Workforce Preparation (pp. 333–352). DOI: 10.4018/979-8-3693-3856-8.ch011

Kusner, M. J., Loftus, J. R., Russell, C., & Silva, R. (2017). Counterfactual fairness. *Advances in Neural Information Processing Systems, 30*, 4066–4076.

Lundberg, S. M., & Lee, S.-I. (2017). A unified approach to interpreting model predictions. *Advances in Neural Information Processing Systems, 30*, 4765–4774.

Mehrabi, N., Morstatter, F., Saxena, N., Lerman, K., & Galstyan, A. (2021). A survey on bias and fairness in machine learning. *ACM Computing Surveys, 54*(6), 1–35. DOI: 10.1145/3457607

Mitchell, M., Wu, S., Zaldivar, A., Barnes, P., Vasserman, L., Hutchinson, B., & Gebru, T. (2019). Model cards for model reporting. *Proceedings of the Conference on Fairness, Accountability, and Transparency*, 220–229. DOI: 10.1145/3287560.3287596

Nambisan, S. (2017). Digital entrepreneurship: Toward a digital technology perspective of entrepreneurship. *Entrepreneurship Theory and Practice, 41*(6), 1029–1055. DOI: 10.1111/etap.12254

Nguyen, T. B., Kumar, M., Sahoo, D. K., Nain, N., Yadav, M., & Dadhich, V. (2025). Mapping the landscape of women entrepreneurs in micro and small enterprises: Trends, themes, and insights through systematic review and text mining. F1000Research, 14. DOI: 10.12688/f1000research.163030.1

Obschonka, M., & Stuetzer, M. (2017). Integrating psychological approaches to entrepreneurship: The Entrepreneurial Personality System (EPS). *Small Business Economics, 49*(1), 203–231. DOI: 10.1007/s11187-016-9821-y

Pankaj, Yadav, R., Naim, I., Kumar, M., Misra, S., Dewasiri, N. J., Rathnasiri, M. S. H., Yadav, M., Balodi, A., Kar, S., & Vihari, N. S. (2023). An Exploratory Study to Identify Effects of Blockchain Technology on Organizational Change and Practices. 2023 IEEE Technology & Engineering Management Conference - Asia Pacific (TEMSCON-ASPAC), 1–8. DOI: 10.1109/TEMSCON-ASPAC59527.2023.10531372

Podsakoff, P. M., MacKenzie, S. B., Lee, J.-Y., & Podsakoff, N. P. (2003). Common method biases in behavioral research: A critical review of the literature and recommended remedies. *The Journal of Applied Psychology, 88*(5), 879–903. DOI: 10.1037/0021-9010.88.5.879 PMID: 14516251

Raji, I. D., & Buolamwini, J. (2019). Actionable auditing: Investigating the impact of publicly naming biased performance results of commercial AI products. *Proceedings of the AAAI/ACM Conference on AI, Ethics, and Society*, 429–435. DOI: 10.1145/3306618.3314244

Rauch, A., & Frese, M. (2007). Let's put the person back into entrepreneurship research: A meta-analysis on the relationship between business owners' personality traits, business creation, and success. *European Journal of Work and Organizational Psychology*, *16*(4), 353–385. DOI: 10.1080/13594320701595438

Ribeiro, M. T., Singh, S., & Guestrin, C. (2016). "Why should I trust you?" Explaining the predictions of any classifier. *Proceedings of the 22nd ACM SIGKDD International Conference on Knowledge Discovery and Data Mining*, 1135–1144. DOI: 10.1145/2939672.2939778

Schlaegel, C., & Koenig, M. (2014). Determinants of entrepreneurial intent: A meta–analytic test and integration of competing models. *Entrepreneurship Theory and Practice*, *38*(2), 291–332. DOI: 10.1111/etap.12087

Shane, S. (2009). Why encouraging more people to become entrepreneurs is bad public policy. *Small Business Economics*, *33*(2), 141–149. DOI: 10.1007/s11187-009-9215-5

Shane, S., & Venkataraman, S. (2000). The promise of entrepreneurship as a field of research. *Academy of Management Review*, *25*(1), 217–226. DOI: 10.5465/amr.2000.2791611

Stewart, W. H., & Roth, P. L. (2001). Risk propensity differences between entrepreneurs and managers: A meta-analytic review. *The Journal of Applied Psychology*, *86*(1), 145–153. DOI: 10.1037/0021-9010.86.1.145 PMID: 11302226

Suresh, H., & Guttag, J. V. (2021). A framework for understanding unintended consequences of machine learning. *Communications of the ACM*, *64*(1), 62–71. DOI: 10.1145/3425716

Tayal, R., Upadhyay, R., Yadav, M., & Singh, R. (2019). The Development and Validation of the Organizational Effectiveness Scale Using Confirmatory Factor Analysis. *Global Business Review*, *22*(3), 097215091881172. DOI: 10.1177/0972150918811720

Trivedi, S., Vishnu, S., Singh, A., & Yadav, M. (2023a). Research Trends in Sustainable E-Payment Systems: A Study Using Topic Modeling Approach. IEEE Transactions on Engineering Management, PP, 1–15. DOI: 10.1109/TEM.2023.3280216

Trivedi, V., Banerji, D., & Yadav, M. (2023b). Expecting the surprises: Role of hope in consumer repurchase intentions in an online shopping environment. In Journal of Strategic Marketing (Vol. 31, Issue 4, pp. 794–816). Taylor & Francis. DOI: 10.1080/0965254X.2021.1996449

Tunio, M. N., Chaudhry, I. S., Shaikh, S., Jariko, M. A., & Brahmi, M. (2021). Determinants of the Sustainable Entrepreneurial Engagement of Youth in Developing Country—An Empirical Evidence from Pakistan. In Sustainability (Vol. 13, Issue 14). DOI: 10.3390/su13147764

Tunio, M. N., & Tunio, S. (2025). *Navigating Digital Transformation: A Systematic Review of SMEs' Transitions and Growth in the Digital Age*. Sukkur IBA Journal of Management and Business., DOI: 10.30537/sijmb.v11i2.1509

Yadav, M., Kumar, M., Alyousef, M. I., Dagar, M., Dewasiri, N. J., & Amoozegar, A. (2025). Mapping Research Trends on Gender Diversity, Work Stress, and Job Satisfaction in Higher Education: A Bibliometric Analysis. *International Journal of Learning. Teaching and Educational Research*, *24*(8), 444–472. DOI: 10.26803/ijlter.24.8.19

Yadav, M., Rangnekar, S., & Srivastava, A. (2019). Demographic variables as moderators between QWL and OCB. *Industrial and Commercial Training, ahead-of-print*. DOI: 10.1108/ICT-04-2018-0040

Yadav, R., Yadav, M., & Vihari, N. (2023). High-performance work system and learning orientation in offline, online, and hybrid workplaces: The mediating role of affective commitment. *The Learning Organization*, *31*(1), 122–136. Advance online publication. DOI: 10.1108/TLO-10-2022-0118

Zafar, M. B., Valera, I., Rodriguez, M. G., & Gummadi, K. P. (2017). Fairness constraints: Mechanisms for fair classification. *Proceedings of the 20th International Conference on Artificial Intelligence and Statistics*, 962–970.

Zhao, H., & Seibert, S. E. (2006). The Big Five personality dimensions and entrepreneurial status: A meta-analytical review. *The Journal of Applied Psychology*, *91*(2), 259–271. DOI: 10.1037/0021-9010.91.2.259 PMID: 16551182

Zhao, H., Seibert, S. E., & Lumpkin, G. T. (2010). The relationship of personality to entrepreneurial intentions and performance: A meta-analytic review. *Journal of Management*, *36*(2), 381–404. DOI: 10.1177/0149206309335187

Chapter 12
The Role of Emotional Intelligence in Entrepreneurship:
AI-Based Measurement Approaches

Narayanage Jayantha Dewasiri
http://orcid.org/0000-0002-5908-8890
Faculty of Management Studies, Sabaragamuwa University of Sri Lanka, Sri Lanka & Qasim Ibrahim School of Business, Villa College, Maldives

Mohit Yadav
http://orcid.org/0000-0002-9341-2527
JGBS, O.P. Jindal Global University, India

Xuan-Hoa Nghiem
http://orcid.org/0000-0003-2292-0257
International School, Vietnam National University, Hanoi, Vietnam

ABSTRACT

Emotional intelligence (EI) is a critical driver of entrepreneurial success, influencing opportunity recognition, leadership, team dynamics, negotiation, resilience, and well-being. Traditional methods of assessing EI, including self-report and ability-based measures, are limited by subjectivity, cultural bias, and static evaluation. Recent advances in artificial intelligence (AI) offer innovative approaches for measuring EI through natural language processing, facial expression recognition, voice analysis, and physiological sensing, providing real-time, objective, and multimodal insights. AI-based assessments can enhance start-up team selection, investor evaluations,

DOI: 10.4018/979-8-2600-1353-3.ch012

coaching, and stress management, while ethical considerations—such as algorithmic bias, privacy, and interpretive limitations—must be addressed. Integrating AI with EI theory enables dynamic, context-sensitive evaluation and development of emotional competencies, fostering more resilient and effective entrepreneurial ecosystems.

INTRODUCTION

Entrepreneurship is an emotionally charged activity by its nature that requires people to operate in uncertainty, manage stress, and build strong relationships with stakeholders (Baron, 2008; Cardon et al., 2012). Emotional intelligence (EI), which is defined as the ability to perceive, regulate and utilise emotions in self and other people (Mayer, Salovey, and Caruso, 2008) has become a key psychological asset in the achievement of entrepreneurial success. Empirical studies indicate that emotionally intelligent entrepreneurs are in a better position to identify opportunities, build teamwork, bargain with investors and adjust to highly changing environments (Ahmetoglu, Leutner, and Chamorro-Premuzic, 2011). Conventionally, EI has been measured through self-report questionnaires and performance-based measures, but they are prone to some weaknesses like social desirability bias and cultural variability (Joseph and Newman, 2010). Artificial intelligence (AI) in the last years has presented new opportunities to the evaluation of EI by taking advantage of natural language processing, machine learning, and multimodal data analytics (Calvo and D'Mello, 2010; Lopes et al., 2020). These artificial intelligence-based approaches offer more objective and dynamic assessments and allow tracking the emotional state of entrepreneurs in the naturalistic setting. With the growing digitalization and globalization of entrepreneurship, it is necessary to explore AI-based EI assessment to improve the psychological competencies of entrepreneurial resilience, leadership, and innovation (Yadav et al., 2024).

Understanding Emotional Intelligence in Entrepreneurship

Emotional intelligence (EI) is largely considered to be a multidimensional concept that involves skills to perceive, comprehend, manage, and use emotion in an adaptive way (Mayer, Salovey, and Caruso, 2008). In the entrepreneurial domain, EI cannot be ignored since, when it comes to entrepreneurship, it is not just a rational strategic process that takes place, but also a highly affective one, which can be characterized by uncertainty, high risk and failure (Baron, 2008; Cardon, Foo, Shepherd, and Wiklund, 2012). EI has five dimensions, namely self-awareness, self-regulation, motivation, empathy, and social skills, which are especially relevant to entrepreneurs (Goleman, 1995). An example is that self-awareness allows entrepreneurs to understand their strengths and weaknesses correctly, and self-regulation helps them to be resilient during stress and ambiguity. Persistence in pursuing opportunities is motivated, stakeholder understanding is improved with empathy, and networking, persuasion, and leadership are all increased with social skills (Boyatzis, 2018; Trivedi et al., 2023a).

Empirical studies always show positive correlations between EI and opportunity recognition, innovation, and entrepreneurial performance (Ahmetoglu, Leutner, and Chamorro-Premuzic, 2011; Mortan, Ripoll, Carvalho, and Bernal, 2014). Increased EI is more effective in enabling entrepreneurs to manage emotional labour, build cohesive teams and build trust with investors and customers (Zampetakis, Beldekos, and Moustakis, 2009). In addition, emotional competencies influence the way entrepreneurs overcome such critical situations as venture failures, negotiations, or intra-team conflicts (Shepherd, 2003). Since entrepreneurship involves both individual and group procedures, EI can be utilized to not only give personal coping and decision-making processes but also the establishment of favorable organizational cultures that facilitate the sustainability of ventures in the long run (Pradhan, Jena, and Singh, 2017).

Since it is an inseparable component, EI has no longer been viewed as a soft skill, but as an essential entrepreneurial ability. However, traditional measurement tools, which are mainly self-report, might not be able to capture the dynamic and situational nature of EI as it is practiced in the context of an actual entrepreneurial situation (Joseph and Newman, 2010). This weakness is the basis of the shift toward AI-based tools that can provide objective, contextualized, and continuous information about emotional competencies of entrepreneurs, a phenomenon that is discussed in the following sections.

Theoretical Foundations

The emotional intelligence (EI) research is based on various theoretical frameworks that theorise the way people perceive, process, and use emotions. The model that was developed by Mayer and Salovey (1997) is the ability model, which identifies EI as a group of cognitive-emotional skills that entail perceiving, using, understanding, and managing emotions. This view considers EI as a quantifiable intelligence that can be used in problem-solving and adaptation. This model was applied in entrepreneurship where it was believed that the ability to read emotional signals among stakeholders or team members may be the direct cause of opportunity recognition, negotiation results and leadership effectiveness (Mayer, Salovey, and Caruso, 2008).

On the other hand, the mixed model proposed by Goleman (1995, 1998) focuses on the combination of emotional competencies, personality characteristics, and social behaviours in a group of domains, which include self-awareness, self-regulation, motivation, empathy, and social skills. This paradigm is very relevant to the needs of an entrepreneur since a successful venture formation often depends on motivation power, the ability to withstand pressure, and good social networking (Boyatzis, 2018). Similarly, the conceptualisation of EI in the trait model proposed by Bar-On (1997) perceives the construct as a set of emotional and social competencies, personality traits, and behavioural dispositions that define the coping mechanisms of individuals in the face of environmental pressures. This strategy highlights the importance of flexibility and resilience to stress, which are essential qualities of an entrepreneur in the face of uncertainty and instability in start ups (Petrides and Furnham, 2001; Yadav et al., 2019).

In addition to EI-specific models, there are wider psychological theories that guide the research of EI in entrepreneurship. The theory of affect-as-information (Schwarz and Clore, 2007) postulates that affect can be used as a source of information that influences judgments and decision making and as such, the theory explains why emotionally intelligent entrepreneurs would incorporate affective information in their cognitive judgments about risk and opportunity. Also, according to the self-determination theory (Deci and Ryan, 2000), intrinsic motivation, which is usually supported by EI-related skills, including self-awareness and emotional control, drives persistence in entrepreneurial activities.

Taken together, these theoretical lenses point to the centrality of EI in entrepreneurship, not as a peripheral aspect of entrepreneurship, the soft skill, but as an essential element of entrepreneurial cognition and behaviour. They also provide a basis of incorporating AI-based tools that operationalise and measure EI constructs more dynamically and objectively, and thus contribute to the development of theory and practice in entrepreneurial psychology.

Entrepreneurial Outcomes Influenced by EI

Emotional intelligence (EI) has been shown to affect a very wide range of entrepreneurial performance, thus determining the personal entrepreneurial behavior as well as the overall performance of the ventures. One of the major results is the opportunity recognition that requires entrepreneurs to identify trends in uncertain and complex environments. The high EI persons have been found to be more skilled in deciphering the emotional and social signals of the customers, markets, and stakeholders and thus help in identifying the unmet needs and new trends (Zampetakis et al., 2009). These entrepreneurs use empathy and perspective-taking to match the innovative ideas with the real-life problems thus increasing the chances of taking advantage of the opportunity (Baron and Tang, 2011).

Leadership and team-building is another imperative outcome that has been shaped by EI. Entrepreneurial businesses are usually run under dynamic resource constrained environments where team cohesiveness and vision is crucial (Ensley, Pearce, and Hmieleski, 2006). Entrepreneurs who have good social awareness and interpersonal skills are able to inspire trust, solve conflicts, and create good team climates. Transformational leadership behaviours, which are fostered by EI, including motivating and empowering employees, are associated with high venture performance and innovation (Côté, 2014; Tayal et al., 2021).

EI is also a crucial factor in negotiation and conflict resolution, especially where the relations with investors, partnership, or customer interaction are involved. Emotionally intelligent entrepreneurs are skilled at managing their own feelings when negotiating important deals as well as correctly reading the emotional state of others, which leads to more favourable deals and relational benefits in the long run (Foo, Elfenbein, Tan, and Aik, 2004).

Moreover, EI also improves resilience and adaptability, which are qualities that are needed in the face of entrepreneurial failures and setbacks. The nature of a start-up environment is volatile; an entrepreneur has to change the strategy often or deal with financial and emotional pressure. The ones who are more EI can view failures as learning experiences and keep on going through the hardship (Shepherd, 2003). This flexibility allows individual well-being and sustainability of organisations.

Finally, EI helps in managing stress and well-being that directly affect entrepreneur endurance and quality of decision-making. The empirical data indicate that emotionally intelligent people can effectively manage stress responses, avoid burn-out, and remain long-term motivated (Pradhan, Jena, and Singh, 2017). Since the entrepreneur is exposed to many hours of work, financial instability, and isolation, EI is an intervention mechanism that maintains the psychological well-being and survival of the business (Trivedi et al., 2023b).

Collectively, these findings demonstrate that EI is a key factor in determining entrepreneurial success, which influences cognitive, social, and emotional activities that are part of opportunity recognition, leadership, negotiation, resiliency, and well-being.

Traditional Approaches to Measuring EI

The emotional intelligence (EI) measurement has always been based on psychometric tools that have been used to measure the emotional skills, capabilities, and temperaments of the individuals. These instruments tend to fall into two categories namely ability based measures and self report or trait based measures.

The conceptualisation of EI as a cognitive ability, such as the MayerSalovey-Caruso Emotional Intelligence Test (MSCEIT) conceptualises EI in terms of ability and measures performance on tasks like the ability to identify emotions in facial expressions, to understand emotional meanings, and to devise effective emotional regulation strategies (Mayer, Salovey, and Caruso, 2002). The MSCEIT is widely used in scholarly studies and in the organisational setting and offers a performance-based approach to EI. However, its critics point out that it has certain problems in terms of objectivity of scoring, cultural differences in expressing emotions, and ecological validity in an entrepreneurial setting (Landy, 2005).

The most common EI assessment techniques are self-report and trait-based measures. The self-perceptions of emotional skills of individuals in areas such as intrapersonal awareness, adaptability, and interpersonal skills are measured in the instruments of the Bar-On Emotional Quotient Inventory (EQ-i; Bar-On, 1997) and the Trait Emotional Intelligence Questionnaire (TEIQue; Petrides and Furnham, 2001). Although these measures are simple to administer and possess good predictive validity in other aspects like leadership and job performance (Van Rooy and Viswesvaran, 2004), they are prone to social desirability bias, self-enhancement tendencies and subjective interpretation of items (Joseph and Newman, 2010).

The ability- and trait-based approaches have been utilized in entrepreneurship studies to explain the role of EI in entrepreneurial intention, opportunity recognition and venture success (Ahmetoglu, Leutner, and Chamorro-Premuzic, 2011). Although they have contributed to it, the traditional approaches traditionally view EI as a fixed phenomenon in contrast to dynamic process that takes place in real-time entrepreneurial decision-making and social interactions. Also, self-report measures can fail to capture the process by which entrepreneurs manage emotions in stressful situations or adjust to new environments where there is a high rate of change-both of which are important in start-up settings (Zeidner, Matthews and Roberts, 2009).

These constraints are indicators of the necessity of more creative and context-sensitive EI testing methods. The development of computational tools has led to the creation of AI-driven tools that can detect emotional cues in language, facial expressions, voice, and physiological reactions. These AI-based approaches will help reduce the biases of the conventional EI measurement and will provide more detailed information on the emotional competencies of entrepreneurs in naturalistic contexts, which is discussed in the next section (Choudhary et al., 2024).

AI-Based Approaches to Measuring EI

With the fast development of artificial intelligence (AI) novel possibilities of measuring emotional intelligence (EI) have been opened with increased objectivity, granularity, and ecological validity in comparison to traditional psychometric tools. Through the use of multimodal data streams, AI-based systems can record emotional cues as they occur in naturalistic settings, which makes them particularly useful in investigating the emotional capabilities of entrepreneurs in dynamic and uncertain settings. These methodologies are based on four major technological streams: natural language processing, computer vision, voice and prosody analysis, and physiological sensing.

Natural language processing (NLP) helps to identify the presence of emotional cues in the verbal and written speech of entrepreneurs. Lexical selection, syntactic and sentiment are analysed by machine-learning algorithms to determine emotional states and regulatory strategies (Pang and Lee, 2008). As an example, the pitch presentation of entrepreneurs, their posts on social media, or even team communications can be analyzed to evaluate the level of optimism, confidence, or stress, hence providing a clue to motivational and social aspects of EI (Kusen, Strembeck, and Conti, 2017).

Facial expression recognition is widely used in the computer vision domain, which allows identifying micro-expressions and affective states in real-time (Ekman and Rosenberg, 2005; Li and Deng, 2020). In the entrepreneurial context, these techniques assess the expression of emotions by entrepreneurs in the process of negotiating with investors or leading a team. Authenticity, empathy and regulatory capacity are the other key elements of EI that are difficult to report on oneself, but can be easily identified through subtle cues such as eye contact, facial tension, and smiles.

The next potential stream is voice and prosody analysis, since such vocal features as pitch, tone, rhythm, speech rate are closely associated with emotional expression (Jiang et al., 2019). Speech analytics AI can assess the vocal delivery of entrepreneurs during a pitch, interview, or meeting with a team to determine stress, enthusiasm, or persuasiveness. One can correlate these insights with domains of EI like self-regulation and social skills, which are the focus of entrepreneurial persuasion and leadership (Afshan et al., 2021).

Finally, these AI-driven modalities provide an all-encompassing, objective, and dynamic system of measuring EI, thus contributing to the theoretical and practical implications of this field to the realm of entrepreneurial psychology.

Last but not least, there are physiological and biometric sensing that provide objective results of the emotional regulation of entrepreneurs. Neural activity, skin conductance, and heart-rate variability can be monitored using wearable devices and sensors thus offering real-time information on stress, arousal and resilience (Picard, 2010). Once these physiological indicators are integrated into machine-learning systems, they allow a multimodal measure of emotional intelligence (EI) to explain conscious control and unconscious emotional reactions (Calvo and D'Mello, 2010).

Combination of these AI-based approaches allows the creation of multimodal systems that triangulate through textual information, facial expression, vocal features, and physiological information to provide a complete EI evaluation (Zeng, Pantic, Roisman, and Huang, 2009). Such systems promise to understand the role of such systems in the regulation and expression of emotions in high-stakes contexts among entrepreneurs, such as fundraising pitches, strategic negotiations, or crisis management. Also, the tools can offer real-time feedback, which allows entrepreneurs to improve their competencies related to EI by using adaptive coaching and training interventions.

Although the current state of AI-based EI measurement is still immature, the possibility of it is in the fact that emotional intelligence can be turned into a dynamic, situational ability, which can be quantified and enhanced objectively. This change is especially applicable to the field of entrepreneurship when the success is frequently determined by the capacity to control emotions in the unexpected and tense circumstances (Tunio et al., 2021).

Integrating AI-Based EI Measurement into Entrepreneurial Contexts

The incorporation of AI-based emotional intelligence (EI) measurement into the entrepreneurial setting provides revolutionary chances to improve decision-making, leadership, and venture performance, in general. Contrary to the traditional, self-reported tests, AI-based tools provide ongoing, context-specific analysis of the emotional competencies of entrepreneurs, which makes them highly relevant to the dynamic and unpredictable nature of the contexts in which entrepreneurship operates.

A major use is in the selection and development of start-up teams. Team dynamics is a decisive factor of venture success and inappropriate interpersonal styles or lack of emotional control usually leads to conflict and failure (Ensley, Pearson, and Amason, 2002). The EI measurement supported by AI is able to provide objective data on the emotional skills of individuals, thus helping incubators, accelerators, and founders to create a balanced team with complementary emotional and social skills. The emergent conflicts can also be detected at an early stage through continuous monitoring and proactive intervention can be taken.

The other area of application is the investor-entrepreneur communication and trust-building. The success of fundraising is often determined by the business model, as well as the capacity of the entrepreneur to exude confidence, authenticity, and empathy (Chen, Yao, and Kotha, 2009). An AI-based pitch presentation analysis, including the analysis of the tone of voice, facial expressions, and other linguistic cues, can provide the feedback on how investors perceive the emotional signs. Investors, in their turn, may utilize such tools to judge the authenticity and emotional control of the entrepreneurs, thereby offering one more dimension of due diligence other than financial metrics.

Another potential application is coaching, mentoring, and training interventions. The AI-based systems can provide real-time feedback on emotional expression and regulation in simulated negotiations, leadership, or speaking engagements. As an example, natural language processing and facial recognition technologies are able to recognize indicators of stress, disengagement, or lack of empathy, and provide an entrepreneur with a personalized set of recommendations on how to enhance EI-related skills (Boyatzis, 2018). These adaptive learning environments have the potential to transform entrepreneurial education through an advancement in theory-based teaching to more experiential, data-driven feedback (Gilal et al., 2020).

Also, AI-based EI measurement has the prospect of stress and burnout forecasting. Uncertainty, workload, and financial pressure make entrepreneurs very susceptible to psychological pressure (Uy, Foo, and Song, 2013). Wearable devices that work with AI will be able to measure physiological signs of stress, including heart-rate variability and galvanic skin response, and indicate when a person is on the brink of burnout. This predictive ability enables timely interventions that protect the well-being of the entrepreneurs in addition to maintaining the performance of the venture.

Finally, the introduction of AI-based EI tools to the entrepreneurial ecosystem has a twofold effect: it allows the entrepreneur to develop their emotional skills and provides the stakeholders, investors, educators, and mentors, with new ways of assessing and advising entrepreneurial talent. With these tools integrated into start-up ecosystems, entrepreneurship can move to a more data-driven concept of the emotional aspects that are at the core of innovation and resilience.

Bias, Ethics, and Limitations in AI-Based EI Measurement

Although AI-based solutions to the measurement of emotional intelligence (EI) could have significant potential, they also present significant issues of bias, privacy, and unethical application, especially in business settings where the results of the assessments will directly affect resource access and opportunity availability.

One of the most urgent problems is algorithmic bias. Emotional recognition AIs trained on biased data can reproduce or enhance cultural, gender, or socioeconomic stereotypes (Buolamwini and Gebru, 2018). To illustrate, facial recognition algorithms are often less accurate with women and darker-skinned individuals, and this may cause systematic misinterpretation of emotional expressions of entrepreneurs during a pitch or an evaluation. These biases do not only undermine fairness but also pose threats to propagate inequalities in entrepreneurial ecosystems.

Privacy and data security is another issue. The application of AI to EI measurement is a regular procedure that presupposes the analysis of sensitive data, such as facial expressions, voice recordings, physiological signals, and linguistic patterns. In the context of entrepreneurship, where privacy of ideas, strategies and negotiations are the most important, misuse or unauthorized access to such information may have dire consequences (Zhou et al., 2021). In that regard, strong data-protection systems and open-consent procedures are required to be responsible.

The moral problems that are related to interpretation and implementation are also subject to examination. In case investors apply AI-based EI measurements in their funding choices, they risk simplifying intricate human qualities to numbers, overvaluing the emotional abilities of an entrepreneur, and overlooking environmental aspects (Jobin, Ienca, and Vayena, 2019). In the same way, the excessive use of AI-based feedback in coaching or training might unintentionally deter the development of self-awareness and reflective learning behaviors among entrepreneurs, which are the basis of developing EI (Chaudhry et al., 2021).

Moreover, contextual and cultural constraints should be taken into consideration. Different cultures have different ways of expressing their emotions and AI models trained in one particular cultural environment may not be able to predict others (Matsumoto, Yoo, and Fontaine, 2008). Under the conditions of globally interconnected entrepreneurial systems, such a mismatch may result in the inaccuracy of the evaluation, thus depriving under-represented regions or cultural groups of entrepreneurs.

Lastly, the problem of dynamic or static measurement is not resolved. Even though the use of AI allows monitoring emotional signals in real-time, the interpretation might not be subtle, as the states of emotion are extremely situational and depend on situational stressors. This poses the risk of false positives (e.g. seeing nervousness as dishonesty) or false negatives (e.g. missing subtle emotional regulation strategies).

To overcome these issues, a multidimensional strategy should be adopted: the creation of more inclusive training data, the transparency of algorithms, the strictest privacy protection, and the integration of ethical principles into the world of entrepreneurship. In their absence, the possible advantages of AI-based EI measurement would be lost in systemic risks, which would invalidate fairness, trust, and utility.

Practical Applications and Future Directions

The implementation of AI-based emotional intelligence (EI) measurement in entrepreneurship is a promise of significant benefits in both practice and research directions. These tools will be able to create more resilient and emotionally skillful entrepreneurial environments by giving psychology, technology, and business a bridge.

In practical terms, EI assessment using AI can transform entrepreneurial training and education. AI-based platforms can be incorporated in curricula by universities, accelerators, and incubators to offer real-time feedback on emotional regulation, leadership, and communication skills. Voice and facial analytics are simulated pitch environments that allow entrepreneurs to tune their persuasion techniques and investor interactions (Li, Chen, and Popovič, 2020). In team-based projects, coaching programs have the opportunity to use AI-generated feedback to develop entrepreneurs in terms of empathy, adaptability, and conflict-management skills (Rashid et al., 2024).

Venture capitalists and angel investors can apply AI-enhanced EI assessments to supplement the existing financial and market analysis in the investment field. Resilience, optimism, and empathy are emotional competencies that are usually critical in uncertainty navigation and venture sustenance (Baron and Tang, 2009). AI-based tests would be able to provide more indicators to determine the potential of the entrepreneurs, thus allowing more comprehensive decision making. However, ethical protection needs to be established to avoid excessive use or discrimination of such tools.

The EI measurement of AI also promises well being and sustainability of organizations. The stress and burnout levels are often high among start-up founders, which negatively impacts their health and survival of the venture (Uy, Foo, and Song, 2013). Emotion-sensing AI and wearables can be used to give early signals of stress overload so that interventions like individualized coaching, wellness programs, or workload can be provided. These technologies can enhance the survival of ventures and ecosystem stability by safeguarding the well-being of entrepreneurs.

Going forward, cross-cultural and context-specific AI-based EI assessment models should be developed as a priority of future research directions. It is due to the fact that emotional expression varies among different societies so models should incorporate cultural norms to be fair and accurate (Matsumoto, Yoo, and Fontaine, 2008). One of the directions is multimodal integration, which is the fusion of linguistic, visual and physiological data streams to obtain a more comprehensive representation of the emotional states of entrepreneurs in real time.

The development of explainable AI (XAI) will also play a significant role in building trust in such systems. The ethical issues can be addressed by using transparent models that help entrepreneurs, educators, and investors understand how EI scores are calculated and encourage adoption (Adadi & Berrada, 2018). Lastly, there is a need to have interdisciplinary partnerships between computer scientists, psychologists and entrepreneurship scholars to come up with tools that are technologically sound and psychologically sound.

Overall, AI-based EI measurement has practical uses in the field of entrepreneurship, including education, investment, well-being, and ecosystem development. The research should be done in future to consider cultural sensitivity, multimodal analysis, and explainability so that these innovations are not only effective but also ethical and equitable. Thoughtfully used AI may change the way emotional intelligence is perceived, learned, and utilized in entrepreneurial practice.

CONCLUSION

EI is an essential factor in the success of an entrepreneur, and it can affect the success of opportunities, leadership ability, team building, negotiation, resilience, and even overall well-being. The conventional ways of measuring EI such as self-report and ability-based measures have produced useful information but are limited by subjectivity, cultural bias and the fixed forms of assessment (Joseph and Newman, 2010; Mayer, Salovey, and Caruso, 2008). With the emergence of artificial intelligence (AI), a novel method of cognition and appraisal of EI in entrepreneurship appears, providing opportunities to measure it in real-time, objectively, and multimodally using natural language processing, facial expression analysis, voice and prosody assessment, and physiological sensing (Calvo and D'Mello, 2010; Zeng, Pantic, Roisman, and Huang, 2009).

The implementation of AI-based EI assessment in the entrepreneurial setting provides useful solutions to team selection, investor assessment, coaching, and stress management, which positively impact the individual and venture-level performance. Simultaneously, ethical aspects, such as algorithmic bias, privacy, and interpretive constraints, should be critically considered to become fair and responsible (Buolamwini and Gebru, 2018; Jobin, Ienca, and Vayena, 2019). Future directions also point to the need to have culturally sensitive, explainable, and multimodal AI systems, interdisciplinary collaborations that cut across computer science, psychology, and entrepreneurship research.

Finally, AI-based solutions have the capacity to make emotional intelligence not a fixed, self-reported phenomenon but a dynamic and operational one. These innovations can make entrepreneurial ecosystems more resilient, adaptive, and successful by helping entrepreneurs, educators, investors, and mentors to improve their understanding of EI and optimize it. The intersection of emotional intelligence theory and AI technology, therefore, is a bright future of both entrepreneurial practice and psychological research.

REFERENCES

Adadi, A., & Berrada, M. (2018). Peeking inside the black-box: A survey on explainable artificial intelligence (XAI). *IEEE Access : Practical Innovations, Open Solutions*, *6*, 52138–52160. DOI: 10.1109/ACCESS.2018.2870052

Afshan, G., Shahid, S., & Tunio, M. N. (2021). Learning experiences of women entrepreneurs amidst COVID-19. *International Journal of Gender and Entrepreneurship*, *13*(2), 162–186. DOI: 10.1108/IJGE-09-2020-0153

Ahmetoglu, G., Leutner, F., & Chamorro-Premuzic, T. (2011). EQ-nomics: Understanding the relationship between individual differences in trait emotional intelligence and entrepreneurship. *Personality and Individual Differences*, *51*(8), 1028–1033. DOI: 10.1016/j.paid.2011.08.016

Bar-On, R. (1997). *Bar-On Emotional Quotient Inventory (EQ-i): Technical manual.* Multi-Health Systems.

Baron, R. A. (2008). The role of affect in the entrepreneurial process. *Academy of Management Review*, *33*(2), 328–340. DOI: 10.5465/amr.2008.31193166

Baron, R. A., & Tang, J. (2009). Entrepreneurs' social skills and new venture performance: Mediating mechanisms and cultural generality. *Journal of Management*, *35*(2), 282–306. DOI: 10.1177/0149206307312513

Baron, R. A., & Tang, J. (2011). The role of entrepreneurs in firm-level innovation: Joint effects of positive affect, creativity, and environmental dynamism. *Journal of Business Venturing*, *26*(1), 49–60. DOI: 10.1016/j.jbusvent.2009.06.002

Boyatzis, R. E. (2018). The behavioral level of emotional intelligence and its measurement. *Frontiers in Psychology*, *9*, 1438. DOI: 10.3389/fpsyg.2018.01438 PMID: 30150958

Buolamwini, J., & Gebru, T. (2018). Gender shades: Intersectional accuracy disparities in commercial gender classification. *Proceedings of Machine Learning Research*, *81*, 1–15.

Calvo, R. A., & D'Mello, S. (2010). Affect detection: An interdisciplinary review of models, methods, and their applications. *IEEE Transactions on Affective Computing*, *1*(1), 18–37. DOI: 10.1109/T-AFFC.2010.1

Cardon, M. S., Foo, M. D., Shepherd, D., & Wiklund, J. (2012). Exploring the heart: Entrepreneurial emotion is a hot topic. *Entrepreneurship Theory and Practice*, *36*(1), 1–10. DOI: 10.1111/j.1540-6520.2011.00501.x

Chaudhry, I. S., Paquibut, R. Y., & Tunio, M. N. (2021). Do workforce diversity, inclusion practices, & organizational characteristics contribute to organizational innovation? Evidence from the UAE. *Cogent Business & Management*, *8*(1), 1947549. DOI: 10.1080/23311975.2021.1947549

Chen, X. P., Yao, X., & Kotha, S. (2009). Entrepreneur passion and preparedness in business plan presentations: A persuasion analysis of venture capitalists' funding decisions. *Academy of Management Journal*, *52*(1), 199–214. DOI: 10.5465/amj.2009.36462018

Choudhary, S., Yadav, M., & Srivastava, A. P. (2024). Cognitive biases among millennial Indian investors: Do personality and demographic factors matter? *FIIB Business Review*, *13*(1), 106–117. DOI: 10.1177/23197145211057343

Côté, S. (2014). Emotional intelligence in organizations. *Annual Review of Organizational Psychology and Organizational Behavior*, *1*(1), 459–488. DOI: 10.1146/annurev-orgpsych-031413-091233

Deci, E. L., & Ryan, R. M. (2000). Self-determination theory and the facilitation of intrinsic motivation, social development, and well-being. *The American Psychologist*, *55*(1), 68–78. DOI: 10.1037/0003-066X.55.1.68 PMID: 11392867

Ekman, P., & Rosenberg, E. L. (2005). *What the face reveals: Basic and applied studies of spontaneous expression using the Facial Action Coding System (FACS)* (2nd ed.). Oxford University Press. DOI: 10.1093/acprof:oso/9780195179644.001.0001

Ensley, M. D., Pearce, C. L., & Hmieleski, K. M. (2006). The moderating effect of environmental dynamism on the relationship between entrepreneur leadership behavior and new venture performance. *Journal of Business Venturing*, *21*(2), 243–263. DOI: 10.1016/j.jbusvent.2005.04.006

Ensley, M. D., Pearson, A. W., & Amason, A. C. (2002). Understanding the dynamics of new venture top management teams: Cohesion, conflict, and new venture performance. *Journal of Business Venturing*, *17*(4), 365–386. DOI: 10.1016/S0883-9026(00)00065-3

Foo, M. D., Elfenbein, H. A., Tan, H. H., & Aik, V. C. (2004). Emotional intelligence and negotiation: The tension between creating and claiming value. *International Journal of Conflict Management*, *15*(4), 411–429. DOI: 10.1108/eb022920

Gilal, F. G., Gilal, N. G., Channa, N. A., Gilal, R. G., Gilal, R. G., & Tunio, M. N. (2020). Towards an integrated model for the transference of environmental responsibility. *Business Strategy and the Environment*, *29*(6), 2614–2623. DOI: 10.1002/bse.2524

Goleman, D. (1995). *Emotional intelligence: Why it can matter more than IQ*. Bantam Books.

Goleman, D. (1998). *Working with emotional intelligence*. Bantam Books.

Jiang, J., Lu, B., Peng, H., Zhu, J., & Ji, Q. (2019). Speech emotion recognition with deep recurrent neural networks. *Proceedings of the IEEE International Conference on Acoustics, Speech, and Signal Processing (ICASSP)*, 6675–6679. DOI: 10.1109/ICASSP.2019.8682629

Jobin, A., Ienca, M., & Vayena, E. (2019). The global landscape of AI ethics guidelines. *Nature Machine Intelligence*, *1*(9), 389–399. DOI: 10.1038/s42256-019-0088-2

Joseph, D. L., & Newman, D. A. (2010). Emotional intelligence: An integrative meta-analysis and cascading model. *The Journal of Applied Psychology*, *95*(1), 54–78. DOI: 10.1037/a0017286 PMID: 20085406

Kusen, E., Strembeck, M., & Conti, M. (2017). Emotional states in social media posts: A case study of Facebook status updates. *Online Social Networks and Media*, *2*, 32–44. DOI: 10.1016/j.osnem.2017.08.002

Landy, F. J. (2005). Some historical and scientific issues related to research on emotional intelligence. *Journal of Organizational Behavior*, *26*(4), 411–424. DOI: 10.1002/job.317

Li, S., Chen, X., & Popovič, A. (2020). How entrepreneurs' emotional expressions shape venture capitalists' evaluations: A multimodal machine learning approach. *Journal ofBusiness Venturing*, *35*(6), 106045. DOI: 10.1016/j.jbusvent.2020.106045

Li, S., & Deng, W. (2020). Deep facial expression recognition: A survey. *IEEE Transactions on Affective Computing*, *13*(3), 1195–1215. DOI: 10.1109/TAFFC.2020.2981446

Lopes, P. N., Nezlek, J. B., Extremera, N., Hertel, J., Fernández-Berrocal, P., Schütz, A., & Salovey, P. (2020). Emotion regulation and the quality of social interaction: Does the ability to evaluate emotional situations and identify effective responses matter? *Journal of Personality*, *88*(1), 111–125. DOI: 10.1111/jopy.12453 PMID: 21395594

Matsumoto, D., Yoo, S. H., & Fontaine, J. (2008). Mapping expressive differences around the world: The relationship between emotional display rules and individualism versus collectivism. *Journal of Cross-Cultural Psychology*, *39*(1), 55–74. DOI: 10.1177/0022022107311854

Mayer, J. D., & Salovey, P. (1997). What is emotional intelligence? In Salovey, P., & Sluyter, D. (Eds.), *Emotional development and emotional intelligence: Educational implications* (pp. 3–31). Basic Books.

Mayer, J. D., Salovey, P., & Caruso, D. R. (2002). *Mayer-Salovey-Caruso Emotional Intelligence Test (MSCEIT) user's manual.* Multi-Health Systems.

Mayer, J. D., Salovey, P., & Caruso, D. R. (2008). Emotional intelligence: New ability or eclectic traits? *The American Psychologist*, *63*(6), 503–517. DOI: 10.1037/0003-066X.63.6.503 PMID: 18793038

Mortan, R. A., Ripoll, P., Carvalho, C., & Bernal, M. C. (2014). Effects of emotional intelligence on entrepreneurial intention and self-efficacy. *Journal of Work and Organizational Psychology*, *30*(3), 97–104. DOI: 10.1016/j.rpto.2014.11.004

Pang, B., & Lee, L. (2008). Opinion mining and sentiment analysis. *Foundations and Trends in Information Retrieval*, *2*(1–2), 1–135. DOI: 10.1561/1500000011

Petrides, K. V., & Furnham, A. (2001). Trait emotional intelligence: Psychometric investigation with reference to established trait taxonomies. *European Journal of Personality*, *15*(6), 425–448. DOI: 10.1002/per.416

Picard, R. W. (2010). *Affective computing: From laughter to IEEE.* IEEE.

Pradhan, R. K., Jena, L. K., & Singh, S. K. (2017). Examining the role of emotional intelligence between organizational learning and adaptive performance in Indian manufacturing industries. *Journal of Workplace Learning*, *29*(3), 235–247. DOI: 10.1108/JWL-05-2016-0046

Rashid, A., Rasheed, R., Ngah, A. H., Pradeepa Jayaratne, M. D. R., Rahi, S., & Tunio, M. N. (2024). Role of information processing and digital supply chain in supply chain resilience through supply chain risk management. *Journal of Global Operations and Strategic Sourcing*, *17*(2), 429–447. DOI: 10.1108/JGOSS-12-2023-0106

Schwarz, N., & Clore, G. L. (2007). Feelings and phenomenal experiences. In Kruglanski, A., & Higgins, E. T. (Eds.), *Social psychology: Handbook of basic principles* (2nd ed., pp. 385–407). Guilford Press.

Shepherd, D. A. (2003). Learning from business failure: Propositions of grief recovery for the self-employed. *Academy of Management Review*, *28*(2), 318–328. DOI: 10.2307/30040715

Tayal, R., Upadhyay, R. K., Yadav, M., & Singh, R. (2021). The development and validation of the organizational effectiveness scale using confirmatory factor analysis. *Global Business Review*, *22*(3), 821–843. DOI: 10.1177/0972150918811720

Trivedi, S. K., Vishnu, S., Singh, A., & Yadav, M. (2023a). Research trends in sustainable E-payment systems: A study using topic modeling approach. *IEEE Transactions on Engineering Management*, *71*, 7511–7525. DOI: 10.1109/TEM.2023.3280216

Trivedi, V., Banerji, D., & Yadav, M. (2023b). Expecting the surprises: Role of hope in consumer repurchase intentions in an online shopping environment. *Journal of Strategic Marketing*, *31*(4), 794–816. DOI: 10.1080/0965254X.2021.1996449

Tunio, M. N., Chaudhry, I. S., Shaikh, S., Jariko, M. A., & Brahmi, M. (2021). Determinants of the sustainable entrepreneurial engagement of youth in developing country—An empirical evidence from Pakistan. *Sustainability (Basel)*, *13*(14), 7764. DOI: 10.3390/su13147764

Uy, M. A., Foo, M. D., & Song, Z. (2013). Joint effects of prior start-up experience and coping strategies on entrepreneurs' psychological well-being. *Journal of Business Venturing*, *28*(5), 583–597. DOI: 10.1016/j.jbusvent.2012.04.003

Van Rooy, D. L., & Viswesvaran, C. (2004). Emotional intelligence: A meta-analytic investigation of predictive validity and nomological net. *Journal of Vocational Behavior*, *65*(1), 71–95. DOI: 10.1016/S0001-8791(03)00076-9

Yadav, M., Rangnekar, S., & Srivastava, A. P. (2019). Demographic variables as moderators between QWL and OCB. *Industrial and Commercial Training*, *51*(7/8), 396–408. DOI: 10.1108/ICT-04-2018-0040

Yadav, R., Yadav, M., & Vihari, N. S. (2024). High-performance work system and learning orientation in offline, online, and hybrid workplaces: The mediating role of affective commitment. *The Learning Organization*, *31*(1), 122–136. DOI: 10.1108/TLO-10-2022-0118

Zampetakis, L. A., Beldekos, P., & Moustakis, V. (2009). "Day-to-day" entrepreneurship within organisations: The role of the trait emotional intelligence and perceived organizational support. *European Management Journal*, *27*(3), 165–175. DOI: 10.1016/j.emj.2008.08.003

Zeidner, M., Matthews, G., & Roberts, R. D. (2009). *What we know about emotional intelligence: How it affects learning, work, relationships, and our mental health.* MIT Press. DOI: 10.7551/mitpress/7404.001.0001

Zeng, Z., Pantic, M., Roisman, G. I., & Huang, T. S. (2009). A survey of affect recognition methods: Audio, visual, and spontaneous expressions. *IEEE Transactions on Pattern Analysis and Machine Intelligence*, *31*(1), 39–58. DOI: 10.1109/TPAMI.2008.52 PMID: 19029545

Zhou, Y., Pan, Y., Wang, C., Venkatesh, V., & Zhang, X. (2021). The dark side of AI-powered emotion recognition: Ethical challenges and future directions. *Information Systems Frontiers*, *23*(6), 1407–1423. DOI: 10.1007/s10796-020-10080-5

Chapter 13
Emotional Intelligence and AI-Augmented Leadership

Bhadralakshmi Jagannathan
http://orcid.org/0009-0000-2449-6985
PES University, India

Shreya Ghosh
http://orcid.org/0009-0008-9309-3424
PES University, India

ABSTRACT

As AI steps in as an active partner in decision-making, leadership is shifting from cognitively exclusive authority to emotionally intelligent partnership. This chapter discusses how Emotional Intelligence (EI) enables leaders to incorporate human empathy, ethical decision-making, and psychological safety in AI-facilitated workplaces. It presents the AIRE Model (Awareness, Integration, Regulation, and Empathy)—a model blending traditional EI theory (Goleman, Mayer & Salovey) with AI-enhanced leadership practices. Practical strategies, case vignettes, and empirical findings illustrate how AI can enhance instead of displace emotional intelligence. It finally details ethical, psychological, and cultural guidelines for designing emotionally aware, sustainable leadership systems.

1. INTRODUCTION

In the AI age, with systems doing analysis and optimizing for us, the leader's distinct contribution increasingly will be emotional intelligence—empathy, moral

DOI: 10.4018/979-8-2600-1353-3.ch013

sense, and awareness of context. However, most organizations suffer from a lack of human-AI integration, as technology development tends to outstrip the growth of emotional skills. Today's entrepreneurial and corporate reality is characterized by volatility, uncertainty, complexity, and ambiguity (VUCA), and leaders must balance technological flexibility with psychological resilience to protect human flourishing in the face of automation and digital transformation. While AI makes decisions more accurate and less mentally taxing, it can also potentially decrease the human communication, amplify prejudice, and push down empathy in managerial relationships and create a paradox that requires leaders to be emotionally intelligent in communicating with both machines and humans.

The rate at which artificial intelligence (AI) is converging in entrepreneurial ecosystems has created a sea change in the ways people thought about work, identity, and ability, and it is forcing a radical psychological and structural change in these aspects. In comparison to the previous technological revolutions that mostly replaced manual, repetitive, or low-skill labour, the present round of AI technology is in direct conflict with the sphere of cognition and feeling that is historically a prerogative of entrepreneurs and organizational leaders. Generative AI systems are now capable of ideation, summarization, solving problems and even replicating features of emotional expression, thus introducing a whole new type of cognitive collaborators. This development weakens leadership, decision making and innovation. Businesspeople, who had been completely dependent on their gut instincts, improvisation, and social sense, are forced to develop the ability to read algorithmic trends, understand the limits of the models, and act in socio-technical paradoxes. However, the growing presence of AI in spite of its sophistication underscores the need that can only be replaced by human emotional intelligence. In cases where AI gives suggestions that lack nuance, empathy or moral thinking, leaders should provide the affective and contextual aspect of information that turns uncritical information into action. The transformation has put a premium on emotional regulation and relational sensitivity, cultural awareness, and reflective judgment skills like these, which are impossible to automate or even outsource to machines.

At the same time, the fast embrace of AI creates an affective turbulence in organizations. At the same time, employees can celebrate the efficiency that AI will bring and at the same time fear losing their jobs, lack of autonomy, and creative agency, or be subjected to more surveillance. When such psychological stressors remain unchecked, they can reduce the level of motivation, increase anxiety at the workplace, and weaken the level of trust in leadership. Already operating in high-pressure settings (a feature defined by the scarcity of resources) and never knowing what to expect next, start-ups are especially susceptible to emotional pressure when it comes to technological disruptions. Lack of emotional intelligence can cause leaders to make things worse- by not conveying the idea of AI integration, not identifying burnout cues, or by overlooking the ethical dimension of technologically-aided decisions. On the other hand, emotionally intelligent leaders cushion these negative impacts by creating open communication pathways, engaging teams in the process of adopting AI, authenticating the experience of emotions, and expressing a common ground that would combine the human and technological advantages. These leaders are bridges between feeling and information, as they make sure the technological change does not overshadow the human dignity, belonging, and psychological health. Therefore, the increasingly AI redefines not only the actions of organizations but also the states of affect, therefore, emotionally intelligent leadership is the stabilizing factor that maintains trust, cohesion and resiliency at all levels of entrepreneurial systems.

Moreover, when AI is incorporated into the decision processes of the entrepreneurs, the leaders have to walk the fine line between the machine-generated insights and the human-centered decision-making. It is no longer about the question of how to use AI but how to use it with wisdom, ethics and in union with the emotional throb of an organization. The computational capabilities of AI extend the reach of leaders, facilitating the quick scenario modeling, mapping consumer behaviour, and talent analytics. However, in the absence of emotional intelligence, these abilities will be used to reinforce algorithmic inequities, subvert psychological safety, or estrange various stakeholders. The leaders should consequently strive to create high-order meta-awareness: a skill to discern the not only the affective conditions of the team but also the emotional content of the algorithm design, data provenance, and model results. This involves identifying situations where AI will get emotional signals wrong on cultural grounds, where automation will make work relationships impersonal and where algorithms will discriminate against under-represented communities. Emotionally intelligent leaders reduce the effects of such limitations by integrating empathy, ethical cogitations, and clear-cut reasoning into decision-making models. They act as bridges between the capabilities of AI and its weaknesses, all of which are used to achieve the prosperity of humanity instead of its decline.

Meanwhile, the emergence of AI redefines organizational expectations on resilience a construction that is entrenched in psychological adaptability. It is no longer possible to trust that entrepreneurs and leaders just grit and find their way out of uncertainty by relying solely on grit or reactive coping instead they have to develop proactive resilience that incorporates emotional awareness with technological acumen. Leaders who are emotionally intelligent emulate adaptive reactions by being calm on explosive situations, displaying candor on uncertainty, and thoughtful in trying moments. These qualities are outgoing that build team culture and create resilience. That resilience is a collective psychological ability that enables human and systems to operate effectively as organizations become more and more dependent on hybrid teams of human and AI. Leaders need to lead people through the identity changes, aid in redefining quality work amid automation by AI, and ensuring the sustainability of human creativity, intuition and relationship richness. Competency to communicate a persuasive story regarding the presence of AI in the organization, where it reduces fear, increases purpose, and drives people to collaborate in an innovative process is a competency that is particularly emotional in its foundation, as it is an innate ability that is influenced by emotional intelligence. This kind of leadership builds on personal and team flexibility but also places the organization in a position to capitalize on AI in a responsible and creative manner. In this regard, the future of AI-enhanced entrepreneurship will not be characterized by being technologically advanced only but the ability of leaders to base innovation on empathy, ethics, and affective intelligence. The key to the successful AI introduction will be ultimately dependent on the leaders who will be able to achieve the dual demands of both technological progress and human welfare equally well, precisely, and compassionately.

Artificial Intelligence (AI), emotional intelligence (EI), entrepreneurship, and organizational psychology are poised to converge, which is reshaping the basics of leadership and work in the twenty-first century radically. AI, which was initially a technical instrument, plays the role of a thought partner and influences decisions, strategies, creativity, communication, and organizational culture. As artificial intelligence systems continue to process data, draw conclusions, and automate processes traditionally the prerogative of human executives, the value of leadership is being redefined to be less cognitively superior and more emotionally, ethically, and socially connected. The entrepreneurial and organizational environment of a volatile, uncertain, complex, and ambiguous (VUCA) digital world needs leaders capable of continuously balancing computational intelligence with emotional intelligence, technological accuracy with human compassion and algorithmic velocity with psychological delicateness.

Business people are today working in the accelerated technological pace like never before. The innovation, strategy, and value creation are being reinvented through the use of Generative AI models, emotion-recognition tools, augmented analytics, and automation platforms. Despite the fact that AI decreases cognitive overload, increases accuracy of decision-making, and widens the scope of creativity, these developments are also associated with ethical issues, socio-psychological disturbances, and cultural complications. The use of algorithmic predictions may inadvertently contribute to biases, eliminate fairness, and destroy trust within the team unless it is emotionally aware leadership. On the same note, over dependence on AI can undermine human interactions, reduce empathy and increase emotional dissociation among workers. This relationship forms a paradox: AI makes the work much more efficient and puts a new type of psychological pressure on people at the same time.

This duality is most apparent in the case of startups and innovation-driven enterprises. Experimentation, agility and quick decision-making are essential to entrepreneurial ecosystems, however, alongside burnout, emotional exhaustion and decision fatigue . With AI tools beginning to infiltrate the workflow of an entrepreneur, leaders need to assist their staff to manage uncertainty without compromising mental health, feeling of inclusion, and strength, which therefore creates a new leadership identity (Syed et al., 2023). Studies reveal that leaders with emotional intelligence have a greater ability to cope with the challenges brought about by AI, maintain unity among their subordinates, and develop work environments where employees feel being valued despite the technological revolution (Cherniss, 2010).

Emotional Intelligence is emerging as a key leadership skill that is impossible to substitute with AI in this developing environment. EI helps leaders with the skills of identifying, both interpreting and controlling emotions, whether their own or that of other people, such that they are able to gain trust, boost morale, resolve conflicts, and maintain ethically sound decision-making. Although AI is excellent in computing, predicting, and identifying patterns, it is not able to simulate an experience of living human experience, culture, moral sensitivity, or real empathy (Jobin et al., 2019). Leaders should then be trained to be highly adept at marrying emotional and artificial intelligence and to develop an environment where AI is used to augment and not to suppress human flourishing.

The chapter presents an elaborate AIRE Model Awareness, Integration, Regulation and Empathy as a holistic approach to emotionally intelligent AI-enhanced leadership. The AIRE Model, based on the classical theory of EI, leadership psychology, affective science, and the latest AI ethics, is a coherent approach that will help leaders navigate the challenges of human-AI collaboration (Mayer & Salovey, 1997). Awareness is the cognitive knowledge of the emotional cues, situational contexts and algorithmic biases. Integration is the process of aligning AI outputs and human judgment, organization ethics, and sensitivity to the situation. The regulation will help leaders balance optimism with caution when adopting AI by regulating their emotional responses under the impact of high-tech pressure (World Economic Forum, 2024). Empathy offers humanity that is needed to create a sense of belonging, cultural sensitivity, and psychological safety in AI-enabled surroundings.

Based on empirical evidence, technology, health, and entrepreneurship case study, cross-disciplinary research, this chapter discusses the application of emotionally intelligent leadership in ensuring that humanness still remains in the core of technological change. It examines the psychological, ethical and organizational implication of AI adoption; provides emotion conscious leadership approaches, and presents evidence based models with the view to developing emotionally intelligent leaders in digital ecosystems. The future of the AI-EI integration, such as culturally adaptive emotional AI, hybrid intelligence systems, and psycho technological well-being, are also noted in the chapter.

This chapter is a prospective scholarly input to the disciplines of organizational psychology, leadership studies, entrepreneurship, and AI ethics because it synthesizes theoretical, practical, and ethical knowledge. It shows that in as much as AI increases cognitive ability, it is the Emotional Intelligence, which balances leadership in humanity, which will ensure that organizations are ethical, resilient, inclusive, and psychologically sustainable in a more digital society.

2. EMOTIONAL INTELLIGENCE AND LEADERSHIP FOUNDATIONS

2.1 The Wonders of Emotional Intelligence (EI) in Modern Leadership.

Emotional Intelligence (EI) has become one of the most topical factors of successful leadership in modern organizational and entrepreneurial environment. Based on the historic publication by (Mayer & Salovey, 1997), EI refers to the ability to effectively recognize emotions, understand their implications, manage the affective reactions, and use the emotional data to influence thought and action. Further it include five of the more crucial aspects of leadership in his paradigm which included self-awareness, self-regulation, motivation, empathy, and social skills, believing that these affective aspects of competence often overshadow cognitive intelligence in predicting effective leadership performance (Goleman, 1995).

In busy and highly innovative entrepreneurial environments, where there is a lot of ambiguity and competitive pressure, EI allows leaders to stay focused, make wise decisions, and maintain relational balance. Empirical studies have shown that the leaders who have a higher EI are more adaptable, have clearer reasoning in uncertain situations, their communication is more convincing, and they are better mobilisers of resources, which are directly related to the entrepreneur performance and the ability to survive through their ventures (Mortan et al., 2014). Since the process of entrepreneurship consistently requires the trade-off between risk, stakeholder responsibility, and negotiating emotionally colored situations, EI will provide the leaders with the affective clarity and cognitive flexibility necessary to make sound decisions and motivate the team. In organizational psychological sense, EI is an important factor of team integrity, psychological safety and trust which are antecedents that strongly predict organizational effectiveness and innovation (Carmeli, 2003). Leaders with high EI develop open channels of communication, employee welfare, and conflict management in constructive ways, which reduce stress and turnover intention at work. EI becomes even more significant in work cultures that are digitally-focused, because often the social background of virtual communication lacks the means to interpret and even discern more complex emotions. In AI-controlled workplaces EI is a humanizing power in a technologically complicated environment. With AI systems increasingly having a larger role in the hiring, assessment, and decision-making processes, leaders need to dissect the emotional implications of automation, algorithmic results, and technological transformation. The reaction of employees to the adoption of AI can be fear, uncertainty, or resistance (Syed et al., 2023). Leaders who possess EI are in a better position to recognize these emotions, act empathetically and guide the teams through change in a transparent and fair manner. Therefore, EI is not merely a positive trait but a leadership skill that could be applied strategically to ensure the organizational health, sound business choices, and performance.

2.2 Psychological Requirements of AI-enhanced workspace Leadership.

The introduction of the Artificial Intelligence into the organizational settings has fundamentally changed the psychological environment of work, thus, placing new emotional and cognitive demands on the leaders. Even though AI enriches the efficiency of operations, predictability, and optimization when making decisions, it also destabilizes traditional leadership roles and interpersonal relations. Leaders will therefore be forced to go through the emotional complexities of technological change such as uncertainty of the employees, threats to their identity and ethical dilemmas. Such problems indicate the necessity of the emotionally intelligent kind of leadership that can address the dual issues of technological competence and human sensitivity (Fountaine et al., 2019). Another principle psychological need is a cognitive and emotional overload. AI devices produce large volumes of data, which requires the leader to analyze multi-layered information and at the same time address employee emotions and expectations. Kolbjørnsrud et al. (2016) note that leaders spend more time on digital coordination, algorithm interpretation, and technological troubleshooting, which leads to a greater load on mental exhaustion. Moreover, the fact that emotionally-charged decisions, like algorithmic-based performance evaluation or AI-aided recruitment put leaders in ethically uncomfortable situations intensifies the emotional impact (Floridi and Cowls, 2019). The other challenge that has arisen is algorithmic responsibility. The decisions made through AI systems are held leaders accountable, despite the lack of full transparency concerning the processes of the algorithms. This is called the black box problem which creates an emotional stress and moral unease. Leaders need to determine the consistency of AI outputs with organizational ideals, laws, and equity in society. Moral failures in AI interpretation can trigger reputational damage or lack of trust within the company (Jobin et al., 2019). Interpersonal disconnection is another challenge that leaders face due to the further mediation of communication in the workplace by digital interfaces.

Excessive use of automation and remote communication reduces the possibility of spontaneous interpersonal bonding, which undermines the possibility of empathetic interaction (Turkle, 2015). As a result, leaders will have to make an extra effort to maintain genuine relationships, promote trust, and promote transparency in online places. Lastly, there is identity change when AI takes up positions of leaders especially in analytics and decision support. The leaders might question their necessity, professionalism, or control in the AI-aroused ecosystems (Syed et al., 2023). The identity shocks may be in the form of insecurity or protective attitude towards AI adoption. Emotional intelligence can counter these challenges by encouraging self awareness, emotional control and adaptive coping mechanisms. Overall, the field of emotionally intelligent leadership is invaluable in the context of the psychological needs of AI-enhanced working conditions.

2.3 AI as a Transformational Division in Entrepreneurship and Organization Behavior.

Artificial Intelligence is not just a working tool but the transformative force, which redefines the way entrepreneurs and organizational leaders are innovative, cooperate, and make decisions. The role of AI does not just lie in the automation of repetitive processes but in the creation of strategic conclusions and innovations, which completely changes the essence of the thinking and actions of an entrepreneur. Brynjolfsson and McAfee (2017) argue that AI will speed up the innovation process because it enhances human intelligence to help leaders expand the range of possibilities faster and more accurately. This augmentation transforms leadership into a human-based activity to a hybrid process that incorporates both computational and emotional abilities. Within the entrepreneurial setting, AI is a cognitive partner, which helps leaders recognize opportunities, analyze the market, forecast, and predict customer behavior. These insights can make entrepreneurs deal with uncertainty more efficiently; nevertheless, they still need to perceive AI-generated outputs in the emotional and contextual terms. Although patterns can be expressed by AI, it is up to entrepreneurs to decide if these patterns comply with human needs, values, and market sensations (Wilson and Daugherty, 2018). Creativity and innovation is also redefined by AI. Generative AI applications assist in ideation, product development, and content, which enhances the speed of the creative processes. However, the creative process of entrepreneurship remains dependent on emotion-based information greatly, on the capacity to put yourself into the shoes of users, understand the emotional response, and work out culturally oriented solutions. Empirical research demonstrates that emotionally intelligent entrepreneurs generate more customer-centered innovations, and develop stronger relationships with their customers (Marques, 2015). In organizational behavior, AI transforms the team interactions by reallocating the roles, redesigning the expertise, and creating new collaboration patterns. Human-AI workgroups need leaders who meet the demands of being technical and emotional at the same time and make sure that technology serves as a tool to make interpersonal relationships stronger and not weaker. As Cherniss (2010) says, the emotionally intelligent leaders would be better fitted to assist the employees in the process of transition, lower the fear of displacement, and strengthen the psychological safety. However, AI creates emotional and cultural dangers. Affect can also be misunderstood by emotion-recognition systems because it is subject to bias in the data set or the differences between cultures, where the evaluation will be incorrect or the decision made will be unjust (Barrett et al., 2019). The leaders need to introduce governance practices that are based on EI to ensure fairness, transparency, and consideration of cultural norms. Without EI, AI use will improve inequalities or destroy trust. Therefore, only through the combination of emotionally intelligent leadership that puts humanity at the core of technological innovation, it can fully realize the potential of AI as a transformative force.

2.4 Emotional Intelligence being an Strategic Asset in AI Intelligence

EI is being understood more as a strategic capability that leaders can acquire to adapt themselves in artificial intelligence-based workplaces. With AI systems taking on an analytical, predictive, and operational quality, emotionally intelligent leadership will enable managers to take care of the human aspect of technology adoption, such as the trust, motivation, ethical and psychological welfare. Goleman proposed the seminal work (1995), which argued that emotional intelligence is what sets apart the exceptional leaders with the competent leaders; in AI-mediated settings, the difference will be even higher, as the EI makes the leadership based on the sense of empathy, ethical awareness, and relationship capability. Emotional intelligence plays a very important role in providing trust and psychological safety, and this aspect is one of the most essential. Fear and resistance are common when the employees feel that AI has threatened their independence or their employment. Leaders with high EI are aware of such respondent affective reactions and respond to them by transparency, assurance, and empathic conversation. Innovation and adaptability can only be promoted through psychological safety, which may be described as a mutual understanding that employees are not afraid of voicing their concerns because of risks of adverse consequences (Edmondson, 2019). Psychological safety is facilitated by the emotionally intelligent leadership that legitimizes emotional experience and fosters the openness of communication. The EI is also another aspect that can boost ethical decision-making within the context of AI. The decisions made by AI may disagree with ethical standards or give biased advice based on the imperfect training information. Such outputs need to be critically examined by leaders, with empathy and ethical reasoning used to reduce harm (Jobin et al., 2019). Emotionally smart leaders thus put the human impacts of AI-driven actions into consideration making sure that people are treated fairly and decisions made suit the organizational values. Moreover, the emotional intelligence enhances the strength of an individual and, therefore, the leaders can stay calm and flexible in the face of the blistering technological change. The skills of resilience include maintaining emotional level, re-framing problems positively and being quick to overcome difficulties. Duchek (2020) argues that emotional awareness and emotional regulation, which are the basic elements of EI, develop resilience. Resilience is a culture of change and learning that leaders who exemplify resilience promote in their subordinates. Lastly, emotional intelligence is the foundation of human-centered digital transformation. Emotionally intelligent managers in organizations implement AI in a manner that is sensitive to the welfare of the employees, cultural sensitivity, and inclusion. EI informs how change processes are designed in a way that they comply with the mitigation of stress, conflict reduction, and social cohesion in order to make technology add value instead of damage human connection. Together, emotional intelligence offers the affective, ethical, and human-centered skills that are vital to responsible, resilient and human-centered AI leadership.

3. THE AIRE MODEL

3.1 Awareness: Emotional, Contextual and Algorithms Consciousness.

The awareness construct is the basic component of the AIRE Model, which refers to the ability of the leader to sense, interpret, and understand the emotional as well as informational messages produced by the human and artificial agents. According to the Emotional Intelligence theory, awareness, especially self-awareness and social awareness, is the foundation onto which the upper-level emotional regulation and interpersonal competence rests (Mayer and Salovey, 1997; Goleman, 1995). In AI-enhanced organizational contexts, the awareness goes beyond the emotional perception and includes situational, cultural, and algorithmic conscious. Self-awareness allows leaders to become aware of the emotional responses that they undergo to AI-generated insights, such as feeling uneasy, being overconfident, feeling anxious or resisting it. These emotional reactions can inform the perception of algorithmic outputs or reaction to technological change in a subconscious way (Cherniss, 2010). Managers with a lack of self-awareness might transfer their fears or biases to AI systems and either excessively trust its automated advice or decline it too soon. On the other hand, emotionally intelligent leaders consider their inner selves and are cognitively open and emotionally based to interact with AI. Social and contextual awareness entails the appreciation of the emotional climate of teams that work in the environment of AI-mediated environments. Due to the adoption of AI, employees can feel unsure about their employment, feel like they are being monitored, or lose control (Fountaine et al., 2019). Highly-aware leaders are able to perceive the smallest emotional signals, including withdrawal, resistance, or anxiety and act pro-emptively to maintain psychological safety. This aspect is especially important with entrepreneurial ecosystems, where emotional volatility and role ambiguity are widespread phenomena. AIRE Model Algorithmic awareness is a new term of EI. It means how leaders are aware of the working mechanisms of AI systems, such as the dependencies of data, limitations, and possible biases. There is no such thing as AI systems being neutral; they are considered to be based on the assumptions they are designed and trained on (Jobin et al., 2019). Therefore, leaders should be aware of epistemic limits of AI, and they should be aware of the cases where outputs can be incomplete, biased, or unsituated. The studies of affective computing also suggest that the algorithms of emotion-recognition often fail to recognize emotional expression in cross-cultural settings, which makes such algorithms to be highly vulnerable to failures (Barrett et al., 2019). Combining emotional, social, and algorithmic awareness, leaders develop the perceptual clarity needed to lead ethically and effectively using AI-supplemented leadership. In the AIRE Model, awareness is the diagnostic step, where the leaders are able to detect the emotional and technological indicators before taking action.

3.2 Integration: Artificial Intelligence and Emotional Intelligence (AI vs. EI).

Integration refers to the ability of the leader to combine emotional intelligence and AI generated data to create balanced, ethical and contextual decisions. Although AI is better at analytical processing, recognizing patterns and making predictions, it is incapable of emotional awareness, moral judgment, and sensitivity to the context (Brynjolfsson and McAfee, 2017). Integration means that AI results are not meant to be interpreted as final results but as inputs that should be perceived based on human knowledge and emotional intelligence. Psychologically, integration displays the principle of EI that relies on emotions to ease cognition (Mayer and Salovey, 1997). The leaders should consider the overlap of the AI recommendations on organizational values, team morale, and social implications. An example is that an AI system will advise on layoffs based on the efficiency ratios; however, leaders with a high EI would determine the human cost of the action, in terms of employee morale, trust, and the overall organizational culture in the long term. In the entrepreneurial environment, integration is of great concern because of the high level of uncertainty as well as speedy decision making. Entrepreneurs are frequently depending on AI tools to analyze the market, predict, and understand its customers, but such tools do not grasp the subtle consumer feelings or cultural connotations, pre-existing social trends (Wilson and Daugherty, 2018). Emotional entrepreneurs combine AI knowledge with opportunistic intuition, stakeholder input, and understanding in their innovation and strategy. The central role of ethical AI governance is also taken by integration. The need to focus on human-in-the-loop systems is emphasized by the research on AI ethics, where leaders should actively monitor, contextualize, and, in some cases, override the algorithmic decisions (Floridi and Cowls, 2019). Leaders who do not combine emotional and ethical reasoning may delegate moral responsibility to machines, which will compromise accountability and trust. In addition, integration also promotes inclusive leadership. AI systems, which are trained on biased data, can be detrimental to some groups of people. Leaders with emotional intelligence are aware of these dangers and incorporate the notion of fairness into the decision-making process, which would allow making sure that the use of AI does not keep inequality alive (Jobin et al., 2019). Therefore, the integration in the AIRE Model makes AI a team player rather than a deterministic decision-maker. In technologically advanced organizations, leaders maintain the human agency, morality, and situational awareness by balancing emotional intelligence with the artificial one.

3.3 Regulation: Emotional Self-Management in High-tech Leadership situations.

Regulation refers to the ability of the leader to control emotional reactions both personal and interpersonal, and to cope with the complexities, ambiguities, and pressures of AI-based settings. The emotion regulation is an essential aspect of emotional intelligence (EI) and demonstrates a strong relationship with the leadership performance, stress and burnout resistance, and moral integrity (Goleman, 1995; Gross, 2015). Emotionally-charged scenarios are a regular occurrence that leaders in AI-enhanced workplaces constantly have to deal with, and they require conscious self-regulation. The implementation of AI is often met with anxiety, resistance or defensiveness and is more likely to occur when automation risks employees their jobs or changes their identities (Syed et al., 2023). Leaders themselves can also have an emotional burden associated with the responsibility of algorithmic decisions, overloading and a lack of confidence with the reliability of AI. Without proper regulation, leaders will have the tendency to respond on the spur, overly reliant on AI, or shut out of emotionally taxing situations. Emotionally intelligent leaders are able to cheque their emotional responses through identifying their triggers and reframing emotions and composure under pressure. This is because they are able to react in a way that is not always automatic, but considered and therefore leads to stability and confidence in teams (Cherniss, 2010). Ethical leadership is also rooted in regulation since emotionally dysregulated leaders tend to be more susceptible to cognitive biases or moral disengagement or decision shortcuts (Bazerman and Tenbrunsel, 2011). Resilience is closely associated with regulation in the context of entrepreneurial ecosystems. Entrepreneurs work under high-risk, high-uncertainty environments where failure and quick change are the norm. Duchek (2020) highlights that resilience is formed due to the ability to regulate emotions and rebound after the adversity, learn and feel motivated. Although AI can make the process of decision-making much faster, it also introduces pressure by increasing the speed and accuracy demands. Therefore, leaders should control reaction to stress to prevent burnout and decision fatigue. Regulation is also an important factor in the relationships between human beings and AI. The leaders need to ensure that they avoid emotional dependency on AI suggestions without being defensive to technological contribution. Balanced control enables leaders to be emotionally open, critical and adaptive. Through emotional stability modelling, leaders foster a psychological safe climate where employees feel encouraged throughout technological changes (Edmondson, 2019). Regulation as a stabilising mechanism in the AIRE Model allows leaders to interact with AI without fearing, operating ethically, and in a sustainable manner without risks of emotional burnout.

3.4 Empathy: Human Connection in AI-Augmented Leadership.

Empathy is the moral and inter-relational core of the AIRE Model, which makes AI-improved leadership the element of human relationship, empathy, and social responsibility. As the ability to understand and sympathize with the emotional state of others, empathy turns out to be a crucial aspect of emotional intelligence and one of the predictors of transformational leadership (Goleman, 1995; Boyatzis, 2018). In the context of AI-mediated workplace, empathy will take on an increasing significance, since digital technologies risk making relationships impersonal and weakening interpersonal contact. The use of AI in decision-making can unwillingly alienate leaders to subordinates by replacing in-person communication with data dashboard, performance measurement, and computerized appraisals. According to empirical research, excessive use of digital communication reduces the accuracy of empathy and destroys interpersonal relationships (Turkle, 2015). Empathic leaders can alleviate this tendency through active listening, emotional validation, and sensitivity and transparency in the explanation of AI-related choices. Besides, empathy plays a crucial role in maintaining psychological security during AI adoption. The employees might have some fears of being monitored, substituted, or evaluated by a biased algorithm. Emotionally intelligent leaders will solve such concerns by validating their fears, clarifying the uses and limitations of AI tools, and reasserting human value in the organizational environment (Edmondson, 2019). Such sympathetic interventions create trust and involvement as well as commitment to the organization.

User centered innovation is based on empathy in the context of entrepreneurship. A business person who listens to customers and stakeholders is in a better position to come up with a product and service that fulfills the genuine human needs, not solely focusing on technical issues (Marques, 2015). Despite the ability of AI to provide understanding of consumer behaviour, empathy enables leaders to provide meaningful and ethical interpretation of the understanding. Empathy is another skill that is critical in cross-cultural AI leadership. Technologies that recognize emotions are often prone to cultural differences in the expression of emotions, which increases the chances of misinterpretation (Barrett et al., 2019). Cultural empathetic leaders are aware of such limitations and prevent the abuse of emotional information. They ensure that the AI-based practices are respectful of diversity, inclusion, and contextual sensitivity. In the AIRE Model, empathy protects the essentially human nature of the AI-enhanced leadership. It translates data into conversation, effectiveness into solicitation and innovation into collective sense. The aspect of leadership that empathy supports in organizations that are increasingly becoming automated is dignity, belonging and ethical responsibility.

3.5 The AIRE Model of a Holistic Approach to Resilient and Ethical AI Leadership.

Although every aspect of the AIRE Model (Awareness, Integration, Regulation, and Empathy) represents a unique leadership competence, the most significant effect of the AIRE Model is an interplay of the different elements as a system of interacting psychological processes. The modern leadership challenges in AI-enhanced settings cannot be managed with the help of isolated affective skills, instead, they require an integrative paradigm in which emotional intelligence is correlated with ethical arguments, technological competence, and organizational stability. The AIRE Model meets this requirement by providing a psychologically based and holistic framework by which leaders may negotiate the complexity that is involved in human-AI collaboration. In the most simplistic sense, the AIRE Model is based on the idea that leadership is not about controlling technology, but is rather a form of stewardship in socio-technical systems. This point of view is in harmony with the systems theory in organizational psychology, the main thesis of which is that the effectiveness of leadership is a result of interactions of individuals, technologies, and institutional environments instead of unique individual characteristics (Katz and Kahn, 1978). This is started by awareness that helps leaders to identify emotional, cultural, and algorithmic cues. Without awareness, the leaders will be susceptible to acting in a reactive manner by either giving in to AI or developing a defensive mechanism. Awareness therefore acts as the cognitive- emotional gateway with the help of which leaders decipher human feelings as well as machine-generated data (Mayer et al., 2016). Integration is based on awareness and the perception is adjusted to judgment. With AI mediated settings, the decision-making process is becoming more about negotiating the conflict between efficiency and ethics, accuracy and fairness, innovation and well-being. Scholarly works concerning the issue of ethical AI governance repeatedly stress the role of human control and situational interpretation, especially with regard to employment, medical, and social integration (Floridi et al., 2018; Jobin et al., 2019). The Inclusion in the AIRE Model makes sure that the leaders do not assume AI outputs to be objective truths but rather as a probable suggestion that has to be considered emotionally, morally, and culturally. This is the process that maintains human agency and accountability and enhances leadership as a moral practice and not a solely technical operation. The stabilizing mechanism in the model is regulation, which allows leaders to achieve a balance of emotions when they are involved in uncertainty, disruption, and ethical complexity. Psychological studies have shown that when dysregulated emotionally, judgment ability is affected, cognitive shortcuts are more likely to be used, and the individual is more exposed to bias, all of which are especially dangerous factors in AI-based decision-making contexts (Bazerman and Tenbrunsel, 2011). Leaders with poor emotional control can either delegate to AI excessively to avoid responsibility or discard AI information due to anxiety or a fear of being threatened by AI (Syed et al., 2023). Regulation enables leaders to be emotionally secure, actively critical, and reflective and thus facilitates the way they make decisions in a consistent and principled manner. The AIRE Model is finished with empathy, which grounds leadership in interpersonal relationship and social responsibility. With the growing percentage of interaction via AI systems, the role of empathy as the main way in which leaders can overcome depersonalization and emotional detachment grows. Empathic leadership has always been associated with increased trust, engagement, psychological safety, and ethical climate through organizational research (Edmondson, 2019; Boyatzis, 2018). In AI-enhanced setting, empathy will ensure that technological effectiveness is not the reason why dignity, inclusion, and well-being are undermined. It is also important in the context of cross-cultural interactions, where AI systems can fail to discern expressive behavior or even strengthen cultural standards (Barrett et al., 2019). Notably, the AIRE Model is similar to the modern resilience theory. Resilience is also being framed not as a simple toughness of an individual, but as a dynamic process that implies emotional awareness, adaptive regulation, social support and ethical coherence (Duchek, 2020). The stressors of working with AI include speed, surveillance, ambiguity, and continual appraisal, and emotionally intelligent leadership might be considered the key to maintaining resilience on both individual and organizational levels. Those leaders who implement the AIRE Model develop an environment where uncertainty is an accepted part of the game, emotions are validated and learning is favored over blame. In terms of entrepreneurship, the AIRE Model covers the psychological fact of the ecosystems based on innovation. Entrepreneurs often work in extremely uncertain conditions, with limited resources, and unstable identity (Shepherd and Williams, 2018). AI tools can also improve the opportunity recognition and scalability, but they also increase the pressure on performance and emotions. As a result, the AIRE framework provides entrepreneurial leaders with the emotional discipline necessary to come out intact after failure, ethical dilemma, and rapid change to stay in touch with the stakeholders needs and social impact. Overall, the AIRE Model contributes to the development of the literature on AI leadership in that it combines emotional intelligence, ethical governance, and resilience into one unified concept. It does not present emotional intelligence as an additional so-called soft skill, but as the psychological foundation of responsible, sustainable, and human-centered use of AI. Having theorized leadership as an emotionally intelligent union between people and machines, AIRE Model provides a future-proof leadership model at the time when intelligent technologies define the era.

4. STRATEGIES, INTERVENTIONS AND CASE APPLICATIONS

4.1 AI-Empathy Dashboards: EI-based Interpretation of Data.

AI-empathy dashboards represent a new organizational intervention that is aimed at tracking the emotion of the employees, their engagement, stress indicators, and the overall emotional climate with the help of AI-based analytics. These systems generally collate the information based on surveys, communication applications, behavioral indicators, and sentiment analysis software to provide the leadership with real time understanding of well-being of their workforce. Even though these dashboards bring huge benefits in size and speed, their overall performance is highly influenced by the emotionally intelligent judgments of leaders (Fountaine et al., 2019). In the context of EI, dashboards are not to be taken as objective emotional facts but to be interpreted in terms of their emotional signals which require contextual and empathic understanding. Emotion is a subjective element that is culturally coded and dependent on the situation (Barrett et al., 2019). In leaders with a high level of emotional awareness, it is understood that AI-inspired emotional information can simplify or distort lived experiences, who are especially featured in multi-diverse or remote teams. The AIRE Model lays stress on Awareness and Integration in this step; the leaders should understand what the data represents, what it does not represent, how it is consistent with human behaviour. With its ethical and transparent use, empathy dashboards can be added to the decision-making of leadership. Empirical studies have shown that trust and engagement are more likely to increase when workers understand the mission of emotional surveillance systems and they believe that they are there to help them and not spy (Edmondson, 2019). Leaders with high emotional intelligence share information concerning the data collection, interpretation, and application techniques, thus supporting the ideas of consent and psychological safety. However, companies still face the threat of ethical risks. Sentiment analysis provided by AI can be violative to privacy or lead to emotional manipulation when abused (Jobin et al., 2019). Leaders should control their reactions to emotional information by consciously not reacting to it with an intervention or punitive action. Rather, supportive measures like the manipulation of workloads, the promotion of dialogue, or the introduction of well-being programs should be informed with the help of dashboards. With the help of EI, AI-empathy dashboards become organizational-care instruments instead of control devices. They facilitate the leaders to notice emotional trends earlier and react in a compassionate way, as well as build resilient, human-focused workplaces in AI-enhanced settings.

4.2 Virtual Emotional Intelligence Training and AI-Simulations.

Virtual Emotional Intelligence (EI) trainings programs represent an interesting innovation in the field of leadership development, where AI-based simulations, chatbots, and immersion technologies are used to enhance emotional competence. These exercises allow leaders to practice emotionally challenging situations, including conflict resolution, ethical dilemmas, and performance feedback, in the safe, psychologically safe settings (Gross, 2015). The use of AI-based simulations provides instant feedback, therefore, enabling leaders to sharpen emotional sensitivity, control and understanding interaction. Experiential learning is considered to be more effective than theoretical alone training in terms of the development of EI competencies on the organizational-psychological level (Boyatzis, 2018). Simulations AI-driven can be used to simulate high-stress leadership scenarios in an emotionally realistic way, exposing leaders to a host of emotional reactions and cultural scenarios. As an example, virtual agents can imitate the feeling of employee panic over automation or ethical issues with AI-driven decision-making. Leaders must find a way of navigating these interactions via empathy and emotional regulation, which strengthens the competencies as specified in the AIRE Model. The potential of virtual EI tools, however, should be taken with a grain of salt. Simulations of AI cannot be fully replicated to create the depth of human feelings or cultural subtleties (Barrett et al., 2019). Leaders that are emotionally intelligent recognize these drawbacks and view simulations as the developmental support and not the replacement of a real-life interaction. The issue of regulation is especially acute; the leaders should not be overconfident about the emotional competence measured by AI and be open to the feedback generated in the context of actual human interaction. Empirical studies show that EI training improves leadership performance, burnout, and resilience when reflected practice and coaching are used to supplement the intervention (Cherniss, 2010). The best efficacy of AI-based training is attained when it is incorporated into larger leadership development systems that include mentoring, peer feedback, and organizational support. Virtual EI training is consistent with human-focused digital transformation in AI-enhanced organizations. It provides leaders with the emotional capability needed to adopt an AI-driven change with compassion, communicate openly and instill trust. As something morally right and psychologically well-informed, AI-driven EI training enhances the leadership without diminishing the authenticity.

4.3 AI-Assisted decision-making by following ethical reflection.

Ethical reflection procedures are organized decision-making points that are integrated into artificial-intelligence-based organizational processes and are meant to curb the inclusion of emotional, ethical and social consequences in the output of technical work. With AI taking on increased control over high-stakes decisions, such as recruitment, promotion, dismissal, and medical diagnostics, organizational leaders are faced with an increased ethical responsibility (Floridi and Cowls, 2019). Implementation of emotionally intelligent leadership is thus important to successfully operationalize ethical reflection in these environments. Ethical AI research anticipates the significance of human-in-the-loop systems, in which leaders engage in probing and situating algorithmic proposals instead of transferring decision making power to automated decision makers (Jobin et al., 2019). The components of the AIRE Model that are particularly relevant are the Integration and Empathy. Reflective questions that the leaders should ask include: Who are the stakeholders that might lose out on the decision? What were the emotional consequences that could arise? Does the decision coincide with the values and social responsibilities of the organization? Leaders who are emotionally intelligent also deal with the moral pressure that comes along with such dilemmas. Ethical decision-making process is often associated with the opposition of efficiency and fairness, profitability and well-being of the employees. According to empirical studies in behavioral ethics, emotional coldness increases the susceptibility of racial blindness especially in moments of time constraint or power diffusion (Bazerman and Tenbrunsel, 2011). Through regulation, leaders are able to stop, introspect and engage in principled thinking instead of the default to algorithmic expediency. These protocols might include multidisciplinary review teams, emotionally intelligent decision lists, and post decision impact analysis. These processes favor accountability, transparency and trust. The higher the level of acceptance toward AI-facilitated decisions is, the more employees feel that their leaders are emotionally astute and ethically based (Edmondson, 2019). In AI-enhanced entrepreneurial ecosystems (where time is of the essence), where impulsive innovation can frequently be the norm, ethical reflection practices alleviate impulsive innovation through the ability to afford moral foresight. They protect against the violation of human dignity by technological advancement, thus ensuring the leadership legitimacy, integrity of the organization.

4.4 AI-Driven Organizations Coaching on Resilience.

The concept of resilience coaching has become central to the intervention of AI-driven corporations, which is charged with suppressing the emotional and psychological impact of relentless technological change. Resilience has been operationalized as the ability to adapt, recover, and prosper during hard times and uncertainty (Duchek, 2020). Artificially intelligence-enhanced environments increase stressors, such as faster decision-making, the ongoing assessment, and increased levels of performance transparency, which, in turn, increases the likelihood of burnout among leaders and their subordinates. Resilience coaching based on emotional intelligence combines evidence-based knowledge and psychological assistance. The artificial intelligence systems are able to identify the stress patterns, measure the workload imbalances, or indicate the patterns of disengagement; but, the emotionally intelligent coach is able to put this information into context through an empathetic conversation and reflexive practice. This strategy also correlates with the dual focus of the AIRE Model on Regulation and Empathy and thus allows leaders to effectively handle stress instead of blurring the emotional reaction. Experienced researchers prove that leaders who are coached on the basis of emotion intelligence (EI) have better emotional regulation, stronger coping mechanisms, and greater adaptability to times of organizational change (Cherniss, 2010). Moreover, resilience coaching helps to re-invent identity, which allows leaders to redefine their functions in the context of AI-enhanced ecosystems where power is being decentralized to intelligent systems (Syed et al., 2023). In the entrepreneurial setting, the concept of resilience coaching gains special importance. Also for entrepreneurs, they easily face repeated failures, situational uncertainty, and emotional instability; it is compounded by AI-based performance demands. Coaching that is enriched with EI helps entrepreneurs to think about failures as learning feedback, maintain intrinsic motivation, and maintain a healthy mind (Shepherd and Williams, 2018). Lastly, resilience coaching reaffirms ethical leadership in that it minimizes the chances of emotionally weak leaders on defensive decisions or moral disengagement in the face of pressure. Their adaptive coping, openness, and emotional honesty have made them an example of such leaders who develop resilient organizational cultures capable of surviving in a world of constant digital disruption.

4.5 Cross-Sector Case Applications of Emotionally Intelligent AI Leadership

Real-world applications across sectors illustrate how emotionally intelligent leadership enhances AI adoption outcomes. In the technology sector, organizations emphasizing responsible AI frameworks demonstrate that empathy and ethical awareness are critical for inclusive innovation. Leaders who prioritize emotional impact assessments alongside technical evaluations foster trust among employees and users, reducing resistance to AI deployment (Microsoft, 2022).

In healthcare, AI-augmented diagnostic tools illustrate the importance of human empathy. While AI enhances accuracy and efficiency, patient trust depends heavily on clinicians' emotional communication and ethical sensitivity. Studies show that when clinicians integrate AI insights with empathic engagement, patient satisfaction and decision quality improve (IBM, 2023). Emotionally intelligent leadership ensures that AI supports—not replaces—human care.

Entrepreneurial ecosystems in emerging markets further highlight the value of EI in AI leadership. Indian startups using AI-driven HR analytics to detect burnout demonstrate how emotionally aware founders integrate data with compassionate intervention. Rather than using emotional data punitively, these leaders employ it to redesign workloads, offer support, and strengthen organizational resilience (Syed et al., 2023).

Across sectors, common themes emerge: AI effectiveness increases when leaders demonstrate emotional awareness, ethical judgment, and empathy. Conversely, AI initiatives fail when emotional dimensions are ignored, leading to mistrust, disengagement, or ethical backlash.

These cases reinforce the central thesis of this chapter: AI's transformative potential is realized only when guided by emotionally intelligent leadership. The AIRE Model provides a transferable framework applicable across industries, cultures, and organizational scales.

CONCLUSION

A fast-fading integration of artificial intelligence (AI) into organizational and entrepreneurial ecosystems has radically changed the leadership, decision-making, and human interaction at the workplace. Due to the growing number of cognitive, analytical, and predictive tasks that AI systems complete, the human element of the leadership process is no longer characterized by advanced information-processing skills but by emotional, ethical, and relational intelligence. The thesis presented in this chapter states that emotional intelligence (EI) is the core human ability that helps leaders to operate in AI-enhanced landscapes in a responsible, resilient, and sustainable way. Based on organization psychology, leadership theory, research in entrepreneurship and the research in AI ethics, the chapter redefines leadership as a human-AI collaboration instead of a contest between human and machine intelligence. Although AI is more efficient, accurate and scalable, it is unaware of emotions, has no moral judgement, cultural sensitivity, and experience of life. In the absence of emotionally intelligent leadership, AI adoption will cause a loss of trust, increased bias, and eroded psychological safety as well as dehumanized organizational relationships (Floridi and Cowls, 2019; Jobin et al., 2019). The identity threat, emotional detachment, surveillance anxiety, and ethical ambiguity are the psychological issues that are associated with AI and highlight the ongoing central role of EI in modern leadership practice (Syed et al., 2023). The main point of this chapter is the AIRE Model known as Awareness, Integration, Regulation and Empathy that is suggested as a universal approach to emotionally intelligent AI-enhanced leadership.

Consciousness allows the leaders to be aware of their emotional signals, situational clues, and algorithms constraints before taking action. Integration is the way to make sure that AI-generated insights are measured using ethical reasoning, emotional understanding, and organizational values. Leaders can be helped to cope with emotional pressure, cognitive overload, and moral pressure in high-tech settings through regulation. Empathy grounds leadership on the human relation, maintains the dignity, inclusion and psychological safety even in the digital transformation. All these elements are the building blocks of a dynamic system that helps to make ethical judgments, resiliency, and adaptive leadership in AI-mediated contexts. The chapter illustrates that emotionally intelligent leadership is especially essential in new entrepreneurial ecosystems, which tend to be characterized by high uncertainty and pressure on innovation coupled with emotional turbulence. The entrepreneurs who work in AI-based markets should work with the rapidity and the prudence, data, and intuition, automation, and thoughtfulness. EI helps entrepreneurs to overcome failure in a healthy way, maintain motivation, and create innovations that are more technologically sophisticated and human-centered, at the same time (Shepherd and Williams, 2018). Likewise, at the organizational level, EI-based leadership is associated with improved employee engagement, trust, and psychological safety, which are the main predictors of innovation and long-term performance (Edmondson, 2019).

The practical parts of the chapter show the ways in which the principles of EI can be realized with the help of AI-empathy dashboards, training in empathy, ethical reflection procedures, and resilience coaching. As the interventions emphasize, AI will only be effective when it is based on the emotional intelligence of its interpretation and ethical regulation rather than merely on a high level of technical sophistication. Applications in technology, healthcare, and entrepreneurship prove the point that AI projects are successful when leaders focus on the emotional appeal, transparency, and empathy, as well as efficiency and innovation. Notably, the chapter plays an important role in the developing the discussion of AI ethics by placing EI as a fundamentally important ethical sense-making mechanism. Instead of considering ethics as an external compliance regulation, the AIRE Model incorporates ethical consideration into emotional awareness, regulation and empathy. This view is consistent with recent demands of human-in-the-loop AI systems and morally responsible governance systems that maintain accountability and moral responsibility (Floridi et al., 2018). As far as resilience is concerned, the chapter highlights that emotionally intelligent leadership promotes adaptive capacity both at individual and organizational levels. Working in an AI-driven environment enhances the pressure on the speed, surveillance, and performance transparency, and emotional regulation and social support can be considered to be vital in supporting well-being. The ability of emotional balance, reflective judgement and empathic engagement as models by leaders develop resilient cultures that can learn, recover and grow through the constant technological disruption (Duchek, 2020).

As Artificial Intelligence continues to evolve from a decision-support tool into an interactive, adaptive, and socially embedded system, future research must increasingly examine AI not merely as a technological artifact but as a developmental partner in leadership formation. One promising direction involves conceptualizing AI as a co-coach in leader development processes. Rather than replacing human mentoring, AI systems can be designed to support long-term leadership growth by providing reflective feedback, emotion-aware insights, and adaptive learning pathways. Such AI co-coaches may assist leaders in tracking emotional patterns, decision tendencies, stress responses, and ethical blind spots over time, thereby influencing leader identity, authenticity, and self-concept (Boyatzis, 2018; Syed et al., 2023). Longitudinal research is needed to examine how sustained interaction with emotionally intelligent AI systems shapes leadership identity construction and psychological maturity.

Another critical avenue for future development lies in the creation of culturally aware affective AI models. Current emotion-recognition and sentiment-analysis systems often rely on universalized assumptions about emotional expression, neglecting cultural display rules and contextual variation (Barrett et al., 2019). This limitation poses serious risks in global organizations, where emotional misinterpretation can lead to bias, exclusion, or ethical harm. Future research should focus on developing EI-aware AI systems that are sensitive to cultural norms, social context, and individual differences in emotional expression. Integrating cross-cultural psychology with affective computing would enable AI systems to support leadership decision-making without reinforcing dominant cultural frameworks or mislabeling emotional behavior.

Policy-oriented research also represents a vital frontier. As AI systems increasingly influence psychological well-being, identity, and interpersonal relationships at work, there is a growing need for mandatory psychological impact assessments (PIAs) for corporate AI technologies. Similar to environmental or data protection impact assessments, PIAs would evaluate the emotional, cognitive, and social consequences of AI deployment on employees and leaders (Floridi et al., 2018). Such assessments could examine risks related to stress, surveillance anxiety, emotional manipulation, and erosion of autonomy. Policymakers, organizational psychologists, and AI ethicists must collaborate to establish standardized frameworks that protect mental well-being while enabling innovation.

Finally, future empirical research should explore hybrid measurement models that integrate Emotional Intelligence indicators with algorithmic performance metrics as predictors of sustainable organizational outcomes. Traditional leadership assessments often separate human competencies from technological effectiveness. However, AI-augmented leadership requires evaluation models that capture both emotional and computational dimensions. Combining EI measures (e.g., MSCEIT, WLEIS) with AI trust calibration indices, decision transparency metrics, and organizational resilience indicators could provide a more comprehensive understanding of leadership effectiveness in digital ecosystems (Mayer et al., 2016; Duchek, 2020). In addition, the future studies should focus on exploring the interdisciplinary synergies between organizational psychology, neuroscience, and AI design, where it is the goal to make sure that the emotionally intelligent systems do not evolve at the expense of human cognitive architecture and ethical reasoning but are instead guided by the short-term performance maximization as well.

Essentially, although AI will keep on transforming the cognitive structure of a working environment, emotional intelligence will be the most notable human strength in leadership. The future of leadership does not exist in opposition to AI or in giving algorithms the keys to power, but in the development of emotionally intelligent leaders, who will be able to unite the technologies with the human. This chapter presents a theoretically based and practically useful structure of leading ethical, resilient, and human-oriented leadership in the era of intelligent machines through the development of the AIRE Model. The more organizations and entrepreneurs venture into the sphere of AI-enhanced futures, the more emotionally intelligent leaders will decide to remain the force that will see the technological advances as an advantage to human prosperity, as opposed to a threat to it.

REFERENCES

Barrett, L. F., Adolphs, R., Marsella, S., Martinez, A. M., & Pollak, S. D. (2019). Emotional expressions reconsidered: Challenges to lhisinferring emotion from human facial movements. *Psychological Science in the Public Interest, 20*(1), 1–68. DOI: 10.1177/1529100619832930 PMID: 31313636

Bazerman, M. H., & Tenbrunsel, A. E. (2011). *Blind spots: Why we fail to do what's right and what to do about it*. Princeton University Press. DOI: 10.1515/9781400837991

Boyatzis, R. E. (2018). *The competent manager: A model for effective performance*. Wiley.

Brynjolfsson, E., & McAfee, A. (2017). *Machine, platform, crowd: Harnessing our digital future*. W. W. Norton & Company.

Carmeli, A. (2003). The relationship between emotional intelligence and work attitudes, behavior, and outcomes. *Journal of Managerial Psychology, 18*(8), 788–813. DOI: 10.1108/02683940310511881

Cherniss, C. (2010). Emotional intelligence: Toward clarification of a concept. *Industrial and Organizational Psychology: Perspectives on Science and Practice, 3*(2), 110–126. DOI: 10.1111/j.1754-9434.2010.01231.x

Duchek, S. (2020). Organizational resilience: A capability-based conceptualization. *Business Research, 13*(1), 215–246. DOI: 10.1007/s40685-019-0085-7

Edmondson, A. C. (2019). *The fearless organization: Creating psychological safety in the workplace for learning, innovation, and growth*. Wiley.

Floridi, L., & Cowls, J. (2019). A unified framework of five principles for AI in society. *Harvard Data Science Review*. Advance online publication. DOI: 10.1162/99608f92.8cd550d1

Floridi, L., Cowls, J., Beltrametti, M., Chatila, R., Chazerand, P., Dignum, V., Luetge, C., Madelin, R., Pagallo, U., Rossi, F., Schafer, B., Valcke, P., & Vayena, E. (2018). AI4People—An ethical framework for a good AI society. *Minds and Machines, 28*(4), 689–707. DOI: 10.1007/s11023-018-9482-5 PMID: 30930541

Fountaine, T., McCarthy, B., & Saleh, T. (2019). Building the AI-powered organization. *Harvard Business Review*.

Goleman, D. (1995). *Emotional intelligence*. Bantam Books.

Gross, J. J. (2015). Emotion regulation: Current status and future prospects. *Psychological Inquiry*, *26*(1), 1–26. DOI: 10.1080/1047840X.2014.940781

IBM. (2023). *Responsible AI and leadership ethics report.* IBM Corporation.

Jobin, A., Ienca, M., & Vayena, E. (2019). The global landscape of AI ethics guidelines. *Nature Machine Intelligence*, *1*(9), 389–399. DOI: 10.1038/s42256-019-0088-2

Kolbjørnsrud, V., Amico, R., & Thomas, R. J. (2016). How artificial intelligence will redefine management. *Harvard Business Review*.

Marques, J. (2015). Empathy in leadership: Appropriate or misplaced? *Journal of Leadership Studies*, *9*(1), 58–67.

Mayer, J. D., Caruso, D. R., & Salovey, P. (2016). The ability model of emotional intelligence: Principles and updates. *Emotion Review*, *8*(4), 290–300. DOI: 10.1177/1754073916639667

Mayer, J. D., & Salovey, P. (1997). What is emotional intelligence? In Salovey, P., & Sluyter, D. (Eds.), *Emotional development and emotional intelligence: Educational implications* (pp. 3–31). Basic Books.

Microsoft. (2022). *Empathy and innovation: Responsible AI initiatives*. Microsoft Corporation.

Mortan, R. A., Ripoll, P., Carvalho, C., & Bernal, M. C. (2014). Effects of emotional intelligence on entrepreneurial intention and self-efficacy. *Journal of Work and Organizational Psychology*, *30*(3), 97–104. DOI: 10.1016/j.rpto.2014.11.004

Shepherd, D. A., & Williams, T. A. (2018). Hitting rock bottom after job loss: Bouncing back to create a new positive work identity. *Academy of Management Review*, *43*(1), 28–49. DOI: 10.5465/amr.2015.0102

Syed, M., Ferris, G. R., & Munir, K. (2023). Identity, work, and artificial intelligence: A review and future research agenda. *Journal of Management Studies*, *60*(2), 295–326.

Turkle, S. (2015). *Reclaiming conversation: The power of talk in a digital age*. Penguin Press.

Wilson, H. J., & Daugherty, P. R. (2018). Collaborative intelligence: Humans and AI are joining forces. *Harvard Business Review*, *96*(4), 114–123.

World Economic Forum. (2024). The future of jobs report. World Economic Forum.
Author Details The authors bring academic and research expertise in psychology, well-being, and human technology interaction, with a focus on positive psychology and digital mental health. Their research interests include resilience, the psychological effects of relationships mediated by AI, and modern uses of positive psychology in digital settings.

Chapter 14
Using Natural Language Processing to Study Entrepreneurial Narratives and Pitches

Mohit Yadav
http://orcid.org/0000-0002-9341-2527
JGBS, O.P. Jindal Global University, India

Narayanage Jayantha Dewasiri
http://orcid.org/0000-0002-5908-8890
Faculty of Management Studies, Sabaragamuwa University of Sri Lanka, Sri Lanka & Qasim Ibrahim School of Business, Villa College, Maldives

Xuan-Hoa Nghiem
http://orcid.org/0000-0003-2292-0257
International School, Vietnam National University, Hanoi, Vietnam

ABSTRACT

This chapter explores the use of Natural Language Processing (NLP) to study entrepreneurial narratives and pitches, highlighting its potential to analyze linguistic, rhetorical, and emotional dimensions of entrepreneurial communication. By applying techniques such as sentiment analysis, topic modeling, and transformer-based models, NLP enables researchers to identify persuasive elements, detect biases, and predict funding outcomes. Case studies from crowdfunding campaigns, venture capital pitches, and real-time pitch coaching illustrate practical applications for entrepreneurs, investors, and educators. While NLP offers transformative insights, challenges such as data scarcity, contextual nuances, cross-cultural biases, and

DOI: 10.4018/979-8-2600-1353-3.ch014

ethical considerations must be addressed. The chapter concludes by outlining future opportunities, including multimodal analysis, AI-driven training, and inclusive ecosystem development, demonstrating the role of NLP in advancing both entrepreneurship research and practice

INTRODUCTION

Entrepreneurial stories and pitches have become the key drivers in the venture creation, growth, and investment acquisition processes. In addition to the presentation of business models and financial forecasts, entrepreneurs are turning to storytelling to convince stakeholders, attract resources and build legitimacy (Martens, Jennings, and Jennings, 2007). Narratives are considered to be the means by which entrepreneurs share their vision, values, and potential impact, whereas pitches, whether in-person, online, or multimedia format, are high-stakes persuasive performances aimed at attaining the interest of investors and customers (Clarke, Cornelissen, and Healey, 2019). Since entrepreneurship is becoming increasingly competitive and global in its operations, the linguistic and rhetorical strategies inherent in these stories have become critical to scholars and practitioners alike.

Natural Language Processing (NLP) is a branch of artificial intelligence (AI), which provides powerful means of analyzing entrepreneurial communication on a large scale. Using computational methods, including sentiment analysis, topic modeling, and semantic similarity, the researchers can reveal trends in how entrepreneurs frame issues, emphasize opportunities, and build credibility (Camacho et al., 2020). An example of this is that studying the tone and emotional appeal of a pitch can provide information about whether it is persuasive or not, and studying recurring themes can give information about the kinds of stories that can appeal to investors or users of the crowdfunding platform (Allison, Davis, Short, and Webb, 2017). The interaction of entrepreneurship research and computational linguistics thus offers an empirical approach to the investigation of the effect of language on entrepreneurial performance.

This intersection has grown in interest because of the academic and practical interests. The importance of discourse and sensemaking in entrepreneurial studies has long been emphasized academically (Lounsbury and Glynn, 2001), but the more traditional approaches, e.g. interviews or manual content analysis, are limited by subjectivity and lack of scalability. NLP is able to overcome these constraints by allowing systematic and reproducible analysis of large volumes of entrepreneurial texts, including pitch transcripts and crowdfunding campaigns, social media posts, or founder blogs (Huang and Knight, 2017). In practice, NLP-based insights may help businesspersons to improve their communication tactics, support the decision-making process of investors, and be a part of the training course, which will improve entrepreneurial storytelling (Yadav et al., 2024).

Irrespective of these opportunities, NLP application to entrepreneurial stories is problematic. The issues of cultural and gender bias in language models, the threat of simplifying complicated rhetorical strategies, and ethical aspects of using sensitive data related to entrepreneurs require thorough consideration (Sun, Nasraoui, and Shafto, 2020). However, NLP and entrepreneurship research synthesis provides an opportunity to further our knowledge of the role of language in the success of entrepreneurs and create the tools that can be used by new and old entrepreneurs. This chapter explores these opportunities through the study of how NLP techniques can be used to examine entrepreneurial stories and pitches, including theoretical backgrounds, methodologies, applications, and future research opportunities.

THEORETICAL BACKGROUND

Entrepreneurial stories and pitches are heavily entrenched in the wider traditions of narrative theory, rhetoric and sensemaking in organizational studies. A narrative is not just a series of events but an organized narration that creates meaning, creates coherence and creates emotional involvement (Fisher, 1984). In the entrepreneurial field, narratives are cognitive and symbolic tools that entrepreneurs use to package opportunities, convince stakeholders, and place themselves in the context of uncertainty (Lounsbury and Glynn, 2001). Stories are not descriptive, but rather performative, i.e. they construct the identities and legitimacy of the entrepreneurship (Martens et al., 2007).

Entrepreneurial pitches are a unique high-stakes narrative communication. They mix narrative and persuasive rhetoric, frequently in condensed form, like elevator pitches, investor pitches, or crowdfunding. Empirical data show that effective pitches contain both factual information such as market opportunity and financial projections and rhetorical tools such as metaphor, analogy, and emotional appeals (Clarke, Cornelissen, and Healey, 2019). The combination of reason and feelings enables entrepreneurs to reach the audience, increase memorability, and impact the decisions on funding. The rhetorical theory focuses on the use of ethos (credibility), pathos (emotional appeal), and logos (logic) by entrepreneurs to make persuasive pitches (Aristotle, trans. 2007; Trivedi et al., 2023a).

Sociologically, entrepreneurial stories play a legitimizing role in harmonizing ventures with cultural values, institutional norms and stakeholder expectations. According to Lounsbury and Glynn (2001), this process is termed as cultural entrepreneurship whereby narratives are used to acquire resources by entrenching ventures in the larger cultural frames. On the same note, Gartner (2007) believes that the process of narrating is core to the very definition of entrepreneurship because it is the process that makes abstract ideas actionable. Narratives also help entrepreneurs and stakeholders to make sense of their situations and thus minimise ambiguity in very uncertain situations (Weick, Sutcliffe, and Obstfeld, 2005).

Recent research has grown to look at differences in entrepreneurial discourses in terms of gender, culture and context. Empirical literature indicates that male and female entrepreneurs can use different narrative styles, and investors are more willing to respond to the traditionally masculine language styles (Balachandra, Briggs, Eddleston, and Brush, 2019). Cross-cultural studies also indicate that the conventions of storytelling vary depending on the institutional and linguistic context, affecting the success of pitches in the international context (Mason and Harrison, 2020). These results highlight the need to study the language of entrepreneurship methodically and cast doubt on the fairness and impartiality of entrepreneurial assessment.

The emergence of digital platforms has also changed the storytelling and pitch of the entrepreneurship, creating new opportunities to analyze it on a large scale. Crowdfunding websites like Kickstarter and Indiegogo have generated thousands of written stories that show how entrepreneurs position their projects to attract scattered audiences (Allison et al., 2017). These electronic texts are prime targets of computation, including NLP, that enables researchers to move beyond small-sample qualitative research to larger-scale, data-driven findings. The combination of NLP and narrative theory and rhetorical analysis thus creates new opportunities to develop the field of entrepreneurship research, particularly the interpretation of the way linguistic patterns influence the entrepreneurial legitimacy, persuasion, and outcomes (Yadav et al., 2019).

INTRODUCTION TO NATURAL LANGUAGE PROCESSING (NLP)

Natural Language Processing (NLP) is an artificial intelligence branch that aims at facilitating computers to comprehend, interpret, and synthesize human language. It combines linguistics, computer science, and machine learning to derive meaning in the text and speech (Jurafsky and Martin, 2023). In the case of entrepreneurship studies, NLP provides a set of methods of the systematic analysis of the language used in stories and pitches, which results in the understanding of persuasion, validity, and appeal to the audience. Whereas the narrative theory focuses on the meaning-making and rhetoric, the NLP transforms these concepts into quantifiable linguistic formulas.

NLP is fundamentally based on a number of processes. Raw textual data undergoes text preprocessing which includes tokenizing, lemmatizing and stop-word removal before being subjected to computational analysis. More complex operations, such as part -of-speech tagging, syntactic parsing, and named-entity recognition (NER), enable scholars to recognize structural elements and entities in the texts of entrepreneurs (Bird, Klein, and Loper, 2009). These methods help to extract important information, such as market, competitor, or customer need references, in pitches.

NLP methods may be divided into shallow and deep methods. Superficial approaches Word frequency analysis, sentiment analysis and keyword extraction are shallow methods that emphasize surface-level linguistic characteristics. As an illustration, sentiment analysis can be used to determine whether a pitch is optimistic, confident, or cautious, which are very important emotional indicators to investors (Liu, 2012). Latent Dirichlet Allocation (LDA) and other topic modeling methods reveal latent themes in entrepreneurial text that include innovation, scalability or social impact (Blei, Ng, and Jordan, 2003; Tayal et al., 2021).

In the past few years, NLP applications have been revolutionized with the introduction of deep learning and transformer-based models. BERT (Bidirectional Encoder Representations from Transformers) and GPT (Generative Pre-trained Transformer) are the models that have proven to be especially able to grasp semantic nuances and contextual meaning in text (Devlin, Chang, Lee, and Toutanova, 2019; Brown et al., 2020). In the case of entrepreneurial research, these models can be used to examine subtle rhetorical strategies, identify storytelling patterns, and even forecast the success of funding on the basis of linguistic patterns. In contrast to conventional approaches, which strongly rely on the handcrafted characteristics, transformer-based models are trained on large corpora, which makes them flexible to any entrepreneurial story.

Despite these developments, NLP should be used with care when applied to an entrepreneurial setting. Pitches and narratives may include textual data that contains domain-specific vocabulary, industry jargon, and cultural allusions that generic NLP models might be unable to capture (Camacho et al., 2020). Moreover, the validity of findings can be impacted by the problem of model interpretability, the presence of biases in the training data, and data quality problems (Sun, Nasraoui, and Shafto, 2020). Researchers should find a balance between the strength of sophisticated computing tools and the critical understanding of their weaknesses, so that the interpretation can be based on the entrepreneurship theory and context (Trivedi et al., 2023b).

Overall, NLP is a powerful method of analyzing the communication of entrepreneurs. Since the measurement of sentiment and thematic structures to the application of the state-of-the-art deep learning models to analyze rhetoric, NLP provides new possibilities in studying how entrepreneurs can use language to persuade, legitimize, and resourceize. Further parts discuss particular methodological strategies and uses of NLP to analyse entrepreneurial stories and pitches.

RESEARCH METHODS OF THE STUDY OF ENTREPRENEURIAL NARRATIVES

The implementation of Natural Language Processing (NLP) in the context of entrepreneurial storytelling requires a methodological design with high rigor to guarantee the accuracy of the language as well as the theoretical applicability. Pitch transcripts, crowdfunding descriptions, or founder interviews are all entrepreneurial texts that have a distinctive mix of technical details, persuasive rhetoric, and stories. In order to capture these dimensions, researchers may use a variety of NLP techniques, including simple text preprocessing to high-level deep learning models.

1. Text Preprocessing and Data Preparation

The first stage of the process of interpreting entrepreneurial stories is the cleaning and structuring of raw textual information. Traditional preprocessing operations are tokenization (dividing text into words or phrases), lemmatization (removing words to their base forms), and stop-word removal (removing high-frequency, semantically irrelevant words, e.g. the or and) (Bird, Klein and Loper, 2009). In entrepreneurial settings, preprocessing can also involve the detection and normalization of domain-specific jargon, e.g., industry abbreviations or industry-specific lingo commonly employed during a pitch. Proper preprocessing will make sure that later analyses are performed on significant linguistic characteristics and not noise (Choudhary et al., 2024).

2. Sentiment and Emotion Analysis

Sentiment analysis is among the most commonly used NLP techniques in entrepreneurial studies. Scholars determine the tone of the emotion of entrepreneurial narratives by categorizing text as positive, negative, or neutral sentiment (Liu, 2012). More sophisticated models are also able to identify fine-grained emotions like optimism, confidence, or anxiety that affect the choices of investors (Davis, Hmieleski, Webb, and Coombs, 2017). An example can be the emphasis on enthusiasm and confidence in a pitch that can be viewed as more believable, and overly cautious wording can cast doubts on the belief of the entrepreneur. This line of analysis is often supported by emotion lexicons and supervised machine-learned classifiers.

3. Topic Modeling and Thematic Analysis

The Latent Dirichlet Allocation (LDA) is a topic modeling technique that can be used to identify latent themes in large volumes of entrepreneurial literature (Blei,

Ng, and Jordan, 2003). When applied to a crowdfunding campaign or a pitch contest, topic modeling may expose common themes, including sustainability, innovation, or social impact (Allison, Davis, Short, and Webb, 2017). Researchers can determine the most effective narrative frames by connecting them to outcomes such as funding success. In addition to unsupervised models, there is also the possibility of supervised topic classification methods that enable scholars to test certain hypotheses about the existence and role of particular themes in the storytelling of entrepreneurship.

4. Rhetorical and Discourse Structure Analysis

Entrepreneurial stories are not only content-related, but the demonstrative and structural ones are also important. Part-of-speech tagging, dependency parsing, and the use of rhetorical structure theory (RST) are examples of natural language processing (NLP) methods that can be used to analyze the way entrepreneurs build arguments and create logical flow (Mann and Thompson, 1988). As an example, syntactic arrangement analysis can be used to determine the use of assertive, tentative, or speculative types of language, and the analysis of rhetorical devices, such as metaphors, analogies, and hyperbole, can be used to identify the use of a figurative language to make complex ideas easier to understand (Clarke, Cornelissen, and Healey, 2019; Afshan et al., 2021).

5. Storytelling Pattern Detection

The essence of entrepreneurial pitches is narrative storytelling. The use of NLP helps in identifying the common storytelling patterns like the problem-solution-benefit pattern, or elements of the hero journey model that is common in many successful stories (Booker, 2004). Computationally motivated methods, such as narrative-arc modelling and sequential analysis, enable researchers to track how entrepreneurs manipulate tension, introduce challenges and resolve them in their enterprises. The identification of these narrative frames can bring new information about the persuasional tools that underlie entrepreneurial communication and how they are adjusted to the expectations of the audience.

6. Advanced Machine Learning and Deep Learning Applications

More advanced paradigms of methodology use word-embedding models (e.g., Word2Vec, GloVe) and transformer-based models (e.g., BERT, GPT) to capture semantic knowledge that goes beyond surface-level characteristics (Devlin, Chang, Lee, and Toutanova, 2019; Brown et al., 2020). These methods are able to analyze subtle rhetorical techniques, analyze inter-pitch similarity, and even predict funding based on linguistic clues (Anglin, Short, Drover, Stevenson, and McKenny, 2018). As an example, deep-learning classifiers that are trained on past pitch data can forecast investor interest and thus provide empirically-supported applications to entrepreneurs who want to perfect their stories (Tunio et al., 2021).

7. Multimodal Integration

Even though the textual analysis is still at the center, most entrepreneurial pitches are multimodal, including speech, gesture, and visual elements. The combination of NLP with speech-recognition and computer-vision methodologies provides a better understanding of the pitches (Chollet, Scherer, Stratou, and Morency, 2015). This synthesis is not just the content but the delivery itself- the connection between verbal content and the prosodic, corporeal and visual informational content. Even in its infancy, multimodal analysis is the future of exploring entrepreneurial communication (Gilal et al., 2020).

Together, these methodological strategies provide a full analytical repertoire of the study of entrepreneurial stories and pitches. Combining the traditional text-mining techniques with the advanced deep-learning and multimodal analysis, the researchers will be able to discover the linguistic and rhetorical predictors of the entrepreneurial performance.

APPLICATIONS IN ENTREPRENEURIAL CONTEXTS

The NLP of entrepreneurial stories is not merely a question of theory but provides solid knowledge to entrepreneurial practice and performance. The systematic study of linguistic, rhetorical, and affective aspects of entrepreneurial communication will provide scholars and practitioners with the resources to discover the factors that drive venture success, evaluate them through biases, and create the tools that can be used to improve training and development in entrepreneurship.

1. Identifying Persuasive Elements in Pitches

One of the fundamental uses of NLP is the identification of persuasive language characteristics in entrepreneurial pitches. It has been empirically established that entrepreneurs who present enthusiasm, confidence, and vision have higher chances of getting finances (Chen, Yao, and Kotha, 2009). These qualities are systematically measured by NLP tools like sentiment analysis and emotion detection, e.g., Anglin, Short, Drover, Stevenson, and McKenny (2018) discovered that a positive set of psychological-capital lexicon, including words representing hope, optimism, and resilience, is related to better performance in crowdfunding. The scaling of NLP analysis allows identifying linguistic features that consistently indicate the level of interest among investors, hence providing practical feedback on pitch improvement.

2. Linking Narrative Style to Funding Success

NLP helps to connect narrative and funding results. Allison, Davis, Short, and Webb (2017) used an elaboration-likelihood model to the crowdfunding campaigns and proved that central-route arguments (e.g., clear product benefits, feasibility) combined with peripheral cues (e.g., emotional appeal) had significant effect on investment choices. Topics modelling and rhetorical analysis offer a mechanism to test these dynamics on large scale data and find out whether sustainability, technological innovation, or social impact are themes that are more appealing to particular groups of investors. These understandings guide the strategic communication of entrepreneurs and the evaluative schemes of investors.

3. Detecting Bias in Entrepreneurial Evaluation

An essential use is related to the recognition of biases in the perception of the entrepreneurial narratives. It has been shown that the gendered language and stereotypes influence investor assessments, which disadvantage female entrepreneurs (Balachandra, Briggs, Eddleston, and Brush, 2019). NLP has the ability to measure differences in framing between male and female entrepreneurs and determine their effect on funding results. On the same note, cross-cultural NLP studies reveal differences in storytelling norms in different settings, indicating the possibility of cultural bias in world entrepreneurial ecosystems (Mason and Harrison, 2020). The identification of these biases encourages fair practices of evaluation (Chaudhry et al., 2021).

4. Supporting Entrepreneurial Training and Education

NLP can also be used in education, where it can provide feedback in real-time or automatically on the quality of the pitch. Sentiment balance, thematic clarity, or storytelling arc can be checked by automated systems on a pitch transcript and suggested improvements are made (Chollet, Scherer, Stratou, and Morency, 2015). Incorporation of these tools in accelerator programs, incubators and university entrepreneurship courses helps entrepreneurs perfect their communication with investors prior to engaging with them. This democratizes coaching resources particularly in resource constrained environments.

5. Enhancing Investor Decision-Making

To investors, NLP applications provide decision-support systems with which analysts can effectively examine many entrepreneurial pitches. The text analysis is automated and indicates which pitches have high levels of linguistic indicators of credibility or innovativeness, so the investor can focus on them (Huang and Knight, 2017). The combination of NLP and predictive analytics can help investors evaluate not only content but also compatibility with successful previous projects to have a more evidence-based perspective that supplements more intuit-based evaluations.

6. Real-Time Pitch Analysis and Feedback

New uses are real-time NLP systems that are used to examine live entrepreneurial pitches. These technologies, often combined with speech-to-text technology, assess the language complexity, emotional coloring, and the rhetorical structure on the fly (Chollet et al., 2015). This technology can develop into pitch assistants, which can provide post-performance feedback that is used to find strengths and weaknesses. This application is still experimental but it represents the transition of post-hoc analysis to dynamic interactive support (Rashid et al., 2024).

Combined, these applications prove the usefulness of NLP in entrepreneurship in practice. In asking linguistic and rhetorical questions about the entrepreneurial stories, NLP enhances the theoretical knowledge and provides practical information to entrepreneurs, educators, and investors. However, such applications should be balanced with ethics and contextual interpretation as it is explained in the later sections.

CASE STUDIES AND EXAMPLES

The practical application of NLP in the entrepreneurial setting can be exemplified with a set of case studies that reveal the ability of NLP to analyze, assess, and improve entrepreneurial stories and pitches. These examples demonstrate how NLP can be used to draw valuable conclusions about large amounts of data, identify patterns of subtle communication, and enhance entrepreneurial action and investor decision-making.

1. Crowdfunding Campaign Narratives

Crowdfunding has become a well-researched field of NLP use in the entrepreneurship domain, with sites like Kickstarter and Indiegogo being sources of large volumes of narrative data, in the form of campaign descriptions, updates, and comments posted by investors. Allison et al. (2017) analyzed more than 50,000 crowdfunding projects and found out that central-route arguments (i.e., facts, feasibility, product description) along with peripheral cues (emotional appeal, sense of community) are predictive of funding success. The topic modelling and sentiment analysis demonstrated that the stories that contain more elements of logic and emotion appeal are more convincing. This example describes the ability of NLP to reveal the linguistic balance that leads to funding results.

2. Detecting Entrepreneurial Passion in Pitches

NLP has been used to predict signs of entrepreneurial passion and readiness in pitch transcripts in venture-capital contexts. The authors of the study by Chen, Yao, and Kotha (2009) discovered that entrepreneurs who exhibited enthusiasm, confidence, and preparedness in terms of the use of language and tone attracted more funding. Later researchers used computational linguistics at a larger scale and proved that positively valenced, visionary language is associated with the greater interest of investors (Anglin et al., 2018). Accelerators and incubators now experiment with automated pitch-feedback tools by training NLP models to identify passion markers, providing an entrepreneur with structured advice.

3. Gender Bias in Entrepreneurial Narratives

One of the landmark cases is the issue of identifying gender bias in entrepreneurial appraisals. Balachandra et al. (2019) determined that women who do not follow the stereotypical communication styles are often punished by investors. NLP analysis of pitch transcripts indicated that there was a difference in the word choice, framing of the narrative, and evaluative feedback between male and female entrepreneurs. The case highlights the diagnostic potential of NLP to reveal the inequity in entrepreneurial ecosystems and informs policy interventions that encourage inclusive funding behaviors.

4. Real-Time Pitch Coaching Systems

The future of real-time NLP in entrepreneurial education is shown by emerging technologies. Chollet, Scherer, Stratou, and Morency (2015) have created an interactive virtual audience system that offers instant feedback regarding speaking to the crowd. The system assesses clarity, sentiment, and rhetorical balance with the help of NLP and speech-recognition and provides specific feedback. Such systems are adapted to entrepreneurship, assisting in refinement of pitch delivery before investor meetings, democratising quality training resources on underrepresented entrepreneurs.

5. Cross-Cultural Entrepreneurial Storytelling

NLP has been also helpful in investigating cultural difference in entrepreneurial communication. Mason and Harrison (2020) examined the phenomenon of investor networks by region and discovered that narrative framing, which highlights the social impact in Europe and technological innovation in the United States, influences investment choices. The cross-linguistic NLP study of pitches and crowdfunding narratives also explains the influence of cultural storytelling norms on the entrepreneurial performance. These results indicate the need to have context-sensitive NLP tools that consider and honor cultural diversity in the context of entrepreneurship.

6. AI-Enhanced Investor Decision Support

A number of venture-capital organizations have recently started testing natural-language-processing (NLP) systems capable of aiding in the filtering of high quantities of startup applications. Huang and Knight (2017) established that linguistic indicators in the context of entrepreneurial pitches (especially those related to credibility and vision) can be operationalised to make investment decisions. These systems allow investors to filter submissions more effectively by ranking applications based on NLP-derived measures of innovation, preparedness and growth potential. Although these tools are not meant to substitute human judgment, but to complement it, they demonstrate a more and more significant role of NLP in professional investment practice.

Taken together, these case studies highlight the scope of NLP applications in the field of entrepreneurship, including identification of persuasive factors and detection of bias up to the training support and facilitation of investor assessments. They also demonstrate that despite the fact that NLP has great analytical and predictive powers the value of NLP is maximised when it is combined with contextual knowledge and human interpretation.

CHALLENGES AND LIMITATIONS

Although NLP provides effective tools of analysis to entrepreneurial stories and pitches, it has a number of limitations that surround its use in entrepreneurship research and practice. These restrictions underscore the importance of interpretative caution, methodological care, and ethical incisiveness in the application of NLP in entrepreneurial situations.

1. Data Availability and Quality

One of the main issues related to the implementation of NLP in the field of entrepreneurial research is the quality of the available datasets. In contrast to typical corpora of news articles or scholarly texts, entrepreneurial stories are usually presented as fragmented ones such as pitch decks, oral presentation, crowdfunding descriptions, and social-media posts. Venture-capital pitch transcripts can be kept confidential, which restricts the ability of researchers to conduct large-scale research (Huang and Knight, 2017). Crowdfunding sites like Kickstarter and Indiegogo have more easily accessible text data, but such stories might not be indicative of high-stakes investment situations. As a result, data sparsity and unequal quality limit the generalisability of results.

2. Contextual Nuances in Language

Entrepreneurial language is often metaphorical, aspirational, and domain specific. The terms like disrupting the industry, scaling fast, or pivoting have a meaning that a generic NLP tool might not be able to sufficiently reflect (Jurafsky and Martin, 2023). The standard sentiment models can either wrongly label entrepreneurial optimism as hyperbole or they cannot differentiate genuine passion and overconfidence. This contextual complexity requires bespoke models and domain-specific lexica which may be expensive to create and test.

3. Cross-Cultural and Linguistic Bias

Entrepreneurship is a universal phenomenon and stories vary according to cultures and languages. NLP models trained on English corpora are likely to miss culturally specific storytelling patterns or rhetoric approaches that are used in non-Western settings (Mason and Harrison, 2020). Besides, automated analysis may strengthen cultural prejudices by favoring Western entrepreneurial discourse patterns, including individualism or visionary leadership, and undermining fairness and inclusiveness in global entrepreneurial ecosystems.

4. Ethical Concerns and Privacy

The application of NLP to entrepreneurial stories generates serious ethical concerns, especially in terms of data privacy and informed consent. Pitch notes and crowdfunding stories frequently include sensitive business details, either intellectual property, market plans or personal stories. In the absence of proper protection, the exploitation of this data may put the entrepreneur at a competitive disadvantage or confidentiality at risk (Zhang and Dafoe, 2019). Also, automated bias-detection systems can unwillingly stigmatize entrepreneurs by labeling their communications as weak or less persuasive, which only reinforces inequalities instead of reducing them.

5. Interpretability and Over-Reliance on Algorithms

An obvious weakness of advanced NLP techniques, especially deep-learning models, is their opaceness. Transformer-based models (BERT and GPT) are capable of predicting the success of funding with great precision, but they tend to be black boxes (Devlin et al., 2019). Such uninterpretability makes it difficult to comprehend the reason why certain linguistic characteristics affect certain results, which may undermine the confidence of researchers and practitioners. The excessive use of algorithmic predictions without a contextual interpretation may lead to the over-simplification of the socio-psychological processes that underlie entrepreneurial communication.

6. Generalizability Across Contexts

The results of NLP analyses are unlikely to be easily generalised in different entrepreneurial contexts. The linguistic indicators of success in crowdfunding campaigns, such as, might vary significantly with the indicators applicable in venture-capital settings, the evaluation criteria vary (Allison et al., 2017). In the same way, findings made after the analysis of written accounts might not be fully applicable to oral pitch presentation that is strongly dependent on delivery style, charisma, and non-verbal feedback. These differences highlight the need to combine multimodal data through text, visual and behavioural information.

7. Resource and Technical Barriers

The use of NLP techniques requires a lot of technical skills and computing capabilities. Resource-constrained entrepreneurs and educators might have no access to complex NLP software or big data or have no professional analyst (Anglin et al., 2018). Such a digital divide threatens to increase inequalities, as well-funded institutions have access to the benefits of sophisticated analytics at the expense of the rest. Therefore, simplified or accessible NLP tools designed to fit the needs of entrepreneurial training are an urgent but not well-covered objective.

Overall, despite the transformative potential of NLP in the study and support of entrepreneurial communication, its obstacles highlight the need to apply the method contextually. To make sure that NLP can be used to benefit the research and practice of entrepreneurship, it is necessary to address the limitation of data access, cultural bias, ethical considerations, and interpretability.

FUTURE DIRECTIONS AND OPPORTUNITIES

With the further development of NLP, new opportunities can be identified to learn more about entrepreneurial communication and to increase the practical use of this phenomenon in the context of entrepreneurial ecosystems. The development of NLP, artificial intelligence, and multimodal analytics can be used in future studies and practice to address existing limitations and expand the field of entrepreneurial research. Some of the potential opportunities are as follows.

1. Multimodal NLP for Pitch Analysis

Future research must go beyond text-based analysis and combine various modalities: Speech, gestures, facial expression and visual pitch materials. The nature of entrepreneurial pitches is the mixture of verbal persuasion and non-verbal communication and visual narration (Chollet et al., 2015). Advances in multimodal NLP and deep learning may be used to support holistic measurements of pitch quality, which would provide more insight into the way entrepreneurs sound credible, passionate, and visionary. The automated pitch-coaching systems might also be refined through such integrative approaches and provide more holistic feedback to the entrepreneurs.

2. Cross-Cultural and Multilingual Applications

Due to the globalisation of entrepreneurship, future research should extend the NLP analysis to other languages and cultural backgrounds. The existing literature is largely based on English data, which can further strengthen Western-centric communication standards (Mason and Harrison, 2020). Investigating the role of cultural values in shaping narrative strategies and investor reactions in creating inclusive, culturally adaptive pitch-evaluation instruments can be achieved by developing multilingual NLP models trained on entrepreneurial corpora across different regions.

3. Predictive Models for Funding Outcomes

Another potentially fruitful avenue is the development of NLP-based predictive models which predict entrepreneurial success using narrative characteristics. Preliminary research has attributed sentiment, narration, and rhetoric style to funding consequences (Allison et al., 2017; Anglin et al., 2018). The next-generation models may take advantage of the large volumes of historical pitch data to increase their predictive power, allowing investors to rank high-potential projects and assist entrepreneurs to detect narrative gaps that can reduce funding opportunities.

4. AI-Driven Entrepreneurship Education

There is also a possibility of incorporation of NLP in the future in the education and training programs of entrepreneurship. Artificial intelligence-based platforms have the potential to provide real-time feedback on drafts of the pitch, simulate investor responses, and suggest ways to improve the storytelling, emotion balance, and structure. These tools would make high-quality coaching democratic, and it would be accessible to entrepreneurs working in resource-bound settings. Additionally, these platforms can help teachers to create a curriculum that emphasizes the successful construction of narratives and persuasion.

5. Addressing Ethical AI in Entrepreneurial Contexts

With the rise in the popularity of natural language processing (NLP) tools in the analysis of entrepreneurial communication, the issue of ethical concerns will become more significant. The next study must explore the frameworks that will bring equity, transparency, and accountability to NLP-based assessments (Zhang and Dafoe, 2019). This kind of work should focus on algorithmic bias, protection of the intellectual property of entrepreneurs, and informed consent in the gathering and analysis of pitch information. Ethical AI should be carefully planned to create trust in businesspeople, investors, and educators, which would make NLP an assistant, not a punitive technology.

6. Real-Time Investor Decision Support

Potential uses would be real-time NLP systems to support investors at live pitch events. NLP tools would provide investors with additional information to make decisions by analysing sentiment changes, rhetorical framing, and thematic clarity when entrepreneurs are presenting. Although such systems are not supposed to substitute human judgment, but are likely to be useful as decision-support systems, particularly in cases where entrepreneurial ventures have to be filtered through large volumes of data.

7. Integration with Entrepreneurial Ecosystem Platforms

NLP tools have a great potential to be incorporated into the entrepreneurial ecosystem platforms like incubators, accelerators and crowdfunding portals. Automated narrative analysis would help entrepreneurs to compare their pitches with successful campaigns, and investors may use NLP dashboards to assess the portfolio risks and opportunities. This integration would institutionalise the use of NLP in entrepreneurial practice, moving it out of the experimental research and into mainstream use.

Collectively, these future directions will highlight the promise of NLP to enhance academic research and at the same time revolutionize the practice of entrepreneurship. NLP can be instrumental in helping to create more effective, inclusive, and data-driven entrepreneurial ecosystems by adopting multimodal, cross-cultural, predictive, and ethically based applications.

CONCLUSION

Natural Language Processing (NLP) is a disruptive method of interpreting entrepreneurial stories and pitches, thus closing the qualitative and quantitative analysis gap. In this chapter, theoretical background, practical examples, methodologies, case studies, obstacles and future prospects of NLP in entrepreneurial situations have been discussed. Together, these discussions shed some light on how NLP can be used to improve the study and practice of entrepreneurship.

Through a linguistic, rhetorical and emotional study of the entrepreneurial communication, NLP provides the systematic information on the factors that affect the success of the venture. Sentiment analysis, topic modelling, rhetorical analysis, and deep learning are some of the techniques that allow researchers to determine patterns of persuasive language, detect biases, and assess the effectiveness of a narrative at a large scale (Anglin et al., 2018; Allison et al., 2017). Such approaches enhance the theoretical knowledge on entrepreneurial storytelling, as well as provide practical resources to entrepreneurs, investors, and educators.

The practical implication of NLP can be demonstrated by case studies based on crowdfunding campaigns, transcripts of venture capital pitching, and pitch coaching platforms in real time. To entrepreneurs, NLP can help understand the influence of passion, clarity, and narrative structure on the perceptions of investors, which can be used to give actionable feedback on pitch refinement. To investors, NLP may serve as a decision support tool and point to promising ventures and reveal linguistic signs of credibility and innovation. Furthermore, NLP helps to identify gender, cultural, and cognitive biases and, thus, make a difference in the more equitable and inclusive entrepreneurial environments (Balachandra et al., 2019; Mason and Harrison, 2020).

In spite of this potential, NLP in the field of entrepreneurship does not lack limitations. The following challenges should be considered carefully: the lack of data, contextual language peculiarities, cross-cultural bias, ethical implications, and interpretability of deep-learning models. NLP requires ethical protection, model training in domains, and multimodal analysis strategies to make it a supportive, fair, and accurate instrument of assessing entrepreneurial stories (Zhang and Dafoe, 2019).

In the future, the combination of multimodal NLP, cross-cultural frameworks, AI-based learning devices, and real-time analysis systems can have massive potential to improve entrepreneurial communication and assessment. Such innovations have the potential to democratise access to high-quality training, enhance investor decision-making and develop more inclusive entrepreneurial ecosystems. NLP can completely transform the research and practice of entrepreneurship by integrating methodological rigor with ethical foresight.

To sum up, NLP is a strong tool in the analysis of the dynamic and complex world of entrepreneurial stories. Its ability to identify patterns in large-scale text data, identify biases that are difficult to detect, and offer actionable information makes NLP an essential resource to researchers, practitioners, and policymakers. With the ever-changing nature of technology, NLP will not just enhance our knowledge of entrepreneurial communication, but will also help in building better, more fairer, and data-driven entrepreneurial ecosystems.

REFERENCES

Afshan, G., Shahid, S., & Tunio, M. N. (2021). Learning experiences of women entrepreneurs amidst COVID-19. *International Journal of Gender and Entrepreneurship, 13*(2), 162–186. DOI: 10.1108/IJGE-09-2020-0153

Allison, T. H., Davis, B. C., Short, J. C., & Webb, J. W. (2017). Persuasion in crowdfunding: An elaboration likelihood model of crowdfunding performance. *Journal of Business Venturing, 32*(6), 707–725. DOI: 10.1016/j.jbusvent.2017.09.002

Anglin, A. H., Short, J. C., Drover, W., Stevenson, R. M., McKenny, A. F., & Allison, T. H. (2018). The power of positivity? The influence of positive psychological capital language on crowdfunding performance. *Journal of Business Venturing, 33*(4), 470–492. DOI: 10.1016/j.jbusvent.2018.03.003

Aristotle, . (2007). *On rhetoric: A theory of civic discourse* (2nd ed.). (Kennedy, G. A., Trans.). Oxford University Press. (Original work published 350 BCE)

Balachandra, L., Briggs, T., Eddleston, K., & Brush, C. (2019). Don't pitch like a girl!: How gender stereotypes influence investor decisions. *Entrepreneurship Theory and Practice, 43*(1), 116–137. DOI: 10.1177/1042258717728028

Bird, S., Klein, E., & Loper, E. (2009). *Natural language processing with Python.* O'Reilly Media.

Blei, D. M., Ng, A. Y., & Jordan, M. I. (2003). Latent Dirichlet Allocation. *Journal of Machine Learning Research, 3*, 993–1022.

Booker, C. (2004). *The seven basic plots: Why we tell stories.* Bloomsbury.

Brown, T., Mann, B., Ryder, N., Subbiah, M., Kaplan, J., Dhariwal, P., & Amodei, D. (2020). Language models are few-shot learners. *Advances in Neural Information Processing Systems, 33*, 1877–1901.

Camacho, S., Nam, T., Kannan, P. K., & Stremersch, S. (2020). The information value of online consumer reviews: A case of review characteristics and consumer perceptions. *International Journal of Research in Marketing, 37*(3), 507–525. DOI: 10.1016/j.ijresmar.2019.12.004

Chaudhry, I. S., Paquibut, R. Y., & Tunio, M. N. (2021). Do workforce diversity, inclusion practices, & organizational characteristics contribute to organizational innovation? Evidence from the UAE. *Cogent Business & Management, 8*(1), 1947549. DOI: 10.1080/23311975.2021.1947549

Chen, X. P., Yao, X., & Kotha, S. (2009). Entrepreneur passion and preparedness in business plan presentations: A persuasion analysis of venture capitalists' funding decisions. *Academy of Management Journal, 52*(1), 199–214. DOI: 10.5465/amj.2009.36462018

Chollet, M., Scherer, S., Stratou, G., & Morency, L. P. (2015). Exploring feedback strategies to improve public speaking: An interactive virtual audience framework. *Proceedings of the 2015 ACM International Conference on Intelligent Virtual Agents*, 114–121. DOI: 10.1145/2750858.2806060

Choudhary, S., Yadav, M., & Srivastava, A. P. (2024). Cognitive biases among millennial Indian investors: Do personality and demographic factors matter? *FIIB Business Review, 13*(1), 106–117. DOI: 10.1177/23197145211057343

Clarke, J., Cornelissen, J., & Healey, M. P. (2019). Actions speak louder than words: How figurative language and gesturing in entrepreneurial pitches influences investment judgments. *Academy of Management Journal, 62*(2), 335–360. DOI: 10.5465/amj.2016.1008

Davis, B. C., Hmieleski, K. M., Webb, J. W., & Coombs, J. E. (2017). Funders' positive affective reactions to entrepreneurs' crowdfunding pitches: The influence of perceived product creativity and entrepreneurial passion. *Journal of Business Venturing, 32*(1), 90–106. DOI: 10.1016/j.jbusvent.2016.10.006

Devlin, J., Chang, M. W., Lee, K., & Toutanova, K. (2019). BERT: Pre-training of deep bidirectional transformers for language understanding. *Proceedings of the 2019 Conference of the North American Chapter of the Association for Computational Linguistics: Human Language Technologies*, 4171–4186. DOI: 10.48550/arXiv.1810.04805

Fisher, W. R. (1984). Narration as a human communication paradigm: The case of public moral argument. *Communication Monographs, 51*(1), 1–22. DOI: 10.1080/03637758409390180

Gartner, W. B. (2007). Entrepreneurial narrative and a science of the imagination. *Journal of Business Venturing, 22*(5), 613–627. DOI: 10.1016/j.jbusvent.2006.10.003

Gilal, F. G., Gilal, N. G., Channa, N. A., Gilal, R. G., Gilal, R. G., & Tunio, M. N. (2020). Towards an integrated model for the transference of environmental responsibility. *Business Strategy and the Environment, 29*(6), 2614–2623. DOI: 10.1002/bse.2524

Huang, L., & Knight, A. P. (2017). Resources and relationships in entrepreneurship: An exchange theory of the development and effects of the entrepreneur–investor relationship. *Academy of Management Review*, *42*(1), 80–102. DOI: 10.5465/amr.2014.0397

Jurafsky, D., & Martin, J. H. (2023). *Speech and language processing* (3rd ed.). Draft. Stanford University. https://web.stanford.edu/~jurafsky/slp3/

Liu, B. (2012). *Sentiment analysis and opinion mining*. Morgan & Claypool. DOI: 10.1007/978-3-031-02145-9

Lounsbury, M., & Glynn, M. A. (2001). Cultural entrepreneurship: Stories, legitimacy, and the acquisition of resources. *Strategic Management Journal*, *22*(6–7), 545–564. DOI: 10.1002/smj.188

Mann, W. C., & Thompson, S. A. (1988). Rhetorical Structure Theory: Toward a functional theory of text organization. *Text*, *8*(3), 243–281. DOI: 10.1515/text.1.1988.8.3.243

Martens, M. L., Jennings, J. E., & Jennings, P. D. (2007). Do the stories they tell get them the money they need? The role of entrepreneurial narratives in resource acquisition. *Academy of Management Journal*, *50*(5), 1107–1132. DOI: 10.5465/amj.2007.27169488

Mason, C., & Harrison, R. (2020). Entrepreneurial ecosystems and the role of angel investors. *Regional Studies*, *54*(8), 1085–1097. DOI: 10.1080/00343404.2019.1680827

Rashid, A., Rasheed, R., Ngah, A. H., Pradeepa Jayaratne, M. D. R., Rahi, S., & Tunio, M. N. (2024). Role of information processing and digital supply chain in supply chain resilience through supply chain risk management. *Journal of Global Operations and Strategic Sourcing*, *17*(2), 429–447. DOI: 10.1108/JGOSS-12-2023-0106

Sun, C., Nasraoui, O., & Shafto, P. (2020). Evolution and impact of bias in human and machine learning algorithm interaction. *PLoS One*, *15*(8), e0235502. DOI: 10.1371/journal.pone.0235502 PMID: 32790666

Tayal, R., Upadhyay, R. K., Yadav, M., & Singh, R. (2021). The development and validation of the organizational effectiveness scale using confirmatory factor analysis. *Global Business Review*, *22*(3), 821–843. DOI: 10.1177/0972150918811720

Trivedi, S. K., Vishnu, S., Singh, A., & Yadav, M. (2023a). Research trends in sustainable E-payment systems: A study using topic modeling approach. *IEEE Transactions on Engineering Management*, *71*, 7511–7525. DOI: 10.1109/TEM.2023.3280216

Trivedi, V., Banerji, D., & Yadav, M. (2023b). Expecting the surprises: Role of hope in consumer repurchase intentions in an online shopping environment. *Journal of Strategic Marketing*, *31*(4), 794–816. DOI: 10.1080/0965254X.2021.1996449

Tunio, M. N., Chaudhry, I. S., Shaikh, S., Jariko, M. A., & Brahmi, M. (2021). Determinants of the sustainable entrepreneurial engagement of youth in developing country—An empirical evidence from Pakistan. *Sustainability (Basel)*, *13*(14), 7764. DOI: 10.3390/su13147764

Weick, K. E., Sutcliffe, K. M., & Obstfeld, D. (2005). Organizing and the process of sensemaking. *Organization Science*, *16*(4), 409–421. DOI: 10.1287/orsc.1050.0133

Yadav, M., Rangnekar, S., & Srivastava, A. P. (2019). Demographic variables as moderators between QWL and OCB. *Industrial and Commercial Training*, *51*(7/8), 396–408. DOI: 10.1108/ICT-04-2018-0040

Yadav, R., Yadav, M., & Vihari, N. S. (2024). High-performance work system and learning orientation in offline, online, and hybrid workplaces: The mediating role of affective commitment. *The Learning Organization*, *31*(1), 122–136. DOI: 10.1108/TLO-10-2022-0118

Zhang, B., & Dafoe, A. (2019). Artificial intelligence: American attitudes and trends. SSRN *Electronic Journal*. DOI: 10.2139/ssrn.3312874

Compilation of References

Abdelmagid, A., Jabli, N., Ibrahim, A., & Teleb, A. (2025). *Generative artificial intelligence (ChatGPT) technology and its impact on the development of digital entrepreneurship skills among university students*. International Journal of Innovative Research and Scientific Studies., DOI: 10.53894/ijirss.v8i2.5885

Adadi, A., & Berrada, M. (2018). Peeking inside the black-box: A survey on explainable artificial intelligence (XAI). *IEEE Access : Practical Innovations, Open Solutions*, *6*, 52138–52160. DOI: 10.1109/ACCESS.2018.2870052

Afshan, G., Shahid, S., & Tunio, M. N. (2021). Learning experiences of women entrepreneurs amidst COVID-19. *International Journal of Gender and Entrepreneurship*, *13*(2), 162–186. DOI: 10.1108/IJGE-09-2020-0153

Ahmad, S., Zhang, Q., Hussain, M. A., & Mahmood, S. (2025). Entrepreneurial success through learning, capital, and work engagement: Market and service orientation perspective. *Acta Psychologica*, *258*, 105188. DOI: 10.1016/j.actpsy.2025.105188 PMID: 40609188

Ahmed, F., Lo, Y., & Chen, S. (2025). Developing Entrepreneurial Mindset Among Non-Business Majors Through Experiential Learning and AI Tools. *European Conference on Knowledge Management*. DOI: 10.34190/eckm.26.1.3762

Ahmetoglu, G., Leutner, F., & Chamorro-Premuzic, T. (2011). EQ-nomics: Understanding the relationship between individual differences in trait emotional intelligence and entrepreneurship. *Personality and Individual Differences*, *51*(8), 1028–1033. DOI: 10.1016/j.paid.2011.08.016

Ajzen, I. (1991). The theory of planned behavior. *Organizational Behavior and Human Decision Processes*, *50*(2), 179–211. DOI: 10.1016/0749-5978(91)90020-T

Akponeware, A., Dawood, N., Rodriguez-Trejo, S., & Dawood, H. (2022). An integrated empirical analysis of UK rail industry's carbon assessment: An industry perspective. *Case Studies on Transport Policy*, *10*(1), 315–330. DOI: 10.1016/j.cstp.2021.12.012

Alameeri, K., Zakaria, N., & Rahman, S. A. (2025). Women's Entrepreneurship in the UAE: Exploring Cultural, Societal, and Structural Challenges through a Conceptual Lens. *International Review of Management and Marketing*, *15*(5), 414–421. DOI: 10.32479/irmm.19844

Alamuri, S., Aluvala, R., & Chittipaka, V. (2025). Innovative Pathways for Empowerment of Rural Women through Sustainable and Diversified Livelihoods. In R. Nagariya, P. Dhaundiyal, K. Mathiyazhagan, & V. Mishra (Eds.), *Proceedings of the International Conference on Sustainable Business Practices and Innovative Models (ICSBPIM-2025)* (Vol. 349, pp. 381–393). Atlantis Press International BV. DOI: 10.2991/978-94-6463-872-1_25

Aldrich, H. E., & Fiol, C. M. (1994). Fools rush in? The institutional context of industry creation. *Academy of Management Review*, *19*(4), 645–670. DOI: 10.2307/258740

Allison, T. H., Davis, B. C., Short, J. C., & Webb, J. W. (2015). Crowdfunding in a prosocial micro-lending environment: Examining the role of intrinsic versus extrinsic cues. *Entrepreneurship Theory and Practice*, *39*(1), 53–73. DOI: 10.1111/etap.12108

Allison, T. H., Davis, B. C., Short, J. C., & Webb, J. W. (2017). Persuasion in crowdfunding: An elaboration likelihood model of crowdfunding performance. *Journal of Business Venturing*, *32*(6), 707–725. DOI: 10.1016/j.jbusvent.2017.09.002

Almalki, A. (2020). Intelligent learning systems: A systematic review and future directions. *Education and Information Technologies*, *25*(6), 5401–5438. DOI: 10.1007/s10639-020-10247-1

Al-Mamary, Y. H. (2025). The transformative power of artificial intelligence in entrepreneurship: Exploring AI's capabilities for the success of entrepreneurial ventures. *Future Business Journal*, *11*(1), 104. Advance online publication. DOI: 10.1186/s43093-025-00533-7

Alpaydin, E. (2021). *Machine learning*. MIT Press. DOI: 10.7551/mitpress/13811.001.0001

Amankwah-Amoah, J., Khan, Z., Wood, G., & Knight, G. (2021). COVID-19 and digitalization: The great acceleration. *Journal of Business Research*, *136*, 602–611. DOI: 10.1016/j.jbusres.2021.08.011 PMID: 34538980

Ammirato, S., Felicetti, A. M., Troise, C., Santoro, G., & Rozsa, Z. (2024). Human resources well-being in innovative start-ups: Insights from a systematic review of the literature. *Journal of Innovation & Knowledge*, *9*(4), 100580. DOI: 10.1016/j.jik.2024.100580

Anglin, A. H., Short, J. C., Drover, W., Stevenson, R. M., McKenny, A. F., & Allison, T. H. (2018). The power of positivity? The influence of positive psychological capital language on crowdfunding performance. *Journal of Business Venturing*, *33*(4), 470–492. DOI: 10.1016/j.jbusvent.2018.03.003

Antretter, T., Lekkas, H. W., Djokovic, D., Souitaris, V., & Wincent, J. (2025). Not what you expected to see? Obesity stereotypes, expectancy violations, and angel investment decisions. *Journal of Business Venturing*, *40*(5), 106510. DOI: 10.1016/j.jbusvent.2025.106510

Ardika, B. S., Setianingrum, A. H., & Hakiem, N. (2017, November). Funding eligibility decision support system using fuzzy logic Tsukamoto:(Case: BMT XYZ). In *2017 Second International Conference on Informatics and Computing (ICIC)* (pp. 1-7). IEEE. DOI: 10.1109/IAC.2017.8280622

Aristotle, . (2007). *On rhetoric: A theory of civic discourse* (2nd ed.). (Kennedy, G. A., Trans.). Oxford University Press. (Original work published 350 BCE)

Audretsch, D. B., & Thurik, A. R. (2010). *Unraveling the shift to the entrepreneurial economy*. Springer. DOI: 10.2139/ssrn.1664466

Autio, E., Pathak, S., & Wennberg, K. (2013). Consequences of cultural practices for entrepreneurial behaviors. *Journal of International Business Studies*, *44*(4), 334–362. DOI: 10.1057/jibs.2013.15

Awad, A., & Abdelaziz, E. (2025). ENTREPRENEURSHIP EDUCATION: A STUDY OF HIGHER EDUCATION INSTITUTIONS IN THE MIDDLE EAST. *Journal of Southwest Jiaotong University*, (2). Advance online publication. DOI: 10.35741/issn.0258-2724.60.2.3

Ayala, J.-C., & Manzano, G. (2014). The resilience of the entrepreneur. *Journal of Economic Psychology*, *42*, 126–135. DOI: 10.1016/j.joep.2014.02.004

Ayoko, O. B., Caputo, A., & Mendy, J. (2021). Management research contributions to the COVID-19: A bibliometric literature review and analysis of the contributions from the *Journal of Management & Organization*. *Journal of Management & Organization*, *27*(6), 1183–1209. DOI: 10.1017/jmo.2021.70

Azad, M., & Marinova, D. (2025). Small Business Entrepreneurship Among Rural Women: A Strategy for Sustainable Development – A Case Study of Mazu Village. *Humanities and Social Sciences*, *13*(5), 486–497. DOI: 10.11648/j.hss.20251305.19

Azoury, N., Subrahmanyam, S., & Sarkis, N. (2024). The influence of a data-driven culture on product development and organizational success through the use of business analytics. [JoWUA]. *Journal of Wireless Mobile Networks, Ubiquitous Computing and Dependable Applications*, *15*(2), 123–134. DOI: 10.58346/JOWUA.2024.I2.009

Bacca, J., Baldiris, S., Fabregat, R., & Graf, S., & Kinshuk. (2014). Augmented reality trends in education: A systematic review of research and applications. *Journal of Educational Technology & Society*, *17*(4), 133–149.

Bachtiar, N. K., Setiawan, A., Prastyan, G. A., & Kijkasiwat, P. (2023). Business resilience and growth strategy transformation. *Journal of Innovation and Entrepreneurship*, *12*(1), 77. DOI: 10.1186/s13731-023-00345-5

BaiDoo-Anu, D., & Ansah, L. O. (2023). Education in the era of generative artificial intelligence (AI): Understanding the potential benefits of ChatGPT in promoting teaching and learning. *Journal of AI, 7*(1), 52–62. https://doi.org/DOI: 10.61969/jai.1337500

Bai, H., & Ertmer, P. A. (2021). Ethical considerations in AI-enhanced learning environments. *Educational Technology Research and Development*, *69*(5), 2553–2571.

Baker, R. S., & Inventado, P. S. (2014). Educational data mining and learning analytics. In Larusson, J. A., & White, B. (Eds.), *Learning analytics: From research to practice* (pp. 61–75). Springer. DOI: 10.1007/978-1-4614-3305-7_4

Bakker, A. B., Demerouti, E., & Sanz-Vergel, A. I. (2014). Burnout and work engagement. *Annual Review of Organizational Psychology and Organizational Behavior*, *1*(1), 389–411. DOI: 10.1146/annurev-orgpsych-031413-091235

Balachandra, L., Briggs, T., Eddleston, K., & Brush, C. (2019). Don't pitch like a girl!: How gender stereotypes influence investor decisions. *Entrepreneurship Theory and Practice*, *43*(1), 116–137. DOI: 10.1177/1042258717728028

Bandura, A. (1986). *Social foundations of thought and action*. Prentice Hall.

Barocas, S., Hardt, M., & Narayanan, A. (2019). *Fairness and machine learning: Limitations and opportunities*. MIT Press.

Barocas, S., & Selbst, A. D. (2016). Big data's disparate impact. *SSRN*, *104*(3), 671–732. DOI: 10.2139/ssrn.2477899

Bar-On, R. (1997). *Bar-On Emotional Quotient Inventory (EQ-i): Technical manual*. Multi-Health Systems.

Baron, R. A. (2004). The cognitive perspective: A valuable tool for answering entrepreneurship's basic "why" questions. *Journal of Business Venturing, 19*(2), 221–239. DOI: 10.1016/S0883-9026(03)00008-9

Baron, R. A. (2006). Opportunity recognition as pattern recognition: How entrepreneurs "connect the dots" to identify new business opportunities. *The Academy of Management Perspectives, 20*(1), 104–119. DOI: 10.5465/amp.2006.19873412

Baron, R. A. (2008). The role of affect in the entrepreneurial process. *Academy of Management Review, 33*(2), 328–340. DOI: 10.5465/amr.2008.31193166

Baron, R. A., Franklin, R. J., & Hmieleski, K. M. (2016). Entrepreneurial stress and well-being. *Journal of Management, 42*(3), 742–768. DOI: 10.1177/0149206313495411

Baron, R. A., & Tang, J. (2009). Entrepreneurs' social skills and new venture performance: Mediating mechanisms and cultural generality. *Journal of Management, 35*(2), 282–306. DOI: 10.1177/0149206307312513

Baron, R. A., & Tang, J. (2011). The role of entrepreneurs in firm-level innovation: Joint effects of positive affect, creativity, and environmental dynamism. *Journal of Business Venturing, 26*(1), 49–60. DOI: 10.1016/j.jbusvent.2009.06.002

Barrett, L. F., Adolphs, R., Marsella, S., Martinez, A. M., & Pollak, S. D. (2019). Emotional expressions reconsidered: Challenges to lhisinferring emotion from human facial movements. *Psychological Science in the Public Interest, 20*(1), 1–68. DOI: 10.1177/1529100619832930 PMID: 31313636

Baum, J. R., & Locke, E. A. (2004). The relationship of entrepreneurial traits, skill, and motivation to subsequent venture growth. *The Journal of Applied Psychology, 89*(4), 587–598. DOI: 10.1037/0021-9010.89.4.587 PMID: 15327346

Bazerman, M. H., & Tenbrunsel, A. E. (2011). *Blind spots: Why we fail to do what's right and what to do about it*. Princeton University Press. DOI: 10.1515/9781400837991

Belguith, M. (2025). *Adoption of AI in entrepreneurship education: University teachers' perceptions*. International Journal of Advances in Educational Research., DOI: 10.62941/ijaer.v2i1.151

Bellotti, F., Kapralos, B., Lee, K., Moreno-Ger, P., & Berta, R. (2013). Assessment in and of serious games: An overview. *Advances in Human-Computer Interaction, 2013*, 1–11. DOI: 10.1155/2013/136864

Bell, R., & Bell, H. (2023). Entrepreneurship education in the era of generative artificial intelligence. *Entrepreneurship Education*, *6*(3), 229–244. DOI: 10.1007/s41959-023-00099-x

Bilgram, V., & Laarmann, F. (2023). Accelerating innovation with generative AI. *IEEE Engineering Management Review*, *51*(2), 18–25. DOI: 10.1109/EMR.2023.3272799

Binns, R. (2018). Fairness in machine learning: Lessons from political philosophy. *Proceedings of the 2018 Conference on Fairness, Accountability, and Transparency*, 149–159. DOI: 10.1145/3287560.3287572

Bird, S., Klein, E., & Loper, E. (2009). *Natural language processing with Python*. O'Reilly Media.

Blei, D. M., Ng, A. Y., & Jordan, M. I. (2003). Latent Dirichlet Allocation. *Journal of Machine Learning Research*, *3*, 993–1022.

Bogen, M., & Rieke, A. (2018). Help wanted: An examination of hiring algorithms, equity, and bias. *Technology Science*. https://techscience.org/a/2018050901/

Bonilla, C. A., & Vergara, M. (2021). Risk aversion, downside risk aversion, and the transition to entrepreneurship. *Theory and Decision*, *91*(1), 123–133. DOI: 10.1007/s11238-020-09786-w

Booker, C. (2004). *The seven basic plots: Why we tell stories*. Bloomsbury.

Bowman, S. R. (2023). Eight things to know about large language models. *arXiv:2304.00612*.

Boyatzis, R. E. (1982). *The competent manager: A model for effective performance*. Wiley.

Boyatzis, R. E. (2018). The behavioral level of emotional intelligence and its measurement. *Frontiers in Psychology*, *9*, 1438. DOI: 10.3389/fpsyg.2018.01438 PMID: 30150958

Brailas, A. (2024). Postdigital duoethnography: An inquiry into human–artificial intelligence synergies. *Postdigital Science and Education*, *6*(2), 486–515. DOI: 10.1007/s42438-024-00455-7

Branicki, L. J., Sullivan-Taylor, B., & Livschitz, S. R. (2018). Entrepreneurial resilience and SMEs. *International Journal of Entrepreneurial Behaviour & Research*, *24*(7), 1244–1263. DOI: 10.1108/IJEBR-11-2016-0396

Brown, T., Mann, B., Ryder, N., Subbiah, M., Kaplan, J., Dhariwal, P., & Amodei, D. (2020). Language models are few-shot learners. *Advances in Neural Information Processing Systems*, *33*, 1877–1901.

Brynjolfsson, E., & McAfee, A. (2017). The business of artificial intelligence: What it can — and cannot — do for your organization. *Harvard Business Review*. https://hbr.org/2017/07/the-business-of-artificial-intelligence

Brynjolfsson, E., & McAfee, A. (2017). *Machine, platform, crowd: Harnessing our digital future*. W. W. Norton & Company.

Bughin, J., Seong, J., Manyika, J., Chui, M., & Joshi, R. (2018). *Notes from the AI frontier: Modeling the impact of AI on the world economy*. McKinsey Global Institute.

Buolamwini, J., & Gebru, T. (2018). Gender shades: Intersectional accuracy disparities in commercial gender classification. *Proceedings of Machine Learning Research*, *81*, 1–15.

Burrell, J. (2016). How the machine 'thinks': Understanding opacity in machine learning algorithms. *Big Data & Society*, *3*(1), 1–12. DOI: 10.1177/2053951715622512

Busenitz, L. W., & Barney, J. B. (1997). Differences between entrepreneurs and managers in large organizations: Biases and heuristics in strategic decision-making. *Journal of Business Venturing*, *12*(1), 9–30. DOI: 10.1016/S0883-9026(96)00003-1

Business Insider. (2025, May 7). *This edtech startup bills itself as the 'Duolingo for exams.' Check out the pitch deck Alice.Tech used to raise $4.8 million*. Retrieved from https://www.businessinsider.com/pitch-deck-alice-tech-funding-ai-edtech-2025-5

Caliskan, A., Bryson, J. J., & Narayanan, A. (2017). Semantics derived automatically from language corpora contain human-like biases. *Science*, *356*(6334), 183–186. DOI: 10.1126/science.aal4230 PMID: 28408601

Calo, R. (2017). Artificial intelligence policy: A primer and roadmap. *U.C. Davis Law Review*, *51*(2), 399–435. https://lawreview.law.ucdavis.edu/archives/51/2/artificial-intelligence-policy-primer-and-roadmap

Calvo, R. A., & D'Mello, S. (2010). Affect detection: An interdisciplinary review of models, methods, and their applications. *IEEE Transactions on Affective Computing*, *1*(1), 18–37. DOI: 10.1109/T-AFFC.2010.1

Camacho, S., Nam, T., Kannan, P. K., & Stremersch, S. (2020). The information value of online consumer reviews: A case of review characteristics and consumer perceptions. *International Journal of Research in Marketing*, *37*(3), 507–525. DOI: 10.1016/j.ijresmar.2019.12.004

Camps, C., Kraus, S., Thomas, A., Tiberius, V., & Jones, P. (2026). Digital Entrepreneurship: A review, research synthesis, and development of a framework. *Technology in Society, 84*, 103124. DOI: 10.1016/j.techsoc.2025.103124

Cantillon, R. (2010). *Essay on the nature of trade in general* (Higgs, H., Trans.). Liberty Fund. (Original work published 1755)

Carayannis, E. G., & Grigoroudis, E. (2023). *Handbook of research on artificial intelligence, innovation and entrepreneurship*. Edward Elgar. DOI: 10.4337/9781839106750

Cardon, M. S., Foo, M. D., Shepherd, D., & Wiklund, J. (2012). Exploring the heart: Entrepreneurial emotion is a hot topic. *Entrepreneurship Theory and Practice, 36*(1), 1–10. DOI: 10.1111/j.1540-6520.2011.00501.x

Carmeli, A. (2003). The relationship between emotional intelligence and work attitudes, behavior, and outcomes. *Journal of Managerial Psychology, 18*(8), 788–813. DOI: 10.1108/02683940310511881

Chadwick, I. C., & Raver, J. L. (2020). Psychological resilience and venture survival. *Entrepreneurship Theory and Practice, 44*(2), 233–255. DOI: 10.1177/1042258718801597

Chamorro-Premuzic, T., Winsborough, D., Sherman, R. A., & Hogan, R. (2016). New talent signals: Shiny new objects or a brave new world? *Industrial and Organizational Psychology: Perspectives on Science and Practice, 9*(3), 621–640. DOI: 10.1017/iop.2016.6

Chatterjee, S., Rana, N. P., Tamilmani, K., & Sharma, A. (2020). The next generation of technology-enabled decision-making: Artificial intelligence and big data. *Journal of Business Research, 124*, 311–320. DOI: 10.1016/j.jbusres.2020.11.015

Chaudhry, I. S., Paquibut, R. Y., & Tunio, M. N. (2021). Do workforce diversity, inclusion practices, & organizational characteristics contribute to organizational innovation? Evidence from the UAE. *Cogent Business & Management, 8*(1), 1947549. DOI: 10.1080/23311975.2021.1947549

Chawla, N. V., Bowyer, K. W., Hall, L. O., & Kegelmeyer, W. P. (2002). SMOTE: Synthetic minority over-sampling technique. *Journal of Artificial Intelligence Research, 16*, 321–357. DOI: 10.1613/jair.953

Chen, C. C., Greene, P. G., & Crick, A. (1998). Does entrepreneurial self-efficacy distinguish entrepreneurs from managers? *Journal of Business Venturing, 13*(4), 295–316. DOI: 10.1016/S0883-9026(97)00029-3

Chen, L., Ifenthaler, D., Yau, J., & Sun, W. (2024). Artificial Intelligence in Entrepreneurship Education: A Scoping Review. *Education + Training*, *2023*(6), 589–608. Advance online publication. DOI: 10.1108/ET-05-2023-0169

Chen, M. H., Chang, Y. Y., & Pan, J. Y. (2018b). Typology of creative entrepreneurs and entrepreneurial success. *Journal of Enterprising Communities: People and Places in the Global Economy*, *12*(5), 632–656. DOI: 10.1108/JEC-07-2017-0041

Chen, X. P., Yao, X., & Kotha, S. (2009). Entrepreneur passion and preparedness in business plan presentations: A persuasion analysis of venture capitalists' funding decisions. *Academy of Management Journal*, *52*(1), 199–214. DOI: 10.5465/amj.2009.36462018

Chen, Y., & Zhang, Y. (2021). Fostering resilience in new venture teams. *Group & Organization Management*, *46*(4), 773–816. DOI: 10.1177/10596011211033164

Cherniss, C. (2010). Emotional intelligence: Toward clarification of a concept. *Industrial and Organizational Psychology: Perspectives on Science and Practice*, *3*(2), 110–126. DOI: 10.1111/j.1754-9434.2010.01231.x

Chollet, M., Scherer, S., Stratou, G., & Morency, L. P. (2015). Exploring feedback strategies to improve public speaking: An interactive virtual audience framework. *Proceedings of the 2015 ACM International Conference on Intelligent Virtual Agents*, 114–121. DOI: 10.1145/2750858.2806060

Choudhary, S., Yadav, M., & Srivastava, A. P. (2024). Cognitive biases among millennial Indian investors: Do personality and demographic factors matter? *FIIB Business Review*, *13*(1), 106–117. DOI: 10.1177/23197145211057343

Chouldechova, A., & Roth, A. (2020). A snapshot of the frontiers of fairness in machine learning. *Communications of the ACM*, *63*(5), 82–89. DOI: 10.1145/3376898

Clarke, J., Cornelissen, J., & Healey, M. P. (2019). Actions speak louder than words: How figurative language and gesturing in entrepreneurial pitches influences investment judgments. *Academy of Management Journal*, *62*(2), 335–360. DOI: 10.5465/amj.2016.1008

Cockburn, I. M., Henderson, R., & Stern, S. (2018). The impact of artificial intelligence on innovation. *The National Bureau of Economic Research Working Paper Series*, (24449), 1–37. DOI: 10.3386/w24449

Cockburn, I. M., Henderson, R., & Stern, S. (2018). The impact of artificial intelligence on innovation: An exploratory analysis. In Agrawal, A., Gans, J., & Goldfarb, A. (Eds.), *The economics of artificial intelligence: An agenda* (pp. 115–146). University of Chicago Press., DOI: 10.7208/chicago/9780226613475.003.0004

Cohen, G., Aiche, A., & Winer, Z. (2025). Matching angels to startups using AI. *China Finance Review International.* Advance online publication. DOI: 10.1108/CFRI-04-2024-0222

Collins, C. J., Hanges, P. J., & Locke, E. A. (2004). The relationship of achievement motivation to entrepreneurial behavior: A meta-analysis. *Human Performance, 17*(1), 95–117. DOI: 10.1207/S15327043HUP1701_5

Colombo, M. G., & Piva, E. (2020). Start-ups launched by recent STEM university graduates: The impact of university education on entrepreneurial entry. *Research Policy, 49*(6), 103993. Advance online publication. DOI: 10.1016/j.respol.2020.103993

Connor, K. M., & Davidson, J. R. T. (2003). Development of the CD-RISC. *Depression and Anxiety, 18*(2), 76–82. DOI: 10.1002/da.10113 PMID: 12964174

Conz, E., & Magnani, G. (2020). A dynamic perspective on the resilience of firms. *European Management Journal, 38*(3), 400–412. DOI: 10.1016/j.emj.2019.12.004

Cooper, A. C., Woo, C. Y., & Dunkelberg, W. C. (1989). Entrepreneurship and the initial size of firms. *Journal of Business Venturing, 4*(5), 317–332. DOI: 10.1016/0883-9026(89)90004-9

Corner, P. D., Singh, S., & Pavlovich, K. (2017). Entrepreneurial resilience and venture failure. *International Small Business Journal, 35*(6), 687–708. DOI: 10.1177/0266242616685604

Côté, S. (2014). Emotional intelligence in organizations. *Annual Review of Organizational Psychology and Organizational Behavior, 1*(1), 459–488. DOI: 10.1146/annurev-orgpsych-031413-091233

Crawford, K. (2021). *Atlas of AI: Power, politics, and the planetary costs of artificial intelligence.* Yale University Press.

Cribben, I., & Zeinali, Y. (2023). The benefits and limitations of ChatGPT in business education and research: A focus on management science, operations management and data analytics. SSRN *Electronic Journal.* DOI: 10.2139/ssrn.4404276

Cummings-Koether, M. J., Durner, F., Shyiramunda, T., & Huemmer, M. (2025). Cultural dimensions of artificial intelligence adoption: Empirical insights for Wave 1 from a multinational longitudinal pilot study. *arXiv.* https://arxiv.org/abs/2510.19743

Darnell, J., & Gopalkrishnan, S. (2024). Entrepreneurship teaching exercises: Integrating generative AI. *Discover Education, 3*(1), 172. Advance online publication. DOI: 10.1007/s44217-024-00261-0

Dash, S. (2025). Sakti Cafe: Empowering Women's Financial Independence and Livelihood Advancement in Odisha, India. *Asian Journal of Education and Social Studies*, *51*(4), 200–210. DOI: 10.9734/ajess/2025/v51i41861

Daugherty, P. R., & Wilson, H. J. (2022). *Radically human: How new technology is transforming business and shaping our future*. Harvard Business Review Press.

Davenport, T. H., & Ronanki, R. (2018). Artificial intelligence for the real world. *Harvard Business Review*, *96*(1), 108–116.

Davis, B. C., Hmieleski, K. M., Webb, J. W., & Coombs, J. E. (2017). Funders' positive affective reactions to entrepreneurs' crowdfunding pitches: The influence of perceived product creativity and entrepreneurial passion. *Journal of Business Venturing*, *32*(1), 90–106. DOI: 10.1016/j.jbusvent.2016.10.006

Deci, E. L., & Ryan, R. M. (2000). Self-determination theory and the facilitation of intrinsic motivation, social development, and well-being. *The American Psychologist*, *55*(1), 68–78. DOI: 10.1037/0003-066X.55.1.68 PMID: 11392867

Deci, E. L., & Ryan, R. M. (2000). The "what" and "why" of goal pursuits: Human needs and the self-determination of behavior. *Psychological Inquiry*, *11*(4), 227–268. DOI: 10.1207/S15327965PLI1104_01

Dell'Acqua, F., ... (2023). Navigating the jagged technological frontier. *Harvard Business School Working Paper*. https://doi.org/DOI: 10.2139/ssrn.4573321

Deng, X., & Yu, Z. (2023). A meta-analysis and systematic review of the effect of chatbot technology use in sustainable education. *Sustainability (Basel)*, *15*(4), 2940. Advance online publication. DOI: 10.3390/su15042940

Deterding, S., Dixon, D., Khaled, R., & Nacke, L. (2011). From game design elements to gamefulness: Defining "gamification." *Proceedings of the 15th International Academic MindTrek Conference*, 9–15. DOI: 10.1145/2181037.2181040

Devlin, J., Chang, M. W., Lee, K., & Toutanova, K. (2019). BERT: Pre-training of deep bidirectional transformers for language understanding. *Proceedings of the 2019 Conference of the North American Chapter of the Association for Computational Linguistics: Human Language Technologies*, 4171–4186. DOI: 10.48550/arXiv.1810.04805

Doshi-Velez, F., & Kim, B. (2017). Towards a rigorous science of interpretable machine learning. *arXiv preprint* arXiv:1702.08608.

Drydakis, N. (2022). Artificial intelligence and reduced SMEs' business risks. *Information Systems Frontiers, 24*(4), 1223–1247. DOI: 10.1007/s10796-022-10249-6 PMID: 35261558

Duchek, S. (2018). Entrepreneurial resilience. *The International Entrepreneurship and Management Journal, 14*(2), 429–455. DOI: 10.1007/s11365-017-0467-2

Duchek, S. (2020). Organizational resilience: A capability-based conceptualization. *Business Research, 13*(1), 215–246. DOI: 10.1007/s40685-019-0085-7

Duckworth, A. L., Peterson, C., Matthews, M. D., & Kelly, D. R. (2007). Grit and perseverance. *Journal of Personality and Social Psychology, 92*(6), 1087–1101. DOI: 10.1037/0022-3514.92.6.1087 PMID: 17547490

Dunan, A., Mudjiyanto, B., Setiawan, A., Syarifuddin, S., Pala, R., Rustam, M., Dirgahayu, D., Buyamin, B., Nuryana, M., & Hartiningsih, H. (2025). Artificial Intelligence in E-Entrepreneurship Training. *International Journal of E-Entrepreneurship and Innovation, 15*(1), 1–22. Advance online publication. DOI: 10.4018/IJEEI.386065

Duong, C. (2025). AI literacy and higher education students' digital entrepreneurial intention: A moderated mediation model of AI self-efficacy and digital entrepreneurial self-efficacy. *Industry and Higher Education*. Advance online publication. DOI: 10.1177/09504222251370089

Duong, C., & Vu, T. (2025). *Entrepreneurial education and higher education students' e-entrepreneurial intention: a moderated mediation model of generative AI incorporation and e-entrepreneurial self-efficacy*. Higher Education, Skills and Work-Based Learning., DOI: 10.1108/HESWBL-12-2024-0390

Dwivedi, Y. K., Hughes, L., Baabdullah, A. M., Ribeiro-Navarrete, S., Giannakis, M., Al-Debei, M. M., Dennehy, D., Metri, B., Buhalis, D., Cheung, C. M. K., Conboy, K., Doyle, R., Dubey, R., Dutot, V., Felix, R., Goyal, D. P., Gustafsson, A., Hinsch, C., Jebabli, I., & Wamba, S. F. (2021). Metaverse beyond the hype: Multidisciplinary perspectives on emerging challenges, opportunities, and agenda for research, practice and policy. *International Journal of Information Management, 66*, 102542. DOI: 10.1016/j.ijinfomgt.2022.102542

Dwivedi, Y. K., Hughes, L., Ismagilova, E., Aarts, G., Coombs, C., Crick, T., Duan, Y., Dwivedi, R., Edwards, J., Eirug, A., Galanos, V., Ilavarasan, P. V., Janssen, M., Jones, P., Kar, A. K., Kizgin, H., Kronemann, B., Lal, B., Lucini, B., & Williams, M. D. (2021). Artificial intelligence (AI): Multidisciplinary perspectives on emerging challenges, opportunities, and agenda for research, practice, and policy. *International Journal of Information Management, 57*, 101994. Advance online publication. DOI: 10.1016/j.ijinfomgt.2019.08.002

Dwork, C., Hardt, M., Pitassi, T., Reingold, O., & Zemel, R. (2012). Fairness through awareness. *Proceedings of the 3rd Innovations in Theoretical Computer Science Conference*, 214–226. DOI: 10.1145/2090236.2090255

Edmondson, A. C. (2019). *The fearless organization: Creating psychological safety in the workplace for learning, innovation, and growth.* Wiley.

Ekman, P., & Rosenberg, E. L. (2005). *What the face reveals: Basic and applied studies of spontaneous expression using the Facial Action Coding System (FACS)* (2nd ed.). Oxford University Press. DOI: 10.1093/acprof:oso/9780195179644.001.0001

Eltanahy, M., Forawi, S., & Mansour, N. (2020). Incorporating entrepreneurial practices into STEM education: Development of interdisciplinary E-STEM model in high school in the United Arab Emirates. *Thinking Skills and Creativity*, *37*, 100697. Advance online publication. DOI: 10.1016/j.tsc.2020.100697

Ensley, M. D., Pearce, C. L., & Hmieleski, K. M. (2006). The moderating effect of environmental dynamism on the relationship between entrepreneur leadership behavior and new venture performance. *Journal of Business Venturing*, *21*(2), 243–263. DOI: 10.1016/j.jbusvent.2005.04.006

Ensley, M. D., Pearson, A. W., & Amason, A. C. (2002). Understanding the dynamics of new venture top management teams: Cohesion, conflict, and new venture performance. *Journal of Business Venturing*, *17*(4), 365–386. DOI: 10.1016/S0883-9026(00)00065-3

Epstein, Z., Hertzmann, A., Akten, M., Farid, H., Fjeld, J., Frank, M. R., Groh, M., Herman, L., Leach, N., Mahari, R., Pentland, A. S., Russakovsky, O., Schroeder, H., & Smith, A. (2023). Art and the science of generative AI. *Science*, *380*(6650), 1110–1111. DOI: 10.1126/science.adh4451 PMID: 37319193

European Commission. (2021). *Proposal for a regulation laying down harmonised rules on artificial intelligence (Artificial Intelligence Act).* COM(2021) 206 final.

Farooqi, A., Das, D., Tripathi, M., Dutta, R., Goyal, N. K., & Sheikh, M. F. (2026). Navigating ethical frontiers in AI-driven geriatric care. In *AI for geriatric care in an aging society* (pp. 243–266). IGI Global., DOI: 10.4018/979-8-3373-5462-0.ch009

Feldman, M. (2021). Gender, leadership, and entrepreneurial ecosystems. *Small Business Economics*, *56*(2), 529–541. DOI: 10.1007/s11187-019-00276-5

Fisher, W. R. (1984). Narration as a human communication paradigm: The case of public moral argument. *Communication Monographs*, *51*(1), 1–22. DOI: 10.1080/03637758409390180

Floridi, L. (2019). *The ethics of artificial intelligence*. Oxford University Press.

Floridi, L., & Cowls, J. (2019). A unified framework of five principles for AI in society. *Harvard Data Science Review*, *1*(1), 1–15. DOI: 10.1162/99608f92.8cd550d1

Floridi, L., Cowls, J., Beltrametti, M., Chatila, R., Chazerand, P., Dignum, V., Luetge, C., Madelin, R., Pagallo, U., Rossi, F., Schafer, B., Valcke, P., & Vayena, E. (2018). AI4People—An ethical framework for a good AI society. *Minds and Machines*, *28*(4), 689–707. DOI: 10.1007/s11023-018-9482-5 PMID: 30930541

Foo, M. D., Elfenbein, H. A., Tan, H. H., & Aik, V. C. (2004). Emotional intelligence and negotiation: The tension between creating and claiming value. *International Journal of Conflict Management*, *15*(4), 411–429. DOI: 10.1108/eb022920

Fossen, F. M., McLemore, T., & Sorgner, A. (2024). Artificial intelligence and entrepreneurship. *Foundations and Trends® in Entrepreneurship, 20*(8), 781–904. https://doi.org/DOI: 10.1561/0300000130

Fossen, F. M., & Sorgner, A. (2021). Digitalization of work and entry into entrepreneurship. *Journal of Business Research*, *125*, 548–563. DOI: 10.1016/j.jbusres.2019.09.019

Foukalas, F. (2025). A Survey of Artificial Neural Network Computing Systems. *Cognitive Computation*, *17*(1), 4. DOI: 10.1007/s12559-024-10383-0

FounderNest. (2021). *FounderNest: AI-powered founder analysis*. https://www.foundernest.com/

Fountaine, T., McCarthy, B., & Saleh, T. (2019). Building the AI-powered organization. *Harvard Business Review*.

Fredrickson, B. L. (2001). The broaden-and-build theory. *The American Psychologist*, *56*(3), 218–226. DOI: 10.1037/0003-066X.56.3.218 PMID: 11315248

Friedman, B., & Nissenbaum, H. (1996). Bias in computer systems. *ACM Transactions on Information Systems*, *14*(3), 330–347. DOI: 10.1145/230538.230561

Games, D., Masli, E., Sari, D., Triani, L., & Komalasari, S. (2025). Generational cohort and technology readiness and acceptance of artificial intelligence among young high-growth entrepreneurs. *Digital Transformation and Society*, 1–21. DOI: 10.1108/DTS-02-2025-0040

Gartner, W. B. (1988). "Who is an entrepreneur?" is the wrong question. *American Journal of Small Business*, *12*(4), 11–32. DOI: 10.1177/104225878801200401

Gartner, W. B. (2007). Entrepreneurial narrative and a science of the imagination. *Journal of Business Venturing*, *22*(5), 613–627. DOI: 10.1016/j.jbusvent.2006.10.003

Gartner, W. B., Carter, N. M., & Hills, G. E. (2019). The development of entrepreneurship: Key factors, challenges, and perspectives. *Journal of Business Venturing Insights*, *11*, e00142.

Gatewood, E. J., Shaver, K. G., & Gartner, W. B. (1995). A longitudinal study of cognitive factors influencing start-up behaviors and success at venture creation. *Journal of Business Venturing*, *10*(5), 371–391. DOI: 10.1016/0883-9026(95)00035-7

Gebru, T., Morgenstern, J., Vecchione, B., Vaughan, J. W., Wallach, H., Daumé, H.III, & Crawford, K. (2018). Datasheets for datasets. *Communications of the ACM*, *64*(12), 86–92. DOI: 10.1145/3458723

Gedeon, S., & Huber, F. (2025). *Using AI-Enabled Images and Comic Narrative to Enhance Entrepreneurship Education*. Entrepreneurship Education and Pedagogy., DOI: 10.1177/25151274251358708

Gilal, F. G., Gilal, N. G., Channa, N. A., Gilal, R. G., Gilal, R. G., & Tunio, M. N. (2020). Towards an integrated model for the transference of environmental responsibility. *Business Strategy and the Environment*, *29*(6), 2614–2623. DOI: 10.1002/bse.2524

Ginting, Y., & Azizurrohman, M. (2025). *Linking Entrepreneurship Education to Entrepreneurial Intentions: A Social Cognitive and Resource-Based Perspective. The Asian Journal of Technology Management*. AJTM., DOI: 10.12695/ajtm.2025.18.1.4

Giuggioli, G., Pellegrini, M. M., & Giannone, G. (2024). Artificial intelligence as an enabler for entrepreneurial finance: A practical guide to AI-driven video pitch evaluation for entrepreneurs and investors. *Management Decision*.

Giulioni, G., Bucciarelli, E., & Silvestri, M. (2012, March). Modeling firms financial behavior in an evolving economy by using artificial intelligence. In *Highlights on Practical Applications of Agents and Multi-Agent Systems: 10th International Conference on Practical Applications of Agents and Multi-Agent Systems* (pp. 333-340). Berlin, Heidelberg: Springer Berlin Heidelberg. DOI: 10.1007/978-3-642-28762-6_40

Goleman, D. (1995). *Emotional intelligence*. Bantam Books.

Goleman, D. (1995). *Emotional intelligence: Why it can matter more than IQ*. Bantam Books.

Goleman, D. (1998). *Working with emotional intelligence*. Bantam Books.

Gonzalez, E. D. S., Kandpal, V., Ozili, P. K., & Chatterjee, P. (Eds.). (2024). *Fintech for ESG and the Circular Economy*. John Wiley & Sons.

Goyal, N. K., Gulati, K., Avasthi, A., Kapoor, S. K., Keswani, B., & Gupta, S. (2026). Securing the imagination: Security and privacy challenges in generative AI systems. In *Generative AI-powered data architectures* (pp. 239–266). IGI Global., DOI: 10.4018/979-8-3373-5616-7.ch010

Graesser, A. C., Fiore, S. M., Greiff, S., Andrews-Todd, J., Foltz, P. W., & Hesse, F. W. (2018). Advancing the science of collaborative problem solving. *Psychological Science in the Public Interest*, *19*(2), 59–92. DOI: 10.1177/1529100618808244 PMID: 30497346

Grégoire, D. A., Corbett, A. C., & McMullen, J. S. (2011). The cognitive perspective in entrepreneurship: An agenda for future research. *Journal of Management Studies*, *48*(6), 1443–1477. DOI: 10.1111/j.1467-6486.2010.00922.x

Gross, J. J. (2015). Emotion regulation: Current status and future prospects. *Psychological Inquiry*, *26*(1), 1–26. DOI: 10.1080/1047840X.2014.940781

Gulla, B. (2025). *The advantages of AI-driven personalized learning paths*. The Training Associates. Retrieved from https://thetrainingassociates.com/ai-personalized-learning-paths/

Guo, K., & Wang, D. (2024). To resist it or to embrace it? Examining ChatGPT's potential to support teacher feedback in EFL writing. *Education and Information Technologies*, *29*(7), 8435–8463. DOI: 10.1007/s10639-023-12146-0

Hamari, J., Koivisto, J., & Sarsa, H. (2014). Does gamification work?—A literature review of empirical studies on gamification. *Proceedings of the 47th Hawaii International Conference on System Sciences*, 3025–3034. DOI: 10.1109/HICSS.2014.377

Hardt, M., Price, E., & Srebro, N. (2016). Equality of opportunity in supervised learning. *Advances in Neural Information Processing Systems*, *29*, 3315–3323.

Hmieleski, K. M., & Baron, R. A. (2009). Entrepreneurs' optimism and new venture performance: A social cognitive perspective. *Academy of Management Journal*, *52*(3), 473–488. DOI: 10.5465/amj.2009.41330755

Hofmans, J., Wille, B., & Schreurs, B. (2020). Person-centered methods in vocational research. *Journal of Vocational Behavior*, *118*, 103398. DOI: 10.1016/j.jvb.2020.103398

Hofstede, G. (2001). *Culture's consequences: Comparing values, behaviors, institutions and organizations across nations* (2nd ed.). SAGE Publications.

Hollan, J., Hutchins, E., & Kirsh, D. (2000). Distributed cognition: Toward a new foundation for human–computer interaction research. *ACM Transactions on Computer-Human Interaction*, *7*(2), 174–196. DOI: 10.1145/353485.353487

Holmes, W., Bialik, M., & Fadel, C. (2019). *Artificial intelligence in education: Promises and implications for teaching and learning*. Center for Curriculum Redesign.

Huang, L., & Knight, A. P. (2017). Resources and relationships in entrepreneurship: An exchange theory of the development and effects of the entrepreneur–investor relationship. *Academy of Management Review*, *42*(1), 80–102. DOI: 10.5465/amr.2014.0397

Huang, L., & Pearce, J. L. (2015). Managing the unknowable: The effectiveness of early-stage investor gut feel in entrepreneurial investment decisions. *Administrative Science Quarterly*, *60*(4), 634–670. DOI: 10.1177/0001839215597270

Huang, M. H., & Rust, R. T. (2018). Artificial intelligence in service. *Journal of Service Research*, *21*(2), 155–172. DOI: 10.1177/1094670517752459

IBM. (2019). *AI in talent management: Identifying intrapreneurs at IBM*. IBM Research. https://www.ibm.com/research

IBM. (2023). *Responsible AI and leadership ethics report*. IBM Corporation.

Jaboob, A., Durrah, O., & Chakir, A. (2024). Artificial intelligence: An overview. *Engineering Applications of Artificial Intelligence*, •••, 3–22.

Jarrahi, M. H. (2018). Artificial intelligence and the future of work: Human–AI symbiosis in organizational decision making. *Business Horizons*, *61*(4), 577–586. DOI: 10.1016/j.bushor.2018.03.007

Jiang, J., Lu, B., Peng, H., Zhu, J., & Ji, Q. (2019). Speech emotion recognition with deep recurrent neural networks. *Proceedings of the IEEE International Conference on Acoustics, Speech, and Signal Processing (ICASSP)*, 6675–6679. DOI: 10.1109/ICASSP.2019.8682629

Jiatong, W., Murad, M., Bajun, F., Tufail, M., Mirza, F., & Rafiq, M. (2021). Impact of Entrepreneurial Education, Mindset, and Creativity on Entrepreneurial Intention: Mediating Role of Entrepreneurial Self-Efficacy. *Frontiers in Psychology*, *12*, 724440. Advance online publication. DOI: 10.3389/fpsyg.2021.724440 PMID: 34497568

Jobin, A., Ienca, M., & Vayena, E. (2019). The global landscape of AI ethics guidelines. *Nature Machine Intelligence*, *1*(9), 389–399. DOI: 10.1038/s42256-019-0088-2

Johnson, L., Adams Becker, S., Estrada, V., & Freeman, A. (2020). *The NMC Horizon Report: 2020 Higher Education Edition*. EDUCAUSE.

Jordan, M. I., & Mitchell, T. M. (2015). Machine learning: Trends, perspectives, and prospects. *Science, 349*(6245), 255–260. DOI: 10.1126/science.aaa8415

Joseph, D. L., & Newman, D. A. (2010). Emotional intelligence: An integrative meta-analysis and cascading model. *The Journal of Applied Psychology, 95*(1), 54–78. DOI: 10.1037/a0017286 PMID: 20085406

Jurafsky, D., & Martin, J. H. (2023). *Speech and language processing* (3rd ed.). Draft. Stanford University. https://web.stanford.edu/~jurafsky/slp3/

Kabudi, T. (2021). AI-enabled adaptive learning systems: A systematic review. *Journal of Educational Technology & Society, 24*(3), 1–15.

Kahneman, D. (2011). *Thinking, fast and slow*. Farrar, Straus and Giroux.

Kahneman, D., & Tversky, A. (1979). Prospect theory: An analysis of decision under risk. *Econometrica, 47*(2), 263–291. DOI: 10.2307/1914185

Kariv, D., Attar, I., Haber, Y., & Elyoseph, Z. (2025). AI-simulated entrepreneurship under uncertainty: Forecasting university-driven capability evolution. *The Journal of Technology Transfer*. Advance online publication. DOI: 10.1007/s10961-025-10306-7

Kaya-Capocci, S. (2023). The trends in entrepreneurship and STEM education studies: A bibliometric study. *İnönü Üniversitesi Eğitim Fakültesi Dergisi, 24*(2), 869–892. DOI: 10.17679/inuefd.1320031

Keh, H. T., Foo, M. D., & Lim, B. C. (2002). Opportunity evaluation under risky conditions: The cognitive processes of entrepreneurs. *Entrepreneurship Theory and Practice, 27*(2), 125–148. DOI: 10.1111/1540-8520.00003

Kelleher, J. D. (2019). *Deep learning*. MIT Press. DOI: 10.7551/mit-press/11171.001.0001

Kelly, A., Sullivan, M., & Strampel, K. (2023). Generative artificial intelligence: University student awareness, experience, and confidence in use across disciplines. *Journal of University Teaching & Learning Practice, 20*(6). Advance online publication. DOI: 10.53761/1.20.6.12

Kilbertus, N., Rojas-Carulla, M., Parascandolo, G., Hardt, M., Janzing, D., & Schölkopf, B. (2017). Avoiding discrimination through causal reasoning. *Advances in Neural Information Processing Systems, 30*, 656–666.

Knight, F. H. (1921). *Risk, uncertainty, and profit*. Houghton Mifflin.

Kolb, D. A. (2015). *Experiential learning: Experience as the source of learning and development* (2nd ed.). Pearson Education.

Kolbjørnsrud, V., Amico, R., & Thomas, R. J. (2016). How artificial intelligence will redefine management. *Harvard Business Review*.

Korzynski, P., Mazurek, G., Altmann, A., Ejdys, J., Kazlauskaite, R., Paliszkiewicz, J., Wach, K., & Ziemba, E. (2023). Generative artificial intelligence as a new context for management theories. *Central European Management Journal*, *31*(1), 3–13. DOI: 10.1108/CEMJ-02-2023-0091

Kosinski, M., Stillwell, D., & Graepel, T. (2016). Mining big data to extract patterns and predict real-life outcomes. *Psychological Methods*, *21*(4), 493–506. DOI: 10.1037/met0000105 PMID: 27918179

Koudstaal, M., Sloof, R., & Van Praag, M. (2016). Risk, uncertainty, and entrepreneurship: Evidence from a lab-in-the-field experiment. *Management Science*, *62*(10), 2897–2915. DOI: 10.1287/mnsc.2015.2249

Krueger, N. F.Jr, & Brazeal, D. V. (1994). Entrepreneurial potential and potential entrepreneurs. *Entrepreneurship Theory and Practice*, *18*(3), 91–104. DOI: 10.1177/104225879401800307

Kumar, M. Yadav, M., & Sahoo, A. (2025). The Importance of Collaboration Skills in Workforce Preparation From Textbooks to Teamwork. In Revitalizing Student Skills for Workforce Preparation (pp. 333–352). DOI: 10.4018/979-8-3693-3856-8.ch011

Kumar, M., Dagar, M., Yadav, M., Choudhury, T., & Luu, T. M. N. (2025a). Navigating the future: Challenges and opportunities in intelligent RPA implementation. In Intelligent Robotic Process Automation: Development, Vulnerability and Applications (pp. 393–420). IGI Global. DOI: 10.4018/979-8-3693-4365-4.ch015

Kumar, M., Jain, A., Mittal, A., Gera, R., Biswal, S. K., Yadav, M., Hung, T. H., & Priya Srivastava, A. (2024). Inclusion of Neural Networks in Higher Education: A Systematic Review and Bibliometric Analysis. 2024 4th International Conference on Innovative Practices in Technology and Management (ICIPTM), 1–6. DOI: 10.1109/ICIPTM59628.2024.10563852

Kumar, M., Yadav, R., Suresh, A. S., Singh, R., Yadav, M., Balodi, A., Vihari, N. S., & Srivastava, A. P. (2023). Mapping AI-Driven Marketing: Review of Field and Directions for Future Research. 2023 2nd International Conference on Futuristic Technologies (INCOFT), 1–5. DOI: 10.1109/INCOFT60753.2023.10425169

Kumari, M., & Goyal, N. K. (2026). Artificial intelligence in the cryptocurrency ecosystem. In *Innovations in cryptocrime and financial fraud* (pp. 245–282). IGI Global., DOI: 10.4018/979-8-3373-0675-9.ch007

Kumari, M., Kumawat, R., Dutta, R., Khan, S. T., Goyal, N. K., & Sheikh, M. F. (2026). Wireless Communication and IoT Integration in Smart Clothing. In Saxena, P., Singh, M., Singh, S., & Rashid, M. (Eds.), *Next-Generation Electronic Textiles and Conductive Materials for Smart Wearables* (pp. 195–232). IGI Global Scientific Publishing., DOI: 10.4018/979-8-3373-4287-0.ch008

Kumari, M., Kumawat, R., Tripathi, M., Suganthi, K., Goyal, N. K., & Sheikh, M. F. (2026). Blockchain for transparency and traceability in supply chains. In *Maximizing operational efficiency at the intersection of supply chain management and marketing* (pp. 35–64). IGI Global., DOI: 10.4018/979-8-3373-3109-6.ch002

Kumar, M., Nain, N., Dagar, M., Luu, T. M. N., & Kaur, K. (2025b). Redefining work and outsourcing in the AI era: Challenges and opportunities. In *Global Work Arrangements and Outsourcing in the Age of AI*. IGI Global., DOI: 10.4018/979-8-3373-1270-5.ch021

Kusen, E., Strembeck, M., & Conti, M. (2017). Emotional states in social media posts: A case study of Facebook status updates. *Online Social Networks and Media*, *2*, 32–44. DOI: 10.1016/j.osnem.2017.08.002

Kusetogullari, A., Kusetogullari, H., Andersson, M., & Gorschek, T. (2025). *GenAI in Entrepreneurship: A systematic review of generative artificial intelligence in entrepreneurship research: current issues and future directions* (Version 1). arXiv. DOI: 10.48550/ARXIV.2505.05523

Kusner, M. J., Loftus, J. R., Russell, C., & Silva, R. (2017). Counterfactual fairness. *Advances in Neural Information Processing Systems*, *30*, 4066–4076.

Lake, B. M., Ullman, T. D., Tenenbaum, J. B., & Gershman, S. J. (2017). Building machines that learn and think like people. *Behavioral and Brain Sciences*, *40*, e253. DOI: 10.1017/S0140525X16001837 PMID: 27881212

Landy, F. J. (2005). Some historical and scientific issues related to research on emotional intelligence. *Journal of Organizational Behavior*, *26*(4), 411–424. DOI: 10.1002/job.317

Langer, M., König, C. J., & Fitili, A. (2019). Information as a double-edged sword: The role of computer experience and information disclosure on applicant reactions to AI-based assessments. *Computers in Human Behavior*, *97*, 123–132. DOI: 10.1016/j.chb.2019.03.029

Lestari, E. D.. (2024). SMEs' business resilience post-COVID-19. *Cogent Business & Management*, *11*(1), 2301135. DOI: 10.1080/23311975.2023.2301135

Levy, M., & Liguori, E. (2023). Algorithms and venture investment decisions: Better, fairer or biased? *Journal of Small Business and Enterprise Development*, *30*(2), 419–422. DOI: 10.1108/JSBED-09-2021-0336

Li, F., Duan, Y., & Fu, Z. (2020). Towards an understanding of the adoption of artificial intelligence in education: A systematic literature review. *Technological Forecasting and Social Change*, *158*, 120–178. DOI: 10.1016/j.techfore.2020.120178

Li, S., Chen, X., & Popovič, A. (2020). How entrepreneurs' emotional expressions shape venture capitalists' evaluations: A multimodal machine learning approach. *Journal of Business Venturing*, *35*(6), 106045. DOI: 10.1016/j.jbusvent.2020.106045

Li, S., & Deng, W. (2020). Deep facial expression recognition: A survey. *IEEE Transactions on Affective Computing*, *13*(3), 1195–1215. DOI: 10.1109/TAFFC.2020.2981446

Li, T., Ji, Y., & Zhan, Z. (2024). Expert or machine? Comparing the effect of pairing student teacher with in-service teacher and ChatGPT on their critical thinking, learning performance, and cognitive load in an integrated-STEM course. *Asia Pacific Journal of Education*, *44*(1), 45–60. DOI: 10.1080/02188791.2024.2305163

Littunen, H. (2000). Entrepreneurship and the characteristics of the entrepreneurial personality. *International Journal of Entrepreneurial Behaviour & Research*, *6*(6), 295–310. DOI: 10.1108/13552550010362741

Liu, B. (2012). *Sentiment analysis and opinion mining*. Morgan & Claypool. DOI: 10.1007/978-3-031-02145-9

Liu, Y., Li, H., & Xu, X. (2021a). Artificial intelligence in human resource management: Applications and challenges. *Journal of Management Science and Engineering*, *6*(1), 1–12. DOI: 10.1016/j.jmse.2025.11.001

Liu, Y., Osmani, V., & Demartini, G. (2021b). Multimodal machine learning for mental health applications: Current developments and future directions. *ACM Computing Surveys*, *54*(5), 1–36. DOI: 10.1145/3214304

Li, Y. (2017). Deep reinforcement learning: An overview. *arXiv*. https://arxiv.org/abs/1701.07274

Longoni, C., Bonezzi, A., & Morewedge, C. K. (2019). Resistance to medical artificial intelligence. *The Journal of Consumer Research*, *46*(4), 629–650. DOI: 10.1093/jcr/ucz013

Lopes, P. N., Nezlek, J. B., Extremera, N., Hertel, J., Fernández-Berrocal, P., Schütz, A., & Salovey, P. (2020). Emotion regulation and the quality of social interaction: Does the ability to evaluate emotional situations and identify effective responses matter? *Journal of Personality*, *88*(1), 111–125. DOI: 10.1111/jopy.12453 PMID: 21395594

Lounsbury, M., & Glynn, M. A. (2001). Cultural entrepreneurship: Stories, legitimacy, and the acquisition of resources. *Strategic Management Journal*, *22*(6–7), 545–564. DOI: 10.1002/smj.188

Luan, L., Lin, X., Dai, Y., Hu, S., & Sun, Q. (2024). Exploring the cognitive dynamics of artificial intelligence in the post-COVID-19 and Learning 3.0 era: A case study of ChatGPT. *Asian Journal of Distance Education*, *19*(2), 1–10. DOI: 10.5281/zenodo.10990472

Luce, R. D., & Weber, E. U. (1986). An axiomatic theory of conjoint, expected risk. *Journal of Mathematical Psychology*, *30*(2), 188–205. DOI: 10.1016/0022-2496(86)90013-1

Luckin, R., Holmes, W., Griffiths, M., & Forcier, L. B. (2016). *Intelligence unleashed: An argument for AI in education*. Pearson.

Lundberg, S. M., & Lee, S.-I. (2017). A unified approach to interpreting model predictions. *Advances in Neural Information Processing Systems*, *30*, 4765–4774.

Malhan, D. Mohan, Preeti, Sushma, Harsh, & Nisha. (2021). Probing Anterior of Entrepreneurial Intentions of Youngsters in India, an Analytical Approach. Academy of Strategic Management Journal, Suppl. Special Issue 6, 20(October), 1–10. https://www.abacademies.org/articles/probing-anterior-of-entrepreneurial-intentions-of-youngsters-in-india-an-analytical-approach-11730.html

Mann, W. C., & Thompson, S. A. (1988). Rhetorical Structure Theory: Toward a functional theory of text organization. *Text*, *8*(3), 243–281. DOI: 10.1515/text.1.1988.8.3.243

March, J. G. (1994). *A primer on decision making: How decisions happen*. Free Press.

Mariani, M. M., Pérez-Vega, R., & Wirtz, J. (2021). AI in marketing, consumer research and psychology: A systematic literature review and research agenda. *Psychology and Marketing*, *39*(4), 755–776. DOI: 10.1002/mar.21619

Marques, J. (2015). Empathy in leadership: Appropriate or misplaced? *Journal of Leadership Studies*, *9*(1), 58–67.

Martens, M. L., Jennings, J. E., & Jennings, P. D. (2007). Do the stories they tell get them the money they need? The role of entrepreneurial narratives in resource acquisition. *Academy of Management Journal*, *50*(5), 1107–1132. DOI: 10.5465/amj.2007.27169488

Mason, C., & Harrison, R. (2020). Entrepreneurial ecosystems and the role of angel investors. *Regional Studies*, *54*(8), 1085–1097. DOI: 10.1080/00343404.2019.1680827

Matsumoto, D., Yoo, S. H., & Fontaine, J. (2008). Mapping expressive differences around the world: The relationship between emotional display rules and individualism versus collectivism. *Journal of Cross-Cultural Psychology*, *39*(1), 55–74. DOI: 10.1177/0022022107311854

Mayer, J. D., Caruso, D. R., & Salovey, P. (2016). The ability model of emotional intelligence: Principles and updates. *Emotion Review*, *8*(4), 290–300. DOI: 10.1177/1754073916639667

Mayer, J. D., & Salovey, P. (1997). What is emotional intelligence? In Salovey, P., & Sluyter, D. (Eds.), *Emotional development and emotional intelligence: Educational implications* (pp. 3–31). Basic Books.

Mayer, J. D., Salovey, P., & Caruso, D. R. (2002). *Mayer-Salovey-Caruso Emotional Intelligence Test (MSCEIT) user's manual.* Multi-Health Systems.

Mayer, J. D., Salovey, P., & Caruso, D. R. (2008). Emotional intelligence: New ability or eclectic traits? *The American Psychologist*, *63*(6), 503–517. DOI: 10.1037/0003-066X.63.6.503 PMID: 18793038

McCaffrey, T., & Spector, L. (2018). An approach to human–machine collaboration in innovation. *Artificial Intelligence for Engineering Design, Analysis and Manufacturing*, *32*(1), 1–15. DOI: 10.1017/S0890060416000524

McClelland, D. C. (1961). *The achieving society*. Van Nostrand. DOI: 10.1037/14359-000

McMullen, J. S., & Shepherd, D. A. (2006). Entrepreneurial action and the role of uncertainty in the theory of the entrepreneur. *Academy of Management Review*, *31*(1), 132–152. DOI: 10.5465/amr.2006.19379628

Mehrabi, N., Morstatter, F., Saxena, N., Lerman, K., & Galstyan, A. (2021). A survey on bias and fairness in machine learning. *ACM Computing Surveys*, *54*(6), 1–35. DOI: 10.1145/3457607

Miço, H., & Cungu, J. (2023). Entrepreneurship education, a challenging learning process towards entrepreneurial competence in education. *Administrative Sciences*, *13*(1), 22. Advance online publication. DOI: 10.3390/admsci13010022

Microsoft. (2022). *Empathy and innovation: Responsible AI initiatives*. Microsoft Corporation.

Mitchell, M., Wu, S., Zaldivar, A., Barnes, P., Vasserman, L., Hutchinson, B., & Gebru, T. (2019). Model cards for model reporting. *Proceedings of the Conference on Fairness, Accountability, and Transparency*, 220–229. DOI: 10.1145/3287560.3287596

Mitchell, R. K., Busenitz, L., Lant, T., McDougall, P. P., Morse, E. A., & Smith, J. B. (2002). Toward a theory of entrepreneurial cognition: Rethinking the people side of entrepreneurship research. *Entrepreneurship Theory and Practice*, *27*(2), 93–104. DOI: 10.1111/1540-8520.00001

Mitchell, R. K., Smith, B., Seawright, K. W., & Morse, E. A. (2002). Cross-cultural cognitions and the venture creation decision. *Academy of Management Journal*, *43*(5), 974–993. DOI: 10.2307/1556422

Mortan, R. A., Ripoll, P., Carvalho, C., & Bernal, M. C. (2014). Effects of emotional intelligence on entrepreneurial intention and self-efficacy. *Journal of Work and Organizational Psychology*, *30*(3), 97–104. DOI: 10.1016/j.rpto.2014.11.004

Motta, V., & Galina, S. (2023). Experiential learning in entrepreneurship education: A systematic literature review. *Teaching and Teacher Education*, *121*, 103919. Advance online publication. DOI: 10.1016/j.tate.2022.103919

Mukherjee, S., Nawazish, M., Padhi, S. S., & Jayaram, J. (2024). Optimal investment in artificial intelligence-driven production activities considering socio-economic concerns. *International Journal of Production Research*, •••, 1–25.

Mulenga, R. (2025). THE DIGITAL EVOLUTION OF BUSINESS, EDUCATION, AND GOVERNANCE IN EMERGING ECONOMIES. *International Journal of Innovative Technologies in Economy*, *3*(51). Advance online publication. DOI: 10.31435/ijite.3(51).2025.3429

Nambisan, S. (2017). Digital entrepreneurship: Toward a digital technology perspective of entrepreneurship. *Entrepreneurship Theory and Practice*, *41*(6), 1029–1055. DOI: 10.1111/etap.12254

Nambisan, S., Wright, M., & Feldman, M. (2019). The digital transformation of innovation and entrepreneurship: Progress, challenges and key themes. *Research Policy*, *48*(8), 103773. DOI: 10.1016/j.respol.2019.03.018

Ndlovu, E., Ebewo, P., Mlotshwa, S., & Shumba, K. (2025). Entrepreneurial Coaching and Self-Efficacy: A Systematic Review of Its Pedagogical Integration into Entrepreneurship Education. *Education Sciences, 15*(2), 237. Advance online publication. DOI: 10.3390/educsci15020237

Neck, H. M., & Corbett, A. C. (2018). The scholarship of teaching and learning entrepreneurship. *Entrepreneurship Education and Pedagogy, 1*(1), 8–41. DOI: 10.1177/2515127417737286

Neck, H. M., Greene, P. G., & Brush, C. (2018). *Entrepreneurship education: Experiential learning approaches*. Routledge.

Nguyen, T. B., Kumar, M., Sahoo, D. K., Nain, N., Yadav, M., & Dadhich, V. (2025). Mapping the landscape of women entrepreneurs in micro and small enterprises: Trends, themes, and insights through systematic review and text mining. F1000Research, 14. DOI: 10.12688/f1000research.163030.1

Nkambou, R., Bourdeau, J., & Mizoguchi, R. (2010). *Advances in intelligent tutoring systems*. Springer. DOI: 10.1007/978-3-642-14363-2

O'Neil, C. (2016). *Weapons of math destruction: How big data increases inequality and threatens democracy*. Crown.

Obschonka, M., & Audretsch, D. B. (2020). Artificial intelligence and big data in entrepreneurship: A new era has begun. *Small Business Economics, 55*(3), 529–539. DOI: 10.1007/s11187-019-00202-4

Obschonka, M., & Stuetzer, M. (2017). Integrating psychological approaches to entrepreneurship: The Entrepreneurial Personality System (EPS). *Small Business Economics, 49*(1), 203–231. DOI: 10.1007/s11187-016-9821-y

Obschonka, M., Stuetzer, M., Gosling, S. D., Rentfrow, P. J., Lamb, M. E., & Potter, J. (2017). Entrepreneurial regions: Do macro-psychological cultural characteristics of regions help solve the "knowledge paradox" of economics? *PLoS One, 12*(6), e0178332. DOI: 10.1371/journal.pone.0178332

OECD. (2017). *Enhancing the contributions of SMEs in a global and digitalized economy*. OECD Publishing.

Pang, B., & Lee, L. (2008). Opinion mining and sentiment analysis. *Foundations and Trends in Information Retrieval, 2*(1–2), 1–135. DOI: 10.1561/1500000011

Pankaj, Yadav, R., Naim, I., Kumar, M., Misra, S., Dewasiri, N. J., Rathnasiri, M. S. H., Yadav, M., Balodi, A., Kar, S., & Vihari, N. S. (2023). An Exploratory Study to Identify Effects of Blockchain Technology on Organizational Change and Practices. 2023 IEEE Technology & Engineering Management Conference - Asia Pacific (TEMSCON-ASPAC), 1–8. DOI: 10.1109/TEMSCON-ASPAC59527.2023.10531372

Park, J., Kim, S., & Lee, S. (2025). AI and Creativity in Entrepreneurship Education: A Systematic Review of LLM Applications. *AI*, *6*(5), 100. Advance online publication. DOI: 10.3390/ai6050100

Petrides, K. V., & Furnham, A. (2001). Trait emotional intelligence: Psychometric investigation with reference to established trait taxonomies. *European Journal of Personality*, *15*(6), 425–448. DOI: 10.1002/per.416

Piaget, J. (1972). *The psychology of the child.* Basic Books.

Picard, R. W. (2010). *Affective computing: From laughter to IEEE.* IEEE.

Podsakoff, P. M., MacKenzie, S. B., Lee, J.-Y., & Podsakoff, N. P. (2003). Common method biases in behavioral research: A critical review of the literature and recommended remedies. *The Journal of Applied Psychology*, *88*(5), 879–903. DOI: 10.1037/0021-9010.88.5.879 PMID: 14516251

Pradhan, R. K., Jena, L. K., & Singh, S. K. (2017). Examining the role of emotional intelligence between organizational learning and adaptive performance in Indian manufacturing industries. *Journal of Workplace Learning*, *29*(3), 235–247. DOI: 10.1108/JWL-05-2016-0046

Primario, S., Rippa, P., & Secundo, G. (2024). Rethinking entrepreneurial education: The role of digital technologies to assess entrepreneurial self-efficacy and intention of STEM students. *IEEE Transactions on Engineering Management*, *71*, 2829–2842. DOI: 10.1109/TEM.2022.3199709

Putri, V. C. C., & Sonni, A. F. (2025). AI-Driven Personal Branding for Female Entrepreneurs: The Indonesian Hijabi Startup Ecosystem. *Journalism and Media*, *6*(3), 131. DOI: 10.3390/journalmedia6030131

Pymetrics. (2020). *How pymetrics works: AI-driven talent matching.* https://www.pymetrics.ai/

Raab, M., Schlauderer, S., Overhage, S., & Friedrich, T. (2020). More than a feeling: Investigating the contagious effect of facial emotional expressions on investment decisions in reward-based crowdfunding. *Decision Support Systems*, *135*, 113326. DOI: 10.1016/j.dss.2020.113326

Radford, A., Narasimhan, K., Salimans, T., & Sutskever, I. (2018). *Improving language understanding by generative pre-training* (Technical report). OpenAI.

Radianti, J., Majchrzak, T. A., Fromm, J., & Wohlgenannt, I. (2020). A systematic review of immersive virtual reality applications for higher education: Design elements, lessons learned, and research agenda. *Computers & Education, 147*, 103778. DOI: 10.1016/j.compedu.2019.103778

Rae, D. (2017). *Entrepreneurial learning: Conceptual frameworks and applications.* Routledge.

Raghavan, M., Barocas, S., Kleinberg, J., & Levy, K. (2020). Mitigating bias in algorithmic hiring: Evaluating claims and practices. *Proceedings of the 2020 Conference on Fairness, Accountability, and Transparency*, 469–481. DOI: 10.1145/3351095.3372828

Rahmi, E., Darmansyah, D., Yulastri, A., & Handrianto, C. (2025). *Bridging Entrepreneurship Education and Digital Transformation: A Novel Experiential Learning Model for Entrepreneurial Mindset Development.* International Journal of Learning, Teaching and Educational Research., DOI: 10.26803/ijlter.24.4.29

Rai, A., Constantinides, P., & Sarker, S. (2019). Next-generation digital platforms: Toward human–AI hybrids. *Management Information Systems Quarterly, 43*(1), iii–ix. https://wrap.warwick.ac.uk/id/eprint/113653/. DOI: 10.25300/MISQ/2019/431E0

Raji, I. D., & Buolamwini, J. (2019). Actionable auditing: Investigating the impact of publicly naming biased performance results of commercial AI products. *Proceedings of the AAAI/ACM Conference on AI, Ethics, and Society*, 429–435. DOI: 10.1145/3306618.3314244

Raman, R., Alka, T. A., Suresh, M., & Nedungadi, P. (2025). Social entrepreneurship and sustainable technologies: Impact on communities, social innovation, and inclusive development. *Sustainable Technology and Entrepreneurship, 4*(3), 100110. DOI: 10.1016/j.stae.2025.100110

Ransbotham, S., Kiron, D., Gerbert, P., & Reeves, M. (2021). Artificial intelligence in business gets real. *MIT Sloan Management Review, 63*(1), 1–14.

Rashid, A., Rasheed, R., Ngah, A. H., Pradeepa Jayaratne, M. D. R., Rahi, S., & Tunio, M. N. (2024). Role of information processing and digital supply chain in supply chain resilience through supply chain risk management. *Journal of Global Operations and Strategic Sourcing, 17*(2), 429–447. DOI: 10.1108/JGOSS-12-2023-0106

Rauch, A., & Frese, M. (2007). Born to be an entrepreneur? Revisiting the personality approach to entrepreneurship. In Baum, J. R., Frese, M., & Baron, R. (Eds.), *The psychology of entrepreneurship* (pp. 41–65). Lawrence Erlbaum Associates.

Rauch, A., & Frese, M. (2007). Let's put the person back into entrepreneurship research: A meta-analysis on the relationship between business owners' personality traits, business creation, and success. *European Journal of Work and Organizational Psychology*, *16*(4), 353–385. DOI: 10.1080/13594320701595438

Raza, H., Riaz, A., Riaz, N., & Ramakrishnan, S. A. L. (2025). *Algorithmic training, future markets, and big data for finance digitalization*. Elsevier., DOI: 10.4018/979-8-3693-6386-7

Ribeiro, M. T., Singh, S., & Guestrin, C. (2016). "Why should I trust you?" Explaining the predictions of any classifier. *Proceedings of the 22nd ACM SIGKDD International Conference on Knowledge Discovery and Data Mining*, 1135–1144. DOI: 10.1145/2939672.2939778

Sajja, R., Sermet, Y., Cikmaz, M., Cwiertny, D., & Demir, I. (2023). Artificial Intelligence-Enabled Intelligent Assistant for Personalized and Adaptive Learning in Higher Education. *arXiv*.

Sarasvathy, S. D. (2001). Causation and effectuation: Toward a theoretical shift from economic inevitability to entrepreneurial contingency. *Academy of Management Review*, *26*(2), 243–263. DOI: 10.2307/259121

Saritepeci, M., & Durak, H. (2024). Effectiveness of artificial intelligence integration in design-based learning on design thinking mindset, creative and reflective thinking skills: An experimental study. *Education and Information Technologies*, *29*(18), 25175–25209. DOI: 10.1007/s10639-024-12829-2

Saura, J. R., & Bužinskienė, R. (2025). Behavioral economics, artificial intelligence and entrepreneurship: An updated framework for management. *The International Entrepreneurship and Management Journal*, *21*(1), 1–33. DOI: 10.1007/s11365-025-01076-7

Sauser, B. (2018). Resilience of SMEs and community impact. *Natural Hazards*, *90*, 79–99. DOI: 10.1007/s11069-017-3034-9

Schlaegel, C., & Koenig, M. (2014). Determinants of entrepreneurial intent: A meta–analytic test and integration of competing models. *Entrepreneurship Theory and Practice*, *38*(2), 291–332. DOI: 10.1111/etap.12087

Schwarz, N., & Clore, G. L. (2007). Feelings and phenomenal experiences. In Kruglanski, A., & Higgins, E. T. (Eds.), *Social psychology: Handbook of basic principles* (2nd ed., pp. 385–407). Guilford Press.

Sekli, M., & Portuguez-Castro, M. (2025). Fostering entrepreneurial success from the classroom: Unleashing the potential of generative AI through technology-to-performance chain. A multi-case study approach. *Education and Information Technologies, 30*(10), 13075–13103. DOI: 10.1007/s10639-025-13316-y

Shahadat, M. M. H.. (2020). Digital technology adoption in SMEs. *Global Business Review*.

Shahriar, M. S., Hasan, K. B. M. R., Hossain, T., Beg, T. H., Islam, K. A., & Zayed, N. M. (2021). Financial decision making and forecasting techniques on project evaluation: A planning, development and entrepreneurial perspective. *Academy of Entrepreneurship Journal*, *27*(4), 1–7.

Shane, S. (2003). *A general theory of entrepreneurship: The individual-opportunity nexus*. Edward Elgar. DOI: 10.4337/9781781007990

Shane, S. (2009). Why encouraging more people to become entrepreneurs is bad public policy. *Small Business Economics*, *33*(2), 141–149. DOI: 10.1007/s11187-009-9215-5

Shane, S., & Venkataraman, S. (2000). The promise of entrepreneurship as a field of research. *Academy of Management Review*, *25*(1), 217–226. DOI: 10.5465/amr.2000.2791611

Sharkey, A. J. C. (2016). Should we welcome robot teachers? *Ethics and Information Technology*, *18*(4), 283–297. DOI: 10.1007/s10676-016-9387-z

Sharma, P., Kumawat, R., Jain, G., Keswani, G., Goyal, N. K., & Sheikh, M. F. (2026). Machine learning-based intrusion detection systems for HIoT. In *Resilient healthcare IoT systems* (pp. 185–214). IGI Global., DOI: 10.4018/979-8-3373-7610-3.ch007

Shepherd, D. A. (2003). Learning from business failure: Propositions of grief recovery for the self-employed. *Academy of Management Review*, *28*(2), 318–328. DOI: 10.2307/30040715

Shepherd, D. A., & Patzelt, H. (2011). Sustainable entrepreneurship. *Entrepreneurship Theory and Practice*, *35*(1), 137–163. DOI: 10.1111/j.1540-6520.2010.00426.x

Shepherd, D. A., & Williams, T. A. (2018). Hitting rock bottom after job loss: Bouncing back to create a new positive work identity. *Academy of Management Review*, *43*(1), 28–49. DOI: 10.5465/amr.2015.0102

Shore, A., Tiwari, M., Tandon, P., & Foropon, C. (2024). Building entrepreneurial resilience using generative AI. *Technovation*. Advance online publication. DOI: 10.1016/j.technovation.2024.103063

Shrestha, Y. R., Ben-Menahem, S. M., & Krogh, G. V. (2019). Organizational decision-making structures in the age of artificial intelligence. *California Management Review*, *61*(4), 66–83. DOI: 10.1177/0008125619862257

Simon, H. A. (1997). *Administrative behavior* (4th ed.). Free Press.

Simon, M., Houghton, S. M., & Aquino, K. (2000). Cognitive biases, risk perception, and venture formation: How individuals decide to start companies. *Journal of Business Venturing*, *15*(2), 113–134. DOI: 10.1016/S0883-9026(98)00003-2

Sirait, H., Basuki, R., Djubair, R., Hardipura, G., & Endri, E. (2025). Exploring the Diffusion of Digital Technologies in Higher Education Entrepreneurship: The Impact of the Utilization of AI and TikTok on Student Entrepreneurial Knowledge, Experience, and Business Performance. *Administrative Sciences*, *15*(7), 285. Advance online publication. DOI: 10.3390/admsci15070285

Somià, T., & Vecchiarini, M. (2024). Navigating the new frontier: The impact of artificial intelligence on students' entrepreneurial competencies. *International Journal of Entrepreneurial Behaviour & Research*, *30*(11), 236–260. Advance online publication. DOI: 10.1108/IJEBR-08-2023-0788

Stewart, W. H., & Roth, P. L. (2001). Risk propensity differences between entrepreneurs and managers: A meta-analytic review. *The Journal of Applied Psychology*, *86*(1), 145–153. DOI: 10.1037/0021-9010.86.1.145 PMID: 11302226

Subrahmanyam, S. (2024a). AI integration in HR processes. In Kaur, J. (Ed.), *Embracing transhumanism and genomics in human resources management* (pp. 69–100). IGI Global Scientific Publishing., DOI: 10.4018/979-8-3693-7668-3.ch004

Subrahmanyam, S. (2024b). Role of data analytics and big data in operational decision-making and performance improvement. In Martínez-Falcó, J., Sánchez-García, E., Marco-Lajara, B., & Visser, G. (Eds.), *Convergence of technology and operations management in modern businesses* (pp. 105–140). IGI Global Scientific Publishing., DOI: 10.4018/979-8-3693-6200-6.ch003

Subrahmanyam, S. (2025a). Business, Digital Transformation, and Entrepreneurship. In Ordóñez de Pablos, P. (Ed.), *Shaping Green and Inclusive Economies Through Innovative Entrepreneurship* (pp. 1–34). IGI Global Scientific Publishing., DOI: 10.4018/979-8-3373-1097-8.ch001

Subrahmanyam, S. (2025b). Human Factors and Workforce Adaptation in Digital Transition. In Martínez-Falcó, J., Sánchez-García, E., & Marco-Lajara, B. (Eds.), *Navigating Digital Transformation Through Business Process Management* (pp. 95–126). IGI Global Scientific Publishing., DOI: 10.4018/979-8-3373-3336-6.ch005

Subrahmanyam, S. (2025c). Shaping Tomorrow's Talent Strategies with Predictive Workforce Intelligence. In Badouch, M., & Boutaounte, M. (Eds.), *Emerging Technologies for Recruitment Strategy and Practice* (pp. 211–236). IGI Global Scientific Publishing., DOI: 10.4018/979-8-3373-6516-9.ch008

Subrahmanyam, S., & El Samra, H. (2025). Startups and AI: Fostering Entrepreneurship in the MENA Region. In Azoury, N., & Yahchouchi, G. (Eds.), *AI in the Middle East for Growth and Business* (pp. 77–92). Palgrave Macmillan., DOI: 10.1007/978-3-031-75589-7_6

Su, C. H., & Cheng, C. H. (2020). A mobile gamification learning system for improving the learning motivation and achievements of students. *Computers & Education*, *75*, 16–27.

Sun, C., Nasraoui, O., & Shafto, P. (2020). Evolution and impact of bias in human and machine learning algorithm interaction. *PLoS One*, *15*(8), e0235502. DOI: 10.1371/journal.pone.0235502 PMID: 32790666

Sunny, B., & Singh, A. (2025). Analysing the Role of Innovation in Enhancing Women-Led Entrepreneurial Ventures. In R. Nagariya, P. Dhaundiyal, K. Mathiyazhagan, & V. Mishra (Eds.), *Proceedings of the International Conference on Sustainable Business Practices and Innovative Models (ICSBPIM-2025)* (Vol. 349, pp. 1073–1089). Atlantis Press International BV. DOI: 10.2991/978-94-6463-872-1_66

Suresh, H., & Guttag, J. V. (2021). A framework for understanding unintended consequences of machine learning. *Communications of the ACM*, *64*(1), 62–71. DOI: 10.1145/3425716

Susi, T., & Ziemke, T. (2001). Social cognition, artefacts, and stigmergy: A comparative analysis of theoretical frameworks for artefact-mediated collaborative activity. *Cognitive Systems Research*, *2*(4), 273–290. DOI: 10.1016/S1389-0417(01)00053-5

Su, Y., & Liu, Z. (2023). A study of ChatGPT empowering college students' innovation and entrepreneurship education in the context of China. *International Journal of New Developments in Education*, *5*(13), 1–7. DOI: 10.25236/IJNDE.2023.051301

Sweller, J. (1988). Cognitive load during problem solving: Effects on learning. *Cognitive Science*, *12*(2), 257–285. DOI: 10.1207/s15516709cog1202_4

Syed, M., Ferris, G. R., & Munir, K. (2023). Identity, work, and artificial intelligence: A review and future research agenda. *Journal of Management Studies*, *60*(2), 295–326.

Tantawy, M., Herbert, K., McNally, J., Mengel, T., Piperopoulos, P., & Foord, D. (2021). Bringing creativity back to entrepreneurship education: Creative self-efficacy, creative process engagement, and entrepreneurial intentions. *Journal of Business Venturing Insights*, *15*, e00239. Advance online publication. DOI: 10.1016/j.jbvi.2021.e00239

Tapalova, O. (2022). AIEd for personalized learning pathways. *Electronic Journal of e-Learning*, *20*(5), 640–651. DOI: 10.34190/ejel.20.5.2597

Tayal, R., Upadhyay, R. K., Yadav, M., & Singh, R. (2021). The development and validation of the organizational effectiveness scale using confirmatory factor analysis. *Global Business Review*, *22*(3), 821–843. DOI: 10.1177/0972150918811720

Tolner, F., Eigner, G., & Barta, B. (2021). Resilience interpretations of SMEs. *IEEE SAMI Proceedings*, 495–500.

Topol, E. J. (2019). High-performance medicine: The convergence of human and artificial intelligence. *Nature Medicine*, *25*(1), 44–56. DOI: 10.1038/s41591-018-0300-7 PMID: 30617339

Tripathi, P., & Trivedi, A. (2025). *Breaking Barriers Through Innovation: The Rise of Women Entrepreneurs*. Cureus Journal of Business and Economics., DOI: 10.7759/s44404-025-05917-0

Trivedi, S. K., Vishnu, S., Singh, A., & Yadav, M. (2023). Research trends in sustainable E-payment systems: A study using topic modeling approach. *IEEE Transactions on Engineering Management*, *71*, 7511–7525. DOI: 10.1109/TEM.2023.3280216

Trivedi, V., Banerji, D., & Yadav, M. (2023). Expecting the surprises: Role of hope in consumer repurchase intentions in an online shopping environment. *Journal of Strategic Marketing*, *31*(4), 794–816. DOI: 10.1080/0965254X.2021.1996449

Tunio, M. N., Jariko, M. A., Børsen, T., Shaikh, S., Mushtaque, T., & Brahmi, M. (2021). How Entrepreneurship Sustains Barriers in the Entrepreneurial Process—A Lesson from a Developing Nation. In Sustainability (Vol. 13, Issue 20). DOI: 10.3390/su132011419

Tunio, M. N., Chaudhry, I. S., Shaikh, S., Jariko, M. A., & Brahmi, M. (2021). Determinants of the sustainable entrepreneurial engagement of youth in developing country—An empirical evidence from Pakistan. *Sustainability (Basel)*, *13*(14), 7764. DOI: 10.3390/su13147764

Tunio, M. N., & Tunio, S. (2025). *Navigating Digital Transformation: A Systematic Review of SMEs' Transitions and Growth in the Digital Age*. Sukkur IBA Journal of Management and Business., DOI: 10.30537/sijmb.v11i2.1509

Turkle, S. (2015). *Reclaiming conversation: The power of talk in a digital age*. Penguin Press.

Upadhyay, A. K., & Khandelwal, K. (2018). Applying artificial intelligence: Implications for recruitment. *Strategic HR Review*, *17*(5), 255–258. DOI: 10.1108/SHR-07-2018-0051

Uriarte, S., Baier-Fuentes, H., Espinoza-Benavides, J., & Inzunza-Mendoza, W. (2025). Artificial intelligence technologies and entrepreneurship: A hybrid literature review. *Review of Managerial Science*. Advance online publication. DOI: 10.1007/s11846-025-00839-4

Uy, M. A., Foo, M. D., & Song, Z. (2013). Joint effects of prior start-up experience and coping strategies on entrepreneurs' psychological well-being. *Journal of Business Venturing*, *28*(5), 583–597. DOI: 10.1016/j.jbusvent.2012.04.003

van Esch, P., Black, J. S., & Ferolie, J. (2019). Marketing AI recruitment: The next phase in job application and selection. *Computers in Human Behavior*, *90*, 215–222. DOI: 10.1016/j.chb.2018.09.009

Van Rooy, D. L., & Viswesvaran, C. (2004). Emotional intelligence: A meta-analytic investigation of predictive validity and nomological net. *Journal of Vocational Behavior*, *65*(1), 71–95. DOI: 10.1016/S0001-8791(03)00076-9

Vankov, D., & Wang, L. (2024). *Education program and experiential learning in Chinese entrepreneurship education: A year-long social cognitive theory intervention's impact on self-efficacy and intention's impact on self-efficacy and intention*. International Journal of Innovation Studies., DOI: 10.1016/j.ijis.2024.07.002

Vecchiarini, M., & Somià, T. (2023). Redefining entrepreneurship education in the age of artificial intelligence: An explorative analysis. *International Journal of Management Education*, *21*(3), 100879. Advance online publication. DOI: 10.1016/j.ijme.2023.100879

Vygotsky, L. S. (1978). *Mind in society: The development of higher psychological processes*. Harvard University Press.

Wachter, S., & Mittelstadt, B. (2019). A right to reasonable inferences: Re-thinking data protection law in the age of big data and AI. *Columbia Business Law Review*, *2019*(2), 494–620.

Wang, S., Sun, Z., & Chen, Y. (2022). Effects of higher education institutes' artificial intelligence capability on students' self-efficacy, creativity and learning performance. *Education and Information Technologies*, *28*(5), 4919–4939. DOI: 10.1007/s10639-022-11338-4

Wang, W., Xu, Y., Wu, Y. J., & Goh, M. (2022). Linguistic information distortion on investment decision-making in the crowdfunding market. *Management Decision*, *60*(3), 648–672. DOI: 10.1108/MD-09-2020-1203

Weick, K. E., Sutcliffe, K. M., & Obstfeld, D. (2005). Organizing and the process of sensemaking. *Organization Science*, *16*(4), 409–421. DOI: 10.1287/orsc.1050.0133

Weng, X., Chiu, T. K. F., & Tsang, C. C. (2022). Promoting student creativity and entrepreneurship through real-world problem-based maker education. *Thinking Skills and Creativity*, *45*, 101046. Advance online publication. DOI: 10.1016/j.tsc.2022.101046

Werbach, K., & Hunter, D. (2012). *For the win: How game thinking can revolutionize your business*. Wharton Digital Press.

Wilson, F., Kickul, J., & Marlino, D. (2007). Gender, entrepreneurial self-efficacy, and entrepreneurial career intentions: Implications for entrepreneurship education. *Entrepreneurship Theory and Practice*, *31*(3), 387–406. DOI: 10.1111/j.1540-6520.2007.00179.x

Wilson, H. J., & Daugherty, P. R. (2018). Collaborative intelligence: Humans and AI are joining forces. *Harvard Business Review*, *96*(4), 114–123.

World Economic Forum. (2024). The future of jobs report. World Economic Forum. Author Details The authors bring academic and research expertise in psychology, well-being, and human technology interaction, with a focus on positive psychology and digital mental health. Their research interests include resilience, the psychological effects of relationships mediated by AI, and modern uses of positive psychology in digital settings.

Xanthopoulou, P., & Sahinidis, A. (2025). Mapping the Intersection of Entrepreneurship, Digitalization, and the SDGs: A Scopus-Based Literature Review. *Sustainability (Basel)*, *17*(18), 8420. DOI: 10.3390/su17188420

Xia, Q., Chiu, T. K. F., Lee, M., Sanusi, I. T., Dai, Y., & Chai, C. S. (2022). A self-determination theory (SDT) design approach for inclusive and diverse artificial intelligence (AI) education. *Computers & Education*, *189*, 104582. Advance online publication. DOI: 10.1016/j.compedu.2022.104582

Xie, Y. (2025). Generative artificial intelligence in entrepreneurship education. *Scientific Reports*. Retrieved from https://www.nature.com/articles/s41598-025-09545-3

Xie, Y., & Wang, S. (2025). Generative artificial intelligence in entrepreneurship education enhances entrepreneurial intention through self-efficacy and university support. *Scientific Reports*, *15*(1), 24079. Advance online publication. DOI: 10.1038/s41598-025-09545-3 PMID: 40618006

Yadav, M., Kumar, M., Alyousef, M. I., Dagar, M., Dewasiri, N. J., & Amoozegar, A. (2025). Mapping Research Trends on Gender Diversity, Work Stress, and Job Satisfaction in Higher Education: A Bibliometric Analysis. *International Journal of Learning. Teaching and Educational Research*, *24*(8), 444–472. DOI: 10.26803/ijlter.24.8.19

Yadav, M., Rangnekar, S., & Srivastava, A. P. (2019). Demographic variables as moderators between QWL and OCB. *Industrial and Commercial Training*, *51*(7/8), 396–408. DOI: 10.1108/ICT-04-2018-0040

Yadav, R., Yadav, M., & Vihari, N. S. (2024). High-performance work system and learning orientation in offline, online, and hybrid workplaces: The mediating role of affective commitment. *The Learning Organization*, *31*(1), 122–136. DOI: 10.1108/TLO-10-2022-0118

Yadav, U. S., Vyas, S., Kanchan, , Ghosal, I., & yadav, A. K. (2024). Impact of entrepreneurial leadership, Social media, digital technology, Entrepreneurial orientation and innovation on business performance in the handicraft sector: Talent management as mediating construct. *Journal of Innovation and Entrepreneurship*, *13*(1), 72. DOI: 10.1186/s13731-024-00434-z

Zafar, M. B., Valera, I., Rodriguez, M. G., & Gummadi, K. P. (2017). Fairness constraints: Mechanisms for fair classification. *Proceedings of the 20th International Conference on Artificial Intelligence and Statistics*, 962–970.

Zampetakis, L. A., Beldekos, P., & Moustakis, V. (2009). “Day-to-day” entrepreneurship within organisations: The role of the trait emotional intelligence and perceived organizational support. *European Management Journal*, *27*(3), 165–175. DOI: 10.1016/j.emj.2008.08.003

Zarsky, T. Z. (2016). The trouble with algorithmic decisions: An analytic road map to examine efficiency and fairness in automated and opaque decision making. *Science, Technology & Human Values*, *41*(1), 118–132. DOI: 10.1177/0162243915605575

Zeidner, M., Matthews, G., & Roberts, R. D. (2009). *What we know about emotional intelligence: How it affects learning, work, relationships, and our mental health.* MIT Press. DOI: 10.7551/mitpress/7404.001.0001

Zeng, Z., Pantic, M., Roisman, G. I., & Huang, T. S. (2009). A survey of affect recognition methods: Audio, visual, and spontaneous expressions. *IEEE Transactions on Pattern Analysis and Machine Intelligence, 31*(1), 39–58. DOI: 10.1109/TPAMI.2008.52 PMID: 19029545

Zhang, B., & Dafoe, A. (2019). Artificial intelligence: American attitudes and trends. SSRN *Electronic Journal*. DOI: 10.2139/ssrn.3312874

Zhang, H. (2025). AI-driven innovation and entrepreneurship education: A K-means clustering approach for Chinese university students. *Discover Artificial Intelligence, 5*(1), 127. Advance online publication. DOI: 10.1007/s44163-025-00341-6

Zhang, L., & Li, J. (2022). Analysis of the influence of entrepreneurial psychology on the index system of digital development of the equipment manufacturing industry. *Frontiers in Psychology, 13*, 1026603. DOI: 10.3389/fpsyg.2022.1026603 PMID: 36425832

Zhang, R., Wang, J., Liu, C., Su, K., Ishibuchi, H., & Jin, Y. (2025). Synergistic integration of metaheuristics and machine learning: Latest advances and emerging trends. *Artificial Intelligence Review, 58*(9), 268. DOI: 10.1007/s10462-025-11266-y

Zhao, H., & Seibert, S. E. (2006). The Big Five personality dimensions and entrepreneurial status: A meta-analytical review. *The Journal of Applied Psychology, 91*(2), 259–271. DOI: 10.1037/0021-9010.91.2.259

Zhao, H., Seibert, S. E., & Lumpkin, G. T. (2010). The relationship of personality to entrepreneurial intentions and performance: A meta-analytic review. *Journal of Management, 36*(2), 381–404. DOI: 10.1177/0149206309335187

Zhou, J., Pan, Y., Wang, J., Vasilakos, A. V., & Fang, B. (2019). Artificial intelligence in personalized education. *IEEE Transactions on Systems, Man, and Cybernetics. Systems, 49*(12), 2153–2164. DOI: 10.1109/TSMC.2019.2915125

Zhou, Y., Pan, Y., Wang, C., Venkatesh, V., & Zhang, X. (2021). The dark side of AI-powered emotion recognition: Ethical challenges and future directions. *Information Systems Frontiers, 23*(6), 1407–1423. DOI: 10.1007/s10796-020-10080-5

Zhu, J., & Luo, L. (2025). Designing the Future of Entrepreneurship Education: Exploring an AI-Empowered Scaffold System for Business Plan Development. 2025 5th International Conference on Artificial Intelligence and Education (ICAIE), 184-193. DOI: 10.1109/ICAIE64856.2025.11158485

Zhu, H., Zeng, W., & Chen, L. (2025). Transforming molecular diagnostics learning: The power of gamification in higher medical education. *Frontiers in Education, 10*, 1502203. DOI: 10.3389/feduc.2025.1502203

Zhu, Q., & Zhang, H. (2022). Teaching Strategies and Psychological Effects of Entrepreneurship Education for College Students Majoring in Social Security Law Based on Deep Learning and Artificial Intelligence. *Frontiers in Psychology*, *13*, 779669. DOI: 10.3389/fpsyg.2022.779669 PMID: 35369210

Zou, J., Han, Y., & So, S.-S. (2009). Overview of artificial neural networks. In *Artificial neural networks: Methods and applications* (pp. 14–22). Springer.

Zuboff, S. (2019). *The age of surveillance capitalism: The fight for a human future at the new frontier of power*. PublicAffairs.

Zulfiqar, S., Sarwar, B., Huo, C., Zhao, X., & Mahasbi, H. (2025). AI-powered education: Driving entrepreneurial spirit among university students. *International Journal of Management Education*, *23*(2), 101106. Advance online publication. DOI: 10.1016/j.ijme.2024.101106

About the Contributors

Samreen Tunio is currently a research scholar at the University of Milan, Italy, in the Department of Social and Political Sciences. In addition to this, she serves as an Assistant Professor and Head of the Department of Commerce at Gulzar-e-Hijri Girls College, Karachi. She is also recognized as an Ambassador for Peace Leader. Ms. Tunio actively participates in various international conferences, where she has presented numerous papers and received the Best Presentation Award. In addition to her conference presentations, she has published several research papers and book chapters, further contributing to her field of expertise. Her research interests include Artificial Intelligence and Machine Learning in Human Resource Management, Intellectual Capital, Organizational Resilience, Sustainability, Green Human Resource Management, Entrepreneurship, and Sustainable Development.

Muhammad Nawaz Tunio Dr. Tunio's dedication to academic excellence is further evidenced by his teaching and administrative roles at various universities, where he has mentored students, organized international conferences, and contributed to developing curricula in Business Administration and Management.

***

Syed Bilawal Ali Shah is an accomplished Petroleum Geologist with a Ph.D. in Petroleum Geology from the University of Malaya, Malaysia. Currently serving as a Lecturer at Curtin University Malaysia and a Post-Doctoral Fellow at the University Malaysia Kelantan (UMK), he possesses extensive expertise in petroleum geological, structural, and geophysical processes. His research contributions encompass reservoir characterization, source rock evaluation, seismic interpretation, and basin modeling, with over 34 published or accepted articles in high-impact peer-reviewed journals. With a strong academic and research background, Dr. Shah has held positions as a Visiting Faculty Assistant Professor at Bahria University Islamabad and worked as a Research Assistant in the Geology Department at the University of Malaya. His professional experience includes industry exposure through internships with Pakistan Oilfields Limited (POL) and Oil & Gas Development Company Limited (OGDCL), where he gained hands-on expertise in petroleum exploration and reservoir assessment. Dr. Shah's research portfolio highlights his proficiency in geological software applications, including Petrel Schlumberger, PetroMod 1D/2D Basin Modeling, and Interactive Petrophysics, which he utilizes for seismic structural interpretation and reservoir characterization. He has been actively involved in research grants, with significant contributions to projects on facies analysis and organic geochemical characterization in Malaysia. Beyond academia, he is also an active reviewer for multiple international journals and has conducted numerous workshops on academic writing, research proposal development, and publishing in impact factor journals. With an h-index of 7 and an i10-index of 7, Dr. Shah continues to contribute to the advancement of petroleum geology through innovative research and academic collaborations.

Syed Haider Ali Shah is an Associate Professor at the Department of Business Administration, Abdullah Gül University, Turkey. With over 11 years of combined academic and industry experience, he brings rich expertise and a dynamic perspective to his teaching and training. Previously, Dr. Shah served as an Associate Professor at Bahria Business School, Bahria University Islamabad, Pakistan, where he dedicated 8 years to teaching, research, and academic leadership. He earned his PhD from the University of Malaya, Malaysia, specializing in Human Resource Practices, Leadership, and Management. His research interests span Green HR Practices, Organizational Behavior, Sustainability, Innovation, Entrepreneurship, Talent Management, CSR, and Pro-Environmental Behavior. Dr. Shah has an impressive record of research publications in impact factor journals, including those indexed in ABDC, ABS, Scopus, and HEC-recognized journals. He has actively contributed to the academic community by presenting papers at numerous national and international conferences, where he has also chaired sessions and served as a reviewer for reputed journals.

Hung Duy Bui is a lecturer at the Banking Academy of Vietnam. Prior to his academic career, he spent more than ten years working at the Monetary Policy Department of the State Bank of Vietnam, where he was responsible for proposing and implementing monetary policy solutions. In 2011, he was awarded an Australian Government Scholarship to pursue a PhD in Economics at Griffith University, Australia. He completed his doctorate in 2016 with a dissertation on Vietnam's exchange rate policy. Dr. Bui currently teaches macroeconomics, microeconomics, and international economics. His research interests include fiscal policy, monetary policy, international economics, and exchange rate dynamics. His works have been published in several reputable academic journals, including the Journal of Economics & Development, the International Journal of Business and Globalisation, and the Journal of the Asia Pacific Economy.

Narayanage Jayantha Dewasiri, Ph.D., is a Chartered Manager at the Chartered Management Institute, UK. He conducts research at the Open University of Sri Lanka and the Sri Lanka Institute of Marketing. He is the founding Editor-in-Chief of the South Asian Journal of Marketing. His research interests are in corporate social responsibility, corporate governance, marketing and sales, management, and finance. He is working as the Head of Field Force at the HMD Global Inc., Sri Lanka. He also serves as a senior lecturer at University of Sabaragamuwa, Sri Lanka. He can be reached at dnjay@ou.ac.lk

Damith Gangodawilage is an award-winning serial entrepreneur has over 20 years of experience in taxation and financial management. Damith is the Founding Managing Director and Chief Compliance Officer of Taxperts Lanka Pvt. Ltd, a fintech company introduced a digital social impact on the taxation ecosystem in the Country. For making a digital social impact on the taxation ecosystem in the country, in 2019, Damith won eSwabhimani from ICTA and NBQSA awards from BCS, Chartered Institute. Further, in 2021, National Ingenuity Award was received from SLASSCOM for best innovation in business process management. Apart from Taxperts, Damith engages with Corporate Business Solutions Pvt. Ltd as the Chief Business Architect and Jt. Managing Partner of Assurance Partners (Chartered Accountants).

Shreya Ghosh is an Assistant Professor at PES University, Bangalore, and a research scholar with a strong passion for inquiry and innovation. Her interests lie in neuroscience, psychology, human relations, and sustainable development. She explores how psychological principles and neuroscientific insights support emotional regulation, cognitive balance, sustainable practices, and elder well-being, while integrating perspectives from wisdom traditions.

Bhadralakshmi Jagannathan is an Honours Psychology scholar at PES University with a strong focus on the practical applications of behavioural science in business and organisational contexts. Her work explores how neural mechanisms shape decision-making, leadership, and organisational behaviour, with a growing emphasis on neuroscience-informed behavioural strategy. She has contributed to empirical research through cross-cultural studies and is particularly interested in bridging research, communication, and applied behavioural design. Her long-term goal lies in working at the intersection of behavioural science, human-centred systems, and innovation while leveraging insights from psychology and neuroscience to drive ethical decision-making, accessibility, and holistic wellbeing.

Fleur Khalil is an Assistant Professor of Audit at the USEK Business School. She joined USEK in 2010 and currently serves as the Associate Dean for Undergraduate Studies. Over the past decade, she has held several leadership roles, including Head of the Undergraduate Department, Head of the Audit Department, Coordinator of CPA courses in the MBA Audit Program, and Head of the EMBA Digital Management Program with ESSCA. Her research focuses on auditing, fraud detection, sustainability, governance, information systems, and digital transformation. She has published in peer-reviewed and Scopus-indexed journals on topics including crowdfunding and sustainable finance, renewable energy, corporate governance and ownership structures, financial literacy and investment behavior, and the application of AI in auditing. She has also contributed case studies, published conference proceedings, and co-authored book chapters, reflecting her interest in bridging academic research with professional practice. Her institutional service includes membership in the Business School Council, the University Admission and Transfer Committee, the AACSB and NECHE accreditation committees, and the Faculty Search Committee. Before transitioning to academia, Fleur built her career in the audit sector in France, where she advanced to a managerial position at a leading international auditing and consulting firm.

MohanKumar has a total of eight years of professional experience in both the corporate sector and academia. He has worked in a Public Sector Bank and a State Government University, focusing on Marketing and Entrepreneurship Development. He completed his PhD on "Motivational Factors and Challenges of Start-Ups in NCR" at the Institute of Management Studies and Research, Maharshi Dayanand University, Rohtak-124001, Haryana. Dr. Mohan specializes in Marketing Management, Human Resource Management, Quantitative Analysis, and Entrepreneurship Development. His research has been published in esteemed national and international journals, and he has actively participated in both national and international conferences, presenting his research findings. In March 2022, he received the "Best Research Paper Award" at an international conference conducted by IITM, GGSIU, Delhi, for his paper titled "Psychological Wellbeing Before & During the COVID-19 Pandemic: A Longitudinal Sample Study of Creative Writers and Directors." Since May 2023, Dr. Mohan has been working at SGT University, Gurugram. He continues to contribute to academia through research, conferences, and workshops, furthering his expertise in his specialized domains.

Fatma Selen Madenoğlu received her Ph.D. degree in Industrial Engineering from Dokuz Eylül University in 2017. She got her B.S. and M.S. degrees both from Erciyes University, Department of Industrial Engineering in 2006 and 2010, respectively. Prior to joining the department of Business Administration at Abdullah Gül University in 2018, she worked as a Research and Teaching Assistant at Dokuz Eylül University during her Ph.D. Her current Research interests focus on operations research, decision making and metaheuristics.

Ali Najeeb is an Associate Professor at the Qasim Ibrahim School of Business (QISB), Villa College, Maldives. His research interests include higher education leadership, governance and management, sustainability, artificial intelligence, industrial relations, employment law and labour issues in small island states, migrant workers, HRM/ER in tourism and hospitality industry. He has published several research papers in refereed international journals, shared his experience in local and international panel discussions and presented his research work in international scholarly conferences. He is a recipient of the Emerald Literati Award for Excellence 2014 – the outstanding paper award from Employee Relations: The International Journal (Q1 and SSCI indexed journal).

Pratiksha Saxena is presently working as Assistant professor in Amity Business School, Amity University, Madhya Pradesh. Her Doctorate degree was awarded in 2022 by Jiwaji University, Gwalior. She completed her MBA from Prestige Institute of Management and Research, Indore in 2012. She has 5 years of Industry Experience in the Banking Sector. She qualified UGC-NET in December 2018.Her area of interest includes Financial Markets and Financial Services. She has attended various National and International workshops, FDP's and Conferences. She holds 10 publications to her credit and an academic experience of more than 4 years.

Mushtaq Ahmad Shah is a finance expert with a PhD in Infrastructure Finance. He teaches banking, finance and economics at Lovely Professional University in India. Dr. Shah has over 8 years of experience teaching and researching at various institutions. He's written articles in academic journals and presented his work at conferences on banking, partnerships between public and private sectors, and behavioral finance.

Satya Subrahmanyam is a distinguished academic leader, researcher, and institutional strategist with over 28 years of experience in higher education, business research, leadership and management. He holds two PhDs and a Postdoctoral qualification from the Polytechnic Institute of Leiria, Portugal. Currently serving as Professor and Dean (Research) at Holy Spirit University of Kaslik (USEK), Lebanon, he spearheads research initiatives that enhance academic excellence and institutional reputation. He played a pivotal role in the development of the Catholic University in Erbil, Kurdistan, where he established new departments, led research programs, and collaborated on international educational projects. As a founding member and Managing Partner of Vignan Institute of Technology and Management, India, he contributed to its transformation into a premier institution. With expertise in AI-driven business strategies, HR analytics, and leadership in technology adoption, he has published extensively, guided PhD research, and led training programs in corporate and academic settings.

Jeayaram Subramanian is an Assistant professor at Jindal Global Business School, O. P. Jindal Global University, India, in the area of Organisational behaviour and Human Resources Management.

Sushma pursuing her PhD from IMSAR, MDU, Rohtak in HR. She has honored with best research paper awards. She is currently working as an assistant professor in Galgotias University, Greater Noida. She writes and presents widely on HR and General Management Topics.

Mohit Yadav is an Professor in the area of Human Resource Management at Jindal Global Business School (JGBS). He has a rich blend of work experience from both Academics as well as Industry. Prof. Mohit holds a Ph.D. from Department of Management Studies, Indian Institute of Technology Roorkee (IIT Roorkee) and has completed Master of Human Resource and Organizational Development (MHROD) from prestigious Delhi School of Economics, University of Delhi. He also holds a B.Com (Hons.) degree from University of Delhi and UGC-JRF scholarship. He has published various research papers and book chapters with reputed publishers like Springer, Sage, Emerald, Elsevier, Inderscience etc. and presented research papers in national and International conferences both in India and abroad. He has many best paper awards on his credit too. He is reviewer of various international journals like Computers in Human Behavior, Policing etc. His areas of interest are Organizational Behavior, HRM, Recruitment and Selection, Organizational Citizenship Behavior, Quality of work life and role.

Index

A

B

C

D

E

F

G

H

I

L

N

O

P

R

S

www.ingramcontent.com/pod-product-compliance
Lightning Source LLC
LaVergne TN
LVHW081532300926
849161LV00006B/1399